Conceptions of Philosophy

ROYAL INSTITUTE OF PHILOSOPHY SUPPLEMENT: 65

EDITED BY

Anthony O'Hear

CAMBRIDGE
UNIVERSITY PRESS

PUBLISHED BY THE PRESS SYNDICATE OF THE UNIVERSITY OF CAMBRIDGE
The Pitt Building, Trumpington Street, Cambridge, CB2 1RP,
United Kingdom

CAMBRIDGE UNIVERSITY PRESS
The Edinburgh Building, Cambridge CB2 8RU, United Kingdom
32 Avenue of the Americas, New York, NY 10013–2473, USA
477 Williamstown Road, Port Melbourne, VIC 3207, Australia
Ruiz de Alarcón 13, 28014 Madrid, Spain
Dock House, The Waterfront, Cape Town 8001, South Africa

© The Royal Institute of Philosophy and the contributors 2009

Printed in the United Kingdom at the University Press, Cambridge
Typeset by Techset Composition Ltd, Salisbury, UK

A catalogue record for this book is available from the British Library

ISBN 9780521138574
ISSN 1358-2461

Contents

Preface   v

List of Contributors   vii

Visions of Philosophy   1
DAVID E. COOPER

Listening to Clifford's Ghost   15
PETER VAN INWAGEN

Metaphysical (Im)mortality and Philosophical Transcendence   37
JOHN HALDANE

My Conception of Philosophy   57
BRYAN MAGEE

Modern Philosophy   71
JONATHAN HARRISON

Philosophical Amnesia   93
NICHOLAS CAPALDI

Philosophy: A Contribution, not to Human Knowledge,
but to Human Understanding   129
P. M. S. HACKER

Can Philosophy be a Rigorous Science?   155
HERMAN PHILIPSE

The Doctor of Philosophy Will See You Now   177
CHRISTOPHER COOPE

Plotinus: Charms and Countercharms   215
STEPHEN R. L. CLARK

What is Humane Philosophy and Why is it At Risk?   233
JOHN COTTINGHAM

Why is There Something Called Philosophy Rather than Nothing?   257
STEPHEN MULHALL

Philosophy and the Sciences After Kant   275
MICHELA MASSIMI

The Inward Turn   313
CHARLES TRAVIS

Philosophy – Wisdom or Technique?   351
ANTHONY O'HEAR

Preface

The essays in this volume are based on The Royal Institute of Philosophy's annual London lecture series for 2007–8. In the series a number of distinguished philosophers were asked to consider and elaborate their own conception of their subject.

In doing so they considered such questions as whether philosophy is an art or a science. Or is it neither? Can we discern progress in philosophy? Do philosophical positions ever really die, or do they just reappear in new guises? Can any philosophical position ever be definitively established? Or refuted? Can we discover wisdom through philosophical reflection, as many earlier philosophers had hoped? Or is philosophy no more than an underlabourer to the sciences, and a clarifier of our day-to-day concepts?

It is fair to say that none of the contributors to the volume thinks of philosophy as no more than an adjunct to the natural sciences. Most, if not all, doubt that in its own methods it should aspire to the methods of the sciences. Their own positive accounts of philosophy's methods and possibilities are, though, varied and at times surprising, and should spark the interest of anyone involved in philosophy.

The Royal Institute of Philosophy would like to thank all the contributors to both lecture series and volume, and also Adam Ferner for preparing the index.

Anthony O'Hear

List of Contributors

David Cooper, University of Durham

Peter van Inwagen, University of Notre Dame

John Haldane, University of St. Andrews

Bryan Magee, Keble College, Oxford

Jonathan Harrison, Universities of Nottingham and Cambridge

Nicholas Capaldi, Loyola University

P.M.S. Hacker, St. John's College, Oxford

Herman Philipse, University of Utrecht

Christopher Coope, University of Leeds

Stephen Clark, University of Liverpool

John Cottingham, University of Reading

Stephen Mulhall, New College, Oxford

Michela Massimi, University College London

Charles Travis, King's College London

Anthony O'Hear, University of Buckingham

Visions of Philosophy

DAVID E. COOPER

I

Characterizations of philosophy abound. It is 'the queen of the sciences', a grand and sweeping metaphysical endeavour; or, less regally, it is a sort of deep anthropology or 'descriptive metaphysics', uncovering the general presuppositions or conceptual schemes that lurk beneath our words and thoughts. A different set of images portray philosophy as a type of therapy, or as a spiritual exercise, a way of life to be followed, or even as a special branch of poetry or politics. Then there is a group of characterizations that include philosophy as linguistic analysis, as phenomenological description, as conceptual geography, or as genealogy in the sense proposed by Nietzsche and later taken up by Foucault.

These characterizations and images – together with any number of others – could, of course, be taxonomized in different ways. For instance, someone might want to gather together the images of philosophy as deep anthropology, therapy and phenomenological description on the ground that philosophy, so pictured, focuses exclusively upon the *human* – on the presuppositions of human thought and talk, on mental health, and on human experiences. But the way I gathered together the various characterizations and images into three groups reflects, I suggest, a fundamental divide in attitudes towards philosophy.

For those who favour the first group of characterizations – philosophy as grand metaphysics, descriptive metaphysics, or deep anthropology – philosophy is an essentially *theoretical, speculative* enterprise. ('Speculative', in the honourable eighteenth-century sense employed, for instance, by Kant.) Its orientation is necessarily and primarily towards Truth – truths about reality or, failing that, about the conceptual schemes we employ for capturing what we take reality to be.[1] For those whose image of philosophy is that of a

---

[1]   Peter Strawson compared the 'analysis' engaged in by the 'descriptive metaphysician' with the enquiries of the theoretical linguist into the 'deep structures' of languages. See his *Analysis and Metaphysics: An Introduction to Philosophy*, (Oxford: Oxford University Press, 1992).

doi:10.1017/S1358246109990026   © The Royal Institute of Philosophy and the contributors 2009

David E. Cooper

therapy, a spiritual exercise, edifying poetry or politics, philosophy is, in essence, a *practical*, *vital* enterprise. Its orientation is towards the Good, towards Life as it should be. The Good in question might be that of the soul, of the mind, of society, maybe of the world as a whole. For all the differences among them, it is this practical, vital orientation that gathers together Wittgenstein's image of philosophy as a cure for 'mental cramps'; the Buddhist's idea of philosophy as wisdom in the service of the overcoming of suffering; the Stoic sage's commitment to philosophy as an exercise aimed at peace of mind; Heidegger's philosophical 'poetry' that will attune us to Being and release us to live authentically; and Marx's embrace of philosophy as an engine of change, not interpretation.[2]

Finally, for those who characterize philosophy as linguistic analysis, conceptual geography, genealogy and the like, the enterprise is essentially defined in terms of its *method* or *style* of enquiry. Philosophy, so considered, has no intrinsic orientation of its own: rather, it can be placed in service to Truth or to the Good, or both. Linguistic analysis, for instance, might be thought of as, in the first instance, an 'under-labourer of the sciences', preparing the ground on which science will unearth its truths. Or it might be seen as, primarily, a method employed in philosophical therapy, a means towards that conceptual clarity that enables us to clear up the confusions that depress us and distort our lives. In Ancient China, a major preoccupation was 'The Rectification of Names', something deemed necessary both in order to align our thought with reality, but also for the proper conduct of government. Nietzschean genealogy, likewise, might be engaged in either for the truths it discovers about our concepts, or for the way that – the *pudenda origo* of our moral systems now exposed – we are released from loyalty to those systems and are free to create 'new tables of values'.

Precisely because characterizations of philosophy in terms of method or style assign to philosophy no orientation of its own, they strike me as being secondary. For they feed upon some prior vision of philosophy's aim and orientation. Maybe philosophy does have, or should have, its distinctive methods and styles of enquiry: but that will be because these are the methods and styles especially appropriate for an enterprise – philosophy – that is already understood in terms of a purpose or orientation.

---

[2] On Heideggerian 'poetry' and Marx's 'politics' as expressions of conceptions of philosophy, see Richard Rorty, 'Philosophy as science, as metaphor, and as politics', in his *Essays on Heidegger and Others*, (Cambridge: Cambridge University Press, 1991).

And if that is so, then the basis divide is between the two visions of philosophy as, respectively, theory or speculation orientated towards Truth, and vital practice orientated towards the Good, towards Life.

II

I have spoken of 'visions' and 'images' of philosophy, and this, I think, is an appropriate vocabulary, especially when it is made to resonate with Wittgenstein's remarks, at the beginning of *Philosophical Investigations*,[3] that distinguish *pictures* and *ideas*. There, the distinction is applied to views about language, and Wittgenstein contrasts particular ideas about language – such as that the meaning of a word is the object it names – from a larger picture of language, as a system of names. But the distinction is clearly intended to apply more widely. Ideas, he tells us, are 'rooted' in pictures, which means that pictures are more basic – so basic, indeed, that they cannot be decisively refuted, since they help to determine what counts as refutation. A Wittgensteinian picture, as one commentator explains, is given up by people only when they have been *converted* and experienced a 'reorientation of interests'.[4]

Talk of 'conversion' and 'reorientation' does not mean that nothing can sensibly be said for or against a picture, so as reasonably to invite or to resist conversion or a change of interest. Indeed, Wittgenstein's own point – when invoking the notions of meaning as use, language games, and the forms of life in which these games are placed – seems to have been to convert his readers away from what he saw as a distorting vision of philosophical enquiry. The vision in question is one of the two great rival visions I identified earlier – the picture of philosophy as theory, as speculation, with its orientation towards Truth. I am sympathetic to Wittgenstein's desire to convert away from this vision, and this is a sympathy I shall be trying to justify in this essay.

Some care, however, is needed in order to see what is really at issue between the rival visions. Champions of philosophy as theory or speculative science will usually concede, or rather boast, that philosophy's achievements can be exploited for bettering the human condition. At the most general level, their point will be that things go better for us when we know what is true, for by acting on the basis of beliefs that match up with how things are we are less liable to

---

[3] Trans. G.E.M. Anscombe, (London: Macmillan, 1969), §1.
[4] Stephen Mulhall, *Inheritance and Originality: Wittgenstein, Heidegger, Kierkegaard*, (Oxford: Oxford University Press, 2001), 36ff.

live in friction with the world. At the same time, proponents of the rival vision of philosophy as a practical, vital enterprise will readily concede that achievement of its practical purposes requires understanding – that philosophers, even if they see themselves as therapists or poets, need to be 'in the truth'. Philosophical therapy, after all, is not like administering a drug, and philosophical poetry is not fantasy.

But these polite concessions do not entail that there is no genuine rivalry. For one thing, the concessions being made are liable to be accused by rivals of not going far enough. For example, there will be those – Fichte, perhaps, or William James – who accuse the champions of philosophy as theory or speculation of failing to recognize that the Truth towards which philosophy is allegedly orientated is, ultimately, inseparable from the Good. In philosophy, at least, the true is what it is good to believe.

Aside from accusations of this kind, and the counter-accusations they are liable to invite, there is surely a genuine rivalry, between the two visions, over the *essence* or *soul*, as it were, of philosophy. Is philosophy essentially Truth-orientated and only accidentally, if at all, a contribution to the Good? Or is it, conversely, an essentially practical endeavour, with whatever concern it needs to have for Truth subordinated to, and shaped by, its pursuit of the Good? Later on, I shall revise this way of putting things. But locating the issue in this way is, I hope, sufficient to allow me to proceed to the business of conveying my sympathy for the practical vision – of defending a conversion away from the vision of philosophy as theory and a reorientation of interests in the direction of the Good. My claim is that the practical vision is more faithful to the origins and continuing impetus of philosophy. So I begin with some remarks on the infidelity of the rival vision to these origins and impetus.

III

Richard Rorty (see note 2) uses the name 'scientism' for the vision of philosophy as theory or speculative science. This is liable to mislead, for 'scientism' is more familiarly applied to a particular, modern version of that wider vision. I am thinking, for example, of the version articulated by W.V.O. Quine, when he writes that 'philosophy is continuous with [natural] science', and differs from the individual natural sciences only in the breadth of the claims it makes. Since 'whatever can be known can be known by means of science',[5] the

---

[5] 'Philosophical progress in language theory', *Metaphilosophy* **1**, 1970, 1.

continuity of philosophy with natural science is just as well. Here we have a good example of a particular 'idea' rooted in the larger 'picture' of philosophy as theory.

Rorty's paradigmatic example of an advocate of 'scientism' is a philosopher who is certainly no Quinean – Edmund Husserl. This is because, Rorty tells us, for Husserl philosophy is founded on the conviction that it can emulate and indeed surpass the natural sciences in establishing genuinely *universal* knowledge'. And that is a pretty good way of characterizing the vision of philosophy as theory or speculative science. In this vision, philosophy is essentially driven by the desire to know, and therefore owes its origins and development to, above all, the challenge of *scepticism.*

Why might this vision be less than compelling? To begin with, it will only be as compelling as the picture it assumes of the special sciences, such as physics, as repositories of objective knowledge of reality. Philosophy, after all, deserves the labels of 'theory', 'speculative science', and 'a quest for universal knowledge' because it is reckoned to emulate and surpass the special sciences. Now ironically, it was Husserl – following the lead of Nietzsche and Bergson, and in turn followed by his student, Heidegger – who helped to render suspect the image, the self-image indeed, of the sciences as mirrors of nature, unclouded or uncontaminated by 'all-too-human' interests, perspectives, prejudices and purposes. If, in the light of the powerful criticisms advanced by these philosophers, this (self) image of the sciences has lost its power to compel, then the comparison of philosophy with the sciences – the invitation to see philosophy as the viable pursuit of 'universal knowledge' – will have back-fired. Like the sciences themselves, philosophy will have been rendered a particular perspective on the world, a particular way of organizing or regimenting human experience. This is not, in itself, to deprecate the philosophical endeavour, but it is to surrender the vision of philosophy as essentially orientated towards Truth.

Another reason for finding the vision uncompelling concerns the assumption that philosophy must be primarily a response to the challenge of scepticism. Here, too, there is a danger of the strategy back-firing. For, even if this assumption is true – which is hardly evident – it is not clear that it helps to secure the vision of philosophy as 'universal knowledge'. And this is because, historically, sceptical challenges were intended more often than not, less as invitations or demands to people that they secure their shaky claims to knowledge, than as challenges to ways of living, to misguided pursuits of the Good. Consider, for example, Pyrrhonism, in both its Hellenistic and early modern forms. The last thing that was wanted by Pyrrho and his heirs, like Montaigne, was to goad people into trying to establish their claims to knowledge. On the contrary, their point was to *deter* people from wasting time and energy on a febrile, frustrating and futile search for certainty. A similar observation applies to scepticism in the context of Indian thought. In defending the *pramanas* ('means to knowledge') against critics, the philosophers of the Nyāya ('Logic') school were not primarily concerned to establish the possibility of certainty, but to defend the exercise of certain capacities – such as perception and testimony – deemed to contribute to 'felicity' and 'release from the wheel of life'. And what some of those sceptical critics, like the Buddhist thinker Nāgārjuna, were interested in arguing was not that we do not really know what we claim to know, but that we should reject the whole conceptual scheme within which calls for evidence, and distinctions between the veridical and the illusory, assume excessive importance. And that is because it is a scheme which puts human beings 'out of joint' with 'the harmonious whole' of the universe.[6]

There is something further that makes questionable the thought that, even if philosophy has often been a response to a sceptical challenge, it must therefore be pictured as, primarily, a theoretical exercise, as the attempt to establish 'universal knowledge'. Sceptical challenges only have the power to disturb if the kind of knowledge whose possibility is challenged is a kind that *matters* to people. Few people would devote a career to trying to secure beliefs that, as Descartes put it, 'no sane man has ever seriously doubted'. But, in that case, attention will shift to the question of why it is that philosophers attempt to secure the possibility of this or that kind of knowledge, of why it is that this kind matters. (For Descartes, it was the potential of scepticism to question the existence of God and the afterlife which made confrontation with it an urgent issue, and that is because scepticism is thereby threatening 'the greatest joy of which we are capable in this life'.[7]) And it will then be tempting to characterize philosophy, not as a theoretical endeavour to establish 'universal knowledge', but in terms of vital goals that are too important to be left as matters of opinion or taste – in terms, therefore, of an orientation towards the Good.

---

[6] See the selections from the Nyāya-Sutras and Nāgārjuna in David E. Cooper and Peter S. Fosb (eds.), *Philosophy: The Classic Readings*, (Oxford: Wiley-Blackwell, 2009).
[7] *Selected Philosophical Writings*, trans. J. Cottingham, R. Stoothoff and D. Murdoch, (Cambridge: Cambridge University Press, 1988), 98.

IV

If it is not *per se* worries about the possibility of knowledge to which philosophy should be seen as a response, what is it that gives to philosophy its impetus and continuing breath? In a couple of books, I have suggested answers that invoke, respectively, the notions of *alienation* and *answerability*.[8] The answers gestured at by those terms are not, I think, at odds with one another: on the contrary, they complement one another. In this section, I shall rehearse those suggested answers, and in the following section indicate what seems to me to be some of their combined merits.

There is nothing original, of course, in the suggestion that philosophy owes its origin and subsequent development to human beings' sense of alienation from the rest of reality. For Hegel, famously, the history of philosophy just is the story of the struggle by Spirit – and by its main 'vehicles', human beings – to overcome alienation. Philosophy's work will be done only when Spirit recognizes that there is, after all, no 'out and out other' to itself. After millennia during which human consciousness has been dominated by alienating dichotomies like mind and nature, or freedom and necessity, philosophy will eventually succeed in enabling us to 'find ourselves in nature' once more and to appreciate that our freedom presupposes rational necessity.[9]

Hegel's story of philosophy is but one attempt – albeit a particularly stirring one – to construe our intellectual history as that of creatures trying to resolve the matter of their status in a universe most of which indeed can strike them as 'out and out other'. And there is no need to subscribe to Hegel's particular story in order to appreciate the element of truth in the wider vision. Once human beings emerged from what Hegel called their 'sunkenness in nature', it must indeed have struck many of them how radically different they seemed to be from just about everything that surrounded them. Only they, it seemed, possessed, *inter alia*, a moral sense, a capacity for freedom, a feeling for beauty, and a tendency to worry about their relationship to the wider world.

The central issue posed for philosophy – the issue which, on this picture, drives the whole enterprise – is how, without cavalier

---

8   *World Philosophies: An Historical Introduction*, 2nd ed., Oxford: Blackwell, 2003; *The Measure of Things: Humanism, Humility and Mystery*, (Oxford: Clarendon Press, 2002).

9   See Hegel's *Encyclopedia of Logic*, §194, and *Phenomenology of Spirit*, §12 and §195.

dismissal of the uniqueness of human beings, they can nevertheless be perceived, and perceive themselves, to be integrated with the rest of reality. How, without rendering them aliens, freaks or danglers – set against and apart from what is 'out and out other' to them – may all that is distinctive of human existence be understood?

One thing, surely, that would soon have taxed our ancestors as they emerged from their 'sunkenness in nature' – from their innocence, as it were – must have been the question of whether what they thought, felt and did *measured up* to or was properly *answerable* to anything beyond itself. To be sure, there is a sophisticated modern, or postmodern, conceit that, as Rorty puts it, the only fidelity we require is 'obedience to our own conventions'.[10] But that is a view – in so stark a form, at least – which few people entertained until recent times. It is a *late* view, and one which, arguably, no one really subscribes to even today. At any rate a case can be made for saying that such a conceit is *unliveable*. Whether or not that is so, it is surely true that, for a very long time, the search has been on for something to which our words, thoughts, feelings, purposes and deeds might be answerable – for what Kierkegaard called a *Maalestock*, a 'measure', a 'qualitative criterion'.[11]

The 'measure' intended here is one of our lives as a whole, and certainly not simply, or mainly, of the accuracy of our beliefs. While it may be impossible finally to isolate the components of belief, feeling, purpose and action in our lives, the initial focus in the search for measure is liable to be upon purpose and action. For the 'metaphysical horror', as Leszek Kolakowski calls it,[12] that impels the quest for something to which our lives our answerable is the dark thought that it just doesn't matter what we do and aim at, that nothing we seek and achieve is worth more than anything else we might have sought or achieved had life gone differently.

The upshot of these reflections on philosophy as grounded in concerns with alienation and answerability is that philosophy is indeed orientated towards the Good. For if this vision is cogent then, to put the matter in a somewhat Daoist idiom, philosophy's enterprise is the dual one of a search for a sense of our integration with the way of things and a quest to find, within the way of things, a measure of our lives. Differently expressed, it is the endeavour to

---

[10]   See the Preface to Rorty's *Consequences of Pragmatism*, (Brighton: Harvester, 1982).
[11]   *The Sickness Unto Death*, in H. and E. Hong (eds.), *The Essential Kierkegaard*, (Princeton: Princeton University Press, 1997), 363.
[12]   *Metaphysical Horror*, (Oxford: Blackwell, 1988).

overcome alienation and to become liberated from the 'horrible' thought that lives are answerable to nothing beyond themselves.

V

But how faithful is the vision articulated in the previous section to the genesis of philosophy and, more importantly, does it capture the continuing impetus of philosophy?

It speaks in favour of this vision, in my judgement, that it places the original enterprise of philosophy in close proximity to religion. The two are close since what philosophy endeavours to establish − the integration of human life with the rest of reality and a measure for the conduct of life − is promised by just about every religion to those men and women who adopt its dispensation. It is no accident, surely, that 'the axial age' in which the great religions emerged is the one in which philosophy is first pursued in a disciplined, critical form. Indeed, for many centuries, making a cut between works of religion and works of philosophy would have been an arbitrary procedure. Were the *Upanishads*, for instance, exercises in religion or in philosophy? A pointless question.

That philosophy emerged in the same climate of concerns as religion does not mean, of course, that every philosophy must be religiously committed. But it does suggest that the philosophies which belong to the main historical current of philosophy have shared the aspirations of religion − integration and measure − even when these aspirations have been pursued godlessly and naturalistically.

The best defence of the vision, however, is that it renders salient, and helps to ground, the discernible rhythms that run through and give form to what I just called 'the main historical current' of philosophy. One does not have to subscribe to a grand History of Philosophy, replete with Laws, Goals and Progress, in order to accept that a relatively small number of theses and antitheses − and the rhythm of their oscillation − gives structure and pattern to philosophy's history.

Fichte may not have been too far wrong when maintaining, at the start of his *Wissenschaftslehre*,[13] that the only real dispute in philosophy has always been between *Idealism* and *Realism* (or *Dogmatism*, as he pejoratively called it). This is the dispute, in all its many shapes, between those schemes (like Fichte's own) which

---

[13] *Science of Knowledge*, trans. P. Heath and J. Lachs, (New York: Appleton-Century-Crofts, 1970), 9ff.

would make the world more mind-like than we usually imagine it to be, and those which (like physicalism) would render the mind more world-like than we might imagine it to be.

It is hard, in my view, to understand the centrality of this dispute between Idealism and Realism – and the constant oscillation between them over the millennia – except as a conflict between two opposed strategies for addressing the issue of alienation. The world can be shown not to be 'out and out other', and hence alien, to human beings *either* by demonstrating that it is much more like us than we thought, *or* by proving that we are much more like it than we thought. To the first strategy belong the attempts, for example, to depict the world as purposive, or as 'constituted' by thought, or as a collection of divine ideas. To the second strategy belong the attempts to establish that, for example, we are purely material beings, or that human freedom and the moral sense are, if not illusions, then reducible to the same nature possessed by everything else that we live alongside. (Dualists, incidentally, do not stand outside the dialectic of alienation. For while they may try to be even-handed in recognizing the irreducible existence of both mind and matter, they are usually anxious to mitigate the alienating effect of the opposition they maintain. They will argue, for instance, that there is divinely established harmony between the two or, as in the case of some Indian schools, that an oppositional engagement with the material world is a precondition for an eventual purification and liberation of the mind.)

If Fichte exaggerates in judging philosophy to be no more than the prolonged battle between Idealism and Realism, this is because he ignores another, though not unrelated, struggle that has gone on for millennia. Here the pattern is one of recoils back and forth between three stances on the issue of whether there is a way reality is independently of how it is conceived of and described. According to one of these stances, which we might label 'humanism', there is no such way. The world is necessarily a 'human world', and no sense can finally attach to the idea that there is a way the world is that transcends our perspectives and 'takes' on it. As Sartre put it, it is only through human being that 'it happens that *there is* a world'.[14] According to the other two stances, there is a way reality absolutely is, irrespective of our 'takes' on it – but a crucial difference separates these two stances. For the first, absolute reality can, in principle at least, be conceptualized and articulated: we can, with enough

[14] *Being and Nothingness*, trans. H. Barnes, (London: Methuen, 1957), 552.

effort and luck, know what it is like. For the second, however, it cannot be conceptualized and articulated: reality must be an ineffable mystery to us. In honour of Kant, we might label these two stances 'dogmatic' and 'transcendental' absolutism respectively. The former is represented by all those metaphysical systems – from Spinozan monism to Logical Atomism, from Berkeleyan idealism to contemporary physicalism – which purport to tell us just how reality fundamentally is. The latter is represented by the many philosophies that invoke a notion – the Dao, Brahman, the Godhead, Being, or whatever – that is deemed to be radically mysterious and 'beyond' whatever can be articulated.

It is difficult, in my judgement, to understand why so many people have devoted so much time, energy and passion to defending or refuting the positions just adumbrated except by reference to a preoccupation with the 'vital' issue of answerability or measure. In relation to this issue, the position of the 'dogmatic' absolutist has its obvious appeal: not only is there a way that reality absolutely is, but we can know how it is and therefore hope to identify how our lives must go if they are properly to accord with fundamental features of reality – with, say, the divine will or with Nature's teleological ends. For both the 'humanist' and the 'transcendentalist', however, this is a pipe-dream, for it fails to appreciate that whatever we can conceptualize and articulate belongs, not to an absolute order, but to a perspectival world, one that is the way it is only in relation to human purposes and interests. For the 'transcendentalist', this cannot, however, mean abandoning the idea of absolute reality, for then our lives would be without anything to answer to beyond themselves. What has to be accepted, though, is that this reality is radically mysterious, and that while we can have intimations of the Dao, Being or whatever – intimations sufficient to provide some measure for our lives – this does not approximate to the crisp, theoretical, propositional knowledge aspired to by the 'dogmatist'.

For the 'humanists', meanwhile, measure and answerability must be, as it were, internal to human existence: for while they reject the appeal to mystery as much as the appeal to an absolute that may be articulated, they are usually unwilling entirely to give up on the quest for measure. The measure or 'criterion' of our beliefs, values and purposes, it might be suggested, is the strength and authenticity of the commitment we have to them. Or the proposal might be that we answer to all that there is to be answerable to when we adopt beliefs, values and purposes without the intrusion of comforting and self-serving illusions – of the kind, it will be added, to which absolutists are prone.

So, to conclude this section, the history of philosophy – its rhythms, patterns of recoils, its alliances and disalliances – falls better into place when it is envisioned as the story of a long enterprise engaged in by human beings who struggle to resolve the 'vital' issues of alienation and answerability. The story manifests the endeavour to live well, to lead lives that are integrated with, and measure up to, the way of things. Thus envisioned, philosophy has been an essentially practical or vital undertaking, orientated towards the Good.

VI

In this final section, I want to consider a predictable objection to the vision I have been recommending. The objection is not, I think, fatal, and it provides a welcome opportunity to guard against a misconstrual of the position I have advanced.

A sympathetic critic might concede that philosophy is thoroughly implicated in the endeavour to live well and with a sense, therefore, of integration with a way of things to which human life is answerable. But this critic will insist that philosophy itself is best characterized as a particular *means* towards the success of this endeavour – a specifically theoretical, speculative, 'scientific' means. Philosophy, then, is a search for truths, albeit ones that may then be practically and vitally exploited for a wider enterprise directed towards the Good.

Well, it was cheerfully conceded in section II that philosophy's way of securing integration and answerability – its angle of approach to the Good, as it were – is that of *understanding*. In that sense, yes, philosophy is orientated towards Truth. But this is not to concede that the understanding philosophy seeks is simply, or at all, a *means* to the resolution of vital issues. And this is because the understanding sought is not finally separable – as a means is from its end – from the Good towards which it is orientated. It is the idea of an *opposition* between orientations towards the True and the Good – one that my earlier remarks might have encouraged – which now needs to be revised in the light of the critic's objection.

The revision will invoke something like the Ancients' equation of knowledge with virtue. This equation was most often employed to stress that a virtuous person must have knowledge. A bad man, as the Stoics urged, cannot be wise. But the equation can be, and has been, employed to emphasize that a person is not possessed of the relevant kind of knowledge – philosophical understanding, in effect – unless he or she is attuned to the Good. For the understanding in question has not been acquired or fully absorbed unless it brings with it precisely that transformation of vision and comportment towards the world which was the purpose in seeking it.

Stoicism furnishes a good example of connection. In Book 3 §2 of his *Meditations*, Marcus Aurelius writes that the Stoic philosopher or sage, who has achieved 'deeper insight into the processes of the universe', will therefore find 'hardly any phenomenon' that does not give him pleasure and invite his respect and admiration. For as he explains later (Bk 10 §21), this 'insight' embraces the appreciation that 'the universe loves to produce all that [is] produced', an appreciation that requires the sage in turn to 'love' the world as a whole. Failure so to 'love' the world – to feel integrated with it, and to find the measure of one's life in it – entails that one is not, after all, a sage, a Stoic philosopher, for one cannot as yet have achieved that authentic 'cosmic consciousness' which is the criterion of sagehood.[15]

Many other examples from the history of philosophy could be given of this insistence that philosophical understanding is lacking or incomplete unless manifested in virtues that are in turn manifested in an appropriate comportment towards the world. For the Buddha, for instance, unless enlightenment or understanding cuts a person free from the 'unwholesome roots' of greed, aversion, and delusion, then it is not enlightenment or full understanding. For properly to understand, and not simply to mouth, such doctrines as that of 'not self' *is* in crucial part to be transformed in the way one sees, and feels and acts towards other people. But there is no need to pile up more examples in order to appreciate the central point being made. The understanding that philosophy seeks is not 'mere' propositional knowledge that may or may not then be exploited for some practical purpose, and that may or may not be employed as a means to the resolution of some 'vital' issue. Rather, it is an understanding that is already invested with an orientation towards the Good, already 'on the way' towards resolution of the 'vital' issues that give philosophy its impetus.

The understanding in question, to give it an old name, is wisdom or *sophia*. So my conclusion, my proposal, could be expressed by saying that philosophy is indeed philosophy, the love and pursuit of wisdom. The journey towards that conclusion has been, I hope, a little less boring than the conclusion itself.

---

[15]   On Marcus Aurelius, see the illuminating discussion in Pierre Hadot, *Philosophy as a Way of Life*, trans. M. Chase, (Oxford: Blackwell, 1995), 190ff and 250ff.

Listening to Clifford's Ghost

PETER VAN INWAGEN

The Clifford of my title is W. K. Clifford, who is perhaps best known as the exponent of a certain ethic of belief – an ethic of belief that he was probably the first to formulate explicitly and which no one has defended with greater eloquence or moral fervor. In the lecture called, appropriately enough, 'The Ethics of Belief,'[1] Clifford summarized his ethic in a single, memorable sentence: 'It is wrong always, everywhere, and for any one, to believe anything upon insufficient evidence'. It will be convenient for us to have a name for this ethical thesis. I will call it 'ethical evidentialism' – 'evidentialism' for short.

Everyone I know of who has written on 'The Ethics of Belief' has taken it for granted that Clifford propounded evidentialism with a certain target in mind, and that that target was religious belief. In the last twenty years or so, however, philosophers have come to realize that a strong case can be made for the thesis that believing things without sufficient evidence is a pervasive feature of human life, a pervasive feature of the way we hold and acquire beliefs in the ordinary business of life, in politics, in matters pertaining to literature and the arts, and in science. And they have noted that failures to observe the dictates of evidentialism in these areas are not in the main 'near misses,' cases in which these dictates might easily have been observed if only people had been a little more careful about what they believed, if only they had taken a little more trouble to collect and examine evidence relevant to their beliefs. It seems, rather, that vast numbers of people believe things (things in no way related to religion or the supernatural) for which it is impossible for them to have sufficient evidence – if not impossible in principle, impossible for those people in the circumstances in which they in fact hold those beliefs.

My concern in this essay is not with religious beliefs or political beliefs or scientific beliefs or the beliefs on the basis of which we conduct the everyday business of our lives. It is with philosophical beliefs. I shall be concerned with the question whether any important philosophical belief is, or ever could be, held by anyone (philosopher

---

[1] *Lectures and Essays, Vol II* (London: Macmillan, 1879). Variously reprinted.

doi:10.1017/S1358246109990038

or not) otherwise than upon insufficient evidence. And I shall be concerned only with philosophical beliefs that satisfy the following two conditions.

(1)	They are positive, not negative. What it means to say that a belief (proposition, thesis, conjecture, theory, hypothesis ...) is positive or negative is hard to explain in any philosophically satisfactory way, and I will not attempt to do so. I shall have to be content to give a few examples of philosophical beliefs or propositions that are paradigmatically *not* positive: 'Formalism is not the correct philosophy of mathematics'; 'Utilitarianism is not an acceptable ethical theory'; 'Knowledge is not simply justified true belief.' And, by the same token, 'Knowledge *is* justified true belief,' although it is no doubt a false thesis, is a positive thesis, and to assent to it is to have a positive philosophical belief. Formalism and utilitarianism — assuming that these terms have been sufficiently well defined that they denote particular propositions — are positive theses, and anyone who accepts formalism or accepts utilitarianism thereby has a positive belief.

(2)	They are not held by almost all human beings. I shall not be concerned with philosophical theses that have been accepted by all sane non-philosophers and have been denied only by a few philosophers — generally practitioners of 'revisionary metaphysics.' I assume that there are such philosophical beliefs because I assume that the denial of a philosophical belief is itself a philosophical belief, and many philosophers have believed things (in, as it were, their professional capacity) that almost everyone — even most philosophers — would deny. Or so it seems at least plausible to maintain. Plausible examples of things that fall into this category would be: 'Change and motion are not real features of the world'; 'One has no reason to suppose that there are minds other than one's own'; 'There are no material objects.'[2] (All these

[2]	I say *plausible* examples, because questions concerning what is uncontroversial on the Clapham omnibus can be extremely controversial in the philosophical lecture-room. Berkeley notoriously maintained that no one but a few philosophers had ever believed in the existence of matter, and my former colleague José Benardete insists that Zeno believed nothing about change and motion that contradicted the beliefs of any of the passengers on the Clapham omnibus. I'll say this: I mean to consider only those philosophical beliefs that are, so to put it, uncontroversially controversial. It will be only these beliefs that will fall within the scope of the question

theses, or my statements of them, contain some sort of negative construction. Nonetheless, all of them are what I would call 'positive' theses. As I said, 'positive' is a very hard term to explain.[3]) Thus, philosophical beliefs like 'Change and motion are real features of the world,' 'One does have reason to suppose that there are minds other than one's own,' and 'There are material objects' do not satisfy my second condition. (I'll sometimes refer to beliefs that do satisfy the second condition as 'controversial,' simply because 'not held by almost all human beings' is a clumsy phrase.)

When I speak of philosophical beliefs, then, I mean my remarks to apply only to positive philosophical beliefs that are not beliefs that are held by almost all human beings. So to restrict my topic is not *severely* to restrict it: a vast range of philosophical beliefs satisfy both the conditions by which I have narrowed my subject-matter.

Let us ask: has any philosopher ever had sufficient evidence for any (positive, controversial) philosophical belief in Clifford's sense of 'sufficient evidence'? This question immediately raises a prior

---

I am asking – whether any philosophical belief is, or ever could be, held by anyone otherwise than upon insufficient evidence.

[3] I would say that the negation of a negative belief must be a positive belief, but that the negation of a positive belief will in some cases also be a positive belief. An analogy is perhaps provided by the concept of positive and negative geographical information. That the spy whose whereabouts we should like to know is not in London is a negative piece of geographical information, and that he *is* in London is a positive piece of geographical information. That he is in the Western Hemisphere is a positive piece of geographical information, but so is the information that he is *not* in the Western Hemisphere – at least given that he must be either in the Eastern or the Western Hemisphere –, for the latter piece of information narrows down our range of possible specific hypotheses as to his location precisely as effectively as its negation does. I might put my point this way: 'Theism is false' is a positive philosophical belief because both theism and its negation, atheism, are philosophical *theories* or at any rate philosophical *positions*. 'Utilitarianism is false' is not a positive philosophical belief because its negation, non-utilitarianism, so to call it, is not a philosophical theory or position. There are many philosophical theories – many ethical theories – that are incompatible with utilitarianism, but non-utilitarianism, or the disjunction of all ethical theories (indeed, of all propositions) incompatible with utilitarianism, is not one of them: it's incompatible with utilitarianism all right, but it's not an ethical theory – and not a theory of any sort.

question: what is that sense? We may well ask, for Clifford never defines the phrase 'sufficient evidence'. Perhaps this phrase requires no definition in the cases Clifford presents as paradigms of belief upon insufficient evidence. (For example, the famous case of the ship-owner who sent his ship to sea without having her overhauled and refitted, and who, although some doubts had passed through his mind as to whether she was really fit to sail, 'succeeded in overcoming these melancholy reflections.') In these cases, perhaps, we can just *see* that a certain belief was held upon insufficient evidence on *any* reasonable definition of 'insufficient evidence'. But philosophical beliefs are not much like the belief that a certain ship is seaworthy, and questions about what counts as evidence – much less, sufficient evidence – for them are more difficult to answer. We shall require some sort of understanding of 'sufficient evidence' if we are to answer the question I have posed, or even to say anything of interest about it.

We shall, in fact, need to have some sort of understanding of three things: of '(a body of) evidence,'[4] of what it is for one to 'have' a certain body of evidence (so understood), and of what it is for a certain body of evidence that one 'has' to be 'sufficient' to support some belief that one has.

I will not attempt to give general definitions of these terms (or accounts of these concepts). That would be a task far beyond my abilities. I will, however, try to say something about what these terms or concepts come to when they are applied to philosophical beliefs.

One form that evidence takes in philosophy is *argument*. One might even suppose that, in philosophy, evidence and argument are so closely related that, with care, the two can be identified. After all, if one has a (good) argument for some philosophical conclusion, then, surely, when one presents that argument to an audience, one presents one's audience with evidence for its conclusion? And if one has evidence that supports a philosophical conclusion, could that evidence not be formulated as or presented in the form of an argument?

Whatever the answers to these rhetorical questions may be, it seems that arguments for philosophical theses are at least *one* kind of evidence for them. Whatever evidence may be, what one's evidence for a certain belief is certainly has a great deal to do with how one

---

[4]   In present-day English, 'evidence' is a mass-term: one cannot (now) speak of 'an evidence' or 'evidences'. And there is no corresponding count-noun. Various idiomatic phrases like 'a piece of evidence' or 'a body of evidence' perform the function of the missing count-noun.

would answer the question, 'Why do you think that?'. More exactly, it has a great deal to do with how one would answer that question when the question is understood in what one might call its epistemic sense. (I oppose 'epistemic sense' to 'psychological or causal sense'. Taken in its epistemic sense, it anticipates an answer like, 'I was there. I saw him do it.' Taken in its psychological or causal sense, it anticipates an answer like, 'Alice has been saying that he did it, and I dislike him so much that I suppose I'm inclined to believe anything discreditable about him.') When this question is understood in its epistemic sense, it seems to be indistinguishable from the question 'What's your evidence for that?' And a philosopher will typically respond to the question 'Why do you think that?' (where 'that' is a philosophical thesis) by presenting one or more arguments for the thesis in question. It is, in fact, not easy to see what other kind of answer to this question there could be. It seems plausible to say that in philosophy evidence is argument – or at least that to *present* evidence is present one or more arguments.

If that is what evidence is in philosophy, what is it to 'have' the evidence for the conclusion of a certain argument that is, or is contained in, or is constituted by, that argument? The answer is pretty clearly this: It is to grasp or understand the argument. Or, if grasping or understanding an argument is a matter of degree: It is *fully* to grasp or understand the argument.

There may be some question as to what, exactly, is involved in grasping an argument. I do not want to build too much into this notion. I take it that one may grasp an argument (even fully grasp an argument) without having considered at length the possible replies to and objections to the argument, without having considered its possible implications, and without having raised the question whether similar or parallel arguments might lead to absurd conclusions. (One might, for example, fully grasp Anselm's ontological argument without having considered the question whether a parallel argument might be used to prove the existence of an island a greater than which cannot be conceived.) I would suppose, too, that it is possible at the same time fully to understand an argument and to believe, mistakenly, that it has false premises – or even to be mistaken about whether the argument is logically valid. (That case is something like this case: You and I are both looking at a sheep in a field; I, for one of those reasons that epistemologists are so skilled at contriving, mistakenly believe I am looking at a mock sheep, artfully crafted of papier-mâché. And you are under no such misapprehension. You and I have the same evidence for there being a sheep in the field; if I have a false belief about my

19

evidence for that thesis – even if I believe that it *isn't* evidence for that thesis –, that fact doesn't prevent its being evidence for that thesis, and evidence that I *have*.)

In light of these considerations, one may want to say that although evidence in philosophy indeed consists entirely of argument, the evidence relevant to a philosophical thesis *p* does not consist entirely of arguments whose conclusion is *p* or the denial of *p*. If we say that such arguments comprise the *primary* evidence relevant to *p*, we may designate those considerations that bear on the cogency of the arguments that comprise the primary evidence as *secondary* evidence that is relevant to *p*. The secondary evidence, like the primary evidence, will consist of arguments, but not arguments whose conclusion is *p* or its denial. The conclusions of the arguments comprising the secondary evidence will rather be propositions that concern the arguments for *p* or its denial: that this argument depends on an equivocation, that that one has a certain suppressed premise that needs to be considered carefully, that this one does not after all depend on an equivocation. (If there is secondary evidence for philosophical theses, there is no doubt tertiary evidence, and so, in theory, *ad infinitum*. But let us not go any further down that road, which is only a byway.)

To have the piece of evidence that is relevant to a philosophical thesis and is, or is contained in, or is constituted by, an argument is, I contend, simply to understand that argument – to understand it fully. Thus, if someone says to me, 'Why do you think that free will is incompatible with determinism?', and if, in reply, I produce a certain argument for that thesis (incompatibilism, it's called) – perhaps I write it on a blackboard – and if that argument is a complete statement of my reasons for accepting incompatibilism (no secondary evidence in this case), then you too will have the evidence for the incompatibility of free will and determinism that is my evidence for that thesis if you inspect the argument written on the blackboard and fully understand it. (And this could be the case even if, say, you believed that the argument contained a logical fallacy when in fact it didn't.)

Now, finally, what is it for a philosophical argument to be or constitute *sufficient* evidence for the philosophical thesis that is its conclusion? I am sorry to have to say that I do not know how to answer this question. Rather than try to answer it, I am going to explore one aspect of the concept of sufficient evidence (in philosophy). My exploration will take this form: I'll present an abstract, schematic case and proceed to ask a question about it. This is the case.

McX believes that p (I mean 'that p' to be a philosophical thesis of the sort I have said I should consider: a positive thesis not held by all human beings). McX has no evidence for this thesis beyond that contained in or constituted by the philosophical argument A (an argument whose conclusion is of course the proposition that p): if you asked him why (epistemic sense) he believed that p, he'd produce the argument A for your consideration, and that would be a complete answer to your question; this answer would leave out none of his grounds for believing that p. McX's colleague Wyman grasps the argument A (fully) and believes neither that p nor that not-p: if you asked Wyman whether p, she'd say (sincerely) something like, 'I don't know' or 'I haven't been able to decide what to think about that' in reply. Although Wyman grasps the argument A fully, she is not convinced by it and remains an agnostic in the matter of the truth or falsity of its conclusion.

And this is the question.

Suppose McX is aware of these facts about himself and Wyman. What, if anything, should he conclude from them? What, in particular, should he conclude about whether he believes that p 'upon sufficient evidence'?

Here is *one* chain of reasoning that might go through McX's mind when he considers these facts.

If my evidence for my belief that p were indeed sufficient evidence, it would lead any intelligent, rational person who reflected on it to believe that p. But Wyman has the same evidence for the proposition that p as I have. I say this because I recognize that my evidence is entirely contained in the argument A, and Wyman – I am convinced – fully grasps that argument. I know that she agrees with me on *this* point: the argument contains no logical fallacy. I am also convinced that she is an intelligent, rational person, and that she has carefully reflected on the argument. I must, therefore, conclude that my belief that p is not based on sufficient evidence.

This chain of reasoning, I say, might occur to McX. But if it does – and if on reflection he accepts its conclusion and proceeds to give up his belief that p – he'll be, as the history of philosophy amply demonstrates, a most unusual philosopher. What alternatives might be open to him (other than ignoring the question of what to think about the

implications of Wyman's failure to be convinced by the argument)?
There would seem to be two alternatives:

He might conclude that there's something wrong with Wyman.
In becoming acquainted with the argument A, she has acquired
sufficient evidence for p — and nevertheless refuses to accept p.
And that implies that she is in some way defective. She's not,
after all, an intelligent, rational person. Or she lacks philosophical
ability or insight — at least in the degree to which he, McX,
displays these qualities. He can *see* that certain propositions
(certain premises of the argument) are conceptual or necessary
truths, and she can't. Or she hasn't considered the disputed premises of the argument with sufficient care — despite the fact that
she said she's been thinking about nothing else for a week. Or
she's intellectually lazy or dishonest: she doesn't want to accept
the conclusion of the argument because it would mean tearing
up most of her own philosophical work and starting over or
because it contradicts philosophical or religious or political
beliefs to which she's strongly emotionally attached — with the
consequence that she has *managed to convince herself* that
propositions that are self-evident are doubtful or even false. In
short, for one reason or another, Wyman is not being rational.

He might conclude that there's nothing wrong with either
Wyman or himself. He might say that he and Wyman are both
being perfectly rational. They've both carefully considered argument A; he's convinced by it, and that's okay; she's unconvinced
by it, and that's okay. That's just how things go in philosophy.

In any real situation, both these alternatives can seem extraordinarily
unappealing. Or, if we include the first alternative that I mentioned in
the range of the alternatives we are considering ('I must, therefore,
conclude that my belief that p is not based on sufficient evidence'),
all three of these alternatives can seem extraordinarily unappealing.

We could sum up the three alternatives that confront McX
this way:

There's something wrong with me. I believe that p, and my
evidence is not sufficient to warrant belief that p (and that's bad).

There's something wrong with Wyman. Her evidence is
sufficient to warrant belief that p, but she does not believe that
p (and that's bad).

There's nothing wrong with either of us. I believe that p and
Wyman does not believe that p and the evidence that each of us

has that is relevant to the truth-value of p is identical. Therefore: either it can be all right to believe something when one's evidence is insufficient to warrant one's belief or (inclusive) it can be all right *not* to believe something when one's evidence *is* sufficient to warrant one's having that belief.

It is important to realize that the abstract story of McX and Wyman is not the mere presentation of a logical possibility. There are real situations of exactly the sort that is laid out schematically in the story. This sort of thing *happens,* and – with few if any exceptions – each of us philosophers confronts alternatives of the sort that confront McX. Asking ourselves what we make of the fact that other philosophers are not convinced by arguments we ourselves find convincing is a task we can avoid only by the ostrich method.

I will cite a concrete case of such disagreement that I have often cited, a case in which I myself figure. I believe that free will is incompatible with determinism.[5] What evidence can I appeal to in support of this belief? The most important part of this evidence can be presented in the form of an argument, an argument I have called the Consequence Argument. To make matters as simple as possible, let us pretend for the moment that the Consequence Argument comprises *all* the evidence I have for incompatibilism. That is to say, if you asked me, 'Why do you think that free will is incompatible with determinism?', I could do no better – and no more – than to write out one or more versions of the Consequence Argument for you and try to explain to you why I thought that each of its premises was true. (I'm going to count my defenses of the premises of the Consequence Argument as parts of the argument. If that sounds incoherent to you, I'll express myself this way: the *Narrow* Consequence Argument is a certain formally valid argument with numbered premises. The conclusion of the Narrow Argument is of course the proposition that free will and determinism are incompatible. The *Wide* Consequence Argument consists of the Narrow Consequence Argument plus everything I have to say in support of the premises of the Narrow Argument. For good measure, I shall include my definitions and explanations of the philosophical terms of art that occur in the Narrow Argument in the Wide Argument.

---

[5]   Despite the negative form of the word 'incompatible', I regard this as a clear case of a positive philosophical belief. Any appearance to the contrary is a linguistic accident – for suppose that instead of saying 'p is incompatible with q' we used an expression that did not have a negative form ('p denies q', perhaps, or 'p logically excludes q').

Peter van Inwagen

When I speak of the Consequence Argument in the sequel, I mean the Wide Consequence Argument.)

David Lewis knew all about the Consequence Argument. In fact, he wrote a characteristically wonderful paper about it called 'Are We Free to Break the Laws?'.[6] (This paper is the best defense of compatibilism that there is. It may well be the best paper about free will that there is.) He and I studied each other's arguments about the compatibility of free will and determinism carefully. We discussed the issues connected with this question carefully and at great length throughout the 1980s. I am therefore, I think, in a position to make this judgment: Lewis fully grasped the Consequence Argument. And he was not convinced by it. (He in fact accepted the denial of its conclusion. I'll presently incorporate this fact into my discussion. But let us pretend for the moment that Lewis simply failed to be convinced by the Consequence Argument; that he considered it carefully and was thereafter an agnostic about its conclusion.) If, therefore, I have no evidence for my belief that free will and determinism are incompatible but the evidence that is contained in or is constituted by the Consequence Argument, Lewis had all the evidence I had for the proposition that free will and determinism are incompatible, and yet did not accept this proposition. What should I conclude from this?

I should, of course, like to believe that I do not, in Clifford's phrase, accept this proposition upon insufficient evidence. But if the evidence I have for this proposition is sufficient evidence, why did Lewis, who had the same evidence, not also accept it? If it is epistemically wrong or irrational to accept a proposition upon insufficient evidence, is it not likewise wrong or irrational *not* to accept a proposition upon *sufficient* evidence? If I have sufficient evidence to support my belief that, say, the earth is more than 6,000 years old, and if I present a Young Earth Creationist with this evidence – if I 'present' this evidence to him in a way that has the consequence that he 'has' this evidence in the same sense as that in which *I* have it – is he not irrational if he does not come to share my belief? As I have said, I do not know how to give an account of sufficient evidence in philosophy (or in any other area of inquiry), but it is certainly plausible to suppose that whatever 'having sufficient evidence' (in any area, philosophy, geology, what have you), may be, it should bear the following relation to rationality: if one has

    6 *Philosophical Papers, Vol. II* (New York and Oxford: Oxford University Press, 1986), 291–98. The paper first appeared in *Theoria* 47 (1981), 113–21.

sufficient evidence for a proposition and does *not* accept that proposition, one is irrational. Or will someone say that one might have sufficient evidence for a proposition one does not accept and not be irrational owing to the fact that one has not carefully considered the implications of that evidence? Well, I don't mind if someone says that. If someone is inclined to, I'll simply add to my statement a clause to accommodate that person's scruple: if one has sufficient evidence for a proposition *and has carefully reflected on the implications of that evidence for the truth of that proposition* and does not accept that proposition, one is irrational. That will not affect the problem with which Lewis's failure to be convinced by the Consequence Argument confronts me, for Lewis had certainly carefully reflected on the implications of the Consequence Argument for the truth of the proposition that free will and determinism are incompatible.

So. How shall I respond to this problem? Shall I say that there's something wrong with *me*? Shall I say, that is, that I do not have sufficient evidence for my belief that free will and determinism are incompatible? Or shall I say that there was something wrong with *Lewis*? Shall I say that, although he *should* have accepted the thesis that free will and determinism were incompatible as a result of considering the Consequence Argument (since that argument constitutes sufficient evidence for its conclusion), for some reason or other he didn't accept it? Or shall I say that there was nothing wrong with either of us? – that it is epistemically permissible for me to be convinced by a certain philosophical argument *and* it was epistemically permissible for him not be convinced by that same argument? (Remember, we are not supposing that he understood the published piece of text that contained the argument differently from the way I did. No, it was the same argument, platonically speaking, that was in my mind and in his.) That is, shall I say that either the Consequence Argument does not constitute sufficient evidence for incompatibilism and it's all right for me to accept incompatibilism on the basis of that argument alone, or that it *does* constitute sufficient evidence for incompatibilism, but it was all right for Lewis not to accept incompatibilism when he was in possession of that evidence?

All these alternatives, as I have said, are remarkably unappealing. I still think that the Consequence Argument shows that free will and determinism are incompatible. I find I can't help thinking that. But why doesn't Lewis see that if it's true? Was Lewis stupid? Lacking in philosophical ability? Intellectually dishonest? I certainly can't believe any of those things. Look, it's *David Lewis* we're talking about here. I can remember a talented young philosopher saying to me in the 1970s, following his first encounter with Lewis, 'Lewis is so smart it's *scary!*'; and that has been more or less the response of all philosophers who have measured themselves against that formidable mind. Nor could anyone suggest with a straight face that Lewis was lacking in philosophical ability – not unless *all* human beings are lacking in philosophical ability. And he was scrupulously honest: he may have believed one or two odd things, but he did *believe* them, and believed them because he thought that they were straightforward objective truths.

Suppose, then, I say that there's nothing wrong with either my being convinced by the Consequence Argument or Lewis's failure to be convinced by it. Suppose I tell myself that that's just how things go in philosophy. There are arguments that some philosophers find convincing and others don't, and it's *okay* to regard the philosophical arguments that one finds convincing as having established their conclusions if one has considered them carefully and responsibly. And it's *okay* for some other philosopher not to find those same arguments convincing provided he or she has also considered them carefully and responsibly. In a word, Lewis and I were both rational – or at least may well have been.

It is now time to take account of a fact that I have been ignoring. I have conceded parenthetically that Lewis did not merely refrain from accepting incompatibilism: he accepted its denial, compatibilism. And he did not accept compatibilism simply because he had examined that thesis and discovered within himself a conviction that it was true. He accepted compatibilism on the basis of certain arguments – arguments whose essential point is as old as Hobbes's debate with John Bramhall, Bishop of Derry, about liberty and necessity. It is necessary to add that these old arguments were not the only ones that played a role in his assent to compatibilism. An argument of *his*, an argument for the conclusion that the Consequence Argument turns on an equivocation also played a role in his assent (this is a case of what I have called secondary evidence). And, having brought that argument into our discussion, I can no longer maintain the pretense that the Consequence Argument constitutes the entirety of the evidence I have that is relevant to the question of the compatibility of free will and determinism. I have some secondary evidence of my own; if nothing else, *my* argument for the conclusion that *Lewis's* argument fails to show that the Consequence Argument turns on an equivocation, is a part of the evidence I have that is relevant to that question.

There were, therefore, other arguments than the Consequence Argument 'in play' in Lewis's and my decade-long discussion of the free-will problem. But, however many arguments were involved in our debate, we both knew about them all and both fully grasped every one of them. Our situation was therefore more nearly symmetrical than I have been making it out to be. I believe that I fully understood all the arguments that constituted Lewis's evidence (primary and secondary) for the proposition that free will and determinism are compatible, and that I therefore 'had' the evidence on which his belief that free will and determinism are compatible was grounded. And, of course, I was not convinced by those arguments. There was, therefore, a certain body of evidence – it comprised the Consequence Argument and all the other arguments that figured in our debate – such that Lewis and I both had this evidence and such that, on the basis of this one body of evidence, I accepted a certain proposition and he accepted its denial.

The position that, in this set of circumstances it was all right for me to accept incompatibilism *and* all right for Lewis to accept compatibilism is not one that it is easy to be entirely comfortable with. (Let's describe the position this way: it was rational for me to accept incompatibilism and rational for Lewis to accept compatibilism.) If I contend that both Lewis and I were rational, I hear Clifford's ghost whispering an indignant protest. Something along these lines (Clifford has evidently acquired, post mortem, a few turns of phrase not current in the nineteenth century).

> If you and Lewis are both rational in accepting contradictory propositions on the basis of identical evidence, then *you* accept one of these propositions – incompatibilism – on the basis of evidence that does not direct you toward incompatibilism and away from compatibilism. (For if it did, it would have directed *him* away from compatibilism, and it would not have been rational for him to be a compatibilist.) But of all the forces in the human psyche that direct us toward and away from assent to propositions, only rational attention to relevant evidence *tracks the truth*. Both experience and reason confirm this. And if you assent to a proposition on the basis of some inner push, some 'will to believe,' if I may coin a phrase, that does not track the truth, then your propositional assent is not being guided by the nature of the things those propositions are *about*. If you could decide what to believe by tossing a coin, if that would actually be effective, then, in the matter of the likelihood of your beliefs being true, you might as well do it that way.

I am unwilling to listen to these whispers. And I find it difficult to answer them. (No doubt these two facts are connected. I am unwilling to listen to the whispers of Clifford's ghost – if I listen to them, it is only because I force myself to – *because* I find them so difficult to answer.)

Could it be that the difficulty I find myself in is based on some false assumption, an assumption hidden somewhere in the various lines of reasoning I have presented? That's certainly an attractive thought. But what might this assumption be – or these assumptions, if there's more than one? Here's a candidate that in some moods I can find appealing: the assumption that all evidence for a philosophical proposition can be presented in the form of an argument. Evidence that can be presented in the form of an argument is essentially public. Any argument can be written down on a blackboard, and – so I have supposed – anyone who studies what's written on the blackboard and understands it thereby 'has' the evidence comprised in the argument. Suppose, however, that there's such a thing as interior, incommunicable evidence for certain propositions: evidence that can somehow be present to one's mind, although one is unable to articulate it, unable to put it into words, unable to present in the form of an argument.

Whether or not there is evidence of this sort for philosophical propositions, there are plausible examples of it in other areas. I sometimes know that my wife is angry when no one else does, for example, and I can't explain to anyone (even to myself) how I know this – I can't give what Plato would call an 'account' of what underlies my conviction that she is angry. It seems to me to be plausible to say that in such cases my belief that my wife is angry is grounded in certain evidence, evidence that I cannot put into words. After all, although I usually turn out to have been right about her being angry, if someone asks me, 'How did you know she was angry?', I can give no answer. Mathematics provides a very different kind of example of this phenomenon. Mathematicians are often intuitively certain that some mathematical proposition is true, although they are unable to prove it. (Gödel, I understand, was convinced that the power of the continuum was aleph-2, but was unable to give any statement of the ground of this conviction.) Since they often later do discover proofs of the these propositions, it seems likely that, prior to their discovery of the proofs, they had some sort of evidence that those propositions were true. Now maybe the evidence they had is exactly the evidence that they would later present in the form of a proof (on those occasions on which they did later produce a proof) although for some considerable period they were unable to articulate it. It is not essential to the suggestion that I am canvassing that 'inarticulable' evidence be *essentially* or *in principle* inarticulable. The suggestion requires only that a person have at a certain time evidence that he is not *then* able to articulate. Might it not be that the following two theses are both true?

(a)   I have sufficient evidence for my belief that free will and determinism are incompatible; some of this evidence is contained in the Consequence Argument, but other parts of it are either in principle interior and inarticulable or else evidence that could in principle be presented in some public form, but which, for some reason, I am at present unable to put into that form.

(b)   Lewis did not have this interior evidence that I have. I thus have more evidence that bears on the thesis that free will and determinism are incompatible than he had. His failure to accept incompatibilism was a rational response to the body of evidence he had, and mine is a rational response to the (more extensive) body of evidence that I have.

It is important to realize that thesis (b) does not imply that I am smarter than Lewis or a better philosopher. The idea is rather this. Owing to some neural accident, I have a kind of insight into the, oh, I don't know, entailment relations among various of the propositions that figure in the compatibilism/incompatibilism debate that was denied to Lewis. I *see*, perhaps, that a certain proposition p entails the proposition q (although I'm unable to formulate this insight verbally) and he was unable to see that p entailed q. And this insight really is due to a neural *quirk* (to borrow a phrase Rorty used for a different purpose). It's not that my cognitive faculties function better than Lewis's. His were as reliable as mine – no doubt more so. But his were not identical with mine, and some accidental feature of my cognitive architecture has enabled me to see an entailment that he was unable to see. (If it's open to me to say this, it would, of course, have been open to Lewis to say the same thing *mutatis mutandis*, to have contended that *he* had a body of interior, inarticulable evidence that *I* lacked and that his total evidence *vis-à-vis* the question of the compatibility of free will and determinism was more extensive than mine. It is imaginable, in fact, that we might both say this – 'this,' of course, being in each case appropriately tailored to the convictions of the speaker –, and might each regard the other as mistaken, perhaps excusably mistaken, perhaps not. Each might suppose that the other had mistaken a merely subjective conviction that some entailment held for *seeing* that that entailment held.)

I have raised the question whether (a) and (b) might not both be true. This question suggests a further question. According to (a), I have sufficient evidence to warrant my belief that free will and determinism are incompatible. According to (b), Lewis had less evidence that was relevant to the question of the compatibility of free will and determinism than I and his belief that free will and determinism were compatible was rational, given the evidence that was available to him. But (b) says neither that Lewis's evidence was sufficient to warrant his belief that free will and determinism were compatible nor that it was not. The 'further question,' of course, is: Was his evidence sufficient to warrant his belief or was it not? I should like to think that it was. I find it uncomfortable to suppose that my evidence was sufficient and Lewis's was insufficient, even if in this case his believing something upon insufficient evidence was somehow excusable. But if I suppose that it was, I face this difficulty: My evidence is, if we interpret this statement very literally, not sufficient to warrant a belief in the compatibility of free will and determinism — not at least if the same body of evidence cannot be sufficient to warrant both a certain belief and its negation (since it is sufficient to warrant my belief that free will and determinism are incompatible). But Lewis's evidence was a *proper part* of my evidence. If Lewis's evidence was sufficient, it would follow that a certain body of evidence was not sufficient to warrant a certain belief, but a proper part of that evidence was sufficient to warrant that same belief. And that seems counterintuitive. It is not clear, however, that this thesis, counterintuitive though it may be, is false. Suppose, for example, that Superman and Lois Lane are looking at a field and that Lois is having visual experiences of the kind that any normal human being who was looking at a field in which there was a single sheep would have. Lois believes that there is a sheep in the field before her, and it would seem that she has sufficient evidence for this belief if any human beings ever have sufficient evidence for any of their beliefs. Superman, more than human, has the evidence that Lois has and more besides: the evidence provided by his X-ray vision, which faculty reveals to him that what appears to the mere human eye to be a sheep is one of those epistemologists' mock-ups of a sheep. It seems therefore that he has sufficient evidence for a certain proposition and that Lois has sufficient evidence for its denial and that her evidence is a proper part of his. Perhaps Lewis's belief and his evidence, on the one hand, and my belief and my evidence, on the other, are related in the same way: my evidence consists of his evidence (the evidence provided by certain philosophical arguments) together with further evidence, interior incommunicable evidence, that is mine alone; nevertheless, despite the fact that his evidence is only a proper part of mine, my evidence is sufficient to support my belief that free will and determinism are incompatible and his evidence was sufficient to support his belief that free will and determinism were compatible.

On reflection, however, the idea that I have evidence, incommunicable evidence, that Lewis lacked, tempting though it is, is hard to believe. At any rate, it's hard to believe that it applies in all cases in which I disagree with other philosophers about some philosophical proposition or other. After all, I accept *lots* of philosophical propositions that are denied by many able, well-trained philosophers. Am I to suppose that in every case in which I believe something many other philosophers deny (that is, in every case in which I accept some controversial philosophical thesis), I'm right and they're wrong, and that, in every such case, my evidence is superior to theirs – owing to the fact that in every such case my evidence incorporates interior, incommunicable evidence that is somehow inaccessible to those other philosophers? If I do suppose that, I must ask myself, is the neural quirk that gives me access to this evidence the same neural quirk in each case or a different one? If it's the same one, what I am postulating looks more like a case of 'my superior cognitive architecture' than a case of 'accidental feature of my cognitive architecture.' If it's a different one in each case – well, that's quite a coincidence, isn't it? All these little evidence-friendly neural quirks come together to give the right results in just one philosopher (no other philosopher agrees with me about very much), and that philosopher happens to be me.

It seems more plausible to reject the idea of interior, incommunicable evidence and to concede (to revert to the case of David Lewis and myself) that I have and Lewis had the *same* evidence in the matter of the problem of free will. But if this is so, then either at least one of us has believed something upon insufficient evidence, or else I accept incompatibilism upon sufficient evidence and Lewis accepted compatibilism upon sufficient evidence and the evidence that the two of us had that bears on the compatibility of free will and determinism is the *same* evidence.

I will not try to say which of these disjuncts is right. I will instead conclude with some remarks about what a philosopher who believes either is committed to.

Suppose a philosopher accepts the first disjunct. (I'll call this philosopher 'you'.) You believe that at least one of the two of us, Lewis and me, accepted a certain philosophical position upon insufficient evidence. Then you must conclude that you and any philosopher who disagrees with you about the truth-value of some philosophical thesis are in the same position: one of you, at least, accepts a certain thesis upon insufficient evidence. Unless you are willing to say that *you* accept the thesis in question upon insufficient evidence (presumably you are not), you must conclude that you accept the thesis upon sufficient evidence and that your colleague accepts its denial upon insufficient evidence. And, surely, you will agree that there are *many* such theses – many positive, controversial philosophical theses that you accept and other philosophers deny? Let me ask you this: Do you really find it plausible to suppose that *in all or most such cases*, one of the two of you accepts a thesis upon sufficient evidence and the other upon insufficient evidence and that *you* are the one with the sufficient evidence? (The alternative is to suppose that you accept a high proportion of the philosophical theses you accept upon insufficient evidence.) We might, indeed, direct this point at Clifford himself – for the simple reason that he is one of us, a philosopher. One very good example of a philosophical thesis that Clifford accepts is, of course, the thesis we have been discussing: ethical evidentialism. Ethical evidentialism is a positive, controversial philosophical thesis. (William James rejected it, and other philosophers – Roderick Chisholm[7] and myself, for example – have expressed doubts about it.) Clifford has, of course, presented arguments for ethical evidentialism – rather good arguments, as philosophical arguments go. But is he really in a position to contend that these arguments constitute sufficient evidence for ethical evidentialism – given that other competent philosophers fully grasp these arguments (have the evidence he has) and do not embrace ethical evidentialism?

Now the second disjunct: that Lewis and I accept contradictory propositions on the same evidence, and that this evidence is in both cases sufficient. I want to make just this point: *Clifford* cannot accept this disjunct. I concede that the second disjunct is not logically inconsistent with Clifford's thesis, with ethical evidentialism. Consider, for example, one of those religious beliefs that were the intended 'target' of ethical evidentialism. The following three propositions are certainly logically consistent:

It is wrong always, everywhere, and for anyone, to believe anything upon insufficient evidence

Professor Dawkins believes that there is no God; the total body of evidence that he has that is relevant to the existence or non-existence of God is E; E is sufficient evidence for his belief that there is no God.

---

[7] See *Perceiving: A Philosophical Study* (Ithaca, N.Y.: Cornell University Press, 1957), 9. and 99–100.

> Archbishop Williams believes that there is a God; the total body
> of evidence that he has that is relevant to the existence or non-
> existence of God is E; E is sufficient evidence for his belief that
> there is a God.

But if the second disjunct is consistent with ethical evidentialism, it is
nevertheless inconsistent with an essential premise of the *argument* by
which Clifford claims to establish ethical evidentialism.

Why does Clifford think that it is wrong to believe things upon
insufficient evidence? The central nerve of Clifford's reason for supposing this is contained in some words I put into his mouth a
moment ago: Of all the forces in the human psyche that direct us
toward and away from assent to propositions, only rational attention
to relevant evidence *tracks the truth*. Believing things *only* upon sufficient evidence is, therefore, the only device we have for minimizing
the extent of our false beliefs, or at least the only such device that
has any prospect of providing us with a useful set of true beliefs.
(One could, of course, very effectively minimize the extent of one's
false beliefs by believing nothing.) If we form our beliefs on any
other basis – if we allow them to be formed by some factor that does
not track the truth –, we are, in effect, believing things at random.
If I form my beliefs on some basis other than rational attention to evidence, no doubt there will be a causal explanation of some sort for what
I believe, but the truth of falsity of those beliefs will not figure in that
explanation. Since there are a lot more ways to be wrong than there are
to be right, beliefs formed by a method that does not track the truth
will, to a high probability, be false. (Recall the 'electric monk' in
one of the Dirk Gently books, who, owing to a malfunction in his
electrical innards, had begun to believe things at random, and who,
at one point in the narrative had spent the morning believing that
forty-seven per cent of all tables were hermaphrodites. The example
illustrates nicely the high probability of a randomly chosen proposition's being false.) A person who believes things upon insufficient
evidence, therefore, is not taking care to minimize the extent of his
false beliefs. And any moral person *will* take care to minimize the
extent of his false beliefs. This is the moral course of action because
a person with false beliefs is *ipso facto* dangerous: a driver on British
roads who believes that in Britain one drives on the right-hand side
of the road is dangerous indeed – as is a ship-owner who believes
that his ship is seaworthy when she is not. Any moral person,
obviously, will want to minimize the danger he presents to himself
and others, and an essential part of realizing that end is to believe
only those things for which one has sufficient evidence.

33

This argument, I contend, is the core of Clifford's defense of ethical evidentialism. There is more to his defense than this core argument, of course. Suppose, for example, that someone had asked Clifford the following rather obvious question: 'Can you really suppose that a philosopher who has false beliefs about the reality of universals or the proper analysis of causation is *ipso facto* dangerous?'. One part of Clifford's defense of ethical evidentialism is, in effect, an answer to this question (and it is a thoughtful and interesting answer). But for my present purposes, I need consider only the core argument. It is evident that anyone who accepts this argument cannot suppose that a certain body of evidence can be sufficient to support both a belief that p and a belief that not-p. For, if that were the case – and particularly if it were a common occurrence –, rational attention to evidence would not track the truth. If you believe that in Britain one drives on the left and if I believe that in Britain one drives on the right, and if the evidence that you and I have that is relevant to the question which side of the road one drives on in Britain is the same, and if this evidence is sufficient in both our cases, then rational attention to evidence does not track the truth – and making sure that one has sufficient evidence for one's beliefs therefore provides no assurance that one is not a dangerous repository of false belief. In the present case, I am a dangerous driver and you, no doubt, are not – but your basing your belief concerning the side of the road to drive on upon sufficient evidence is not what prevents you from being a dangerous driver, for I did the same thing and everyone had better steer clear of me – literally – when I'm behind the wheel. If, therefore, one accepts the second of the disjuncts on offer, one can accept ethical evidentialism, if at all, only on some basis other than the argument by which Clifford defends it.

Can the philosopher who accepts ethical evidentialism say anything in defense of his or her accepting any positive and controversial philosophical thesis? (And remember: ethical evidentialism is itself a positive and controversial philosophical thesis.) I cannot see any very plausible avenues for the ethical evidentialist to explore. I conclude that philosophers should find ethical evidentialism an unattractive thesis – as I do. But what are philosophers to say in response to Clifford's argument for ethical evidentialism? It certainly does seem clear that, for just the reason Clifford cites, *many* propositions are such that a moral person will accept them only upon sufficient evidence. Might a philosopher contend that that this stricture does not hold for all propositions, and that philosophical propositions are among those for which it does not hold? Supposing that Aristotle was right to think that universals exist only *in rebus* (they might ask), did Plato's belief that universals exist *ante res* make him a dangerous man? Might this philosopher not appeal to the authority of Hume in the matter of errors in philosophy: While errors in religion (and, presumably, in politics and medicine and many other areas, including the Highway Code) are dangerous, '. . . errors in philosophy are only ridiculous.'? There is much that might be said in response to the thesis that false philosophical beliefs are harmless. Two of the things that might be said, and they're the only ones I will say, are that history demonstrates that wrong ideas in philosophy have done a lot of harm, and that Plato's political beliefs did not exist in isolation from his metaphysical beliefs.

If it is conceded that it is wrong to accept philosophical prop-ositions − positive, controversial ones − otherwise than upon suffi-cient evidence, and if it is conceded that the same evidence cannot be sufficient for contradictory propositions, and if it is conceded that interior, incommunicable evidence plays no significant role in philosophy, there seem to be only two choices open to a philosopher who is unwilling to embrace immorality. (I will remark that I have encountered only one philosopher who has made the first of these choices and only one who has made the second.) First, the philosopher might insist that he *does* have sufficient evidence for his philosophical beliefs and that those philosophers who disagree with him on any substantive philosophical point do *not* have sufficient evidence for their beliefs; those other philosophers are irrational or lacking in philosophical ability or unintelligent or unin-formed or intellectually dishonest or exhibit some other such cognitive or epistemic defect. I can only say that I regard any philo-sopher who embraces that option as a comic figure. Secondly, the philosopher might choose to accept *no* philosophical theses (other than negative theses and uncontroversial ones) − not even the thesis that accepting no philosophical theses is the only morally permissible course of action for a philosopher. This philosopher I regard not as a comic but as an heroic figure. I have nothing to say about such heroism other than that few of us other philosophers are likely to imitate it. I certainly am not.

Metaphysical (Im)mortality and Philosophical Transcendence

JOHN HALDANE

I. Introduction

There is a lapidary saying owing to Etienne Gilson, that is often misquoted or adapted – with 'metaphysics' taking the place of 'philosophy' – and which is invariably reproduced in isolation. It is that 'Philosophy always buries its undertakers'. Understanding this remark as Gilson intended it is relevant to the issues of the nature of philosophy, and of what conception of it may be most appropriate or fruitful for us to pursue. The question of the mortality or otherwise of philosophy in general, and of metaphysics in particular, is a significant one for ongoing intellectual enquiry, and it is also relevant to the current position of academic philosophy in Great Britain and in the English-speaking world.

Although I am unable for reasons of space to make the case that would be required to establish the claim, my belief is that in the last thirty years philosophy has lost ground in the academy and in intellectual and educated circles more generally. In the decades following the second world war philosophers held the headships of a string of colleges and universities: Mary Warnock and Bernard Williams at Cambridge; Justin Gosling, Stuart Hampshire, Anthony Kenny, Anthony Quinton, and Geoffrey Warnock in Oxford; Malcolm Knox at St Andrews, A.D. Lindsay at Keele, and others elsewhere. Something of this continued with Onora O'Neill at Cambridge, Alan Ryan at Oxford, and Stewart Sutherland at Kings London then at Edinburgh, but by then the trend was away from the previous disposition in which philosophy was looked to as somehow comprehending the diversity of approaches represented by the different arts, humanities and sciences.

Of course, the ongoing and accelerating ramification of knowledge has led to levels of specialisation that make it impossible to comprehend the whole of even a major part. Yet still the hunger for understanding of human nature and of the universe is pressed, but whereas intelligent questioners might for generations have directed themselves to philosophers for general guidance they now are more

doi:10.1017/S135824610999004X

likely to look and listen to popularising scientists, historians and biographers. Again I recognise that advances in biology and in physics have elevated the standing and increased the claims to fundamental relevance of these sciences; but in understanding the trend away from philosophy as a general guide one also has to look to the practice of professional academic philosophers themselves and to how they conceive their activities – and their responsibilities. Certainly 'applied' philosophy has got going, but in the areas and approaches that enjoy intellectual prestige among philosophers themselves the favoured styles of enquiry and theorising have served to isolate philosophy from general literate culture. There is also the fact, with which I shall be concerned shortly, that philosophy in general, and metaphysics in particular once seemed to promise possibilities that contemporary professional practitioners have generally either disavowed or quietly moved away from, or of which they are altogether ignorant.

These are, I realise, fairly sweeping statements, and as previously noted, I am not here in the business of trying to construct a detailed argument about the movement of philosophy to the margins of intellectual culture, or its descent down the table of academic disciplines, but I would encourage readers to consider these general observations and to think how, if the situation is as I have suggested, it might now be rectified. In this connection it is worth remembering that philosophy is a discipline that depends for the most part on patronage and patrons have a right to ask about the general interest of the activities they support.

II. Gilson's insight

Returning then to the issue of the mortality or otherwise of philosophy, it is especially worth looking at the context within which Gilson's resonant words about it always burying its undertakers were first inscribed, for it reveals how his observation is connected with a broader understanding of the nature of philosophical enquiry and in particular metaphysical speculation – an understanding that also has implications for the study of the history of these disciplines.

The source is a book published in 1938 when the threat to western intellectual traditions was keenly felt. The text derived from a series of four lectures given by Gilson in Harvard in 1936–7, immediately following the publication in English of *The Spirit of Medieval Philosophy*, the subject of his earlier Gifford Lectures at Aberdeen.

Having raised the study of medieval and modern thought to new standards of scholarship and insight, he was interested in the possibility of drawing broader conclusions about the phases and movements within philosophy. The result is in four parts: 'The Medieval Experiment', 'The Cartesian Experiment', 'The Modern Experiment', and finally that from which the book takes its title: 'The Unity of Philosophical Experience'.[1]

Having observed oscillations between speculation and scepticism in the periods surveyed in the earlier parts, Gilson claims that these cannot be wholly explained in terms of biography, literary history, or even history of 'ideas' (understood as historical systems of thought). His suggestion is that we must instead see philosophers and their doctrines as 'ruled from above by an impersonal necessity' (307); for, as he then says, 'Philosophy consists in the concepts of philosophers, taken in the naked, impersonal necessity of both their contents and their relations' (308) ... [and hence] ... "the ultimate explanation of the history of philosophy has to be philosophy itself" '(308). Recurrence and oscillation, therefore, are not to be explained entirely by reference to historical, economic or sociological factors but by the inevitable dialectic of ideas.

The points are deep and important ones for the conduct of historically-oriented academic inquiry in philosophy, and in other fields such as art and science where concepts and conceptions play an important role in structuring and animating first-order practice. Those who look for causes and effects of ideas in the surrounding personal, social, cultural, economic and material environments risk the danger of losing sight of the conceptual and rational ordering of thought and thought-laden products. Historians of ideas may be sensitive to this, but their interests, like those of biographers, do not, as such, require them to assess the intrinsic merits of their chosen subjects. It is enough that an idea has a significant history, was entertained here and there, explains this and that; just as it is enough that a figure lived in a time and place, was influenced by and influenced others, acted in various ways, had certain relationships, and so on. By contrast, in considering the descriptive, normative explanatory, and expressive content of philosophical, as of artistic or of scientific, endeavours it is always necessary to relate them to other thoughts and works in point of response and comparison by reference to common purposes, and to evaluate them accordingly. Typically advances in these areas take the form of solving, or improving

---

[1]   Etienne Gilson, *The Unity of Philosophical Experience* (London: Sheed & Ward, 1938).

treatments of inherited problems. But those solutions themselves give rise to new difficulties or questions, all against a background of enduring common concerns. Art, science and philosophy, at least in their fundamental expressions are essentially dialectical, and that is more than a matter of historical ordering and consequence. While this is not the occasion to explore the issue, these points are relevant to the issue of the nature and extent of progress in philosophy.[2]

From the identification of the dialectic of ideas, Gilson proceeds to derive a number of 'laws' or conclusions, the first of which introduces the oft-quoted phrase. He writes:

> Now the most striking of the recurrences which we have been observing together is the revival of philosophical speculation by which every sceptical crisis was regularly attended ... The so-called death of philosophy being regularly attended by its revival, some new dogmatism should now be at hand. In short, the first law to be inferred from philosophical experience is: *Philosophy always buries its undertakers*. (311–2).

Significantly, Gilson's remaining conclusions make explicit reference to metaphysics in terms that invite comment:

'*by his very nature man is a metaphysical animal*' (314).

'*metaphysics is the knowledge gathered by a naturally transcendent reason in its search for the first principles, or first causes, of what is given in sensible experience*' (315).

'*as metaphysics aims at transcending all particular knowledge, no particular science is competent either to solve metaphysical problems, or to judge their metaphysical solutions*' (316).

'*the failures of the metaphysicians flow from their unguarded use of a principle of unity present in the human mind*' (318).

'*since being is the first principle of all human knowledge, it is a fortiori the first principle of metaphysics*' (319); and finally

'*all the failures of metaphysics should be traced to the fact, that the first principle of human knowledge has either been overlooked or misused by the metaphysicians*' (323).

---

[2]   See John Haldane, 'Has Philosophy made a difference and could it be expected to?' in Anthony O'Hear (ed.) *Philosophy at the New Millennium* (Cambridge: Cambridge University Press, 2001); also published as *Philosophy* Supplement **48**.

III. Metaphysics causality and existence

Gilson regards metaphysics, classically, as the study of being – *ente per se* (ονηου) – and he thinks that it belongs to the nature of mankind to reflect upon particular beings and to proceed from that to asking about the causes of them, proximate, distal and ultimate. Since *cause* is an analogical notion, however, such enquiries involve more than tracing lines of efficient, or 'movement', causation.

Certainly one may ask what previous *event* was responsible for some *occurrence*, and then ask about the *events* prior to that. But one may also ask about what makes some *particular* to be the *species* of thing it is, and from there ask what makes such a *species* to be what it is and so on. Again one may ask what a thing is *made of* and then ask about the nature of the composing *material*, and then about that of which its stuff is composed; or one may ask what a thing is *doing*, or what it is *for*, and then ask in turn about the point of the identified *aims* or *functions*. One may also enquire as to why some things do not exist that might have been expected, and in pursuing this question come to realise that while the causes of non-existence may in some cases be impediments in others they may be absences, privatory causes.[3]

In one or more of these ways (by pursuing efficient, formal, material, final and privative causes) one is brought, so Gilson would say, to the question of being as such – and from that to the issue of the cause of being. Traditional defenders of the arguments presented by Aquinas at the outset of the *Summa Theologiae* (*Prima pars*, q2. a3) often make a point of trying to explain how these are not directed at establishing the existence of a *first cause within* a series, but rather a cause of there being various kinds of causal series: *a first cause outwith.*

They are not always successful in this effort, in part because Aquinas himself gives examples of causal series and says that there must be a first member, or else subsequent members could not ensue – as when he writes 'anything in process of change is being changed by something else. Moreover, this something else, if in process of change, is being itself changed by yet another thing, and this last by another ... Hence one is bound to arrive at some first

---

[3] On the matter of privatory causes, and on the analogicality of the idea of 'cause' and the suggestion that this has more than four analogates (efficient, formal, material and final) see, respectively, John Haldane, 'Privatory Causality', *Analysis*, Vol. 67, July 2007, and 'Gravitas, Social Efficacy and Moral Causes', *Analysis*, Vol. 68, January 2008.

cause of change not itself being changed by anything, and this is what everybody understands by God'.[4]

A more important obstacle to these expositors' efforts, however, is the persistence of a style of thinking about dependence that is so strongly cast that people find it almost impossible not to suppose that if it is said that 'not b unless a', then the relation in question must be either logical, or causal in the efficient sense. It is just such a cast of mind that makes one miss, or dismiss, the conclusion of the passage I just quoted, which, even though it is expressed in connection with a causal series, is not that there must exist a first cause in the series of changes, but that there must exist a cause of change per se, and hence of the series of changes – be it finite or infinite.

In some ways the distinctive and pre-modern character of Aquinas's style of argument is better expressed, and its difference better registered, in the reasoning from beings to being that St Thomas presents in his *Commentary on the Sentences of Peter Lombard*. This turns on the famous distinction between being and essence. Consider the claim that something, *A*, does not exist 'through itself'. Most naturally this will be understood as saying that *A*'s existence is an effect of the activity, and hence the existence, of another. A is contingent upon, in the sense that it is causally dependent on, something else. Need a sequence of such dependent beings itself be dependent, in the sense of caused? Not obviously. Maybe the sequence just exists.

Still, there is another way of approaching the matter which suggests that the sequence, and its members, must after all be dependent – not in the way of necessarily having to have an antecedent originator – but because their existing does not follow from their nature. The difference between things that have one kind of causal ancestry and those that have another is an extrinsic difference. The difference between things that need causes and those that do not, because they exist through themselves, is an intrinsic one. The former are contingent the latter non-dependent.

Abstractly specified, non-actual possibilities of different sorts, the possibility of a cat and the possibility of a dog, say, differ in content but are alike in being non-actual. By contrast, the difference between an abstractly specified non-actual possibility and an actuality of the same sort, the distinction between the possibility of a cat, and an actual one, is not a difference of content (essence) but of existence (being). The possibility and the actuality are alike in species but are

---

[4]   *Summa Theologiae*, Vol 2. Existence and the Nature of God, trans. Timothy McDermott (London: Eyre and Spottiswode, 1964), 15.

unalike in that the latter exists. One may formulate this reasoning either with regard to the extensions of concepts or with regard to concepts themselves. The issue can be put by saying that from the concept of f-ness, it does not follow that there are any fs (that the concept has an extension), or that there exists a universal nature *F-ness* existing antecedently to, and independently the concept of fness.

So there is a metaphysical difference expressible in terms of 'existing through itself' which is not, as such, that of having or not having an antecedent cause (though it connects with this), but is the difference between (a) having a nature of a sort that might be merely possible, and whose actualisation therefore depends for its being realised upon something else, and (b) having a nature of a sort that includes actuality. Things whose essence does not include existence, be it one, several or an infinite series of such, depend for their existence on other things from which their being is derived. Ultimately the existence of dependents flows from some being (or beings) whose essence includes existence and the causal power to communicate being, i.e. to *create* entities, and not just to change pre-existing ones.

Famously, Aquinas criticises an ontological proof, presumably that of Anselm, quoting the same passage from the psalms 'The fool said in his heart, There is no God' but in this case citing it to confirm that 'the opposite of the proposition "God exists" can be thought'.[5] (the thinker may have been a fool, and in error, but his atheism was not conceptually incoherent). He continues:

> I maintain that the proposition 'God exists' is self-evident in itself (*per se nota*), for as we shall see, its subject and predicate are identical, since God is his own existence. But because what it is to be God is not evident to us, the proposition is not self-evident to us, but needs to be made evident. This is done by things which though less evident in themselves are nevertheless more evident to us, by means, namely of God's effects.

Put in terms of concepts, Aquinas's position is that the notion 'essence-that-includes-existence' (E-E) is not the concept of a specific, determinate essence E, such that the concept E-E guarantees the existence of E's actualisation; rather E-E is the concept of a property concerning which it remains to be established whether any essence exemplifies it.

The argument of the *Sentences Commentary* progresses as follows: first it distinguishes *essence* and *existence*; then it shows that things

---

[5] ST Ia, q. 1, 1, *sed contra*; op. cit. 5.

whose nature does not include existence, things which do not exist *through themselves*, must derive their existence from antecedent actualities; and from this it proceeds to the conclusion that a fully sufficient source of being must not *derive* its being but possess it by nature, which is to say, in the *Summa* terminology, in the source 'subject and predicate must be identical'. Accordingly, the proof is not purely conceptual but proceeds from dependent existence to that which is and gives existence.

In this, the Gilsonian progress is evident. Beginning with observed beings, one moves up to thinking about being and its conditions, and from there rises higher to recognise the necessity of a transcendent cause of the being of beings, which is itself Being.

Here I have jumped to the uniqueness of the first principle, whereas a moment ago I spoke of some being (or beings) whose essence includes existence and the causal power to communicate being. An argument for singularity is given in the following question of the *Summa*, which concerns the simplicity of God. Anything whose essence includes existence cannot derive that existence from anything external or internal to it, for otherwise by nature it would be only potentially existent, and so could not be an originating cause of the existence of anything else. An originator, so conceived, is pure actuality, it has no metaphysical parts or potentialities, and hence there could be no ontological ground for plurality, no basis for numerical diversification.

It is of course possible to retrace the steps of the preceding argument, object at every point, and then skip sceptically forward again: are we really sure that we have experiences? If we do, do we know that their objects include extra-mental existents? If that is assured, do we know that these have causes? If we do, do we know that there is a real distinction between the nature of a thing and its actuality? If so, can we then properly infer that actualities are dependent? If we can, do we know that there must therefore be non-dependent actuality? If there is, must it belong intrinsically and essentially to the nature of what has or is it? If so, can we conclude that the sufficient cause of the being of beings is being itself? If we can be sure of each and every preceding part, how do we know that Being is not many?

There has long been a population of philosophers treading up and down these stairways: the ascenders often avowedly pursuing the metaphysics of ultimate being; the descenders sometimes wanting to rest metaphysics at a lower level, and sometimes wanting to raise it to the ground. While acknowledging that not every stairway is equally easy to ascend, I share the belief of Aquinas and of Gilson that there is a structure of being, that it really does rise to the highest imagined level, and that the ascent is humanly possible. Now, though, I want to move from that traditional debate to consider a different issue, namely in what sense, other than that already explored, might the practice of metaphysics lead to transcendence?

IV. Metaphysics empiricism and science

There is no question but that there was a significant revival of metaphysics in English-language philosophy during the last quarter of the twentieth century, and it continues today. Whereas philosophers directly influenced by Austin, Ryle and Wittgenstein tended to avoid or to tread minimally into ontology, those inspired by Kripke, Lewis and Plantinga have marched to and fro across the field and been busy surveying, laying foundations and building within it. Interestingly, however, the new-found interest in metaphysics has not often been accompanied by existential or transformative concerns, such as characterised the approach of earlier figures like Bradley and McTaggart, or Bergson and Gilson. No doubt many factors contribute to this difference, some of them extra-philosophical. Yet there are some important features of contemporary Anglo-American philosophy that are relevant to this. Here I wish to mention two.

The first has been commented upon by Rorty[6] and Putnam[7], and by some others (though by the latter more often in the style of prefatory injunctions not subsequently heeded). This is the widespread assumption, particularly among American analytical philosophers influenced by Quine, that metaphysics is essentially the abstract

---

[6] See Richard Rorty, *Philosophy and the Mirror of Nature* (Princeton, NJ.: Princeton University Press, 1992), *Consequences of Pragmatism* (Minneapolis, MN: University of Minnesotta Press, 1982) and *Truth and Progress* (Cambridge: Cambridge University Press, 1998). For a late statement of his views particularly in relation to the 'scientific' aspirations of analytical philosophy see 'How many grains make a heap?' *London Review of Books*, 20 January 2005. This is a review of Scott Soames two volume history of analytical philosophy *Philosophical Analysis in the Twentieth Century* (Princeton, NJ: Princeton University Press, 2003).

[7] See Hilary Putnam, *Renewing Philosophy* (Cambridge, MA: Harvard University Press, 1992) and 'Is Analytic philosophy a good thing?' unpublished.

end of empirical theorising.[8] On this account philosophy takes up issues raised by natural science and helps clarify them, or draws from them conclusions more general and more abstract than would interest most trained scientists. Examples abound in the areas of substance, property, event, causality, identity, laws and modality, and space and time.

One apparent merit of this approach to the subject is that it answers the question sometimes raised by non-philosophers, and posed with a particular edge within universities where the competition for resources and prestige is most intense: *what is the use of philosophy?* The idea that it is a well-ordered and empirically respectful discipline that takes up the really hard questions raised by physics or evolutionary biology, or promises to sharpen canons of evidence and methodology, provides a clear answer satisfactory to many, if not to the incurious practitioners.

This scientific self-conception brings other institutional and professional benefits: the development of research programmes, determinate projects with specifiable aims and outcomes, the creation of research teams, a structured division of labour with graded expertise and training opportunities; a sense of an agreed agenda of well-defined questions, addressed through a consistent and shared methodology of enquiry, leading to clear and conclusive answers. One might capture all of this is in a slogan that some philosophers might now be happy to have inscribed within their offices: *funded progressive research.*

Although I offer this motto in a spirit of irony (which I testify to and record now in case the suggestion is actually adopted), I do not suppose that the scientific conception is entirely inappropriate, and there are branches of the subject, for example, philosophy of science, philosophical psychology, logic and philosophy of language, and philosophy of mathematics, where it may be both relevant and fruitful. I do want to point out, however, (and again I am here echoing others) that this contrasts markedly with another model of academic reflection which is that associated with humane learning. Here the latest is not presumed, even weakly, to be the best; the goal is not new knowledge but deeper understanding of long-familiar features of human experience and practice; and the methods are not theoretical and scientific, but descriptive and reflective.

---

[8]   Quine himself was happy to say that philosophy is not just continuous with science but is even part of it. For an engaging and accessible discussion of Quine's views on the nature of philosophy see his interview with Brian Magee 'The Ideas of Quine' in Magee (ed.) *Men of Ideas: Some Creators of Contemporary Philosophy* (London: BBC, 1978).

Elsewhere, in a previous Royal Institute of Philosophy lecture (in a series on Philosophy at the New Millennium) I addressed the question of whether philosophy in the twentieth century had made any difference to the resolution of the issues it inherited from earlier periods[9] and used the phrase 'intimations of "undeniable progress"' to characterise the tone struck by some eminent contemporary philosophers, including Derek Parfit, and perhaps more surprisingly Thomas Nagel. An example worth repeating is that of Paul Churchland who writes as follows:

> The [folk psychology] of the Greeks is essentially the same FP we use today, and we are negligibly better at explaining human behaviour in its terms than was Sophocles. This is a very long period of stagnation and infertility for any theory to display, especially when faced with such an enormous backlog of anomalies and mysteries in its own explanatory domain.[10]

The point here is not to discuss the merits of Churchland's scientific neurophilosophy but to suggest the contrast between this view and that of the humanistic philosopher who would think that human behaviour needs to be interpreted as personal, and hence related to the meanings and values that structure the existential and phenomenological space we inhabit.

Continuing on, he or she is likely to suppose that the human world has not much changed through recorded history, and that descriptions and interpretations offered by acute observers from any time or place are as likely to be as valuable as those of here and now. Indeed, for a variety of reasons, including the increasing influence of scientific styles of thinking about humanity, it might be that sources from a more humanistic culture are of greater value in the effort to see ourselves as persons. And if those sources seem confused about aspects of our behaviour then maybe that is a more appropriate response, for perhaps we are conflicted beings presenting the same anomalies and mysteries today as in antiquity, though we may now be less aware of them through a falsely applied scientific consciousness.

So much for the influence of science turning philosophy toward *scientism*. The second idea I wish to mention is connected with aspects of the modern scientific world view as that developed in the

---

[9]   See John Haldane, 'Has Philosophy made a difference and could it be expected to?' op. cit.
[10]   P. Churchland, 'Eliminative Materialism and the Propositional Attitudes' *Journal of Philosophy*, 1981, 73–5.

wake of the renaissance, but philosophy itself did much to shape and sharpen it.

Scientific corpuscularism and related theories of matter, space and motion (re)introduced the idea that in itself the universe is quite unlike the everyday world of experience. Conjoined with the empiricist thesis that all knowledge begins with the senses, this has a paradoxical result, namely, that our only primary source of knowledge is systematically deceptive. Things look coloured, sound noisy, taste sweet or sour, feel warm or cold, apparently diminish as they recede, and so on; but in reality it is quite otherwise, and moreover there is no naturally intelligible connection between the way things are in themselves and the ways things seem to the senses.

One reaction to this radical difference between the word of visible appearance and the hypothesised reality follows a line suggested by Cardinal Bellarmine ('Master of Controversial Questions') writing on April 12, 1615 in reply to the Carmelite provincial Paolo Foscarini's regarding the Galileo affair:

> ... it seems to me that Your Reverence and Galileo did prudently to content yourself with speaking hypothetically, and not absolutely, as I have always believed that Copernicus spoke. For to say that, assuming the earth moves and the sun stands still, all the appearances are saved better than with eccentrics and epicycles, is to speak well; there is no danger in this, and it is sufficient for mathematicians.[11]

In other words one may hold to the appearances and remain agnostic about the hypotheses. On the other hand one may embrace the latter and demote the former. How far they may be demoted is a further issue, but the scientific temper of modern times has increasingly been inclined to regard them as practically ineliminable, but ontologically superficial and even phenomenal. Put into the key of epistemology, modern philosophy remains attached to a Lockean corpus of melodies. We may, and indeed we can only begin with experience, but that is an interaction between surfaces, one of which happens, mysteriously, to be sensitive, and what we should seek to infer is the internal nature and structure of substance, the permanent substructure around which our senses seem to see wrapped all manner of decorations.

Of course it is in the nature of the 'interior' as here conceived of that it cannot be an object of experience, for that could only be of another

---

[11] For the full text of the letter (in English translation) see The Galilean Library: Manuscripts at http://www.galilean-library.org/bellarmine1.html

exposed surface. And so the world as real knowledge seeks to reconstruct it an essentially theoretical affair. Furthermore it lacks the features apparent to experience in the ordinary sense of the term, according to which we can be said to see beliefs being formed, desires being expressed or suppressed, purposes being pursued, things being said and done; animals hunting and rearing their young; trees and plants growing; and so on.

In the philosophy of mind Cartesianism and Lockeanism gave rise to the problem of how one can have knowledge of other minds. Generalised throughout philosophy they give rise to the problem of how one can have knowledge of anything other than what can be hypothesised as an underlying cause of appearances – and even knowledge of self, seemingly immune to this general scepticism, in fact remains silent on the inner substance of mind.

V. Metaphysics and transcendence

Evidently there is a marked contrast and a large intellectual gulf between the Thomistic metaphysics of Gilson and the Lockean scientism that characterises much contemporary philosophy. In the case of the former the link between metaphysics and transcendence was clear: metaphysics is the movement from experience of beings, to intellectual recognition of Being. Superficially this may seem to share a common structure with the position of the Lockean scientific realist, since both hope to lead consciousness from the world of everyday experience to that of abstractly inferred reality.

But the resemblance is only passing. For the point of the Gilsonian position is that the objects of common experience are not at all unreal, and that what one comes to know through the ascent of metaphysics is not something abstract and theoretical but something real communicated to and expressed in the world of experience: beings show Being. The Lockean position by contrast denies that what is known to sense are real beings, properly speaking; and insists that what is real, supposedly, is not available other than as theoretically postulated. Equivalently, whereas the Gilsonian contrast is between being as object of experience and as object of metaphysical recognition; the Lockean one is between objects of sense and postulates of science.

The latter, in effect, simultaneoulsy establishes dualities of sense and intellect and of appearance and reality, and its further philosophical contribution is to direct serious attention and interest away from the first to the second in each pair. No surprise then that this school of study, made more intensely scientific for reasons mentioned

John Haldane

earlier, has little interest in possibilities of personal transcendence or transformation, and little interest in philosophy as the practice of the love of wisdom.

For the Gilsonian, by contrast, the philosophy that always buries its undertakers is both metaphysically and existentially transcendent in its aspirations. The metaphysical aspect has already been discussed and the existential follows from it in two ways. First, the ascent from beings, to the being of beings, to Being itself, is an intellectual movement of the person revealing his or her capacity to reach beyond common starting points. That implies much which I will here just point at by observing that the reflexive knowledge achieved in metaphysics supports an ennobling understanding of human nature.

One aspect of this concerns the issue of philosophical materialism and the question of whether this may be refuted by reflection upon human mental activity. Consider in this connection an argument for the immateriality of thought that derives from Aristotle (following a line of reasoning developed by Plato) but which is most fully developed in the writing of Thomas Aquinas and other medieval and scholastic Aristotelians. In *Summa Theologiae* Prima Pars, question 75, articles 5 Aquinas writes as follows:

> Whatever is received into something is received according to the condition of the recipient. Now a thing is known in as far as its form is in the knower. But the intellect knows a thing in its nature absolutely: ... Therefore the intellectual soul itself is an absolute form, and not something composed of matter and form. For if the intellectual soul were composed of matter and form, the forms of things would be received into it as individuals, and so it would only know the individual: just as it happens with the sensitive powers which receive forms in a corporeal organ; since matter is the principle by which forms are individualized. It follows, therefore, that the intellectual soul, and every intellectual substance which has knowledge of forms absolutely, is exempt from composition of matter and form.[12]

The terms in which the argument is cast are drawn from Aristotelian metaphysics, and some explanation of these follows below, but the essence of the argument may be represented as follows:

1. Intellectual acts are essentially constituted by conceptualized universal natures.
2. No materially instantiated property is universal.

[12] *Summa Theologiae*, Ia, q.75, a 5.

3.   Therefore, conceptualized universal natures are not materially instantiated.
4.   What is essentially constituted by non-materials is itself non-material.
5.   Therefore intellectual acts are non-material.
6.   Acts follow from and express the nature of the agent whose acts they are.
7.   Therefore intellectual agents are non-material.

Setting aside exegetical details arsing with the fact that the same or similar arguments appear in different parts of the Thomistic corpus in slightly different forms, I shall suggest a reading of the argument according to which it may well be sound.

As stated in the quoted passage the argument presupposes the Arsistotelian thesis that cognition involves a reception of the form of the thing known into the intellect where it is deployed as a concept informing an intellectual act.[13] That is a counterpart of an analogous claim made by Aristotle and adopted by Aquinas that in the case of sense-cognition the sensible form of the object is received into the sense. In the case of the latter, St Thomas holds that the process of reception, and the realization of the form in the sense (which come to the same thing) are material processes.

As regards universals or general natures Aquinas holds a mediate position between *universalia in rebus* and nominalistic conceptualism. For him natures are as such neither one nor many, but many in things and one in the mind (*De ente et essentia*, and *Commentary on the Metaphysics*, V, 1). To each member of a natural kind K belongs an individualized nature: the kness-of-a, the kness-of-b, and so on. These natures are numerically distinct, being individuated by the matter they inform; but they are formally or specifically alike, and this formal identity provides the basis for a general nature produced by the mind in abstraction from particulars.

---

[13]   The analysis of cognition in terms of the reception and exercise of species becomes particularly intricate in the writings of later Thomists, often involving additions to and changes of terminology. The best account of the subject as it is treated by St Thomas himself is Bernard Lonergan, *Verbum: Word and Idea in Aquinas* (ed.) David Burrell (London: Darton, Longman and Todd, 1968), and for Aquinas and later Thomism more generally see John Peifer *The Concept in Thomism* (New York, NY.: Record Press, 1952) reprinted as Volume 3 of *Modern Writings on Thomism*, selected and introduced by John Haldane (London: Thoemmes Continuum, 2004). Piefer's book is unduly neglected and rewards study.

John Haldane

In sense cognition individualised forms corresponding to those in the objects of sense are formed under the material conditions appropriate to the particular sense organ. In intellectual cognition, by contrast, the principle of cognition is not an individualized form but the universal. When I look at Orbit the dog, both Orbit and my eyes feature individualsed sensible forms of the colours of her coat. When I think that dogs are animals, by contrast, the content of my mental act is not a particular dog, or the members of the set of existing dogs; rather it is dogness per se. Dogness per se, however, is an abstract entity, an immaterial universal. So if intellection involves a cognitive faculty receiving forms in this way, then that faculty and its acts are themselves immaterial. Put another way, if purely conceptual thought involves universals and is thereby immaterial, then since acting follows upon being (*agere sequitur esse*) the faculty or power is itself immaterial.[14]

Aquinas's argument has been charged with committing a fallacy of equivocation confusing two senses of *receiving a form*, in this case a universal formed by abstraction. The original source of this criticism, I believe, is an article by Joseph Novak who writes as follows:

> The difficulty in Aquinas's argument does not lie [in the claim that] spiritual accidents must have spiritual substances in which they inhere ... one can readily grant [this]. Rather the problem lies in attributing the property of being immaterial [intentionally] and immaterial [ontologically] in the same sense. A representation seems to possess the property of being immaterial [intentionally] while the intellect itself seems to possess the property of being immaterial [ontologically]. Moreover, one cannot argue from the immaterial quality of the form as representation to its immaterial quality as inhering accident, since the former possesses only intentional, while the latter possesses ontological, immateriality.[15]

Writing in terms more readily intelligible to a non-scholastic readership Pasnau formulates the same point as follows:

> It seems to me that Aquinas has fallen victim to what I call the content fallacy: the fallacy of conflating facts about the content of our thoughts with facts about what shape or form those thoughts take in our mind. When Aquinas characterizes the

---

[14] Here one may recall the affinity argument for the immateriality of the soul presented by Socrates in Phaedo, 78–80.

[15] Joseph Novak, 'Aquinas and the Incorruptibility of the Soul', *History of Philosophy Quarterly*, Vol. 4, 1987, 413.

soul as 'having one power through which it makes things actually immaterial by abstracting from the conditions of individual matter, a power which is called the agent intellect' (79.4 ad 4) it seems to me that he has fallen victim to an ambiguity in the phrase 'abstracting from the conditions of individual matter'. That phrase might mean that the agent intellect produces an entity that is immaterial rather than material ... or that the agent intellect changes the representational content ... making it so that the newly formed intelligible species no longer represents 'the conditions of individual matter'.[16]

The common complaint is that there is a distinction between *epistemological* or *representational* abstraction on the one hand, as when one moves from an idea or representation of Orbit to a concept or representation of dogness, and *metaphysical* or *ontological* abstraction on the other whereby a material particular yields an abstract universal. In the case of the latter there is an existential difference between a material and an immaterial entity, while in the case of the former the difference is in intentional content. And granting that the process of intellectual abstraction may effect the latter, producing universal ideas (*concepts*) from particular representations (*percepts*) it does not follow that in crossing this intentional divide one has also crossed the ontological one between the material and the immaterial.

In order to assess this argument it is necessary to distinguish between thoughts as *mental acts* and thoughts as *intentional contents*. If at the same time during a particular day in 1999, Paul and Pauleen both thought that the second millennium is coming to an end then we can say that they had the same thought (content) while yet having different thoughts (episodes). Different criteria of identity and individuation apply to acts and to contents, but for the materialist whatever thoughts (as mental acts or states) are about, numbers, say, they themselves are certainly material entities; whereas for an absolute idealist whatever thoughts may be about, stones, for example, they are, in themselves, immaterial.

For Aquinas, sensory acts have particular sensibles as their objects and are themselves sensible particulars. Both sensings and what they represent (sensible characteristics) exist under material conditions, individuated by the quantities of matter that they characterise. Through a process of intellectual abstraction, however, particulars

---

[16] Robert Pasnau, *Thomas Aquinas on Human Nature* (Cambridge: Cambridge University Press, 2002) 315–6.

John Haldane

(states of the sense-faculties) having particular contents (being of this or that individualised sensible form) are employed to form general conceptions. The challenge of the critics is that Aquinas fallaciously moves from what might be termed 'content de-particularisation' to 'ontological dematerialisation', whereas there is nothing in the former that either requires or supports the latter, and so far as abstractness of content is concerned that is compatible with it being carried by a material representation. Just as for Bishop Berkeley thoughts of rocks were made of mind, so for the materialist Aquinas's thoughts of God may be made of brain.

Three points are relevant by way of response. First, while intellectual judgements may be accompanied by conscious imagery or by none, their intrinsic content is abstract. Second, while the conceptual contents of such acts may have actual or possible empirical extensions (as in the judgement that dogs are animals), equally they may be such as could not possibly have anything like empirical realization conditions since they concern *abstracta* or *entia immaterialia*: as in a universally quantified mathematical formula, or in the judgement that every number is a species unto itself. The third point undercuts the distinction deployed in the charge of equivocation. In the case of sensory-cognition Aquinas's account of this involves material causation and therefore encourages the thought that presentational content per se is compatible with materiality. A generalisation from that might take the form of distinguishing act and content and deploying this in the ways considered above. But there is another possibility compatible with the materiality of sensory cognition but which blocks the act/content distinction as formulated and thereby denies the critics use of it against Aquinas. Suppose that instead of distinguishing representations as vehicles of content from representational content as such, one identifies sensory acts with their sensuous contents, and intellectual acts with their conceptual contents, treating both as pure *Vorstellungen* or cognitive presentations. On that account the presentation of a material particular as content is identical with the occurrence of a material particular, a state of the sensory system of the subject. Similarly the presentation of an abstract universal, being immaterial in content is thereby immaterial in substance. This provides an interpretation of Aquinas's argument in which it does it not rest on a fallacy, a suggestion that, as Pasnau remarks of his own analysis, involves a 'not very charitable explanation'[17] of his confusing intentional and ontological abstraction. It also suggests an understanding of intellection as the highest

---

[17] Pasnau, 351.

realisation of the power of cognition, and as an activity transcendent of material particularity.[18]

The second way in which metaphysical and existential transcendence may be linked is by coming to see that the world has a basic ontological structure that unites it, and out of which beings emerge as entities to which existence has been given, one may make something of the idea that what experience introduces us to, and what metaphysics confirms, is that reality is not something unknowable behind an opaque barrier; and nor is it essentially different from what we observe of our surroundings and ourselves. Seen as realities, other human beings emerge as co-knowers, other animal species as co-inhabitors, and the world more broadly as a community of beings, no doubt often sources of competition and of danger but neither perplexing appearances not unknowable substances. Metaphysics in the tradition I have been recommending has the potential to induce a kind of spiritual transcendence by confirming that the world is real, and that it is the place of our first being, but with the further hint that there may be more in store and that this might provide some kind of intellectual and existential completion by uniting us with the source of being itself.

[18] The previous eight paragraphs overlap with the final section of an essay on the subject of ontological nature of mental acts: 'The Metaphysics of Intellect(ion)' in M. Baur (ed.) *Intelligence and the Philosophy of Mind*, Proceedings of the ACPA, Vol. 80, 2006 (Charlottesville, VA.: Philosophy Documentation Center, 2007).

My Conception of Philosophy

BRYAN MAGEE

There is general agreement, which I share, that among the earliest of Western philosophers were three of the very greatest: Socrates, Plato and Aristotle. Each of these is on record as saying something – and it is almost the same thing – about the nature of philosophy itself that goes to the heart of the matter. Aristotle said: 'It is owing to their wonder that men now begin, and first began, to philosophise' (*Metaphysics*, i.982). And Plato wrote, putting his words into the mouth of Socrates: 'This sense of wonder is the mark of the philosopher. Philosophy indeed has no other origin' (*Theaetetus*, section 155).

None of us chooses to be born; and when we come to consciousness we find ourselves existing in a world, a world of experience. Perhaps most of us accept it as we find it, and take up, and carry on as best we can, the unasked-for task of being in it. But some of us are struck with wonderment at it, and are moved to try to understand it. This wonderment – or its distant relation, curiosity – can be very powerful indeed for some individuals, enough to dominate their lives. It may turn them into philosophers, but it can also turn them into contemplatives of other kinds, including religious kinds; or it may encourage them to become creative artists, or scientists. Such people may all be trying to penetrate the mysteries of the world in which they find themselves, and to deepen their understanding of it; and their activities can for that reason have important characteristics in common. Philosophizing is far from being the only way of putting wonderment into practice. But philosophy is distinct from those others in significant respects, as indeed they are from one another, though it was not always the case.

Historically, philosophy began when some people started publicly trying to understand the world around them by the use of reason. This was a milestone in human development. Before then, claims to knowledge, or attempts at understanding, had appealed to authority, either human or supra-human. It could have been the authority of a person or a social class or a body of doctrine, or a priesthood, and could have expressed itself through laws or rituals or schools or traditions or social conventions or the use of armed men. Anyone who publicly flouted it was punished and cast out, usually killed. Rulers, teachers and priests, through institutions of what may

doi:10.1017/S1358246109990051

sometimes have been quite primitive kinds, passed down from generation to generation an inviolate body of doctrine that called itself knowledge. Frequently it claimed divine origins, and was therefore difficult if not impossible to change. The appearance of the first teachers who tried to attain knowledge and understanding through reasoning had, among its many revolutionary consequences, a knock-on effect: they taught their pupils to reason too, and to think for themselves – and therefore to put forward ideas of their own: to discuss, debate, argue, criticize. No longer was there any handing down of something inviolate. Teachers did not expect even their own pupils to agree with them. Conflicting views between generations became the norm.

It was in the sixth century BC that these developments began, in the world of the ancient Greeks. They launched a runaway growth of knowledge and understanding that is without parallel in human history.

Those first philosophers, whom we now call the pre-Socratic philosophers, were concerned above all to understand the physical world around them, and their concerns would be characterized nowadays as scientific rather than philosophical. The first questions of the person conventionally taken to be the first philosopher, Thales, were 'What is the world made of?' and 'What is sustaining it?' Actually the chief interest of most of the pre-Socratics might be said to have been cosmology. The one among them who is usually said to have invented the term 'philosophy' was also the first to apply the word 'cosmos' to the universe – Pythagoras. The impersonality of their concerns was one of the chief criticisms made of them by Socrates, who was in conscious reaction against them. What difference – he asked, referring to some of their well-known questions – what difference could it possibly make to me or my life to know how far the sun is from the earth; or whether the sun is roughly the size of the Peloponnese or bigger than the whole world? What I need to know is how to live my life – and for that I need to know what is good, what is right, what is just: these are the questions we ought to be discussing . . . And as everyone knows, he went on to achieve immortal fame for the particular manner in which he discussed them.

But other philosophers went on asking those other kinds of question, as well as taking up Socrates' questions. His most gifted pupil, Plato, is as good an example of this as any. He made contributions of genius over the whole range of Socrates' field of enquiry, but then went on to produce an entire cosmology, in which mathematics plays an essential part, along with what we would now term physics. The ablest of Plato's pupils, Aristotle, then did the same again, and indeed coined the term 'physics'. For generation after generation all attempts to understand the world by the use of reason continued to come under the general umbrella term 'philosophy'. The attempt to understand nature became known as 'natural philosophy'. Newton's great work was entitled '*Philosophiae Naturalis Principia Mathematica*', 'The Mathematical Principles of Natural Philosophy'. It was not until the eighteenth century that science began to be distinguished from philosophy, and the word 'scientist' was not coined until the nineteenth century. I am told that to this day there is an ancient university in Scotland where the professor of physics has the official title 'Professor of Natural Philosophy'.

Even after science had established intellectual independence of philosophy it retained an enormous amount in common with it, above all the imaginative propounding of explanatory theories that are then subjected to logical analysis and critical discussion. The principal characteristic that distinguished the two was that the propositions of science were testable not only intellectually in this way but also empirically, by measurement, experiment or direct physical observation. Empirical testability made so much difference to intellectual enquiry that, once science was independent, it started achieving results with almost unbelievable speed. By the nineteenth century more and more people had begun to believe that science had put in our hands the key to understanding everything, so that all meaningful questions about what actually exists would sooner or later be answerable by scientific methods. Philosophy itself ingested that view. It was central to logical positivism, which was the reigning orthodoxy when I first began to interest myself in academic philosophy. The view was that all statements that are not tautologies must, if they are to mean anything at all, make *some* noticeable difference to *some*thing, a difference that is observable at least in principle; otherwise they are empty. And therefore their truth or falsehood must be empirically decidable, again in principle. This means that when it comes to finding out truths about the world, the methods of science have the potential to fill all the available space, and there is nothing separate for philosophy to do. It has, as people used to say, no first-order tasks. Its function is a second-order function: not to tell us directly about the world but to elucidate and make more perspicuous our talk about the world. It is, as Gilbert Ryle famously put it, talk about talk. Scientists talk about the world, and philosophers talk about talk about the world. Philosophy's job is to deepen our understanding of the concepts we are using, and to make our use of them less ambiguous, to critically evaluate arguments; and to analyse, and possibly improve, our intellectual methods. Philosophy was still seen as important, because all these things were seen as important. And they were seen as being germane not only to the activities of professional scientists but to all significant utterance. But they were nevertheless seen as being unavoidably parasitic on the activities of first-order enquiry.

It would be difficult to exaggerate what a break this was with the whole of philosophy's previous history. I do not believe it had occurred to any of the great figures of philosophy before then, with only one or two arguable exceptions, to think of the subject-matter of philosophy as being in any way linguistic. They wrote as if they regarded themselves as confronting problems presented to them by an essentially non-linguistic reality. In fact they shared, I think, the attitude expressed towards his former self by one of the first major philosophers to move away from an exclusively first-order conception of philosophy, Bertrand Russell, who was older than the logical positivists and revered by them, but never wholly one of them. In his book *My Philosophical Development* (14) he tells us that until about 1917 – in which year, please note, he was forty-five years old, and had his most original and lastingly influential work already behind him – 'I had thought of language as transparent – that is to say, as a medium which could be employed without paying attention to it.' In other words, although philosophy could be expressed only *in* language, it was not *about* language: the objects of its concern were nearly always non-linguistic. As Schopenhauer had put it many years before, philosophy as it should be done is carried on *in* concepts but (except for logic) is not *about* concepts. To the day of his death Russell believed that the central task of philosophy was to understand the world. He says this baldly in his best known book of all, his *History of Western Philosophy* (411): 'A philosopher's job is to find out things about the world by thinking rather than observing.' Although it was in fact Russell's work that launched the logical analysis of statements in ordinary language on its triumphant career in professional philosophy, he believed to the end of his life that his successors had pursued this kind of analysis much too far, and had transmogrified what he had only ever intended as an ingenious and powerful tool into a subject matter, a whole conception of philosophy. But his view about that was to become a minority view, and has remained so.

It is worth observing that developments of this kind did not occur only in philosophy. They happened at the same time in literature, and the study of literature. Academics in those fields too began for the first time to regard, let us say, novels not as primarily concerned to explore reality, the world, people, human relationships, life in all its aspects, but as being primarily concerned to explore language and the uses of language. And some creative writers who were to make big reputations – James Joyce is an obvious example, but there were others – produced novels in which that was indeed the primary concern. In literature too, as in philosophy, it was an almost complete break with the past, and was declared to be such by its practitioners. Some of the best known among philosophers felt that there was no longer much point in reading the philosophy of the past – Wittgenstein was famous for the meagreness of his acquaintance with it. My supervisor, Peter Strawson, said to me on two separate occasions that he regarded Kant's *Critique of Pure Reason* as the greatest work of philosophy to have been produced since the ancient Greeks – and I agree with that judgement – but one of his colleagues, a woman who had spent a long career teaching philosophy at Oxford, told me with unembarrassed complacency that she had never read it.

The equation of subject matter with language spread to one subject after another, for instance to psychology, and to sociology. In field after field, language was credited with a level of importance, indeed a centrality, that no one had ever thought of according it before.

I think this helps to explain an exceedingly strange aspect of philosophy's overall development, at least in the English-speaking world, in the twentieth century. Logical positivism had given rise to the view, and provided the intellectual foundations for it, that philosophy could not give us direct knowledge of reality, but was confined to a second-order function of examining what can be said in language. Eventually logical positivism was abandoned. But what was not abandoned was the view of philosophy's relationship to language for which it had provided the basis. The foundations had been removed, yet the superstructure was left standing. Through all the changes and developments that have happened here in philosophy since – and there have been many changes – most professional philosophers have pressed on as if their activity were a second-order one whose subject-matter consisted of linguistic formulations of first-order ideas. They are still devoting themselves primarily to the elucidation of concepts, and to the ancillary tasks that doing that involves.

Now it is my contention that this approach is misconceived – that as a conception of philosophy it is a mistake. Let me straight away make one thing clear. I am not against analytic activity in itself. I am against its being a conception of philosophy. I am against its being seen as philosophy's main concern. In fact I take the same view as did Bertrand Russell – who as the father or godfather of modern linguistic analysis can scarcely be thought to have been against it in principle. It is my view, as it was his, that a new weapon that should have been seen as a valuable addition to our armoury has been allowed, as in a horror story, to take on a life of its own, and to take over. And my chief complaint is not even this, which would be a wholly negative one. My chief complaint is that because a mistaken conception of philosophy has held sway, alternative conceptions of philosophy have not been pursued as they should have been, except by mavericks. On this point I am again with Russell. Near the end of *My Philosophical Development* he says (230): 'The most serious of my objections is that the new philosophy seems to me to have abandoned, without necessity, that grave and important task which philosophy throughout the ages has hitherto pursued. Philosophers from Thales onwards have tried to understand the world... I cannot feel that the new philosophy is carrying on the tradition.'

Well, I'm afraid that is still true. And although I am out of step with most of my contemporaries on this, almost the whole of philosophy's history is on my side, not theirs. What has happened during the last half century and more has been a diversion, in both senses of that word; it has been fun, but it has been a detour, though admittedly a *détour de force*. In the remoter past of philosophy there were other detours, blind alleys, garden paths, which were sometimes followed for generations. I advocate a return to the main road. Philosophy should once more view its main task as that of trying to understand the world, not least the enigma of our existence in it, and also the nature of our experience.

I said at the beginning that other people too were seriously engaged in this task and I referred to religious thinkers, scientists and creative artists. Philosophy differs from religious enquiry because it proceeds without appeal to faith or authority. Philosophers should be the last people inclined to treat any text as sacred. They should insist on subjecting everything to reason. I am not suggesting that the world is totally explicable by reason. In fact, I do not think it is totally explicable at all. But the task of philosophy is to take us as far as reason can take us. The role of reason is evaluative and analytic, and in that sense critical; so reason has to have something to work on that it does not itself produce. And for the philosopher, that something is first and foremost experience, and then the explanations of experience that we grasp at, or more consideredly offer ourselves, or receive from others. The creative writer too is exploring experience; but the philosopher differs from him in that he is trying to express himself in utterances that are literally true. Philosophy differs from science in that although its claims to truth are indeed testable by logical and methodological analysis, and critical discussion generally, they are not testable by empirical procedures. What are the foundations of commonsense knowledge, of science, of mathematics, of logic? These are not questions within those fields, they are questions about them. They are questions for philosophers, including of course philosophers of science, of mathematics and of logic. No science can tell us what is the provenance of ethics and values, or what a right is, or what makes something a work of art. Yet all these are questions that can be rationally addressed and critically discussed; and furthermore they are fundamental to our lives. They are philosophical questions, and that is what makes philosophy so important. We need to pursue them with a perpetually self-critical awareness that extends, yes, to our use of language, of concepts, of analysis and of argument, but such things are among the auxiliaries of method: they must never be seen as constitutive of what it is we are investigating – unless, of course, our investigations are themselves in the philosophy of, shall we say, language or logic. To take just one example, philosophical questions about time are not 'really' about temporal concepts, or our use of language. They are about time. They are *not* about 'time'.

If I may summarize my view of what the central task of philosophy is as expressed up to this point, it is to formulate and criticize rational explanatory theories about the nature of reality, theories that address themselves to problems of substance, not usually of language, but theories that for some good reason are not empirically decidable, even though they are rationally criticizable. Problems of this character present themselves about questions of importance across the whole range of our human experience: I have given several examples, and shall give more. Our curiosity, our wonder, drives us to want answers to these questions; and science alone can never give us all the answers we look for.

It is salutary to remember that creative artists too may be involved, also in a professional and disciplined way, in trying to deepen their insight into, and understanding of, the world, and our experience of it, and to communicate their findings. I want to say a word about the arts in this context, because they help me to make an essential point about the role of language. Painting and sculpture can express insights into the nature of space, and of physical objects, and of the relationship of physical objects to space – and thus, more generally, the nature of the world around us – that are not expressible in language. They may also express inner states that are not expressible in language. The fact that something is not expressible in language does not necessarily mean that it is deep: works of art may be clichéd and superficial, and many are. But they need not be. The greatest art can be as profound as anything that can be experienced or expressed by human beings. And I do not see how anyone can seriously claim that language is in any way central either to the reality being experienced by the visual artist or to the artist's communication of it. Music is an even stronger example of the same truth. Many people claim that the profoundest experiences and insights they ever have, the deepest sense of being in contact with the inner significance of things, come from listening to great music. But again, it would be impossible to claim that language is in any way constitutive either of the experience being had or of the composer's expression of it. The philosopher, unlike the painter and the composer, cannot communicate his work without the use of language; but his work is not thereby *about* language, or *about* the concepts expressible in language. They are no more constitutive of what is being dealt with in the philosopher's case than in the artist's. If I may quote Russell one last time: 'The essential thing about language is that it has meaning – i.e. that it is related to something other than itself, which is, in general, non-linguistic.'

I am as sure as anyone is entitled to be about anything that lies in the future that the importance accredited to language which so differentiates the last eighty or ninety years from everything that went before will come to be seen as wholly disproportionate. It is not the case that language is the most important single contributory element in the conception we form of the world. Seeing, to which much more of the brain is given over than to language, and only a few aspects of which are expressible in words, does more to provide us with our conception of the world. Or, to take a different sort of example: it has now long been treated as a truism that the single thing that most differentiates us human beings from the animals is language, but I should say that this is not so: I should say that morality is the most important *single* distinguishing factor.

If one thinks about it seriously, not all that much human experience is satisfactorily expressible in language. None of the things most important to us is, like being in love, or our grief at the loss of those we love, or our own fear of death, or our relationship to our children, even the taste of our food and drink, or our feelings about our work. And language is, anyway, a johnny-come-lately phenomenon, recently arrived on the surface of just our one particular planet. The planet itself is little more than a speck in the cosmos. It therefore cannot be the case that language is constitutive of the reality in which we find ourselves, which we are trying so hard to understand, and with which we have to deal, and of which indeed we are part.

In its most basic features, this world that the philosopher finds himself wondering at, and finds himself wondering at his own existence in, seems to consist of a container whose most clearly perceptible contents are material objects. The container itself has four dimensions, three of space and one of time, and the material objects in it have their being in those dimensions. The objects are continuously in interaction with one another, and these interactions are for the most part causal in character, so that it is usually possible to give causal explanations of the motion of matter in space. The search for causal explanations has always been among the central preoccupations of science. Characteristically, scientific explanation reduces the phenomena to be explained to connections between fundamentals. In physics these may include mass, energy, change, distance, time; and the connections between them are likely to be expressed in mathematical equations. The most famous equation to be formulated in the twentieth century was $E = mc^2$ – the amount of energy embodied in a material object is equal to its mass times the square of the velocity of light – a simply incredible discovery, fraught with consequence. But if you were to say to the physicist: 'You are using mathematics here. How is mathematics to be justified? What are its foundations? How can they be validated?'; or 'What actually *is* a causal connection, in itself? What is it for one thing to cause another?'; the scientist excuses himself and bows out. These are not scientific or mathematical questions. They are questions *about* science, and *about* mathematics. They are, in fact, among the classical, and still unsolved, problems of philosophy. The amount of knowledge that science has provided us with is prodigious, and has transformed our understanding of the world, but science cannot explain everything. What is characteristic of science is the reduction of explanation to a basic level *that is then left unexplained*. Schopenhauer, who revered science, and was very knowledgeable about it, and appreciative of its power and significance, said that in relation to ultimate explanation it was like meeting a group of people and being introduced to each of them in terms of his or her relationship to the others – this one was that one's brother, that one was this one's cousin, the other one was another's niece, and so on – so that by the end you were left saying to yourself: 'Yes, I've got all that straight – but who on earth are they all?' This fact that science explains things without itself being explained is one of the factors (there are others) that precludes it from ever providing us with ultimate understanding of the world. This point was taken up and repeated by Wittgenstein in the *Tractatus* (6.52): 'We feel that even when *all possible* scientific questions have been answered, the problems of life remain completely untouched.'

Science gives rise to many, many questions that it cannot itself answer. Problems about the nature of time are notorious. Einstein believed that there was no such thing as an objective now, a now not relative to an observer, and therefore no such thing as an objective flow of time. But Karl Popper disagreed with him about that, and they had a face-to-face argument about it. The status of science itself is contentious, and there is disagreement among eminent scientists about what constitutes acceptable scientific method. It is more usually the philosopher of science than the scientist who tries to sort out their differing views. (In that matter, incidentally, Einstein endorsed Popper's basic formulation.) Anyone attached to a university will have on all sides of him people (by no means all of them scientists in a narrow sense) who believe that all significant questions about the nature of reality are ultimately soluble by scientific methods. Such people seem not to recognize that this belief is not in itself a scientific belief, but is a belief about science. It is not itself susceptible of scientific investigation. It is a metaphysics, and one that, it so happens, stands up very badly to critical discussion; in fact it does not stand up at all. Its uncritical acceptance is an act of faith, not rationally sustainable.

The status of mathematics is problematic in a quite different way. In philosophy of mathematics the ur-question is, is mathematics a product of the human mind, as natural languages are, or does it exist independently of the human mind? To give a specific instance from within the subject, are the natural numbers human constructions? I personally have heard world-famous mathematicians argue on each side of that question; and the question itself is not to be solved by mathematics.

All these are areas of questioning that are fundamental for philosophers, and cannot be answered by science. Ordinary, everyday life too is such an area, I am tempted to say the most fertile of all. We cannot stir an inch in any direction without running into enigmas. For instance, all of us here believe 100% that tomorrow will come, and after that another day, and another day after that – and so on indefinitely. The time-unit 'day' is local to our world, and if in the future the earth is drawn into the sun there will be no more days; but whatever units of time are appropriate, we assume that one will be positioned after another. Does this mean that we, here, now, are living in time without end, eternal time – that we are already living in eternity? Or is time bounded? Or will it stop? How could that happen? What could it even mean? Are there any other possibilities?

If so, what are they? That is only one example. Our ordinary here-ness and now-ness bristles with such fundamental philosophical enigmas. The space we find ourselves in: is that infinitely extended? Could it be? Or is it bounded? If so, how could *that* be? What sorts of things do we know about the physical objects that seem to be sharing our space, and how do we know them? What difference does it make that we ourselves are physical objects, each one of us always and inescapably located in a particular place at a particular time, with the result that all our perceptions and all our experiences are perspectival?

Here we come to a point which, in my opinion, is more than any other fundamental to philosophy. Everything of any kind that we can do – including all our knowing, experiencing, apprehending, thinking and imagining – can be done only with the physical appar-atus we have. So only what that apparatus can mediate is apprehen-sible by us, and it is apprehensible only in the forms that the apparatus makes available to us. But that is not to say that only such things can exist or be the case. *Anything* else, provided it is not self-contradictory, can exist or be the case, but is just not appre-hensible *by us*. Now the fact that we have the physical apparatus that we do have is a contingent truth, not a necessary one, as is the fact that the forms it makes available to us are whatever it is they are. Likewise the fact that the reality external to ourselves is whatever it is is also a contingent and not a necessary truth. So our situation is that of an only partially and contingently equipped observer trying to under-stand a contingently existing and contingently characterized reality that may extend immeasurably beyond him. An inescapable con-clusion is that what we take reality to be can exist for us only in what-ever terms our little bit of contingently possessed apparatus makes available to us. But those terms are perforce already limited to what is apprehensible by us. This is a permanently unsatisfactory situation. The only conceptions of reality we are capable of forming are such as are apprehensible to us, yet we have the strongest possible rational grounds for believing that reality extends beyond that, and is not confined to the terms in which we are able to conceive it. So it may well be that by far the greater part of it is not explicable to us in terms that we are able to understand at all, and must therefore remain permanently unintelligible to us. J. S. Haldane – who was, I believe, always a materialist – once asserted that the universe is not only queerer than we imagine, it's queerer than we *can* imagine.

This luminous and entirely rational insight was pioneered most influentially by Kant, richly developed by Schopenhauer, and taken up from Schopenhauer by Wittgenstein in the *Tractatus*. I do not think Wittgenstein added to it very importantly, but he understood it profoundly, and gave it wonderfully incandescent expression. This line of development within Western philosophy contains, I do believe, the most insightful of the thinking available to us so far on these utterly fundamental matters.

I could go on and on giving examples of philosophical questions about matters that are fundamental to our existence; and they would all be among the questions with which philosophy could and should concern itself. None of them is a question primarily for science, because the investigations and conjectures of science are confined to the realm of empirical testability – though this does mean that science can often give our enquiries helpful support. Also, scientific theories can rule out metaphysical theories. None of these enquiries is primarily about our use of concepts or of language, though we need always to be critically self-aware in such use. They are enquiries into the nature of reality, the way things actually are. As with the novelist and the playwright – who may be superior masters of the use of language – it is important that we never confuse the medium we are communicating in with the reality we are communicating about. Only one small corner of the field should ever be given over to concern with the medium itself.

Many of the philosophical questions I have mentioned so far come from areas in which philosophy finds itself in a neighbouring territory to science or mathematics. This reflects the mainstream development of the subject for most of the last four hundred years, if not during the last few. There was a period of hundreds of years before that, during the Middle Ages, when philosophy was closer to religion. The balance and the emphasis have differed in different historical periods. I am sure the balance will continue to change. An outsider might be forgiven for supposing that in the study of philosophy, intellectual fashion would have no place; but everyone in this room knows that intellectual fashion is an exceedingly powerful force. There is one aspect of philosophy's potential that has never had such a period of dominance although it has always existed, and has always intrigued me, namely philosophy that shares concerns with, and takes account of, the creative arts. I would approach it in the following way.

As I have already stressed, we do not just *inhabit* a world of material objects existing in a container of space and time: we ourselves are material objects. Opinions differ as to whether we are wholly and solely our bodies. Many people believe that we are, others that we are our bodies plus something else, and yet others that the real, essential 'I' is a something else whose existence is independent of space and time. But whichever of these alternatives is correct, if any is, while we are in this world we are unquestionably embodied. Whether *or not* we have spirits or souls or disembodied minds, and whether *or not* our experience will ever include any world other than this one, while we are in this world we are unquestionably living in, or with, or through, if not as, material objects, the material objects that are our bodies. Whatever the explanation may be, each one of us in this world is a material object that knows itself from inside. And for each one of us, his own body is the only material object that he knows from inside.

Inside ourselves we have an unending welter of experiences that range from the superficial and trivial, or the workaday and mundane, to the compelling and the profound. Some of our inner experiences are almost overwhelmingly powerful, and are of the very highest interest and importance to us. But they are not subject to rational enquiry in the normal sense, because they are accessible to only one person. Our bodies – including our brains, our nervous systems and our sense organs – are fully available to the investigations of science, but our experiences are not. It is very properly a principle of science that for any claim to have scientific status, what it claims must be inter-subjectively observable, checkable, testable – and our inner experiences are not. Yet they are the most immediate experiences we have, and this gives them an inescapable importance for philosophy. As Descartes famously claimed, the only things of which I can be indubitably certain are that I am having whatever immediate experiences I am currently having, and that in the having of them I know myself to exist as, at the very least, a something that has these experiences. If I try to enlarge on this in any way at all – for instance, by describing any of the experiences in language, or by drawing logical inferences from them, or by trying to establish what sort of a something I am – I make myself liable to error. But in knowing that whatever I am is having whatever pre-linguistic experiences I am currently having I cannot err. This has what might appear to be the paradoxical consequence that our only absolutely certain knowledge is permanently ring-fenced from science and scientific investigation.

This does not, however, mean that it is ring-fenced from all investigation. Much of it belongs to the province of the creative artist, although it is not the whole of his province. Creative artists can have what are perhaps the profoundest of all insights into inner states, and can give public expression to those insights in works of art. But some of the same territory also belongs to the philosopher. Substantial contributions to its investigation have been made not only by Kant and Schopenhauer, whose work ranged across the whole of philosophy, but, after them, more narrowly, by Nietzsche and Husserl. It has always been central to the concerns of existential-ist philosophy – first, in the nineteenth century, with Kierkegaard, and then in the twentieth with philosophers as different as Heidegger and Merleau-Ponty. Some other philosophers who confine themselves within analytic traditions coterminous with science and mathematics have been suspicious of these thinkers, if not downright hostile to them, because of the unamenability of these aspects of their subject matter to enquiries that embody scien-tific principles. But this is surely an error on their part. It is manifestly a mistake for a philosopher trying to understand the nature of material objects, and the nature of our knowledge of them, to rule out of consideration his direct knowledge and experience of the one and only material object that he experiences and knows from inside. How can it not be obvious that if he wants to deepen his under-standing of the inner nature of things, at least one legitimate place to start is with the only thing of whose inner nature he has immediate, direct, unmediated perceptions? Of course, what he then goes on to say must be subjected to rigorous logical analysis and critical discus-sion, like all other philosophical utterances. His statements may not be empirically testable, but nor are most of the statements of most other philosophers – it certainly does not mean that they are not *tes-table*; and, as with others, their tenability will depend on their success in withstanding detailed and prolonged criticism. If a philosopher produces utterances that cannot be rationally criticized at all then they will not be philosophy. They may have other interest: they may be metaphysical rhapsody of a kind that some religious people value, or they may be poetry, perhaps even great poetry. On the other hand such a philosopher may produce utterances that claim to be literally true, and are rationally criticizable, and are interesting. All the philosophers I have just mentioned did that. And in all such cases they were writing – there should be no serious question about this – philosophy.

Modern Philosophy[1]

JONATHAN HARRISON

Crafty Men Contemne *Studies*; simple Men Admire them; And
Wise Men Use them; For they teach not their own Use: But
that is a Wisdom without them, and above them, won by
Observation.

Francis Bacon

There is hardly any view so paradoxical that some philosopher somewhere or other has not propounded it. That everything is air, fire,
water; that the world contains nothing but atoms and the void; that
nothing (that is, *pace* Sartre, not anything) exists; that we know
nothing; that the world is an idea in the mind of God; that matter
does not exist; that the absolute does exist and that everything else
is only appearance; that there is no past and no future; that what
seems to be reality is an illusion; that propositions about the world
that we have neither been able to establish nor refute are neither
true nor false; that truth is relative, and that all matter is just a holo-
gram in a one-dimensional space, is just a selection from such paradoxical contentions.

It needs only a little reflection to dismiss most of them. But what
often happens when one challenges one of them is that it turns out
that the man who put it forward did not quite mean what he said.
He did not really mean to say that no-one knows anything in any
sense that would make it necessary to pay attention to what he said.
He did not go to the lengths of suggesting that I act on his belief
that there might be no such thing as food, and so appear to die for
what would seem to be the lack of it. He did not think that I ought
only to ignore someone else's 'relatively true' belief that I am dead
if I myself think I am still alive. If everything in the world is water,
it is water that sometimes answers to all the tests of being wine.
The world might not have a past, but eating what must then be my
quite delusive breakfast allays the pangs of what one might think

[1] I am grateful to my nephew, Keith Bradbury, for reading the print-
out, and making many corrections and helpful suggestions.

doi:10.1017/S1358246109990063

was present hunger as well as any real breakfast would have done. Space may have eleven dimensions, but I can find my way about London just as if there were only three. Propositions about the future may be neither true nor false, but one can bet on them just as profitably as if they were. Physicists quote with admiration the ancient view that there are only atoms and the void, but it has been rejected by Einstein, who thought that, though there are atoms, there is no void.

Not only do philosophers wisely tend to prevent their views from cutting any ice, which results in the curious philosophical vice of giving back with one hand what you have taken away with another. Often when a philosopher – or sometimes a scientist – propounds an apparently paradoxical view, he has a fall-back position, which is the one he defends when the view he claims he holds is under attack; he adopts some manoeuvre which nullifies it and deprives it of its sting. His more controversial view is what gives what he says interest. The fall-back view is what gives it plausibility. Confusing the two makes it seem as if he was saying something *both* interesting *and* plausible, which usually he is not. I once heard Derrida maintain that there was no such thing as giving, but he did not appear to mean that no-one could give anyone anything. He was really talking about 'true giving', on which topic his remarks were fairly platitudinous. They *seemed* important because he gave the impression that he was talking about actual giving. I thought he must have a terrible time at Christmas.

One difficulty in refuting such thinkers is that those who dismiss them are condemned to defending rather obvious and unexciting truths. The contradictory of what is exciting is usually (not necessarily) dull. Hardly anyone makes himself a great reputation by arguing that not everything is made of water, that there really are chairs and tables and that we know that there are, and that there are such things as beliefs. To gain such a reputation one has to say some such thing as that there are not any such things as beliefs. This, on the assumption that one believes what one says is, though logically consistent, pragmatically inconsistent; the person putting forward this view, if he is sincere, must *believe* that there are no such things as beliefs. Few arouse much interest by saying that there really are material objects, or that the universe has had a past and will have a future. So great is the hunger of philosophers and their readers to come to paradoxical, or at least adventurous, conclusions the easy way, by using only philosophical techniques without empirical premises, that philosophers seldom learn to reject the novel and exciting in favour of the dull and mundane. Their tendency to set aside the obvious is not diminished by their relying on arguments that are much more likely to be invalid than the common or garden views that they set aside are likely to be false. Fortunately, however, that a view is absurd does not necessarily mean that exposing the fallacies in the arguments used to establish it is not sometimes exciting. Much of this kind of work by G. E. Moore, for example, *is* exciting, partly because of the intensity and logical rigour with which the views he is criticising are exposed. Many philosophers with more enterprising views are intellectually flabby by comparison.

The men and women who are more impressed by what is obscure and pretentious than by plain truth expressed in simple, clear English often put down the fact that they find the former difficult to its being profound, when usually it is only muddled. And conversely, when the truth is so lucidly expressed that they do quite easily understand it, they think it must be trivial. One of the more recent ways of producing spurious problems is sometimes to be found in work put in the terminology of Logic, that branch of Philosophy usually most worthy of respect. For even the terminology of Logic sometimes gives rise to problems that do not appear when they are formulated in ordinary good English.

For example, there seems to be no way of simply saying 'perhaps' and 'whether' in the language of the propositional calculus. There is nothing at all wrong with saying that *perhaps* there is life on Andromeda, though no-one knows *whether* there is or not. There is no need to say that there *is* life on Andromeda, and (sic) no-one knows that there is. And I think it is desirable to translate, when possible, sentences in the symbolism of symbolic logic into normal English, to make sure they make sense, or at least to make sure you really do understand them.

Most advanced Philosophy – Logic apart – is mistaken. Aristotle said that there is only one way of going right, many ways of going wrong. There is so much different philosophy written in answer to the same philosophical questions that it cannot all be right, and most of it must be erroneous. (If I have produced some of this myself, my excuse is that I didn't know at the time *which* of what I wrote was mistaken.) The history of Philosophy is the history of error, and the histories of Philosophy themselves often concatenations of half-truths about the philosophers whose views are expounded, often too briefly for accuracy or proper comprehension.

Philosophy once used to be defended for its lack of progress by saying that it consisted in a residue of the unsolved problems which were left behind when its more successful branches – Psychology, for example – split off and became sciences. But the number of such problems should then get progressively smaller, whereas in fact it gets larger.

In reply to the jibe that philosophers say what everyone knows in a language that no-one can understand, it can be said that if no-one can understand philosophers' language, how could anyone know that what they say is what everyone knows? And one can add that there is a large amount of perfectly comprehensible philosophy which laymen do not read because, though not technical, it is closely reasoned, and demands more application than laymen are accustomed to give to have informed views on problems that they do not hesitate to talk about. One can also say that laymen themselves are to some extent responsible for the incomprehensibility of some, especially French, Philosophy. They are in some respects like the people who complain of being misled by some journalists, who might prefer to tell the unvarnished truth, but know that their newspapers would not be bought if they were to.

The triviality of much Philosophy is also a cause for reflection, if not for concern. A layman would not think that the nature of the relationship between a proper name and what it stood for was a matter of great moment. As John Stuart Mill said, proper names name rather than describe or classify, and one might think (wrongly, as it happens) that that is all that one really needs to know about them. But the amount of man-power and intellectual weight that has gone into attempting a solution of the problem of proper names – and some cynical person might say into making it – must be simply enormous. Indeed, in some cases one suspects that there sometimes wouldn't be much of a problem if the rewards for seeming to solve it had not seemed so great. (I sometimes suspect that American influence has done as little for our Philosophy as it has for our waist-lines.) But this does not mean that the people who devote themselves to trying to solve philosophical problems are not very able, or the literature they produce not of a very high quality. And the relative triviality of much Philosophy does not alter the fact that the subject of Philosophy includes matters of the greatest moment, and that it is sometimes highly influential. There is after all the story of the philosopher whose later editions were bound in the skins of those who laughed at the first (though nowadays one would have been lucky to be sufficiently read to be laughed at, or to cause as many deaths as one might have liked). And neither the kudos attached to philosophical writing nor its actual merit varies with its (practical) importance.

In defence against the charge that there is too much Philosophy one might reply that Philosophy, like every other academic subject, is infinite. But that knowledge is infinite does not mean that more than a tiny part of it is worth having. It is worth knowing that Charles I had his head cut off, but one doesn't need an account of the behaviour of every molecule in his head, his neck, the axe that removed it or the block on which it rested. Knowledge is supposed to be valuable for its own sake, but such pieces of knowledge aren't valuable at all.

Some argue that philosophical questions arise naturally in the course of life. It is natural to ask who we are, how we got here, and why there is something rather than nothing. So it is, but I doubt whether these questions make sense. There is no answer to them more profound than the following. (1) I am Jonathan Harrison, a retired Professor of Philosophy. (2) My father fell in love with my mother at a dance during the first world war, and I was the result. (I didn't say 'the immediate result'.) (3) One cannot ask for an explanation of the existence of the universe, over and above the existence of the things in it. You can ask the question: 'Why was there a fire in that house, but not in those other houses?' because there are other cases, often cases of houses in which there was no fire. But the question: 'Why in those cases, was there a universe when in those other cases there was not?' does not make sense. By definition there can only be the one case. To use more pretentious language, it involves a transcendental application of the categories. The universe is as it is. And there is no point in philosophers trying to discover the meaning of life. Life doesn't have a meaning. Some try to draw religious or metaphysical conclusions from the improbability of their existence, but though it is true that on the information available at the beginning of the universe the chances of its containing a person like me must have seemed very small, yesterday these chances were extremely good, and today leave no margin of error. Incidentally, I do have religious experience, which I value, but I don't think that it is veridical.

Philosophers do not investigate the world at first hand, and so are unlikely to come honestly, by an application of Philosophy alone, to any truths about it. They *can* come to such truths, but only in conjunction with premises supplied by those who do investigate the world at first hand (together with, in Moral Philosophy, Philosophical Psychology and the Theory of Perception, the results of a certain amount of rudimentary first-hand observation).

One permissible thing philosophers can do *viz-a-viz* science is to familiarise themselves with the more elementary work of those who can and do come to conclusions about the world. One result of doing this is the realisation of just how paradoxical some of these views are. That since time is a fourth dimension, nothing really changes, is just one of these paradoxical views. I think it is quite wrong to claim that the universe is static for the reason that a language which mentions things changing is replaced by one in which adjacent slices of a four-dimensional universe are described as being similar or dissimilar to one another. Adjacent time-slices of things in the universe being dissimilar to one another *is* the substances whose time-slices they are changing. And I myself am highly suspicious of physicists (and philosophers) who talk of men travelling rapidly through space coming back much younger and healthier than those they left behind, or than they would have been if they hadn't travelled. They could well be healthier, but they can't be younger. If they leave on the 1st of January and come back on the 1st of January a year later they are (by definition) just one year older. The earth has been once round the sun in that time, and that is what being a year older means. It is not that I dispute what physicists say about the behaviour of clocks at high velocities; that would be an exercise in hubris. Whether one is in a spaceship travelling at a very high velocity (that is, fast) or not, one's chronological age is determined by the number of revolutions of the earth that have elapsed between the time at which one started on one's journey and the time at which one returned; this does not vary with the speed at which one travels. The speed of the clocks with which, on one's journeys, one measured this time is different from the speed of our clocks, as is the speed of one's aging process. But their clocks, measured by the revolutions of the earth, are just slow. If one was born in 1950 AD and died in 2050 AD one is one hundred years old, even though one has led a more interesting life and looks better preserved at the time of one's death than other men of one hundred. Of course, it is a matter for decision how one measures time-intervals, but the convention is that on the earth one uses revolutions of the earth round the sun, and we are on the earth. If the whole solar system were to start travelling through the galaxy at a different rate, the case might be different. And despite the eminence of some of the theoretical physicsts who have espoused it, time-travel is a nonsense.

The situation in Philosophy is not improved by a system which demands that all professional philosophers produce a certain amount of published work in order to gain promotion or keep the respect of their colleagues, whether they want to publish or not, whether anyone wants to read what they write or not, and whether they have anything to say or not. It is as if Tantalus had been condemned to be buried in enormous quantities of grapes which he was not only compelled to eat until they made him ill, but also forced to work in order to produce even more grapes.

As a result of there being too many philosophers, when a new problem crops up, philosophers throw themselves upon it like a pack of hungry wolves, worry it to what would be extinction were it not that the problem seems to thrive on the treatment, and then pass on to something else. They leave its mangled remains to the history books – if there are any sufficiently detailed to notice – to record another failure. And PhD students are set to work to write theses presupposing current views, without being taught to develop the independence of mind which might enable them to see that some of the views they are working to elaborate and refine are simply mistaken. It might even be that neither student nor supervisor has much incentive to discover this.

The result of the increasingly large number of academics in Philosophy is too many philosophers chasing too few important problems; everything gets excessively complicated and diversified, and philosophers themselves become excessively specialised. The number of philosophical problems expands in proportion to the number of people employed to solve them. There is a constant stream of ephemeral writing in periodicals which, until a human eye falls on them, are simply vast collections of dead paper-molecules. Heads of departments, of which I was once one, are not to be blamed for this overproduction. It is their duty to 'encourage' their staff to write. But the results of everybody's doing their duty can be disastrous – though in this case 'disastrous' would be an exaggeration. Philosophical writing is funded by the tax payer. (The tax payer, of course, could and does fund far worse things.) If philosophy, like sudoku cubes, were simply a form of mental exercise and entertainment it could easily be justified, were it not that, unlike sodoku, there is no way of checking whether one has got the correct answer. But one would like to think that Philosophy was something more than a game.

In the sciences, specialisation pays dividends. You can work on an area yourself, and take on trust at least some of the results of scientists working in areas in which you are not a specialist. (I am told by a friend who is a scientist that this is no longer true; the volume of publications is so enormous that it is impossible to check it all.) In Philosophy one cannot trust one's colleagues to get things right, and whole areas of enquiry are often based on fundamental mistakes.

All search for knowledge should in the last resort be justified by there being a chance of discovering something that, directly or indirectly, satisfies a human need, even if the need is only curiosity. (Curiosity is biologically useful and so commendable by the way.) All of what claims to be worth finding out should be either useful or agreeable, both of which features tend to depend, among other things, upon its scope and its certainty. (On this latter virtue Philosophy falls rather low.) It is, of course, the end result that should be agreeable, not the search; assessed simply as a search, Philosophy comes out rather well. But what human need much Philosophy satisfies is doubtful.[2] Quite a lot of people seem to think they can do without it.

It is not difficult to see ways in which Philosophical work can multiply. One way is this. First of all some philosopher puts forward a view. Then a second philosopher puts forward reasons for thinking that this view is incorrect. Then a third philosopher puts forward reasons for thinking that the second philosopher's reasons for thinking that the first philosopher's view is incorrect are incorrect. Then a fourth philosopher puts forward the view that, though the second philosopher's reasons for thinking this view is incorrect *are* incorrect, the view *is* nevertheless incorrect, but not for reasons given by the second philosopher. Then a fifth philosopher comes along and says that the third philosopher is mistaken about the first philosopher's view, which is in fact no different from the view the third philosopher himself put forward on some past occasion, and has been ignored. And, alas, all these variations on a theme seem to have acquired names.

With longer work, it is the first step that counts, and the first step is more often than not wrong. And the tendency to think in jargon, like 'truth conditions', 'assertion conditions', 'defeasibility', 'rigid designators', 'best explanation', 'existential choice', and so on, causes possibly erroneous views to get enshrined in what becomes familiar language, and so to escape proper scrutiny. (The quantity of jargon associated with the language of possible worlds is horrific.) And it produces clichés. The greatest gift a philosopher can have is the gift of not understanding things, especially things that everyone else thinks they can understand.

Peer assessment may produce a high minimum standard, but inhibit originality. Philosophers read too many books and pay too little attention to actual experience, especially moral and perceptual experience. There has, I believe, been a decline in teaching by official lecturing. Lecturing has always been a questionable way of disseminating information. There are usually books which treat the subject of the lecture better by a person who knows more about it than does the lecturer. And lectures are too often given over to discussion, where the strong and vociferous tyrannise the weak and inarticulate.

---

[2] See my 'The Importance of Being Important' (1978).

But it does sometimes save the lecturer a lot of the trouble necessary for systematic presentation. Discussion in small groups is a different matter. Bacon wisely said: 'Reade not to Cotradict, and Confute'. But, since what philosophers say is usually wrong, this is just what a philosopher should do when reading the work of another philosopher. But it does slow you down.

Of course Philosophy is not the only subject having difficulties. History was in my day largely a matter of learning one damn thing after another, and I remember turning with relief to Economic History, which involved some kind of rationale. English, apart from the set texts, which were wonderful, was a matter of learning the right kind of thing to say. French, my inability to do which was the cause of my academic success, was the same, except that here one had to learn the language, something which was supposed to be unnecessary when one was studying English. (I wonder, by the way, why English children often have to wait until they are eleven to learn French when French children, who one hopes are not cleverer than English children, can learn French from the age of nought.)

To some extent the situation I have described is produced by too sharp a division between arts and science. On an extreme view, too much of an arts education consists in learning to produce the right kind of waffle. I am not suggesting that producing the right kind of waffle does not demand intelligence, and that those who are good at it often deserve and get better degrees and better-paid jobs than those who are not – though I do note that business people are complaining about the kind of educated person being turned out by schools and universities. (This may partly because the examination system in arts, though scrupulously fair, is very inaccurate.) But the result of the separation between arts and science – I don't just mean physics by 'science' – sometimes involves a divorce from reality which results in the feeling that in academic thought anything goes so long as you can find enough people to agree with what you say. In my experience the kind of thing I am complaining about is often to be found in most speculative Theology, especially that trying to reconcile Christianity with what the speculators accept to be the fact that there is no omnipotent, omniscient perfectly good being. My remarks also apply especially to some Literary Criticism and certain types of French Philosophy. (Sartre, I used to think, was a brilliant novelist and playwright, but a rubbish philosopher.) Indeed, I see there is one French philosopher who holds that nothing is real. One might think that he intended to defend the view that everything is an illusion – in which case I am sure that it would have turned out to be an illusion which precisely resembled reality – but all he seemed to have meant is that man's values are hollow and can give no permanent satisfaction, a view which I seem to have heard before.

If the people who produce all this had some elementary training in science, which is more rigorous than arts, perhaps some of it might be avoided. Indeed, the best thing might be for all students to have to study a small amount of science – not necessarily an exact science – through the whole of their university careers, which would then have to take longer. In Philosophy some of the benefits of science are produced by Logic, and it might be a very good thing if students other than philosophers, as well as philosophers, had to do some Logic at some time or other, though I think there are better ways of making people think more rigorously than learning Logic; one needs to think more rigorously about one's own subject. But what is needed in much – not all – 'analytic' philosophy is a standard of rigour which emulates mathematics. (I don't, incidentally, think that *all* Philosophy must be analytic, whatever analytic Philosophy may be. It was once associated with the view that all philosophers can do is to analyse common sense; a view which is certainly mistaken. ('Common sense' is a misnomer, incidentally. It is a matter of common sense that you should change your wet socks; it is not a matter of common sense that you have socks.) Reflections on human life and morals, politics, the satisfactoriness of cosmological speculations, the destiny of man, the nature of wisdom and the possibility of an after life are all quite proper subjects for philosophical enquiry, and these involve reaching substantive conclusions, not just analysing things. And getting to these conclusions does presuppose having a certain amount of empirical information.

It might also be a good idea if scientists were compelled to read some arts subjects, partly because some arts subjects do help us with the proper enjoyment of life – though I don't see why enjoying life should be made compulsory. Studying English – at least to the extent of reading good literature, rather than hearing people talk about it – might enable scientists to write up their results and communicate with other scientists and laymen more lucidly than they do. It has been suggested to me (by a scientist, as it happens) that reading some arts subject might improve scientists' powers of disseminating important warnings. There are some important warnings – about global warming, for example – that they have failed to give, or at least effectively to bring home to us. But the main failing concerning global warming is the ignorance of science both among politicians and the general public, which more science in schools and universities might have remedied. With more science among the population politicians would not be able to get away with their present pusillanimity, which is the result of the electorate itself being so short-sighted, so self-indulgent and so badly informed. As it is, politicians are usually too ignorant and too terrified of losing votes to do anything effective. They commonly argue that we are such a small country that our emissions can make no appreciable difference to the eventual outcome, but if every country (and every individual) whose limiting emissions made no difference refused to limit them, the result would be disaster. But hope for the future is more likely to be dependent on technologists finding new sources and new ways of producing energy than on politicians learning self-control. One only hopes that the politicians do not muck things up.

Another reason why a certain amount of science might be a good discipline for arts people is that the subject matter at least of the exact sciences, unlike that of Philosophy, is inexorable; if you make a mistake about it, it punishes you, perhaps with your own or, worse, someone else's life. I sometimes think it might be a good idea if the same fate sometimes befell philosophers who made mistakes, but then few people would write Philosophy. In science, making a mistake slows you down; you have to go back and do it correctly. In Philosophy, it speeds you up, and may add to your list of publications by provoking someone to point out the error. If so you may score a double by replying to him. Even in mathematics, which has no empirical content, mistakes are easier to spot, and wrong mathematics may lead to actual experiments going wrong or predictions being falsified. (My favourable remark about science does not always apply to writing about science, as opposed to doing it.)

Of course, the exact sciences cannot give one the whole truth. They don't give one moral judgements – which most people seem to think they can make – though to make moral judgements is often to use a bludgeon when it would be better to use a scalpel. That men should *act* morally is necessary to mankind – we would not have evolved to be moral beings otherwise – but it is difficult to defend the rationality of the moral judgements men make, though one can point out the bad consequences of not acting on them, hoping one's audience will care. The more set in their ways of thinking morally they are – and I am not convinced that deontological morality involves more than being set in one's ways of thinking – the less they will be inclined to care. And the exact sciences are *too* exact to be useful in many spheres of life. The trouble with science and mathematics as disciplines is that, though they train people to think clearly on subjects which admit of precise measurement, it is enormously important that men and women be trained to think well on subjects where such precision is impossible. To some extent subjects such as Economics, Psychology, Sociology, and perhaps some Politics might fit this bill. Though I understand that they are to some extent taking students away from more demanding sciences, they might also take students away from the less demanding ones. But it is unavoidable that much, if not most, intellectual activity is a matter of making correct assessments, which involves coming to uncertain conclusions on inadequate evidence.

It is not to be inferred from my admiration of science that I think that Physics is perhaps the preeminent science – whatever this may mean – from whose conclusions all the facts investigated by the other sciences can be deduced. In fact I think this is very great rubbish. And in any case, even if it were true, an entailment of the other sciences by Physics would not be enough. One would need an equivalence. Without the equivalence all the allegedly derivative sciences could quite happily go on – as in practice they can – even though Physics were false. And an equivalence seems even more implausible than an entailment.

Most of people's opinions beyond the immediate province of their everyday life – and many that are not – are highly irrational. It is a good thing that man is an irrational animal in *behaviour*. A rational man would be something of a monster. But to gain truth he must be rational – that is, where empirical matters are concerned, scientific – in all walks of life. This includes being rational about problems concerning the existence of God; the efficacy of prayer; the superiority of Islam; the relative intelligence of black, white and other varieties of people – a subject which should be approached scientifically and dispassionately with a view to finding out the facts, not used as an excuse for moral exuberance. It includes being rational about the value of marriage; the success of various different methods of education; the evils of segregation by colour; religion or nationality; the efficacy of prison; the desirability of wars, and so on almost indefinitely. But most men's opinions are based on inadequate information and prejudice. More fundamental science teaching in schools might do something to combat this, especially if the 'hard' sciences could be supplemented with subjects that more concern probability and have to do with people's behaviour. Some elementary knowledge of statistics could well help people – especially doctors – to think more rationally. As the Duke of Wellington nearly said, statistics are the guide of life. (I am thinking of people who don't use the MMR vaccine, do use homeopathic medicine, believe in astronomy, go for psycho-analysis, trust bookies and financial advisers, can't compare the safety of trains with that of cars, grossly over-estimate the chances of being killed in some accident, don't know that obesity is bad for you, gamble heavily on the national lottery, believe in dowsing, are guided by astrologers, are convinced that their chances of finding a quarter of a million in a sealed box are improved by their willing that it should be there, and who sacked the England manager because England did not win the World Cup.) Just as we have evolved to be creatures who eat and drink too much and exercise too little in the circumstances of modern living, so we have evolved to be creatures who take quick decisions even when they have time to base them on thought that is more rational. But in trying to achieve all this sophistication, we might well be expecting too much from teachers, who waste too much of their time wrestling with unruly classes whom they are not allowed to discipline.

I understand that British engineers are relatively poorly paid, and not in the top jobs; these are then sometimes occupied by men and women without the technical knowledge to do them properly. This may be a regrettable manifestation of the fact that science, perhaps especially technology, is underrated in this country. Though the British Empire was won on the playing fields of Eton, the battle to prevent global warming may have been lost in the class rooms of Harrow. It is scientists, and more particularly engineers and technologists, that we will increasingly have to rely on to solve the problems raised not only by global warming, but by the world population's outgrowing its food supply, and multiplying too rapidly. They may even, by brain modifications and additions, eliminate man's disposition to violence, group intransigence, and religious bigotry. (Religion, I suspect, is like alcohol. Though individual people may benefit from both, the world would be a better place without either.) Scientists will almost certainly be able to increase man's intelligence. If they were allowed to use genetic engineering, they could considerably improve the quality of men and the lives of men. Prison may come to seem an even cruder way of dealing with dishonesty and violence than it does now. (Having the satisfaction of punishing people can be purchased at too high a cost.)

My critical remarks about Philosophy do not mean that some Philosophy is not highly desirable, at least in preventing bad Philosophy, and sometimes bad thinking, which can be a dangerous. It can offer very great enlightenment, interest and intellectual satisfaction, which does not exclusively consist in escape from previous error. And the best philosophers do work of the very highest order. Part of the difficulty with at least the central problems of Philosophy, is that there is no elementary part which those of more pedestrian ability can master and build on. In History, say, it is important to remember what one has been taught, even if one does not understand it. In Philosophy just remembering (and when necessary regurgitating) is valueless.

Descartes' remedy for avoiding error was to be guided by clear and distinct ideas. (Of course one can't always tell when one's ideas are clear and distinct, but one can try.) Berkeley's remedy for much Philosophical error was always to clothe one's words with ideas. Not writing in good, ordinary English is one of the most common causes of *not* clothing one's words with ideas. For example, a bête noire of mine is the artificial language of possible worlds. If Leibniz had only said that this world could not be any better than it is, think what a lot of muddled thinking would have been avoided. Quine, writing more than fifty years ago, and arguing against the metaphysician McX, pointed out that Pegasus was not a possible object, inhabiting another sphere of reality. 'Possible' is not a word for an attribute at all. To say that Pegasus is possible is not to describe anything, and certainly not to describe a kind of horse, but is just to say that something answering to a certain description – the description of Pegasus (a winged horse) – might possibly or could conceivably have existed. And to compare two things they must both exist. You cannot compare an object with another object that might possibly exist but doesn't. For example, you cannot raise the question whether the Albert Hall is larger than Valhalla. All you can do is to say that there might have been a place answering to the description of 'Valhalla' which would then have been larger than the Albert Hall. Whether Smith is identical with the man who broke the bank at Monte Carlo (i.e. *is* the man who broke the bank) is a perfectly genuine question, if someone did break the bank at Monte Carlo. The question whether Smith is identical with the man who broke the bank, when no-one actually broke the bank at Monte Carlo, is just muddled. If no-one broke the bank at Monte Carlo, there is no-one to be identical or not identical with the man who broke the bank at Monte Carlo. The problem of transworld identity is just confused.

One thing that limits speculative Philosophy is the fact that almost all first-hand knowledge of the universe on which such speculation must be based can be obtained only by empirical investigation of a kind which philosophers are not usually qualified to undertake. However, one does not oneself have to make the basic discoveries of science in order critically to discuss them, and perhaps to build on them, though it would be nice to understand more of the relevant mathematics. And in order sometimes to see that something is wrong with what even eminent physicists like Einstein say about the world, it is not necessary to have knowledge of the specific details of their science. Sometimes all that is necessary is imagination and a certain kind of logical rigour. The main function of all academic work is to discover facts about and understand the universe or parts or aspects thereof, and the function of Philosophy, by acting as a preventive to erroneous thinking, could help this enterprise to no inconsiderable extent. (What help the view that the morning star is necessarily, instead of only contingently, identical with the evening star is to astronomy, however, I can't think. It won't make a blind bit of difference which it is.)

There are also some very important moral and political questions involving philosophy coming up or getting more serious. Global warming will produce moral questions concerning whether whole communities may be allowed to perish. Partly as a result of global warming nationalism may come to be considered as a vice; unfettered nationalism may, among other things, mean that a country which does not cut its emissions will have to be compelled to do so, which implies an international organisation capable of enforcing such reductions. War, international crime and international business, faster-moving populations, globally infectious diseases, space exploration and the need for ever more energy are further reasons for international government. International government is a (logically) interesting case, as it is something that is necessary, but may not be possible. (To be more serious – but the point shows how important it is to use English correctly – it is *having* international government that is necessary, *getting* it that is impossible.) No individual nation can solve these problems itself, or enforce the relevant solutions. And, as the speed of a convoy is the speed of its slowest ship, the speed of a democracy is the speed of its slowest and most ignorant voters, so the necessity for decisive and prompt action to stop global warming quickly enough may spell the death of democracy. (In this case, the people who write extolling democracy's virtues will probably write condemning it.) The steady increase in longevity will increase the seriousness of questions concerning euthanasia and assisted suicide and whether women should have licences to reproduce. Our present often ridiculous attitude to contraception, abortion and euthanasia must become much more permissive if we are to survive in an over-populated planet. A lot of quite imaginary rights, many of which are the result of prolonged moderate affluence such as the supposed right to have as many children as one wishes and to do what one likes with one's own body will probably have to go. And the development of brain technology will mean we will have to decide when to allow and how to control the production of super-intellects, whether ganic or (more likely) organic, whether detached from our brains or partly ingrained in them or embedded in them. Advances in genetic engineering will revolutionise human beings. Satisfactorily to anticipate and discuss such problems it is necessary – though not sufficient – to have a certain knowledge of science. But whether such academic discussion will make much difference to the outcome, I very much doubt.

Despite my complaints about the quantity of professional Philosophy, I think that *elementary* Philosophy should be indulged in by everybody. Some of it is, after all, a more rigorous attempt to think about questions that many will think about anyway. It would be nice if it could be taught – but taught informally, without being examined – in schools. Some elementary Philosophy is really indispensable to a properly educated man or woman. The trouble is finding the people to teach it. I suspect that teaching elementary Philosophy in schools is more, not less difficult than teaching advanced Philosophy in universities. And though in an ideal world there would be no lawyers and no physicians, everybody would be a philosopher and, in an ideal world, a good one.

Perhaps the world would be an academically better place if people did not raise philosophical problems, but were content with knowledge of the world, of *a priori* subjects like Logic and Mathematics, and perhaps also with epistemological questions – the solutions to which are a species of *a priori* knowledge – concerning how such knowledge is arrived at. (It *could* be held that all other philosophical questions are meaningless.) The question whether or not we know something is on this view not really a matter for a philosopher, but for the specialists in whatever branch of knowledge is at issue. One should ask a historian how one knows historical truths, and a scientist how one knows scientific ones – though I very much doubt whether either would be able to give a satisfactory answer. Philosophers should, for example, ask how we know that this is, say, a chair, rather than interminably considering the question whether we really do know that it is one. The former question is surprisingly difficult to answer, and involves explaining how we conflate or synthesise actual sense-data or views (and to a lesser extent feels) of an object, with remembered views seen from different places, to build up a picture of an object as a whole, and an object in space.

But what is the cure for that academic disease of which some but not all Philosophy is just one symptom? To allude again to education, though it has never really interested me very much, one should try to induce more students to read science, mathematics, medicine and certain subjects that are predominantly technological or sociological. A reluctance to do difficult science is entirely understandable, but an inability to do it – often the result of poor teaching and lack of discipline in schools – should mean that one cannot profit from the level of education to which one is being subjected. One would then hope that certain of the less demanding subjects would wither away – but not completely so – and perhaps also absorb some of the stringency demanded by the sciences. Conversely, scientists should not be allowed to devote themselves to science only. I am not quite sure why, but I cannot imagine anything more dreadful than a scientist who knows only science. But a scientist who is taught only science can learn other things in the course of living. An arts person who is taught no science is usually condemned to that ignorance for ever. Where at least the exact sciences are concerned, getting more people to read them would mean paying science teachers, both in schools and universities, more than others, and perhaps giving science students more financial help – but bread and butter before jam. And perhaps what was first done for money will come to be done for love. Since, or so I am told, there are so many bad science teachers already employed, change could not be brought about quickly enough without sacking or redeploying some of them. Substituting the International Baccalaureate, which has a higher science content than A-levels, might help, but probably wouldn't be enough. It is obvious, really, that the expenditure on scientific research ought to be drastically increased. The future of our country and indeed the world depends on scientists – and to some extent on the scientific knowledge of the whole population, especially politicians. The survival of mankind does not depend on those who teach English Literature or Latin and Greek, and still less on Film Studies. Culture is indeed valuable – though I'm not sure why – but it is not always worth its expense. (Philosophy, by the way, is an excellent subsidiary subject, especially for scientists.)

The cure for bad Philosophy, trivial Philosophy, obscure and pretentious Philosophy, muddled Philosophy, is not no Philosophy, but better Philosophy – which I myself think would involve less Philosophy. The benefits of doing Philosophy well are great. It should broaden the mind, prevent one from taking things on trust, reduce slavish conformity, cultivate the imagination, and produce accurate thinking and lucid expression. You would think the difficulty of its problems would produce humility, but the amount of hubris necessary to tackle them and to stand out against the majority opinion when one thinks this mistaken to some extent militates against this. A person even more pessimistic than myself might say that the trouble is that I have presented an ideal which is what many of us are trying to achieve and failing. But we don't always fail; it is just very difficult to know whether we have or have not succeeded, especially with so many helpful colleagues telling us that we haven't. Magna est veritas, and one hopes that it may often prevail. (If truth in Philosophy did prevail, we would all be out of jobs.) But in Philosophy it may be better to travel hopefully than to arrive, though one doesn't know what arriving would be like.

We will not arrive in our own lifetime, if ever. But when one considers the billions of years during which the earth will be able to support human life if human beings themselves do not wreck it, the chances of what one does now making more than a tiny and temporary bit of difference to the future are nil, especially when one considers the appreciable possibility of human brains being supplemented by implants that will greatly increase their owners' intelligence. Perhaps they will be too intelligent to do Philosophy at all. When one considers this fact, watching philosophers competing for publishing space at the cost of more useful or more entertaining activities is like watching men queue for the privilege of tipping what is done at the cost of their most valuable possession, time, over a cliff into the sea. (It is not a criticism only of having money that you can't take it with you; you can't take anything with you.)

I have space very briefly to discuss only four of the numerous philosophical views that I consider to be erroneous.

(1)   If we look upon the world what we see and feel or introspect is spatially extended coloured patches, specks of colour, flashes of light, pains, itches, bodily sensations, the agonisings caused by intense thought and deliberation, and the pains of unrequited love. We do not, especially when we look inwards, come across anything like the description of an electron or an atom or a molecule, and that we should try and dismiss the former phenomena is the result of rejecting the evidence of our senses and of introspection in favour of what we think physicists tell us in books. In my youth the object of many philosophers was to reduce statements about unobserved entities such as protons and electrons to statements about observed entities, which they supposed to be sensedata. This was misguided. Nowadays the object of many philosophers is to reduce statements about observed things to statements about unobserved things like electrons, which is even more misguided.

(2)   It is obvious that our perception of objects is mediated. Even if what we see 'immediately' and without inference are the front surfaces of material objects – and there is no reason in the

definition of sense-data why what we see should not both be the surface of a material object and a sense-datum – 'sense-datum' is the word for what is immediately given in perceptual experience – we still cannot without investigation know that what we see is the front surfaces of what we take to be objects to find out what lies on the other side of them. If we try to do this, what we do then see is just new surface still – if you are determined to be pessimistic – 'getting in the way'. But if we were not aware of the front surfaces of objects, one could know nothing whatsoever about them. In order to get a complete picture of an object we have to go round to the back and piece it together with what we remember to be its front. (This is a process of synthesis, not one of inference.) It is partly because the sense-datum theory has been rejected that much brilliant and constructive work by philosophers like Bertrand Russell, C. D. Broad and H. H. Price, not to mention certain aspects of the work of Locke, Berkeley and Hume, have been misunderstood and neglected.

(3) One bad result of confusing sentences with propositions, and ascribing truth to the former, is Conventionalism. The rules determining the meaning of words and sentences are fixed by convention, but that does not at all mean that the things we use the sentences to say are true by convention. It is a matter of convention that the sentence 'The earth is round' expresses the fact that the earth is round, and not that it is flat, but not a matter of convention that the earth is round. If 'round' had not meant round, the fact that the earth is round would have had to be expressed in different words – perhaps in the sentence 'The world is flat' – but this would not alter the fact that the earth is round or make it a conventional one. It is a matter of convention that the words in the sentences. 'Two and two make four' and 'Things that are equal to a third thing are equal to one another' mean what they do, but that does not mean that the fact they express is true by convention. How could one change either of these obvious facts by legislation? All that one does by changing 'equals' from meaning what 'equals' means to meaning what 'is larger than' means is to cause the sentence 'Two and two make four' to express a different (eternally) false proposition; but this does not mean that it has changed the truth of the proposition that these words expressed before their meaning was changed to express a false proposition. If truth were a property of sentences, one would have changed the truth of

something; but all one has in fact done is to change what truths these sentences express. Conventionalism in mathematics is open to the same objection, together with the further one that if mathematical truths were the result of human convention bridges would fall down and aero-planes crash, for human conventions are precarious to an extreme.

(4)   The view that there are possible worlds other than this was refuted by Quine before it was propounded (by Kripke). Quine points out, when criticising the metaphysics of Wyman (in 'On what there is') that 'possible' is not a word for an attribute of, say (Quine thought) the Parthenon, or of anything else. And it should be obvious that it is not the world that is possible, but the proposition that there is or should be such a world. In my youth the 'probables' had to play the 'possibles' at football − I was never either − but this was not a football match between two different worlds of school-boy, but between those of whom it was the case that they would probably be selected and those who would only possibly be selected. To suppose that being possible is an attribute of worlds is a mistake nearly as absurd as the much-ridiculed mistake of supposing that being average is an attribute of men. Think what a lot of sophistry Leibniz would have avoided if, instead of saying that this is the best of all possible worlds, he had simply said that this would could not be any better than it is.

Scoring own goals is another bad habit of Philosophers. They assert as truths propositions to the effect that all propositions are false. They accurately reveal the fact that nothing can be accurately revealed. They attempt to prove that nothing can be proved, and claim to know that there is no such thing as knowledge. They obstinately refuse to revise their opinion that all opinions are subjct to revision. Many are certain that nothing is certain. Some believe that belief is impossible; others think that there is no such thing as thought. They authorise the translation of learned philosophical works that claim that translation is impossible, and write with the greatest lucidity words that mean that there is no such thing as meaning. They eloquently describe the ineffable. Some advance good inductive evidence for thinking that science may proceed counter-inductively and others give reasons for thinking that though the past is no guide to the future, there is every reason to suppose that a hypothesis that has once been refuted will go on being refuted in years to come. They provide inductive proofs that induction is untrustworthy, via the inductive generalisations that all inductive generalisations eventually break down. Some produce causal explanations of the fact that all causal explanation is impossible. Some write books proclaiming that it is absolutely true that all truth is relative. Others argue as if it were unequivocally true that there is a third possibility to truth and falsehood. They offer *a priori* proofs that there is no such thing as *a prior* proof. They maintain as an analytic proposition that there is no such thing as analyticity, and that there is, of necessity, no such thing as necessary truth. They build great edifices on the premise that Foundationalism is false. They hold it as a scientific fact that not all facts are scientific, and as a truth of philosophy that there is only scientific truth. They propound as a philosophical truth that there are no philosophical truths, but only techniques for dissolving problems. They take immense trouble stating convincing arguments for what they take to be the truth that it is not truth, but continuing the conversation, that matters. They argue with deep sincerity that it is important to play with ideas, rather than believe them, and then, though one would have thought they wanted to convince us, defeat this end by telling us that when they said this, they were only playing. They assert that all intellectual remarks are ironic, and expect this remark to be taken as being literally true. Having themselves transcended the limits of thought, they feel themselves to be in the best possible position to tell us that thought has limits. Sometimes they provide logical proofs of the validity of Logic, thus pressupposing the truth of what they are trying to prove. At other times they provide logical proofs of logic's invalidity, thus presupposing the truth of what they are trying to disprove. They are worried in case it is not consistent to hold that some inconsistencies can be true. Without having established the whole truth about anything, they announce that nothing short of the whole truth about everything is worthy of belief, and claim to know the partial truth that there is no such thing as partial truth. Without themselves understanding the whole of any one language, they state that it is impossible to understand anything in isolation from the whole of language, and appear to think they understand what they themselves say, isolated though their remark is. They are convinced of the useless truth that only what is useful can be true. They try to prove that in reality nothing is real, and that it is no illusion that everything is illusory. They provide rational arguments for the desirability of faith, but nevertheless put their faith in reason. From the centre of the self they lament that the self has no centre. As a result of careful reflection upon the function of material sense organs they conclude that there is no such thing as matter. They argue most rationally in favour of irrationalism. They provide their readers with the most moral reasons for believing that it is wicked to be good. They altruistically proclaim that all men should seek their own interest, and not bother about the interest of the person making this proclamation. They think that there are no opinions that may not be legitimately expressed, but try to prevent people from expressing the opinion that there are some such opinions. They immodestly proclaim their modesty, openly adocate the advantages of deception, and hold that not forgiving one's neighbours deserves severe punishment in this world and the next. They listen to the story of the Pharisee who thanked the Lord that he was not as other men are, and thank the Lord that they are not as that Pharisee. They insist that anarchism should be imposed by force upon the protagonists of government. Their concern for the welfare of man is such as to make them deplore universally doing good because of the harm it would do. They write as if moderation were a virtue that one could not have to excess. Though, like honest men, they say nothing of which they are not sure, they are, on the basis of past experience, rightly convinced that most of what they say must be wrong. I myself am one hundred percent serious in saying that I am only ninety-five percent serious about everything I say. And the fact that I have taken so much trouble to criticise certain aspects of modern Philosophy before an audience that contains so many distinguished members of this species must show that I have a greater respect for a much loved subject than my words must sometimes indicate.

Philosophical Amnesia

NICHOLAS CAPALDI

Many Individuals currently identified within the academic world as '"professional"[1] philosophers' spend a great deal of time arguing about the meaning of their discipline. The situation has recently become so critical that the *Cambridge Dictionary of Philosophy*, for example, self-consciously excludes the term 'philosophy' from its list of entries.[2] An outsider might get the impression that members of the profession suffer from a recurrent kind of intellectual *amnesia*[3] and need constantly to be reminded about who they are and what their function is.

The simple response to this predicament is that most of us do know what philosophy is. The present puzzlement if not obfuscation is the result of three factors: (1) intellectual flaws in the two dominant movements in the profession today (analytic philosophy and deconstruction); (2) the locus of those movements is the university; and

---

[1] This is a reflection of the fact that 'philosophy' is now identified with an academic department in the modern university and that these academics belong to academic associations. This has important consequences that we shall discuss below.

[2] See Robert Audi (ed.), *The Cambridge Dictionary of Philosophy* (Cambridge: 1995), preface, xxv–xxvi. Audi believes that the meaning of the term will emerge from consideration of the particular entries. In effect, this privileges one of the alternatives I discuss below: the notion that the whole becomes intelligible by accumulated knowledge of the parts is a specifically Aristotelian (to be defined below) inductivist assumption. The *Blackwell Companion to Philosophy* (1996) has two entries on contemporary Philosophy but none on 'philosophy' per se. The online *Stanford Encyclopedia of Philosophy* also lacks an entry on 'philosophy'. The *Internet Encyclopedia of Philosophy* has no entry. *The Oxford Companion to Philosophy* (1995) has a substantial entry by Antony Quinton which acknowledges the controversy surrounding the term. The older (1967) *Encyclopedia of Philosophy*, ed. Paul Edwards, has a long and useful entry by John Passmore, but it too acknowledges controversy.

[3] In less charitable moments I am inclined to identify the intellectual malady as a form of 'Alzheimer's disease' since many of those afflicted occasionally seem to regain a sense of personal identity, sometimes brilliantly so. Seriously, this is a helpful metaphor in that I do believe there is a common ground that is occasionally recaptured and then lost again.

doi:10.1017/S1358246109990075   © The Royal Institute of Philosophy and the contributors 2009
Royal Institute of Philosophy Supplement **65** 2009   93

Nicholas Capaldi

(3) the university has become the home of self-alienated intellectuals.[4] We shall have more to say about this later.

The complex response to this situation can be summarized in the
following argument:

1.   There are alternative and conflicting perspectives[5] on what
     constitutes philosophy.
2.   These views are articulated within the framework of a larger
     conversation[6] or cultural context.
3.   These conflicting perspectives on what constitutes philosophy
     have been present from the very beginning of the history of the
     discipline.
4.   Within this seemingly vast variety of perspectives we can ident-
     ify *three fairly stable patterns in constant dialogue with each other*.
5.   Each of these three alternatives provides both an account for
     why there are alternative and conflicting views, that is, on
     why (1) is the case; proponents of each of the recognized per-
     spectives in (1) provides an account of the alleged errors in
     the other perspectives.
6.   There is at present no consensual[7] or conceivable way in which
     to adjudicate among these perspectives. That is, there is no set

---

[4]   Eric Hoffer, 'Men of Words,' 130–142 in *The True Believer* (2002); E.
Shils, 'The Traditions of Intellectuals,' in Huszar (ed.) *The Intellectuals*
(The Free Press 1960); Leszek Kolakowski, 'The Intellectuals' in
Modernity on Endless Trial (University of Chicago Press 1997); Julien
Benda, *The Betrayal of the Intellectuals* (2007); Raymond Aron, *The
Opium of the Intellectuals* (2006).

[5]   We shall identify these perspectives below.

[6]   The term 'conversation' is borrowed from Michael Oakeshott, whose
views have profoundly influenced this essay.

[7]   Richard Rorty, *Philosophy and the Mirror of Nature* (1979) and
Consequences of Pragmatism (1982); A. MacIntyre, *Three Rival Versions of
Moral Inquiry* (1981); – Jean-Francois Lyotard, 'Introduction: The
Postmodern Condition: A Report on Knowledge,' 1979: xxiv–xxv.
'Simplifying to the extreme, I define postmodern as incredulity toward
metanarratives. This incredulity is undoubtedly a product of progress in
the sciences: but that progress in turn presupposes it. To the obsolescence
of the metanarrative apparatus of legitimation corresponds, most notably,
the crisis of metaphysical philosophy and of the university institution
which in the past relied on it. The narrative function is losing its functors,
its great hero, its great dangers, its great voyages, its great goal. It is being
dispersed in clouds of narrative language elements–narrative, but also
denotative, prescriptive, descriptive, and so on [...] Where, after the metanarratives, can legitimacy reside?'

94

of premises on which all of the disputants can agree and from which we can deduce a specific and contentful conception of philosophy.[8]

[8] Tris Engelhardt has made the following powerful case against the possibility of a philosophical resolution of moral diversity. It applies as well to why there is no resolution of the conflict among rival versions of philosophy. It is not simply the case that there are significant moral disagreements about substantive issues. Many if not most of these controversies do not appear to be resolvable through sound rational argument. On the one hand, many of the controversies depend upon different foundational metaphysical commitments. As with most metaphysical controversies resolution is possible only through the granting of particular initial premises and rules of evidence. On the other hand, even when foundational metaphysical issues do not appear to be at stake, the debates turn on different rankings of the good. Again, resolution does not appear to be feasible without begging the question, arguing in a circle, or engaging in infinite regress. One cannot appeal to consequences without knowing how to rank the impact of different approaches with regard to different moral interests (liberty, equality, prosperity, security, etc). Nor can one without controversy appeal to preference satisfaction unless one already grants how one will correct preferences and compare rational versus impassioned preferences, as well as calculate the discount rate for preferences over time. Appeals to disinterested observers, hypothetical choosers, or hypothetical contractors will not avail either. If such decision makers are truly disinterested, they will choose nothing. To choose in a particular way, they must be fitted out with a particular moral sense or thin theory of the good. Intuitions can be met with contrary intuitions. Any particular balancing of claims can be countered with a different approach to achieving a balance. In order to appeal for guidance to any account of moral rationality one must already have secured content for that moral rationality. See *The Foundations of Christian Bioethics* (2000).

Not only is there a strident moral diversity defining debates regarding all substantive issues, but there is in principle good reason to hold that these debates cannot be brought to closure in a principled fashion through sound rational argument. There does not seem to be a rational way of securing moral agreement in our culture. The partisans of each and every position find themselves embedded within their own discourse so that they are unable to step outside of their own respective hermeneutic circles without embracing new and divergent premises and rules of inferences. Many traditional thinkers find themselves in precisely this position. They are so enmeshed in their own metaphysics and epistemology, so convinced that they are committed to 'reason' when what they are committed to is a particular set of premises and rules, so able to see the 'flaws' in the positions of others who do not accept the same rules, that they quite literally do not understand the alternative positions or even how there can be other positions. More important, they fail to understand the character of contemporary moral debate. What

Nicholas Capaldi

7.   My claim is that the recognition of the foregoing is a profound truth that (a) tells us something important about ourselves, and (b) has normative implications for the practice of philosophy as a discipline. This claim is an instance of one of the perspectives.[9]

Alternative Accounts of Philosophy[10]

To say, as I do, that there are alternative accounts of philosophy is to recognize the following historical claims: (a) the classical Greeks first articulated alternative accounts of philosophy; (b) much of the classical intellectual inheritance, including these philosophical viewpoints, was preserved as well as incorporated by Christianity and then transmitted to modernity; (c) the vast variety of perspectives can be fairly neatly categorized as one of three that I identify as Platonic, *Aristotelian, and Copernican*; (d) all philosophical movements up until now can be explained by reference to this Platonism-Aristotelianism-Copernicanism categorization; (e) the alternatives perspectives have an on-going history of interaction. This dialogue is integral to the history of philosophy; it *explains why philosophy can never truly distance itself from its history;*[11] and why part of the great philosophic conversation is the question 'What is Philosophy?'

---

is peculiar about contemporary moral debate is not just the incessant controversy but the absence of any basis for bringing the controversies to a conclusion in a principled fashion. Philosophy has gone into a deep coma, or a state of clinical death.

[9]   It is the Copernican perspective to be addressed below. This entire essay is self-consciously Copernican. Hence, it follows the dictum that philosophy 'leads to no conclusions which we did not in some sense know already.' (Collingwood, *Philosophical Method*, 161). Note Macintyre's observation that 'A tradition then not only embodies the narrative of an argument, but is only to be recovered by an argumentative retelling of that narrative which will itself be in conflict with other argumentative retellings' *The Tasks of Philosophy Cambridge*, 2006), 12.

[10]   The following account and categorization is historical. While I do attempt to draw some generalizations from the historical record, all such generalizations reflect the past and make no claim to any other status. The charge that this is merely a set of historical observations and of no philosophical significance is itself an expression of the Aristotelian perspective.

[11]   'Philosophy…has this peculiarity, that reflection upon it is part of itself.' Collingwood, *Philosophical Method* (1933), 1.

Platonism[12]

1.   The model is geometry.
2.   A good explanation, therefore, is a deduction from first principles or axioms.[13]
3.   First principles are *a priori*:
      a.   not derived from experience;
      b.   pass the logical test of non-self-contradiction.
4.   The explanation of the physical world is by reference to an ideal world of mathematical forms imperfectly *copied* by our experience (e.g. point, line).[14]

---

[12]   Recall Whitehead's remark that all philosophy is a footnote to Plato. The pre-Socratics including Pythagoras did not work out fully formed views but they anticipated and inspired both Plato and Aristotle.

[13]   There is no explanation for why deduction from first principles is the standard model of explanation in philosophy other than the historical fact that Plato took Pythagoras and geometry so seriously. See Toulmin, *Human Understanding* (1972).

[14]   '**Platonic Metaphysics:** In the Platonic tradition (e.g. Plato, Plotinus, Porphyry, Augustine, Descartes, Leibniz, Berkeley, and Frege, to mention just a few) ... the world of everyday experience cannot be understood on its own terms. As a consequence, a distinction is introduced between the world of appearance (or everyday experience) and ultimate reality. Platonic metaphysics is marked by a series of derivative dualisms. In its modern form, it is claimed within Platonism that although science can account for the world of appearance, science cannot account either for itself or for ultimate reality. Hence, metaphysics is a kind of non-empirical *pre-science*. Ultimate reality is conceptual or logical, (consisting of forms, ideas, or universals, etc.), not a system of physical objects. The conceptual entities that comprise ultimate reality are related to each other in logical fashion. *Platonism, moreover, rejects any distinction between a thing and its properties.* A thing is a particular set of properties (ideas, forms, etc.). Platonists do distinguish between essence (meaning) and existence (reference) as well as insist upon the irreducible and fundamental nature of meaning. The distinction between meaning and reference is derivative from the distinction between ultimate reality (which is conceptual) and the world of everyday experience. Finally, Platonists insist upon the dualism of subject and object, a dualism in which the subject's knowledge of itself is more fundamental than the subject's knowledge of objects.' Capaldi, *The Enlightenment Project in the Analytic Conversation* (1998), 112–113. See also Steven Weinberg, 'Nature, as we observe it, is but an imperfect representation of its own underlying laws.' *New York Times*, May 10th, 1974, 56.

5.   The social world is always construed as utopian (e.g. Republic).[15]
6.   In ethics,
     a.   there are external absolute standards (utopia) for judging society;
     b.   to know the good = to doing the good.
7.   Hence, politics is defined by the ethical.
8.   (6b) accounts for why there is an intellectual elite and why they are identical with the moral elite. The elite are intellectuals who through contemplation grasp the ideal world order. Practice should conform to the order so grasped. (T/P)[16]
9.   Since the world is not self-explanatory, *philosophy is the discipline which goes beyond the limits of the special sciences.*

Aristotelianism[17]

Aristotelianism is also known as naturalism.[18] Naturalism[19] is the view that the world is fully intelligible in its own terms. Its

---

[15]   Platonists see history as a series of events that imperfectly manifest an ideal. Moreover, since values are *a priori*, Platonists can dispense with a separate conception of empirical social science or history. This allowed thinkers to harmonize traditional values with their other intellectual pursuits. Think here of Augustine and Descartes, for example. The closest that Plato comes to an historical account is the logic of decay: Philosopher kings → timocracy → oligarchy → democracy → tyranny.

[16]   Platonists (e.g. Rousseau) are rarely advocates of revolution in the modern sense since they do not believe in actualizing the ideal. Aristotelians (e.g. Marx), on the other hand, do believe that the 'form' is 'in' 'matter' and hence that ideals can be actualized in practice.

[17]   My teacher in the history of philosophy, John Herman Randall, Jr. argued strenuously that Aristotle was a kind of methodological pluralist and that only later (medieval) thought turned Aristotle into a rigid system. This is a plausible reading of Aristotle, but it does not belie the point that others have found enough in Aristotle to turn him into a rigid system.

[18]   Taking the pre-Socratics as the earliest philosophers, it is plausible to argue that naturalism is the oldest version of philosophy. The entire subsequent history of philosophy can then be viewed as a dialogue between naturalism and it critics. Think here of Raphael's painting *The School of Athens*.

[19]   Naturalistic Aristotelian philosophy can be contrasted with religion. Religion's narrative is *dualistic* (we can only make sense of the world by appeal to something supernatural); *mysterious* (there is an ultimate mystery at the heart of the universe, a pre-conceptual domain that is not

narrative is monistic; rationalistic (everything is in principle conceptualizable); impersonal (the ultimate principles of intelligibility have no direct reference or concern for human welfare); and *secularly Pelagian* (despite the world's impersonality, humanity, we are assured, can solve its problems on its own and by exclusive reference to the natural order). The most sophisticated and influential version of naturalism is Aristotle's.[20]

1. Aristotle's model is teleological biology.[21] While systematic philosophers pretend to establish their principles in an independent, abstract, and premeditated fashion (wholly autonomous reason), the fact is that in every case we can identify the specific previous intellectual practice from which it is drawn. Subsequent versions of Aristotelianism substitute the latest fashionable science.

2. A good explanation is a deduction from first principles – a notion borrowed from Plato.[22]

3. First principles, the major premises of a good explanation, are *abstracted* from experience. Truth is established through correspondence. *The whole history of epistemology in western philosophy deals with the obsessive and continuous failure of Aristotelians to explain knowledge in a naturalistic manner.*

---

itself conceptualizable); *personal* (the supernatural pre-conceptual ground of our own existence is a person who cares for us); and involves grace (humanity needs divine aid in order to deal with the human predicament).

[20] Aristotle survives in a distinct version when supplemented by Christianity; what is said about 'Aristotelianism' does not always apply to this Christian version. The Christianized version, in fact, is closer to 'Platonism'. Critics would argue that it survives the criticism made of purely naturalistic Aristotelianism by appeal to the '*deux ex machina*'. To my mind, the Christianized Aristotelianism is an indirect acknowledgement of the shortcomings of the purely naturalistic Aristotle. See previous note.

[21] A clear case can be made that each major philosophical perspective takes as its paradigm the most extensive and coherent body of knowledge available to it at the time of its articulation. Despite its claim to be premeditated, the content of a philosophical perspective is always drawn from a previous practice. This lends weight to the Copernican position outlined below.

[22] Toulmin, S.E. (1972). *Human Understanding.*

Nicholas Capaldi

Copernicanism[29]

Copernicanism is Kant's Humean inspired revolution in philosophy, specifically a reaction to the hopeless failure of Aristotelian naturalist epistemology, especially in response to developments in modern physics.[30]

1. Model: *human action*, not contemplation, is primordial. Reflection is always ultimately reflection on prior practice.
2. Explanation is not the grasping of an external structure but the subject's imposition or projection of structure.
3. First principles: social practice is the pre-theoretical ground of all theoretical activity. How we understand ourselves is funda- mental, and how we understand the non-human world is derivative. We cannot, ultimately, understand ourselves by reference to physical structures.
4. Physical world: Newtonian (atoms already in motion); science is not the observation of nature but experimentation on and with nature. It is *technological*.[31]
5. Social world is the interaction of self-directed individuals. Social knowledge and understanding do not consist of the

---

[29] Copernicanism as a separate philosophical perspective is entirely lost on MacIntyre. He completely fails to see the difference between Hume and Kant on the one hand and the French *philosophes* and later positivists on the other. In *After Virtue* (1981), MacIntyre argued that we in the Western World have lost our way in morality. We are besieged with a cacophonous pluralism wherein no common understanding of morality is ever possible. There can be so single impartial justification for our moral judgments. Why has this occurred, according to MacIntyre? The Enlightenment epis- temological and moral theories of Bacon, Hume, and Kant, not to forget Diderot, by default lead to logical positivism and its offsprings, emotivism and post-modernism. We now recognize the failure of the Enlightenment. The failure puts us in the perplexing position of having to choose between Nietzsche or Aristotle – either moral relativism or a radical conservatism in which humans are seen as having an essence, as social beings who need friendship and who work out over time traditions which give structure to their lives and call forth a set of virtues. Nietzsche's thought is incoherent, so only a return to Aristotle can save us.

[30] One can profitably view Copernicanism as, in part, the development of Aristotle's conception of practical reason as opposed to the primacy of theoretical reason.

[31] Gaukroger, Stephen. *The Emergence of a Scientific Culture; Science and the Shaping of Modernity 1210–1685*. Oxford: Clarendon Press, 2006.

discovery of absolute (timeless and contextless) standards
external to humanity but involve, instead, the clarification of
standards implicit within the human mind and/or social
practice.[32] Axiologically it is possible to defend the reality
and universality of norms but only as part of the internal
structure coupled with the contention that epistemological
norms are derivative from axiological norms, that is, by making
axiology primary and metaphysics and epistemology secondary.

6. Ethics is the clarification of individual autonomy and
   responsibility.[33]

7. Politics is classical liberalism,[34] understood as limiting the
   power of the state in the interest of expanding human
   autonomy.

[32] There are no hidden rigid substructures to social practice such that
once one knows that substructure one can predict (or normatively require)
future permutations of that practice (there are no rules for the application
of rules) and no structures that would show the 'secret' logic of a practice.
Hence the application of an understanding of a practice to a novel set of circumstances requires judgment and imagination. No culture dictates its own
future. Human beings are always free to accept, reject, or redeploy their
inheritance.

The notion of 'verstehen' as developed by neo-Kantians such as Dilthey
and Weber, historian-philosophers such as Collingwood, or philosophers
such as Wittgenstein, Heidegger, Oakeshott and Gadamer, makes clear
that all understanding, even science, is interpretation.

[33] 'Almost all modern writing about moral conduct begins with the
hypothesis of an individual human being choosing and pursuing his own
directions of activity.' M. Oakeshott, 'The Masses in Representative
Democracy,' 367 in *Rationalism in Politics and Other Essays*, (ed.) Fuller
(1991). Autonomy entails some version of the freedom of the will.
Autonomy leads in politics to classical liberalism, wherein individuals set
their own goals and require liberty as a means to freedom. 'Moral philosophy' as opposed to 'ethics' comes into being in the 17th century. It reflects
the recognition that there is no natural teleology (as in Aristotle) so that the
question of how the interests of the individual are related to the interests of
others or to society as a whole (i.e. our moral obligations) becomes a real
issue. Aristotle would never have raised such an issue because he saw a seam-
less web of the individual and society.

[34] When liberalism is fully 'Aristotelianized' (in the sense I have
defined) it becomes communitarian or modern liberal as opposed to classical
liberal. Communitarians postulate a social good that takes precedence over
the good of individuals. Aristotelian naturalists, as I have contended
above, do not take internal freedom (i.e. autonomy) seriously. As a result,
they are apt to see individuals as constrained by circumstances rather than

8   Since the pre-theoretical ground is not itself conceptualizable, there can be no intellectual elite!

9.   Philosophy[35] is both (a) the explication of the logic (procedural norms) of each and every human activity[36] and (b) the articulation of the larger vision of how these activities relate to each other. It is both analytic (conceptual clarification) and synthetic (larger vision);[37] but it is not the accession of an independent cosmic order. Neither is it a form of advocacy.[38]

An over-simplified summary of these perspectives is to say that Aristotelians believe that philosophy is about the intelligibility of the world in itself; Platonists and Copernicans disagree that the world is intelligible in itself; Platonists appeal to something outside of nature; Copernican think philosophy is about the interaction of humans with the world as seen from the human perspective.

---

as choosing how to respond to circumstances. As a further consequence, they are likely to see socials problems like poverty as something that requires redistribution.

Classical liberalism is also conceptualized in Aristotelian terms by philosophers such as Hobbes and Locke (Natural law versions). I would argue that this is another version of pouring the new wine into old bottles. The consequences of doing so are (1) endless confusion and debate, (2) reading Hobbes as a covert authoritarian, and (3) attempts to use Locke to derive communitarian versions of liberalism.

One can, of course, defend a version of classical liberalism (or any political philosophy) using 'some' of the philosophical vocabulary derived from Aristotle (or almost any philosopher). The adoption of a vocabulary is not to be confused with adopting a system or conceptual framework such as I have described.

[35]   These views are clearly expressed by R. G. Collingwood in his works *Philosophical Method* (1933) and an *Essay on Metaphysics* (1940).

[36]   Philosophy awakens 'our sensitivity to realities which underpin our ordinary lives and activities . . . things which are usually just out of sight of unreflective consciousness, but they are things which we all know, but darkly.' Anthony O'Hear, *Philosophy in the New Century* (London: Continuum, 2001), 191.

[37]   This permits us to see that the alternative philosophical perspectives do achieve a kind of consensus on the procedural norms of discourse (analysis proper) within the larger cultural context; where disagreement exists is in speculative thinking or synthesis.

[38]   Philosophers may, of course, be advocates in other contexts but not as part of their professional activity. Philosophers can, in their professional capacity, point out with regard to social practices when others have asked irrelevant questions or spoken inappropriately.

Another way of putting this is that Platonists think about 'thinking', Aristotelians think about 'the world', and Copernicans think about 'thinking about the world'.

The History of Philosophy Illustrated by the PAC Categorization

Let me briefly note some examples of the on-going dialogue among the three main philosophical perspectives. One might refer to these as alternative accounts of the alternative accounts.[39] A good deal of the history of philosophy can be understood as a conversation among these three conceptions of philosophy.

1. The Sophistic claim that 'Man is the measure of all things' is an early (anachronistic) expression of Copernicanism, and Socrates' attack on Protagoras is an early 'Platonic' reaction to it.
2. Recall that Aristotle's initiation of philosophical discussion typically begins with a seemingly condescending review of the inadequacies of his predecessors all of which contribute to a teleological progression to his own views.
3. Aristotle's relation to his predecessors is recapitulated by Aquinas' treatment of his predecessors. Aquinas refers to Aristotle as 'The' philosopher not 'a' philosopher.
4. Varro and even Cicero recognized the unique character of historical explanation as opposed to (Aristotelian) philosophical explanation. Both of these writers heavily influenced Hume. Hume's *History of England* is a Copernican account of the rise of modern commercial republics as opposed to Hobbes' and Locke's appeal to the original contract, an Aristotelian notion.[40]
5. Notice the usual epistemological classification of medieval philosophers as either Realist (Platonic), Conceptualist (Aristotelian), or Nominalist (Copernican).
6. Epistemological skepticism is a recurrent position throughout the history of philosophy. I understand 'skepticism' generically

---

[39] These alternative views may be profitably seen as Weberian ideal types; they may also be seen as Kuhnian paradigms. It is remarkable to note the extent to which one position will accuse a second position of not answering a question when the point of the second position is to delegitimate that question.

[40] Rousseau's account of the original contract is Platonic. Note Rawls' Aristotelian critique of Hume's Copernican critique of the idea of an original contract.

to mean a recognition of the limits of discursive reason, limits revealed by identifying whatever is the failed current version of Aristotelian naturalism. All Aristotelian naturalistic anthologies of the so-called problems in philosophy invariably begin the epistemology section with a critique of skepticism.

7. Aristotelian naturalists (e.g. Spinoza and Hobbes) can find no room for the radical 'freedom of the will'. Platonists from Augustine to the present and some Copernicans (e.g. Kant) take this (internal) 'freedom' seriously and they do not confuse it with 'liberty' (mere absence of external constraint).

8. Hume holds the most radical version of the Copernican position; he claims only to identify how human beings structure their experience ('as long as the human mind remains the same'[41]); he speculates on physiological, psychological, and cultural reasons for this structuring; but he denies that either he or anyone else can give a further explanation.[42]

9. Kant 'Platonizes' the Copernican revolution by insisting on the absolute and timeless character of the mind.

10. Hegel 'Aristotelianizes' the Copernican Revolution both by collapsing the subject-object distinction and construing ultimate reality as teleological.[43] If there are no further permutations, then Hegel should be the last philosopher to offer a system of philosophy. And so he is.

11. When modern Aristotelians need to respond to the incontrovertible historical dimension to thinking that modern philosophers (usually Copernicans of some sort) have identified, they invariably teleologize that history. Positivists, for example, even though they deny the relevance of history nevertheless *endorse* (without being able to establish intellectually) a progressive reading of the history of physical science such that objective truth is what scientists ultimately and eventually will agree upon 'in the end.'[44]

[41] Enquiry Concerning Human Understanding, Section V, Part I.

[42] See the qualifications in the *Treatise*, Appendix: '...all my hopes vanish, when I come to explain the principles, that unite our successive perceptions in our thought or consciousness. I cannot discover ant theory which gives me satisfaction on this head.'

[43] Hegel's teleology allows him both to answer the Kantian (Platoniz) question of the conditions of human knowledge and to provide an account of the developing self-consciousness of God.

[44] The quote is from C.S. Peirce. For the failure to prove that science progresses see Kuhn's critique of Popper and Feyerabend's critique of Lakatos. There is an additional respect in which Analytic philosophers

12.　　One modern version of Aristotelianism is Enlightenment Project scientism: *The Enlightenment Project is the attempt to define and explain the human predicament through physical science and a derivative social science as well as to achieve mastery over it through the use of a social technology.* This project originated in France in the eighteenth century with the *philosophes.* The most influential among them were Diderot, d'Alembert, La Mettrie, Condillac, Helvetius, d'Holbach, Turgot, Condorcet, Cabanis, and Voltaire. The Project continued during the nineteenth century in the work of Comte, the founder of positivism.[45]

13.　　This vision of philosophy is proclaimed in the Positivist Manifesto of 1929 in which Comte is himself named as a precursor. The leading spokesperson for positivism was Carnap, and it was Carnap who officially co-opted and incorporated the work of Bertrand Russell. Moritz Schlick once characterized positivism as the rejection of the view that there are synthetic *a priori* truths. Here we have the Aristotelian rejection of Kant's version of Copernicanism.

14.　　The dominant Aristotelian view in the profession today is analytic philosophy.[46] Given its position of dominance, it is

---

(who are Aristotelian) appeal to teleology. They frequently present a two tier view of human nature in which everything is mechanistic on the physiological level but miraculously and unaccountably there is a parallel level of human consciousness in which we act teleologically. See Capaldi, op. cit., 14.

[45]　Von Wright (1971), 9–10: 'It would be quite wrong to label analytical philosophy as a whole a brand of positivism. But it is true to say that the contributions of analytical philosophy to methodology and philosophy of science have, until recently, been predominantly in the spirit of positivism … It also largely shares with nineteenth-century positivism an implicit trust in progress through the advancement of science and the cultivation of a rationalist social-engineering attitude to human affairs.'

[46]　'The Dominant mode of philosophizing in the United States is called "analytic philosophy". Without exception, the best philosophy departments in the United States are dominated by analytic philosophy, and among the leading philosophers in the United States, all but a tiny handful would be classified as analytic philosophers. Practitioners of types of philosophizing that are not in the analytic tradition … feel it necessary to define their position in relation to analytic philosophy. Indeed, analytic philosophy is the dominant mode of philosophizing not only in the United States, but throughout the entire English-speaking world.' Searle (1996), 1–2.

important to examine whether it and the discipline are illuminated by the PAC categorization. I have done so at length in my book *The Enlightenment Project in the Analytic Conversation*.[47] I specifically exclude from the designation 'analytic philosophy' the movement known as ordinary language philosophy that originated with G.E. Moore. OLP was Aristotelian but it was never scientistic.[48]

15. Wittgenstein's revolt against analytic philosophy was a Copernican reaction to positivist Aristotelianism. Carnap understood early on that Wittgenstein was not a member of the club. Michael Dummett's Aristotelian response to Wittgenstein's Copernicanism is to call Wittgenstein a 'defeatist'. Analytic philosophers like to critique their Copernican opponents as 'anti-foundationalist.'

16. Heidegger's philosophical relationship to Husserl is parallel to Wittgenstein's relationship to Russell. In both cases we have a Copernican rejection of Aristotelianism.

17. Collingwood has critiqued positivism (what I mean here by analytic philosophy) for assimilating philosophy 'to the pattern of empirical science'[49] and for being anti-philosophical.

18. In *Whose Justice? Which Rationality?* (1988) MacIntyre developed his theme of cultural cacophony, but also defended a special kind of Aristotelianism – the Thomistic theistic version, as the most coherent account of the moral life and its justification. He sets forth the thesis that some traditions are superior to others. His criterion is that a tradition is superior to others if it can resolve the problems and anomalies in those other traditions in such a way that supporters of the other traditions can come to understand why they cannot resolve those problems using only their own intellectual resources. MacIntyre illustrates this by showing how Aquinas' synthesis of Aristotelianism and Augustinianism produces a tradition allegedly able to resolve problems unresolvable in both of its predecessors. He would later retract

---

[47] Capaldi (1998), op. cit.

[48] N. Capaldi, 'Analytic Philosophy and Language,' in *Linguistics and Philosophy, The Controversial Interface*, (ed.) Rom Harre and Roy Harris (Oxford: Pergamon Press, 1993; Language & Communication Library series), 45–107.

[49] Collingwood, *Philosophical Method* (7) and (147).

that claim and admit that you could not prove the superiority of any of the alternatives.[50]

Allow me to offer one extended example. Modern philosophy is usually focused on seven thinkers: Descartes, Spinoza, and Leibniz (so-called rationalists) as well as Locke, Berkeley, and Hume (so-called empiricists), and finally Kant. This traditional and almost universally despised distinction nevertheless survives largely because so many contemporary philosophers are engaged in the intellectually incestuous activity of thinking that philosophers only read other philosophers and because of the continuing obsession with naturalistic epistemology.

In reality, the great ages of philosophy and the great philosophers are responding to much larger intellectual challenges. It is impossible to understand modern philosophy, that is, the philosophy of the sixteenth through eighteenth centuries, unless one realizes the extent to which that philosophy was a response to developments in modern science. It is no accident that Descartes, a mathematician and scientist, is almost always singled out as the first modern philosopher. Among other things, modernity begins with the collapse of the Aristotelian medieval world view with its organic, teleological, and hierarchical conception of the world. One simple way to capture that difference in scientific terms is to say that whereas Aristotelian physics was based on the assumption that rest was the natural state, modern physics from Galileo on starts with the assumption that motion is the natural state.

Confronted with this new view of the physical universe, how did *scientists* respond? They responded in two different ways that became identified with Descartes and Newton. Descartes argued for a homogeneous and pleonastic universe in which there is no

---

[50]   In *Three Rival Versions of Moral Enquiry* (1991), MacIntyre backed away from claiming that you could prove the superiority of one version. He contrasts the ninth edition of the Encyclopedia Britannica, the idea of pure unencumbered rationality, Nietzsche's Genealogy of Morals, the idea that such rationality is simply another expression of the will to power, and Pope Leo XIII's *Aeterni patris*, which sought to establish Thomism as the official doctrine of the Roman Catholic Church. Each of these traditions has irresolvable internal problems. Specifically, Leo XIII misunderstood Thomism by building in a modernist program – of treating Thomism as an epistemological theory like Encyclopedia rather than as a coherent metaphysical and moral system. MacIntyre reject's any God's eye neutral nonpartisan interpretation as an illusion. Genuine rational inquiry requires membership in a particular type of moral community.

distinction between space and matter; Newton took up and advocated Gassendi's atomism (along with Galileo's momentum). We thus had two conflicting scientific paradigms.

How did *philosophers* respond to the new science and its major protagonists? Some poured this new wine into old bottles and others fashioned a new bottle. The old bottles were the philosophies of Plato and Aristotle. Committed as they were to the belief in an autonomous reason, these philosophers could not see that Platonism and Aristotelianism were themselves constructs based on earlier views of the physical universe. To be a Platonist in this context is, among other things, to believe in a dualistic universe within which first principles are allegedly known a priori. To be an Aristotelian in this context is, among other things, to believe in a monistic universe within which first principles are allegedly 'abstracted' from experience.

The new bottle is expressed as the Copernican Revolution in Philosophy, wherein the first principles are structures that we project onto the world. The Copernican turn is the full articulation of looking at the world from a Newtonian point of view.[51]

The geography of modern philosophy looked like this:

[51] I would argue that Copernicanism is Newtonianism writ large: motion, not rest is fundamental (action not contemplation is basic); motion is in a straight line, not cyclical (history does not repeat itself endlessly); every entity interacts with and influences every other entity (we cannot talk about things in themselves – only in relation to us); first principles cannot be explained – theory can only be the explication of ongoing practice. An organic (Aristotelian) universe and social world would see individuals as derivative from their communal roles; an atomistic universe would see individuals as primordial and the community as an historical construct. Individuals are not simply 'atoms', rather they are atoms with a history of past interaction. The historical relation, however, is not an organic relation.

Although atomism has an ancient lineage (Democritus, Epicurus), I would suggest that modern atomism was embraced as much if not more so for its social implications. Gassendi gave both ontological and theological significance to monads as endowed with original motion by God; Bacon and Hobbes were atomists; atomism appealed to the practical success of seeing mechanical objects from an atomistic point of view; Newton's first law of motion, I suggest, has a theological origin, certainly not an empirical origin; it is, so to speak, a projection from the human and social realm onto nature. In this it bears a striking similarity to the later doctrine of evolution, which originated in history and was then projected onto biology. See N. Capaldi, *David Hume: The Newtonian Philosopher* (1975).

(Cartesian Physics)   (Newtonian[52]
                                                  Physics)
Descartes   **Locke**
(Platonic Philosophy)[53]
                                                  (Aristotelian[54]
                                                  Philosophy)
(Cartesian Physics)[55]   (Newtonian[56]
                                                  Physics)
Spinoza   **Berkeley**
(Aristotelian   (Platonic
  Philosophy)[57]   Philosophy)[58]
(Newtonian
  Physics)[59]

                                                  (Newtonian
                                                    Physics)[60]

Leibniz   **Hume**
(Platonic
  Philosophy)[61]
                                                  (Copernican)[62]
                        (Newtonian Physics)
              KANT
                        (Copernican Revolution)[63]

[52] Recall Locke's claim that space is a simple idea given in sensation as well as his defense of the existence of a vacuum (empty space) as opposed to Descartes' pleonasm.

[53] For Descartes physics is founded on a dualistic metaphysics; first principles are clearly *a priori*; he distinguishes between the order of knowing and the order of being; there is a clear dualism between finite human reason and infinite will, and error is the result of the exercise of the freedom of the will. See n. 14.

[54] Nothing could be more Aristotelian than Locke's critique of innate (a priori) ideas and his insistence on the distinction between primary qualities (in the object) and secondary qualities.

[55] Like Descartes, Spinoza rejects Aristotelian teleology (no final causes) in favor of determinism.

[56] See Berkeley's *De Motu* (1721) for his analysis of Newton and Leibniz.

[57] For Spinoza, God = Nature; one substance, no dualism; his epistemology is an empiricist-physiological account; freedom consists of knowledge of causes over which we have no control. See n. 23.

[58] Berkeley's praise of Platonists can be found in *Siris* (1744) on Tar Water; in addition he is an immaterialist who believes that things are collections of ideas not something independent of them; he supports a dualism that distinguished between ideas in God's mind and ideas in human minds; epistemologically, he is the foremost critic of Locke's Aristotelian idea 'abstraction'; finally, he believes that we have direct intuitive knowledge of ourselves.

Nicholas Capaldi

Current Debate on the Meaning of Philosophy: Is the Existence of Alternatives a Problem? a Crisis?[64]

If competing conceptions of philosophy is the historical norm, why is there a current debate? The current debate reflects a peculiar intellectual crisis. But what kind of crisis is this? No Copernican, for example, would be surprised by the existence of alternative conceptions of philosophy. That is exactly what one would expect in a world where order is a construct of the human imagination. I shall have more to say about this below. Moreover, a Platonist might be saddened but never surprised. There are those who see and those who do not; the latter live in the world of shadows.

The current crisis reflects the following:

1. Philosophy is now housed within the University.
2. The recent history of the university has involved three competing models described below as the Ivory Tower Model, the German Research Model (Enlightenment Project scientism), and the Utilitarian Model.
    a. The German Research Model has combined with the Utilitarian model,[65] and given the spectacular success

---

[59] Space and time are relative ideas not entities as in Cartesian physics. Leibniz worked out the calculus independently of but at the same time as Newton; the calculus enables us to deal with matter in motion, matter that is not reducible to space.

[60] See N. Capaldi, David Hume: *Newtonian Philosopher*.

[61] Leibniz's model is the calculus instead of geometry; in his epistemology, he criticizes Locke for arguing against the existence of innate (a priori) ideas; his dualism, like Berkeley's, distinguishes between God as infinite monad and humans as created finite monads; monads 'mirror' and essentially act like Platonic forms; his God reminds us of the *Timaeus* because 'HE' is persuaded to act in accordance with the ultimate essences; finally, human beings always act for the seeming best and err only out of ignorance.

[62] Hume was never a simple minded empiricist: all of our most important ideas are complex ideas involves the structuring activity of the mind. In the *Abstract* he cites this as his most revolutionary idea.

[63] 'The Copernican Revolution in Hume and Kant,' *Proceedings of the Third International Kant Congress*, ed. Lewis White Beck (Dordrecht, Holland: Reidel, 1972), 234–40.

[64] 'The present is a time of crisis and chaos in philosophy.' Collingwood, *op. cit.*, 6.

[65] The utilitarian model by itself was originally intended to promote agricultural and technological development. The German Research model

112

of the physical sciences[66] and government subvention,
they have jointly triumphed over the Ivory Tower
Model.

b.   As a consequence the traditional humanities (philosophy, history, and literature) have declined.

3.   Philosophy has survived by becoming a social science. In its
analytic form, philosophy aspires to be the social science of
science.

4.   Demise of philosophy as a legitimate discipline.

a.   If scientism is correct, then philosophy is superfluous.

b.   Analytic philosophy has failed intellectually to legitimate
scientism. (Quine → Kuhn → Feyerabend)

c.   Analytic philosophy, by espousing a model of social
scientific thinking called exploration, has failed in its
attempt to deal with norms, that is, to identify, explicate,
or legitimate them.

d.   Exploratory analytic philosophy has given rise to
deconstruction.[67]

e.   Deconstruction has abandoned the Socratic role of philosophy and substituted an adversarial role.

The locus of philosophy is now in the academy. Philosophy as a
discipline is being marginalized in the academy (higher education).
Philosophy is being marginalized in three ways: absolutely, relatively,
and intrinsically. Philosophy is being marginalized *absolutely* and this
can be seen in the declining numbers of jobs and programs.[68] It is
being marginalized *relatively* in the sense that even where apparent

---

originally on its own was committed to the pursuit of truth and not any particular social agenda. The combination of the two has led to what we now
describe as 'political correctness'.

[66]   The larger cultural context has embraced an uncritical and unreflective commitment to scientism. This has reinforced the perception that we do
not need anything other than the sciences.

[67]   Deconstruction is the, among other things, the latest incarnation of
so-called continental philosophy as opposed to Anglo-American
philosophy.

[68]   Few *new* colleges and universities (e.g. Cal State Monterey Bay, UC
Merced), have a philosophy department or even offer a philosophy major or
minor. In most cases, a token philosopher is hired into a general humanities
department and pressed into service teaching composition or rhetoric to
round out a teaching load that cannot be filled by the few philosophy
courses (usually applied ethics and logic/critical thinking) offered.

growth takes place it is at a lower level than within other disciplines. Most of all, it is being marginalized in the sense that few people within the academic community see any crucial or central disciplinary role for philosophy in higher education, and the number dwindles as we speak.[69]

Why is Philosophy as a Discipline Being Marginalized? Try to understand the sense in which this question is being raised. We should not be misled by the willingness of people outside the academic world to pay lip service to the importance of philosophy. In reality, the educated public finds most of what academic philosophy has produced in the last half-century unintelligible and/or boring. Nor should we be misled by the self-congratulatory and reasonable surmise within the academy that academic philosophers are probably brighter than academics in other fields. Idiot savants get the same recognition. Nor should we be lulled by the frenetic activity we see at national meetings.

How did Philosophy lose its place? Philosophy lost its essential place along with the other humanities. So a further question is how did the humanities in general lose its place? This presupposes that we answer the question what *was* the place of the humanities? Going back to their origins at the University of Paris in the Middles Ages, the humanities were custodians of the *Ivory Tower* and as such their essential task was the articulation, preservation, critique and transmission of the fundamental values of civilization. Higher Education was understood as *the initiation into that inheritance and as an adventure in self understanding.* This conservative conception of education was 'what ancient Athenians [had] called paideia...it was passed on...from the schools of the Roman Empire to the cathedral, the collegiate, guild and grammar schools of medieval Christendom. Moved by a vivid consciousness of an intellectual and moral inheritance of great splendor and worth, this was the notion of education which informed the schools of renaissance Europe and which survived into... [British] grammar and public schools and their equivalents in continental Europe.'[70]

---

[69] It would be easy enough to point out that the academic world in general is going through an economic downward spiral. But this in itself does not explain why when asked to cut the budget, Deans immediately think of eliminating programs and positions in philosophy.

[70] Michael Oakeshott, 'Education: The Engagement and Its Frustration,' in *The Vocie of Liberal Learning* (Indianapolis: Liberty Fund, Inc. 2001) 83.

The humanities defined and explicated the human condition. This role has been lost. Its usurpation began in the last half of the eighteenth century with the Enlightenment Project: (a) the cosmic order can be accessed through an autonomous human reason, freed of any higher authority, that (b) the human condition can be exhaustively defined by the sciences, and (c) that all human moral, social, and political problems could be resolved through a derivative social technology. Recall that this Project was doctrinairely and programmatically espoused by French *philosophes*. The Enlightenment Project was developed further in the 19th century by both Comte and various schools of German scientific materialism, and transmitted to the contemporary university with the German research model of higher education during the last half of the 19th century.

For almost a century, three paradigms vied for the attention of the university: the *ivory tower paradigm, largely in liberal arts colleges with a religious affiliation*, the German Research model and the utilitarian paradigm. The German research model is the disinterested pursuit of knowledge, perceiving the university as a set of graduate programs training professionals by focusing on the accumulation of knowledge in the spirit of the Enlightenment Project.

The utilitarian paradigm is the one wherein the university is seen as an institution for solving various and sundry social problems. In this model, the university exists as a means to social ends defined externally to the university itself. The spectacular successes of science and engineering and government subvention of higher education combined to make it possible for the German research model and the utilitarian model to unite[71] in the form of the Enlightenment Project and displace the ivory tower, and along with it went the displacement of the humanities. We are familiar with this transition in the work of C.P. Snow on the 'Two Cultures.'

Philosophy survived as a discipline by embracing the Enlightenment Project. Philosophy survived as the discipline which, allegedly, articulated the fundamental truths about Science, as the social science of Science, as well as the progenitor of scientific hypotheses about social phenomena from knowledge acquisition to public policy. In practice, this is indistinguishable from other social sciences. Philosophy becomes one of the social sciences! We see as well in the academy the (pseudo)social scientization of the other humanities (history, literature, and the arts).

---

[71] The German research model pursuit of knowledge is disinterested (i.e. apolitical); when it combines with the utilitarian model it is transformed into the Enlightenment Project; that is, it acquires a social agenda.

115

Analytic philosophy is the current embodiment both of Aristotelianism as a conception of philosophy in general and the Enlightenment Project in particular. Aristotelians, as we have maintained above, are keenly interested in the operation of institutions. They see healthy institutions as having a clearly defined goal and successful individuals as those who help in the pursuit of that goal. Analytic philosophy as a version of Aristotelianism thereby tends to be hegemonic and monopolistic.[72] Aristotelians in the form of analytic philosophy insist upon an extraordinary intellectual hegemony, but they have been incapable of achieving it. My claim is that the intellectual failure of analytic philosophy, a form of Aristotelianism, exacerbates the loss of academic (and cultural) legitimacy.

The problem with the role that analytic philosophy has assumed is that it only makes sense if science is the fundamental way of accessing the cosmic order and the place of humanity with it. Philosophy as such is the self-appointed supreme discipline only if scientism is true. By **scientism** I understand the doctrine that science is the truth about everything and the ground of its own legitimacy. The difficulty is that science cannot legitimate itself intellectually. The Great tradition of Western philosophy has known this and repeatedly asserted this for about two thousand years (repeated critiques of Aristotelian naturalistic epistemology), but we had to spend the last half of the twentieth century waiting for most analytic philosophers to acknowledge this state of affairs. Please note that this is not a problem for the hard sciences, for they make no cosmic claims. It is a problem for those whose status depends upon the enthronement of scientism.

There is an even stronger way of identifying the crisis. If science could legitimate itself intellectually, what need would it have of philosophy (as its social science)? Philosophy appears as no more than a pre-scientific intellectual endeavor that has been superseded by science. Technology has passed philosophy by. To establish its importance in its own eyes, analytic philosophy needs the premise that scientists, as opposed to science, are incapable of articulating self-legitimation. Philosophy is the (self-appointed) supreme discipline because it alone has the rhetorical and intellectual resources to legitimate a practically powerful science whose practitioners, it is alleged, nonetheless cannot provide for its foundation.

---

[72] Platonists and Copernicans have become the marginalized within the marginalized. For the latter raising the issue of competing conceptions of philosophy is both about (a) one's role in the profession and (b) the role of the discipline in the larger cultural context.

Unfortunately, Aristotelians in the guise of analytic philosophers have failed to legitimate scientism. The current story of the demise of *scientism* is by now a familiar one.[73] In 'Two Dogmas of Empiricism', Quine undermined traditional empiricism by asserting (a) that there is nothing independent of different conceptual schemes and (b) that different conceptual schemes are alternative readings of experience. Thesis (a) is an ontological relativism that *contradicts* the ontological empirical realism of (b). That is, Quine denied that there is an independent position from which to judge whether a conceptual scheme matches reality but embraced the semantic enterprise by asserting that the totality of knowledge must match reality. Kuhn in the *The Structure of Scientific Revolutions* used the history of science to discredit the conception of scientific theories as experimentally confirmable or disconfirmable. As Kuhn showed, scientists operate with paradigms that structure the way in which experiments are interpreted. Kuhn's work was followed by the more radical views of Feyerabend, who, in *Against Method*, argued that paradigms constituted the entire pre-theoretical context within which theoretical science operated. Science could not, therefore, serve as the arbiter among competing paradigms.[74]

By the time the failure of scientism was recognized, analytic philosophy had already done irreparable harm to the discipline. It had modeled the profession as a pseudo-social science with all of its trappings. Philosophers and students of philosophy read only articles by other philosophers in philosophical journals. The issues discussed therein were deemed worthy of discussion because other philosophers had discussed them. Whatever the larger framework that had given rise to the discussion was soon forgotten.[75]

For the explication of fundamental norms it has substituted research programs. It engages in a form of speculation I call **exploration**, that is, beginning with our ordinary understanding of how things work it goes on to speculate on what underlies those workings. It aims to change our ordinary understanding. The new understanding does not evolve from or elaborate the old understanding; rather, it replaces the old understanding by appeal to underlying structures. The underlying structures are allegedly discovered by appeal to

---

[73]   See N. Capaldi, 'Scientism, Deconstruction, and Nihilism,' in *Argumentation*, 9: (1995), 563–575.
[74]   This turns analytic philosophy into an ideology, the advocacy of scientism without subscription to realism.
[75]   Cohen (1986), 138–39.

Nicholas Capaldi

some hypothetical model about those structures. Unlike legitimate physical science, the alleged hidden structures to which pseudo-social science appeals never get confirmed empirically. What we get is an unending series in which one faddish language replaces another. 'As a consequence immense prestige is accorded to those individuals skillful in formulating clever, ingenious, and sometimes bizarre hypotheses. Ingenuity becomes the benchmark of success, and like present day movements in the arts leads to sudden shifts in fashion. Philosophy is the only discipline where whole careers and reputations are made on the basis of failed research programs.'[76] In addition to these spurious research programs, we find *bogus intellectual enterprises* like philosophical psychology and artificial intelligence. In real science the hidden structure explanation saves the phenomena; in bogus philosophical psychology we dismiss or we redefine the phenomena to fit the theory. The appearances are called 'folk psychology' or we deny that beliefs and desires cause action.

A further consequence has been the special damage to axiology. By turning philosophy into a speculative social science, analytic philosophy revives the whole issue of the relationship between facts and values and thereby puts itself in the position of being hopelessly unable to deal with norms. In place of the identification and explication of fundamental norms, we are given hypotheses about the hidden structure of those norms. We have witnessed things as preposterous as the idea that one can provide a 'theory'[77] of 'justice'.

It works something like this. The 'theorist' identifies in some arcane fashion a particular set of practices; the theorist speculates on the hidden structure behind those practices and formulates a model of that structure, complete with seemingly technical vocabulary; the alleged substructure licenses the theorist to decide which parts of the surface practice are legitimate and which are not. This turns axiology into a mask for private political agendas.[78]

---

[76] Capaldi, op. cit., 454.

[77] Rawls is not simply providing an account; he is providing an exploration; this is a special kind of explanation that ultimately masks a private political agenda. Rawls, to his credit, went on to modify his account in later wirings, but it is the earlier work that is taken seriously and has become canonical for those working in axiology.

[78] 'This [Rawls' book] is certainly the model of social justice that has governed the advocacy of R.H. Tawney and Richard Titmus and that holds the Labour Party together,' (Stuart Hampshire in his review of the book in the *New York Review of Books*, 1972). Rawls's conclusions have 'enormous intuitive appeal to people of good will,' Ronald Dworkin in

118

And it gets worse. The only growth areas in philosophy are 'applied' ethics, bioethics and business ethics.[79] To begin with, this creates the misleading impression that axiology is the application of a theory to practice – again, another invitation to promote private agendas. Many textbooks in these areas begin by treating the work of axiologists like Kant and Mill as theories called 'deontology' or 'utilitarianism'. This is not only a caricature of the work of great philosophers but a gross misrepresentation. To make matters even worse, the textbooks go on to provide summaries of the major alleged flaws in these alleged theories, thereby leaving the reader with both a new ethical vocabulary and a cynical nihilistic attitude about normative issues. Curiously, applied ethicists are in great demand for providing you with a (sophistic) choice depending upon whatever public policy conclusion you want to legitimate.

The ultimate irony of the social-scientization of philosophy is that it has legitimated deconstruction.[80] Michel Foucault and Jacques Derrida embrace scientism by arguing that mathematical science is the best and only defensible ideal construct for thinking. They relentlessly pursue the consequences to which the scientific ideal has led. They begin with a hidden structure analysis of some text[81] or social phenomenon. They then find themselves confronted with the existence of a multiplicity of competing exploratory hypotheses. Denied independent and objective criteria for choosing among rival hypotheses, committed to the notion that their own hypothesis has some superior validity,[82] they offer a hidden structure analysis of the

---

Magee (1982), 213. Nozick, by the way, does exactly the same thing but ends with a different agenda.

[79] See D. Solomon, 'Domestic Disarray and Imperial Ambition,' in T. Engelhardt (ed.), *Global Bioethics* (Scrivener, 2006), 335–361. 'The principal irony of the turn to the ethical in the 1960s was that the academic disciplines of theology and philosophy were called on for help at precisely the moment in their history when they were least able to provide it.' (345).

[80] 'Deconstruction' is a controversial term coined by Derrida in the 1960's but never defined. It is not an alternative view of philosophy. I understand deconstruction to be a method, a form of exploration.

[81] I do not deny the potential value of reading texts in a novel fashion; what I do challenge is the view that human beings can be understood in terms of hidden (social) structures.

[82] See Rorty's critique of Derrida in 'Deconstruction and Circumvention' *Essays on Heidegger and Others* (Cambridge: Cambridge University Press, 1999).

Nicholas Capaldi

faults of rival hypotheses.[83] That is, they offer a hidden structure analysis of other hidden structure analyses. Instead of civil discourse we see the rhetorical assassination of the character of our opponents. Socratic clarification has given way to adversarial confrontation.

Far from establishing the hegemony of analytic philosophy (scientistic Aristotelian naturalism), analytic philosophers have brought philosophy into disrepute, and they have opened the flood gates to irresponsible deconstruction. By making philosophy a kind of social science, analytic philosophy has promoted exploration as the model of thinking. Exploration encourages the formulation of hypotheses about hidden structure. Deconstructionists have carried this form of thinking to its logical conclusion. Both analytic philosophers and deconstructionists have abandoned the explication of the larger cultural context and have substituted programs of radical reform. They are no longer Socratic but adversarial. We have moved from the idea of rival visions of philosophy to the question of whether there is any such thing as philosophy!

Retrieving Philosophy

What they, namely, analytic writers and deconstructionists, should both argue, but have failed to, is that the pre-theoretical context of human values cannot be explained by any kind of theory about hidden structure. It is the failure to see this point that makes both groups anti-philosophical.

What is this pre-theoretical context? We find ourselves immersed in the world, a world in which it is not possible to talk about either it or ourselves independently of that immersion. How are we to understand ourselves? Our interaction with this world is not given to us ready made but requires an interpretive response on our part. Both our freedom and our responsibility are revealed in these interpretive responses. To be sure, our interpretive response does not occur in a vacuum but originates in a cultural context, that is, a context which is both social and historical. Epistemology is always social. Nevertheless, the cultural context does not dictate the response. There are no rules for the application of rules. This cultural context is itself something that we confront, that must be apprehended. In the course of that apprehension we are free to recognize its dissonant voices and internal tensions, to challenge parts of the

---

[83]   For MacIntyre's critique of Foucault see Alasdair MacIntyre, *Three Rival Versions of Moral Enquiry* (Notre Dame, 2006).

120

cultural context, to reject parts of it, to modify parts of it. We are also free to extend the cultural context in ways that are not dictated by the context itself. What we are not free to do is to pretend[84] that we can stand outside all frames of reference and by the appeal to an alleged autonomous reason privilege certain practices and de-legitimate others. Analytic philosophy proceeds from the assumption that we can rent the luxury skybox at the Archimedian Point. This is worse than epistemic hubris (thinking one can *find* the luxury skybox at the Archimedian Point); it's bad metaphysics—there is no skybox to rent because there is no Archimedian Point.

How can we best characterize this larger context? Since the time of the classical Greeks there has been a continuous set of reflective activities called philosophy. Those activities are designed to identify the norms of the other activates in the larger cultural context. As such, these activities fall into two categories:

First, philosophy has sought to identify the *procedural norms* of our thinking and discourse. We know this as analysis: explications of the logic of certain practices, and the clarification of the concepts that inform that practice. This is something that all three versions of philosophy can share. The analytic part is something that can always be taught and learned in varying degrees; from this springs the tendency for so much of philosophy to revert to a kind of scholasticism, especially in the academy.[85]

Let me list just a few of the prominent **analyses** from the history of philosophy. Notice that most if not all of these are negative in their import.

1. Logic
    a. Socrates' stress on the importance of non-contradiction
    b. The recognition that first principles cannot be proven (Plato's Socratic notion of *reminiscence*, Aristotle's conception of *teleology*, Hume's notion of *custom*, Kant's conception of the synthetic *a priori*, Gödel on *incompleteness*, Wittgenstein's notion of *practice*, and Heidegger's '*retrieval*')
    c. Aristotle's insistence that validity is not truth
    d. Epistemological skepticism is self-defeating (everybody)

---

[84]   This is always pretense and not a claim since we can identify the particular historical practice that is privileged with elevation ('Euclidean' geometry, teleological biology, computer technology, etc.).

[85]   Whenever academic philosophers are at a loss to justify their professional existence they always fall back on the value of identifying the procedural norms, that is, logic.

      e.   Discursive reasoning has limits (Kant)
2.   Science
      a.   The substitution of Newtonian science for Aristotelian science means that all causation is efficient causation (Hume)
      b.   The principle of verification is not itself an empirical truth
3.   Social world
      a.   We cannot directly apprehend the self
      b.   Norms are not 'facts' (but 'facts' presuppose norms)
      c.   The Distinction between causes and reasons
4.   Philosophy
      a.   philosophy is not a body of specific knowledge
      b.   philosophy is a meta-engagement of human immersion, studying the other forms of immersion/activity and their relation to each other (Socratic)
      c.   argumentative discourse is only one form of discourse, and it presupposes a larger cultural context that is more than discourse
      d.   When philosophy is detached from the larger context it becomes dogmatic and eristic (Adversarial)

Second, there is the identification of the norms[86] that undergird the larger cultural context. This is **synthesis**, the attempt to achieve a coherent vision of a culture's practices. The synthetic activity requires a breadth of imagination that is much rarer and cannot be taught in the sense that there is an algorhythm.

Let me note just a few of the prominent **syntheses** from the history of philosophy.

1.   Aristotle's[87] explication of the Greek Polis.
2.   Augustine's explication of Christianity integrating its Hebrew, Greek and Latin sources.
3.   Locke's explication of modernity integrating science, commercial economies, and representative government.
4.   Oakeshott's delineation of a civil association.

---

[86]   To identify these norms is not the same thing as saying that you must agree with them. Different individuals will have different narrative accounts of their own engagement with those norms.

[87]   The Aristotle who performed this task did not appeal to or believe in hidden social structures.

Notice what all of these syntheses have in common: they are conservative. They are conservative[88] in the senses that they presuppose a prior moral community; they seek to identify the norms inherent[89] in current institutional practice and to raise the issue of their coherence.[90]

What distinguishes the exploratory thinking of so many analytic philosophers and deconstructionists is that their agenda is to delegitimate current institutional practice. They are adversarial. It is not the case that being adversarial is always wrong; it is the case that being adversarial[91] requires or presupposes agreement on, or explication of, a prior normative framework. What analytic philosophers and

---

[88]   We may characterize the differences among the three philosophical perspectives when they engage in synthesis as follows: Platonists see current practice as an imperfect copy of the ideal which if actualized would render perfect coherence; Aristotelians see current practice as aiming, albeit imperfectly, at achieving its built-in end; Copernicans see the on-going evolution of a series of practices which creates periodic tensions requiring further explication.

[89]   Traditions are fertile sources of adaptation. The development of a tradition or inheritance is not a philosophical act; it may be either legal or political.

[90]   This is where I think the Sheffer stroke ($|$) is illuminating. Sheffer showed (and so did Peirce, independently) that all logical operators of the first order predicate calculus can be reduced to a single operator meaning 'is incompatible with' (or 'not and'). In furtherance of my point, all (logical) argumentation is about identifying (and avoiding) incoherence. The question then becomes: Coherence with, between, or among what and what? For the analytic philosopher, what counts is coherence between extant practices or institutions and the hidden structure (e.g. Rawls's reflective equilibrium). For the Copernican, what counts is coherence among the elements of extant practices or institutions. Another way to say this is that what H.L.A. Hart in *The Concept of Law* calls the 'internal point of view' on a practice is the only point of view – or at least, the only alternatives to it are other 'internal' points of view. His student, Raz, goes on to argue that all normative statements about the law are statements from a point of view – the point of view of one who accepts the law. My response to Raz, then, would be something like: 'And what normative statements do you suppose are *not* like that?'

[91]   One is reminded here of Hume's critique of Locke's attempt to justify revolution. Hume argues that you cannot have a theory of revolution since this presupposes an authoritative reference point. The whole point of revolution is to reject a specific authority. Situations may in the minds of some call for revolution, but it is philosophically absurd to provide a justification. Ritual appeals to those who already agree with you are not justifications.

deconstructionists have done is to be adversarial without prior philo-sophical explication.[92] This is disingenuous. Current attempts to address normative issues by both analytic philosophers and decon-structionists[93] are a travesty of philosophical speculative thinking.

Summary

Philosophy has a special role to play. That special role is comprised of two parts, pedagogical and cultural. The pedagogical role is making us self-conscious, aware of our basic presuppositions. This is analysis; it can be taught; and, thankfully, it can be practiced outside of the dis-cipline, the profession and the academy. The cultural role is the fash-ioning of a narrative that brings the presuppositions of an entire array of cultural practices into some sort of coherent synthesis. This is a role that has been unique to philosophy or to those we identify as great philosophers, even though many of them have played that role outside of the academy.[94]

This is a special role, but it is not an authoritative role.[95] To engage in this activity is to offer a vision that is not an argument, although it may contain arguments within it. Moreover, identifying presupposi-tions is different from the application of those presuppositions or the challenging of some of those presuppositions in the light of others. It is a role that acknowledges the freedom of the imagination, the auton-omy of choice, and in the contemporary context the goodness or val-idity of a *civil*[96] association. It is a role that can never be played by

[92]   What is wrong with academic business ethics? – it is wholly adversar-ial to its subject matter. Indeed, to its practitioners and to many others, the whole point and purpose of the business ethics course is to be 'equal time' for the critics of business – as if the FCC's long defunct Fairness Doctrine somehow applied to b-school curricula.

[93]   This is why it was impossible to get a straight answer from Derrida on the status of his pronouncements.

[94]   Questions can certainly be raised about the detrimental effect on philosophy of being situated within the present day academy.

[95]   An individual thinker may choose to do both. However, the legiti-macy of the policies derived from the vision in no way follow from the value of the vision. Others can in retrospect appreciate the value and impor-tance and influence of the vision without endorsing the derived policies. We value Aristotle's analysis of the polis, but most of us would choose not to live in one.

[96]   For those not familiar with Oakeshott, an enterprise association has a collective goal to which everything and everyone is subordinated; a civil

self-alienated and self-proclaimed elites who strive to reveal to others their respective roles and beliefs and actions within an *enterprise* association. So many prominent members of the profession are so unreflectively hostile to modern commercial societies that they have incapacitated themselves from providing a vision: Rorty, MacIntyre, Blackburn, Derrida, Foucault, to name just a few.[97] A large part of the hostility of many intellectuals to modern commercial societies[98] is that such societies are not enterprise associations requiring a clerisy.[99]

Let me elaborate. Oakeshott distinguished between an enterprise association and a civil association. An enterprise association has a collective goal to which everything and everyone is subordinated; when the society overall is an enterprise association it is traditional, authoritarian or even totalitarian; no other enterprise associations are tolerated. A civil association has no such collective goal but is characterized by procedural norms within which individuals pursue their personal goals. A society which is overall a civil association may contain within it a multitude of enterprise associations (families, religions, the military, a business, etc.) such that individuals may voluntarily enter and exit from them. This is what a liberal society is in the generic sense. Modern western polities are civil associations held together by agreement on the procedural norms (e.g. due

---

association has no such goal, rather it is characterized by procedural norms within which individuals pursue their personal goals.

[97] Richard Rorty, who has influenced my thought in many positive ways, is an example of a peculiar sort of failure. In the end he found no special role for philosophy, but his professed skepticism was a claim to exempt from criticism political principles which he held (and inherited) but could not make into a coherent narrative, specifically, 'the demands of self-creation and of human solidarity,' which he asserted were 'equally valid yet forever incommensurable.' Rorty, *Contingency, Irony, and Solidarity* (Cambridge, 1989), 15.

[98] Joseph Schumpeter, *Capitalism, Socialism, and Democracy* (1975); Bertrand de Jouvenel, 'The Treatment of Capitalism by Continental Intellectuals,' in *Capitalism and the Historians*, ed. F. A. Hayek (1974); Ludwig von Mises, *The Anti-Capitalist Mentality* (1975); Peter Klein, 'Why Economists Still Support Socialism,' *Mises Daily Article* (11/15/06); Robert Nozick, 'Why Do Intellectuals Oppose Capitalism?' *Cato Policy Report* (1998).

[99] See Paul Hollander, *Political Pilgrims: Western Intellectuals in Search of the Good Society* (1997). Philosophy, for many, is the articulation of a moral vision for those hostile to substantive religious communities.

process). Different individuals may belong to a variety of different substantive moral communities which function for them as enterprise associations.

In civil associations such as our own, intellectuals do not play a leadership role. At best they may help to identify the procedural norms and even offer a larger vision of how the norms of various institutions interact (see below), but they cannot offer an authoritative account of the substantive norms of the entire society. Intellectuals (including clergy) cannot offer an authoritative account of the good life for that is something that each individual determines for herself or himself. In civil associations such as ours leadership comes from the business and legal community. Both Platonists and traditional Aristotelians reflect the enterprise associations of the classical and medieval world, and that is why they (a) find appeals to group membership irresistible and (b) invariably favors top-down direction of society by the government. The adherence to classical models in the modern context leads to hostility to modern economic, political, legal, and social institutions. You cannot provide a comprehensive philosophical understanding of a cultural context to which you are in permanent adversarial opposition. Modern civil associations are best captured by Copernicans.

The further analogy I would like to draw is the following. Just as Platonists, but Aristotelians especially, are unhappy with modern civil associations so they are unhappy with the idea of living with competing conceptions of philosophy. They are inexorably driven by the logic of their position to seek hegemony.

The existence of rival versions of philosophy leads to rival versions of the university. Each of these rival views has a different conception of epistemology and therefore of academic practice. Consider some of the current standard alternatives: Bloom's notion of the Great Books is to select them, read them and discuss them from a pre-modern but non-theological Aristotelian point of view. Analytic philosophers focus on the lecture as the authoritative presentation of fact, but offer quasi-socialist hidden structure analyses of social institutions disguised as scientific fact. Deconstructionists use the lecture as a rhetorical discrediting of the analytic agenda and the 'smuggling in' of their own. MacIntyre advocates a university where 'rival and antagonistic views of rational justification' can be debated and where teachers "initiate students into conflict." What all of these foregoing views share in common is hostility to modern commercial societies.

For Oakeshott, on the other hand, liberal learning is the unique ordering of our experience in our imagination. It is what makes us individuals with a voice of our own. Before we can have that voice we must participate through the voices of others. Our inheritance is a set of cultural achievements and practices, not a doctrine to be learned (contra Bloom and MacIntyre). The inheritance is recreated through appropriation, is not homogeneous and has no definitive formulation. The Great Authors do not speak as one voice with one message, but they do provide the context in which we achieve and sustain our freedom. To hear and respond to different voices is not to be initiated into conflict. The teacher who facilitates this initiation both into the inheritance and into discovering one's own voice, in the end, helps others to discover their own freedom and responsibility. It is only through interaction with our inheritance that we become what we are. It is in this sense that *education is a conversation with many voices*. The role of the teacher is to help the student come to know his/her voice by hearing it echoed in the conversation and to join the conversation first by speaking in the voices of others and, eventually, in his/her own voice. Rather than initiation into conflict, the student learns the ethics of conversation.

If the discipline of Philosophy is to play a significant intellectual role, then it must provide a coherent narrative of our intellectual inheritance, situate itself within it, and accept the challenge of achieving a coherent cultural framework. In its present major forms, the discipline is unable or unwilling to do that. Contemporary philosophy must find an alternative way of proceeding if it is to avoid being marginalized within the larger cultural context, and if it is to play a significant role in the articulation of our fundamental procedural values. We are not suggesting an entirely new direction. On the contrary, we have urged a return to the main track of western philosophy, a recapturing of the richer understanding of ourselves that is preserved in the western philosophical inheritance.

The act of retrieving this common framework is neither reactionary nor anachronistic. Retrieving our framework is not a simple matter of uncritically returning to the past. Instead, it is the re-identifying of something that is a permanent part of the human condition even though it is always expressed in specific historical contexts. The framework is not a rigid structure but a fertile source of adaptation that not only evolves but also expands to incorporate things that might from an earlier perspective seem alien. The fact that these truths are always contextualized means that the act of retrieval through explication inevitably involves a reformulation. To encompass the past is to make it our own in some fashion. Since the retrieval is not solely an intellectual act, we should not be surprised that there is (a) no definitive articulation, (b) inevitable controversy over its articulation, and (c) a necessary act of faith in its continuing apprehension.[100] Controversy is not a problem to be solved but an inevitable condition that requires a moral response.

In sketching an alternative to analytic philosophy and deconstructionist philosophy, we can recapture the central cultural role of philosophy – the articulation of the inheritance and the provision of a coherent framework.[101] Philosophy can be restored as the conscience of the culture and in a way that is Socratic. As long as professional philosophy confuses its *Socratic* role with an *adversarial* stance it cannot perform that role. A coherent narrative does not preclude (a) different voices, (b) internal tensions, or (c) critique, but it does presuppose the endorsement of the fundamental norms of one's community of discourse. Given the present estrangement of University intellectuals from modern culture, perhaps this is a welcome opportunity for philosophy as a discipline to provide constructive leadership for the entire intellectual and academic world.

[100] These observations were suggested by Jaroslav Pelikan, but I do not recall the specific writings.

[101] 'The idea of system is inevitable in philosophy, and...no attempt to deny it can succeed unless it is pushed to the point of denying that the word philosophy has any meaning whatever.' Collingwood, *Philosophical Method*, op. cit., 186.

Philosophy: A Contribution, not to Human Knowledge, but to Human Understanding

P. M. S. HACKER

1. The poverty of philosophy as a science

Throughout its history philosophy has been thought to be a member of a community of intellectual disciplines united by their common pursuit of knowledge. It has sometimes been thought to be the queen of the sciences, at other times merely their under-labourer. But irrespective of its social status, it was held to be a participant in the quest for knowledge – a cognitive discipline.

Cognitive disciplines may be *a priori* or empirical. The distinction between what is *a priori* and what is empirical is epistemological. It turns, as Frege noted, on the ultimate justification for holding something to be true.[1] If the truths which a cognitive discipline attains are warranted neither by observation nor by experiment (nor by inference therefrom), then they are *a priori*. Otherwise they are empirical. The natural and moral sciences (the *Geisteswissenschaften*) strive for and attain empirical knowledge.[2] The mathematical sciences are *a priori*.

Cognitive disciplines have a distinctive subject matter, concerning which they aim to add to human knowledge. Physics deals with matter, motion, and energy, chemistry with the constitution of stuffs out of elements, biology with the nature of living beings, history with 'the crimes, follies and misfortunes of mankind' (Gibbon), and so forth.

The empirical sciences aim not only to discover truths but also to *explain* the phenomena they study. The natural sciences produce theories (typically with predictive powers) to explain the facts and laws they discover. The moral sciences too aim to explain the phenomena they study – although not to the same extent by way of theory and general laws; and their predictive powers, if any, are more limited.

---

[1] Frege, *Foundations of Arithmetic* (Blackwell, Oxford, 1959), §3.
[2] Of course, that does not mean that they contain no *a priori* propositions. But these belong to the method of representation and do not describe what is represented.

doi:10.1017/S1358246109990087
129

P. M. S. Hacker

Mathematics and logic strive to produce theorems by means of proofs, and are not subject to confirmation or falsification by experience.

If philosophy is a cognitive discipline, then the truths it attains need to be characterized. Are they *a priori* or empirical? To answer this question, we should cast around for established philosophical truths – examine the fund of philosophical knowledge achieved over two and half thousand years. But two disturbing features immediately spring to the eye:

First, if one asks a physicist or biologist, a historian or a mathematician what knowledge has been achieved in his subject, he can take one to a large library, and point out myriad books which detail the cognitive achievements of his subject. But if one asks a philosopher for even a *single* book that will summarize the elements of philosophical knowledge – as one might ask a chemist for a handbook of chemistry – he will have nothing to present. There *is* no general, agreed body of philosophical knowledge – although there are libraries full of philosophical writings from antiquity to the present day, which are in constant use.

Secondly, each cognitive discipline has its own object of study. But if we examine the history of modern philosophy, it appears to be *a subject in search of a subject matter.* In the modern era, great philosophers recurrently attempted to isolate a distinctive subject matter for philosophy, and a proper method for achieving the knowledge, which, they held, had evaded their predecessors. Descartes thought that the task of 'first philosophy' was to disclose the foundations of all human knowledge, and to erect a certain and secure structure of knowledge on indubitable truths. The key to achieving this was his new *method*. Only thus could philosophy participate in the quest for knowledge. Hume supposed that the subject matter of philosophy was the human mind, and the task of philosophy to explain how it functions. Philosophy must do for psychology what Newton had done for physics, and must introduce *the experimental method of reasoning* into the study of the mind. Kant held that philosophy must determine the *a priori* categories of thought and the *a priori* principles of conceptualized experience. It must, above all, explain how synthetic *a priori* knowledge is possible. Only then will metaphysics be set upon the true path of a science. Russell thought that the subject matter of philosophy consists of the most general truths about the universe, and its task to discover them and catalogue their logical forms. Only by adopting *the scientific method in philosophy* can genuine progress be achieved. And so on.

The striking feature of these programmatic objectives is that none survived for long. Each collapsed, for one or another of four reasons:

130

(i)   A vital assumption proved unsustainable. So, for example, it was a Cartesian error to suppose that genuine knowledge must be indubitable; or resistant to hyperbolic doubt. It was erroneous to suppose, as Russell did, that propositions of logic are all generalizations that describe the most general features of the universe. On the contrary, propositions of logic need not be general (e.g. 'Either it is raining or it is not raining' is, *contra* Russell, a proposition of logic), and they describe nothing at all (e.g. the latter tautology tells one nothing about the weather).

(ii)   The subject matter, correctly understood, was taken over by an empirical science. So, for example, the experimental study of the exercise of human cognitive faculties that Hume allocated to philosophy was taken over by experimental psychology.

(iii) The goal proved to be chimerical: the conception of knowledge as resting on indubitable foundations is wrong. Hence the goal of displaying the structure of human knowledge as a hierarchy based on subjective experience is illusory. The Kantian goal of explaining how synthetic *a priori* truths are possible foundered over the misconception of such truths as propositions to which nature *must* conform, rather than as expressions of norms of representation.

(iv)   The method proved broken-backed: Cartesian method is not a reliable way of discovering truths, Kant's Copernican revolution is misconceived, and Russell's scientific method in philosophy is a chimera.

This should give us pause. How can it be that after two and a half thousand years of endeavour philosophy has still not reached the status of a science, has no agreed subject matter, and has no fund of philosophical knowledge? How is the poverty of philosophy, construed as a cognitive discipline, to be explained?

2. Philosophy as the midwife of the sciences

Many questions that were opened by philosophers were subsequently handed over to scientists, for example questions concerning the constitution of things, the infinity or finitude of the universe, the nature of the stars, the origin of life, the innateness of ideas. Physics, although it continued to be known as natural philosophy down to the nineteenth century, became independent of philosophy in the seventeenth. Psychology broke free of philosophy at the end of the nineteenth century, and mathematical logic is doing so today. This midwifery has been invoked (by Russell and Austin, for example) to explain the poverty of the results of philosophy – namely that once questions are sufficiently sharply formulated to be answerable, they are handed over to an independent science, which then contributes to the extension of human knowledge.[3]

This is misleading, for four reasons:

First, although independence was achieved by such sciences, new areas of philosophical investigation were thereby generated, e.g. philosophy of physics or philosophy of the psychological sciences. But it would be misguided to suppose that questions in the philosophies of the special sciences remain philosophical only because they are insufficiently clearly understood to be handled by a new meta-science.

Secondly, although these sciences achieved independence, it would be mistaken to suppose that they achieved freedom from conceptual confusion. The conceptual confusions of the sciences, in physics, psychology, neuroscience, economics (not always recognized as such by scientists) are grist for *philosophical* mills – not philosophical problems for experimental investigation. (Of course, scientists may grind the grist too – we are not concerned with trade union disputes, but with distinguishing different forms of intellectual enquiry.)

Thirdly, the birth of an independent science does *not* free philosophy from a host of questions which have always been on the philosophical agenda associated with the subject matter of that special science. Despite the fact that investigations of matter in motion had achieved a degree of clarity that made it possible for them to be handled by an independent science of physics, such questions as: What distinguishes substances from properties? How are substances related to events and which is ontologically prior? – such problems were *not* allocated to physics. Similarly, even when questions about what material things are made of, what the ultimate chemical elements are and what kinds of chemical combinations they enter into, were sufficiently clearly understood to be handed over to chemistry, other questions, such as how things (substances) are related to the stuff of which they consist, remained exactly where they had always been – on the agenda of philosophy. And the autonomy of psychology has not removed from the domain of philosophy the fundamental questions in philosophical psychology, such as 'What is the mind?' or 'How is the mind related to the body?'

---

[3]   B. Russell, *The Problems of Philosophy* (Oxford University Press, Oxford, 1967), 90; for a similar view, see J. L. Austin, 'Ifs and Cans', *Philosophical Papers* (Clarendon Press, Oxford, 1961), 180.

Fourthly, the suggested explanation is implausible when we turn to practical philosophy (in Kant's sense of the term) – to ethics, political and legal philosophy. Moral philosophy has not and will not give birth to a science of morality, and so called ethicists are not moral scientists. The emergence of political science in the nineteenth century was not a result of philosophical midwifery, and legal philosophy is not going to be displaced by a science of law. Moral, legal and political philosophy do not give birth to new sciences, but contribute to the emergence of new moral, legal and political distinctions, principles and constitutional arrangements.

So, the poverty of philosophy qua cognitive discipline cannot be explained as a consequence of the fact that once knowledge is achievable the subject becomes a science.

3. 'Philosophy has only just come of age'

There is another move here, that might, in honour of its recent advocates, be called the Wykeham Chair gambit. Thirty years ago, Professor Michael Dummett, Wykeham Professor of Logic at the University of Oxford declared that 'philosophy has only just very recently struggled out of its early stage into maturity: the turning point was the work of Frege, but the widespread realization of the significance of that work has had to wait for half a century after his death...'[4] Recently, Professor Timothy Williamson, Dummett's successor but one in the Wykeham Chair of Logic at the University of Oxford, declared that we have only now (in 2005) arrived at 'the end of the beginning' of philosophy.[5] Well, one can blow the Last Trumpet once, but not once a generation.

Less parochially – the suggestion that philosophy has not achieved the results of a science because the subject is so difficult that only NOW has it been discovered how it may do so, has been advanced by numerous great philosophers who were not holders of the Wykeham Chair of Logic at the University of Oxford. They all enjoyed the brief illusion that they had, at long last, found the real key to unlock

---

[4] M. A. E. Dummett, 'Can analytic philosophy be systematic and ought it to be?', repr. in *Truth and Other Enigmas* (Duckworth, London, 1978), 457. Frege died in 1925. Half a century later is 1975, two years after the publication of Dummett's, *Frege's Philosophy of Language* (Duckworth, London, 1973).

[5] T. Williamson, 'Must Do Better', in P. Greenough and M. Lynch, (eds.) *Truth and Realism* (Oxford University Press, Oxford, 2005), 187.

the riches promised by philosophy, to achieve real philosophical knowledge and to set philosophy at last upon the true path of a science. Descartes thought that his new method of analysis and systematic doubt would enable anyone to establish *the indubitable foundations of knowledge*, and to derive *all possible knowledge* in absolutely sure and certain steps. Locke thought that with his new Way of Ideas, he would be able to determine for the first time the *scope and limits of human knowledge*. Hume proposed 'a compleat system of the sciences, built on a foundation almost entirely new, and the only one upon which they can stand with any security'. Kant, comparing the method of his critical philosophy to the Copernican revolution, supposed that by following the principle that 'objects must conform to our [*a priori*] knowledge', rather than our *a priori* knowledge conforming to objects, he would at last be able explain how synthetic *a priori* knowledge is possible, and to place metaphysics 'upon the true path of a science'. Russell too recognised the scandal that 'Philosophy, from the earliest times, has made greater claims, and achieved fewer results, than any other branch of learning.' He boldly declared 'that the time has now arrived when this unsatisfactory state of affairs can be brought to an end.'

The promise that after two thousand years of irresponsible adolescence, philosophy will at last produce a flood of truths and well-founded theories – tomorrow, has been made, and proven empty, far too often to carry conviction. Moreover, such declarations of the incompetence of one's predecessors does scant justice to the endeavours of some of the greatest geniuses of mankind. And it renders it well nigh unintelligible that we still read, and *should* still read, the works of Plato and Aristotle, Aquinas and Scotus, Descartes and Kant. (Scientists do not need to read the works of Galen or Paracelsus, Tycho Brahe or Kepler.) Finally, it is implausible to suppose that twenty-five centuries of endeavour by some of the greatest minds of our culture should have failed to come up with some solid philosophical knowledge *because the problems of philosophy are so much more difficult than problems in the sciences*. Is the philosophical problem of what a substance is, and how substances are related to the stuffs of which they are made *so much more difficult* than the question of what are the elements of which all things are made? Is the philosophical problem of what knowledge is so much more difficult than the question of the descent of man? Is the relation of mind to body so much more complex than the Krebs cycle? Is *that* why we can discern so little achievement in this 'sector in the quest for knowledge' (as Dummett once put it)? Surely the difficulty of philosophical questions is not to be compared to that of scientific questions *in degree*, but *in kind*.

When bombarded throughout the ages with incompatible claims about the subject and unfulfilled promises of how this is going to be set right, the correct move is to challenge the fundamental assumption that is taken for granted by all participants in the debate, namely the assumption that philosophy is a cognitive discipline.[6]

4. Philosophy as a quest for understanding rather than knowledge

Philosophy is not a contribution to human *knowledge*, but to human *understanding*. It is neither an empirical science nor an a priori one, since it is no science. The difficulty of philosophy does not consist in the difficulty of discovering new, let alone arcane, truths about the world; nor yet in producing proofs concerning its existence[7], the existence of recherché 'entities' like universals[8], or of common or garden 'entities' like events.[9] *It is a quest for understanding, not for knowledge.*

As a slogan, this is correct. Like all slogans, it needs clarification and qualification. First, some clarification:

If one claims that philosophy is a contribution to human understanding, one must explain what the object of understanding is, and how achieving understanding in philosophy differs from adding to one's fund of knowledge.

---

[6]   This radical move was made by the later Wittgenstein and, following him, by many of his distinguished pupils; in a somewhat different form, by the Vienna Circle; and subsequently by many members of the Oxford group of philosophers between 1945 and 1970.

[7]   As G. E. Moore attempted to do in his famous proof of the existence of the external world.

[8]   Williamson recently declared (*The Philosophy of Philosophy* (Blackwell, Oxford, 2007), 19) that the task of metaphysics is to discover 'what fundamental kinds of things there are', for example 'substances and essences, universals and particulars'. Physicists, it seems, discover the existence of fundamental particles such as neutrinos or mesons, meta-physicists discover the existence (or non-existence) of fundamental things such as universals or essences.

[9]   Donald Davidson, in 'Causal Relations', *Journal of Philosophy* **64** (1967) offered a proof that events exist. As Waismann remarked apropos Moore's attempt to prove the existence of the external world: 'What can one say to this – save perhaps that he is a great prover before the Lord' ('How I see Philosophy', in *How I see Philosophy and Other Essays* (Macmillan, London, 1968), 1).

P. M. S. Hacker

It has been suggested that philosophy seeks not knowledge of new facts but an understanding of old facts; or that its role is that of organizing the knowledge we already possess. These suggestions are partly right and partly wrong.

Scientists seek to understand why the phenomena they investigate are as they are and behave as they behave. They do so by way of empirical explanation, which may take various forms, e.g. hypothetico-deductive, inference to the best explanation, or explanation by reference to intervening mechanisms. All these are subject to empirical confirmation or refutation. To that extent it is misleading to suggest that philosophy seeks not for knowledge of new facts but for an understanding of familiar facts – as if science did not satisfy that need. Philosophy cannot explain phenomena *in that sense* at all. So whatever its quest for understanding is, it is not akin to the understanding achieved by the empirical sciences.

Nevertheless, philosophy *can* contribute in a unique and distinctive way to understanding in the natural sciences and mathematics. It can clarify their conceptual features, and restrain their tendency to transgress the bounds of sense. It is a Tribunal of Reason, before which scientists and mathematicians may be arraigned for their transgressions. Indeed, the sciences (and to a lesser degree mathematics), in our times, are the primary source of misguided metaphysics – which it is the task of philosophy to curb, not to encourage. Disabusing a Hilbert of the character of Cantor's paradise contributes to the deeper understanding of arithmetic in general and of the calculus of transfinite arithmetic in particular.[10] Explaining that alternative geometries are not alternative theories of space but alternative grammars for the description of spatial relationships contributes to a better understanding of the enterprise of geometry. Making it clear that parts of the brain are not possible subjects of cognitive predicates contributes to a better understanding of the manner in which neuroscience *can* explain the neural foundations of our cognitive powers. Nevertheless, it would be misleading to suggest in general that the understanding that philosophy seeks is parasitical on the sciences in this way. For the illumination philosophy can thus contribute characterizes primarily the philosophies of the special sciences.

Similarly, there is some truth to the claim that philosophy does not add to the sum of our knowledge of the world (or of mathematics), but

---

[10]   Wittgenstein was told of Hilbert's remark that no one would drive him out of Cantor's paradise, to which he replied that he would not dream of driving anyone out of paradise, he would just get them to open their eyes and look around – then they would leave of their own accord.

rather *organizes* what we already know. Certainly distinctions that philosophers have progressively drawn since the days of Aristotle have contributed to clarity regarding the sciences. It is thanks to philosophy that we distinguish the empirical sciences from logic and mathematics, the natural from the moral sciences, deductive from inductive reasoning, a priori from empirical probability, nomothetic from idiographic explanation, causal from hermeneutic explanation, and so on. These distinctions are crucial for a proper understanding of the manifold scientific (as well as non-scientific) enterprises of trying to gain knowledge and understanding of the world we live in, of ourselves within it, and of the mathematical apparatus we have invented to quantify it. Nevertheless, it would be misleading to characterize the task of philosophy as being to organize, or to put order into *the knowledge we already possess*. Insofar as philosophy has to organize material, what it has, *above all*, to organize are *forms of description* (or *norms of representation*) by means of which we present what we know and what we strive to know. I shall elaborate this below.

The kind of understanding philosophy pursues is distinctive. It can be described in various more or less misleading ways:

In the metaphysical mode: philosophy strives for an understanding of the *a priori* natures of things and of internal relations between things (but there are no 'metaphysical facts' to be discovered, and internal relations are creatures of reason, not of nature).

In the conceptual mode: philosophy strives for an overview of the structure of (parts of) our conceptual scheme and of logico-grammatical relations between its elements (but that does not make concepts the special subject matter of philosophy).

In the linguistic mode: philosophy strives for an overview of segments of our language that in one way or another, give rise to conceptual problems (but philosophy is not in general *about* language).

Correctly understood, these are descriptions of one and the same enterprise. Of course, investigating the use of a word *need not* be a logico-grammatical investigation into the concept it expresses. It may be a non-philosophical, purely linguistic, investigation into etymology, phonetics, syntax, morphology, and so forth. But a *philosophical* investigation into the use of a word *is* an investigation into the concept expressed, for it is an investigation, geared to philosophical purposes, into the presuppositions, implications, compatibilities and incompatibilities linked with the use of the word in sentences. For the most part, philosophers will abstract from irrelevant local differences between languages. A philosophical investigation into the use of 'know', for purposes of epistemology for example, will yield much the same results as a philosophical investigation into the uses of 'wissen' and 'kennen', the manifest differences often being irrelevant to the investigation.[11] For the investigation, whether conducted in English or in German, is an investigation into those features of usage that determine the common concept of knowledge.[12]

The *a priori* nature of things is fixed by the sense-determining rules for the use of expressions signifying things.[13] To suppose that things, their properties and relations have an a priori nature in any *other* sense is to fall victim to illusion. For it is to take for 'objective (language independent) necessities' what are actually no more than the shadows cast on the world by grammar. To describe the nature of substance, for example, *is* to characterize the categorial concept of substance, just as describing the nature of events is to characterize

[11]   Note that even where a philosophically relevant feature is picked out by reference to an aspect of a given language not shared by some other language, it does not follow that the distinction thus marked is not capable of being drawn in the second language and demonstrated by features of its use. Whether a verb has a progressive form or not is often an important clue to the character of the concept expressed, e.g. that 'to know' lacks a progressive form shows that it does not signify an activity or process. But German does not have a progressive tense! Nevertheless, that knowledge is no process can be made clear in German too, for there is no such thing as interrupting someone in the middle of knowing, and it makes no sense to ask someone whether he has finished knowing something.

[12]   But it would be mistaken to suppose that there are not sometimes philosophically important differences between different languages and cultures. An investigation into the use of 'mind', for example, will differ interestingly from investigations into the use of 'Geist' and 'Seele', or 'anima', or 'psuche', or 'nephesh' and 'ruach' – which betokens differences in the way different languages and different cultures articulate characteristic human powers. It is important to note too that a philosophical enquiry into a categorial concept need not be an investigation of the use of the category-word in question. An investigation of the nature of substances (i.e. persistent things of a kind) is not an investigation of the use of the word 'substance' ('substantia' or 'ousia') – which is a term of art in philosophy – but rather an investigation into common features of usage of a large subclass of concrete count nouns, the common form of which is signified by the formal concept of substance.

[13]   To avert misunderstanding, I am *not* suggesting that such rules for the use of words typically or even commonly take the form of analytic definitions that specify necessary and sufficient conditions for the application of their definienda. Things may have a nature, even though they have no essence – as in the case of propositions, numbers or games (the concepts of which are family-resemblance concepts).

the concept of an event and to describe the nature of the mind is to characterize the concept of mind. But there is no way to characterize a concept other than by describing the relevant features of the uses of expressions that express that concept or belong to the category of concepts it subsumes. So to describe the nature of substance just is to spell out, *and order*, the salient sense-determining rules for the use of that subclass of concrete count nouns that signify substances, and their similarities to and differences from other kinds of nouns. This may be done in the formal mode or (more commonly) in the material mode. To state the nature of events just is to describe (directly or indirectly) the constitutive features of event-designating expressions, and to compare and contrast them with the use of other general types of expression, such as material object names. And to describe the nature of the mind is to describe and order the relevant features of the use of the expression 'the mind' and its cognates, and of psychological predicates ascribable only to creatures that can be said to have minds.

Philosophy has no subject matter *in the sense in which the empirical sciences do*. It deals with philosophical questions, which are different in kind from questions in the empirical sciences and in mathematics. What philosophical questions are is best displayed by an array of uncontroversial and incontrovertible examples. These will be very various: 'What is ...'-questions (e.g. what is the mind, knowledge, truth); 'What is the difference'-questions (e.g. what is the difference between knowledge and belief? or between a reason and a motive?'); 'How possible'-questions (such as 'How is it possible to measure time, given that the present has no extent, the past no longer exists and the future does not yet exist?', 'How is it possible for Achilles to overtake the tortoise, given that he has to traverse an infinite number of spaces in a finite time?'; 'Why necessary'-questions? (Such as 'Why *must* 2 and 2 make 4? or 'Why can't something be both red all over and green all over?') and 'Do so-and-so's exist-questions?' (Such as 'Do universals exist?','Do objective values exist?'). But the form of questions is little guide as to whether they are philosophical. 'What is matter?' can be a philosophical question in an appropriate context, but it can be a scientific one in another context. 'What is a dodo?' is no philosophical question, but 'What is belief?' is. 'Do dragons exist?' is not a philosophical question, but 'Do universals exist?' is. 'Why can't I go back to Africa?' is not a philosophical question, but 'Why can't I go back to the reign of Queen Elizabeth I?' is. Philosophical questions cannot be circumscribed by their form. Nor can they be circumscribed by their content, since they can, in principle, be concerned with any subject matter at all − *any subject matter that gives rise to conceptual confusions and unclarities.* These questions cannot be resolved by the empirical sciences, since they are not empirical questions. *They are all questions that are, directly or indirectly, solved, resolved or dissolved by conceptual investigation.* One might therefore say, as above, that, in one sense, philosophy has no subject matter; but one might also say that, in another sense, philosophy has everything as its subject matter.

5. Philosophy and conceptual investigation

Philosophy is a conceptual investigation. This assertion can easily be misunderstood. Does it mean that philosophy has a subject matter after all – namely concepts? That would be misleading. Being a conceptual investigation does not mean being solely *about* concepts. The traditional questions of whether an omnipotent, omniscient and benevolent God who created the universe exists, whether we have an immortal soul, whether we are free, are philosophical. They are *about* whether God (thus conceived) exists, whether human beings have immortal souls and whether we are free agents. But they are answered by conceptual investigations, not by observation and experiment.[14] These investigations involve scrutiny of the concepts of God[15], the soul, and voluntariness. Similarly, the questions of whether machines can think or whether the brain can think, are philosophical. Neither can be answered by experimental science. To deny that they are about machines, brains, and what it is to think, would be misleading. But to suggest that they are not, *in a very distinctive sense*, about the concept of thinking and its intelligible applicability or inapplicability to machines and brains would be grossly to misrepresent the investigation. For such questions are concerned with *what does or does not make sense*. And the way to examine whether something does or does not make sense, for example whether it makes sense to say that computers think or that the prefrontal cortices think, requires methodical investigation of the use of the verb 'to think' and its

---

[14]   Of course, philosophers sometimes engage in what they misleadingly call 'thought-experiments'. But a thought-experiment is no more an experiment than monopoly money is money.

[15]   To be sure, *if* the concept of god as an omnipotent, omniscient and benevolent creator of the universe (the god of the philosophers) is coherent, and if the ontological argument for the existence of such a god is invalid, then whether there is such a god is an empirical question, not a conceptual one.

ramifying logico-grammatical connections and presuppositions. It would be mistaken to suppose that if a question is about a concept it is not *also* be about what falls under the concept – as if Hart's *Concept of Law* were not also about the law, or Ryle's *Concept of Mind* were not also about the mind. In truth, 'about' is no jack with which to lift the vehicle of philosophy.

The conceptual investigations that characterize philosophy are a priori. It is the characterization of our current concepts and the description of their relations within the conceptual field to which they belong that can contribute to the resolution of philosophical problems. The features of our concepts that are marshalled for philosophical purposes are specified by conceptual truths. Conceptual truths – for example: that events occur at a time, but do not exist at a time; that they may need space but do not occupy space; that they lack spatial dimensions; that they may have phases; that they can move, not as objects move, but in the sense that their successive phases occur at different places; and so on and so forth – are not empirical, but *a priori*. They describe aspects of the nature of their subject; they characterize the concept at hand; and they are manifest in the use of words.

That philosophy is an *a priori* investigation does not mean that it is an *a priori science*. Mathematics is *a priori*. But it is not a science after the manner of the natural sciences. It does not discover new facts about the realm of numbers and spatial relations as physics or chemistry discover new facts about the realm of nature. The mathematician is an inventor, not a discoverer.[16] What he invents are new forms of mathematical description. For mathematics is the *grammar* of number and space. Its business is *concept-formation by means of proof*. A proof grafts a new conceptual articulation onto the body of mathematics. The concepts thus formed have their *ultimate* (though not necessarily their proximate) rationale in providing rules for the transformation of empirical statements involving magnitudes, quantities, and so forth. Philosophy, by contrast, does not consist of a body of theorems at all. Nor is it the task of philosophy to form novel concepts by means of deductive proofs. It does not produce new rules for the transformation of descriptions of empirical phenomena. Its task is *concept-elucidation* for the purpose of resolving philosophical problems. That philosophy can be done in an armchair does not

---

[16] See Wittgenstein, *Remarks on the Foundations of Mathematics*, 3rd ed. (Blackwell, Oxford, 1978), 99. For elaboration, see G. P. Baker and P. M. S. Hacker, 'Grammar and Necessity' in *Wittgenstein: Rules, Grammar and Necessity* (Blackwell, Oxford, corrected edition, 1992), 263–349.

show that it is an *a priori* science, any more than the fact that it can be done peripatetically shows that it is an *a posteriori* one. It is not a *science* of any kind, not even in the Pickwickian sense in which mathematics might be said to be. But the fact that philosophy is not an *a priori* science does not mean that it is not an *a priori* investigation. The distinction between a priori investigations and empirical ones is categorial. Hence it is as deep as any categorial gulf. No philosophical question can be answered by scientific enquiry, and no scientific discovery can be made by philosophical investigation. Philosophy can reveal the incoherence, not the falsity, of a scientific claim.

6. Philosophy and linguistic investigation

Philosophy is a conceptual investigation by means of which philosophical questions are answered, or shown to be confused or incoherent. In order to answer or dissolve philosophical questions, the relevant concepts have to be examined, the presuppositions of their employment brought into view, their logico-grammatical relationships spelled out, the conceptual field within which they are embedded characterized, the human needs they fulfil specified, and the behavioural and cultural contexts in which they are at home described. But concepts are no more than abstractions from the uses of symbols, and concept-possession is no more than mastery of the use of concept-expressing symbols. So a conceptual investigation is inevitably and unsurprisingly also an investigation into the uses of words, phrases and sentences.

Linguistic investigations pertinent to philosophical enterprises are, however, very different from those of linguists. Language is the subject matter of linguistics. It is not the subject matter of philosophy. Of course, philosophy of language concerns itself with the conceptual network formed by such concepts as *word, sentence, meaning, understanding, truth, reference, predication, description, quantification*, and so forth. Philosophy of language is indeed about the nature of language – also about the concept of language and about aspects of the use of the word 'language'; and so forth. But philosophy in general is not. Philosophy's general concern with language is twofold. First, confusions and unclarities of one kind or another about the uses of words, phrases and sentences is *one* source, a *major* source, of philosophical puzzlement and confusion. Secondly, describing the uses of words is *one* method, a *major* method, for answering or dissolving philosophical questions, for removing philosophical puzzlement and eradicating conceptual incoherence.

Moreover, the aspects of the uses of words, and indeed the very words and phrases, that interest philosophers are, by and large, very different from those that interest linguists. It is of little interest to a linguist to investigate whether, and in what sense, one can say that events move, or whether it makes any sense to speak of visual sensations, or whether the term 'person' is a substance-noun. The linguistic investigations that are pertinent to philosophy in general are precisely those that shed light on philosophical problems, which are not usually of concern to linguists. Furthermore, by contrast with linguistics, no theories are involved in, and no *new* linguistic information is relevant to, the philosophical description of the uses of words – merely reminders of the familiar, and realization of the obvious. How can this be?

Philosophy is concerned with questions that require, for their resolution or dissolution, the clarification of concepts and conceptual networks. But, apart from the philosophies of the special sciences, most of the concepts that need to be thus clarified are ordinary ones, familiar to any mature speaker of the language, expressed by such words as 'know', 'believe', 'doubt', 'certainty', 'mind', 'body', 'thought', 'understanding', 'true' and 'false', 'good' and 'evil', 'beautiful' and 'ugly'. These concepts are constituted by the sense-determining rules for the use of the words that express them. These are rules that we follow in our daily discourse. They determine the meanings of the words we use. So we are perfectly familiar with them – otherwise we would not understand what we say or know what we mean.

It is important not to conceive of such rules in too formal a manner – we are not dealing with the rules of a calculus, nor yet with regimented grammar or lexicography, let alone with rules inaccessible to consciousness 'buried deep within the mind/brain' (as Chomsky and his followers put it). Rather, we are concerned with the familiar rules of a human practice which all normal human beings master. Their mastery of the practice is exhibited in their uses of words in sentences, in the contextualized explanations which they give, or would accept, of what they mean and of what the words thus used mean. Sense-determining rules for the use of words can be given in various forms. They are not necessarily expressed by a meta-linguistic assertion. They may be expressed by such utterances as 'Vixens are female foxes', which is used as a definition. The meaning-determining rules that are the business of philosophy are commonly expressed by a priori propositions that look like descriptions but are normative in function.[17] So, for

---

[17] I use the term 'normative' to signify what pertains to a rule (a norm), expresses a rule or is rule-governed.

example, 'Understanding is an ability, not a mental state or process' is tantamount to the grammatical explanation that to say that someone understands something is not to say what mental state he is in or what process is taking place in his mind, but to indicate something he can do. Similarly, the statement that red is a colour, employed as an explanation of meaning, amounts to specifying the rule that anything that can be said to be red can be said to have a colour, just as the explanation 'That ☞ ☐ is white' supplies a rule for the use of the word 'white', namely that anything that is *that* ☞ ☐ colour can be said to be white. They may be articulated by explicative utterances such as 'A proposition is true if things are as the proposition describes them as being' – which is an explanation of a salient aspect of the use of the truth predicate. Exclusionary rules may be expressed by modal propositions about what cannot be the case. Despite looking like descriptions of *de re* necessities, these are tantamount to asserting that there is no such thing as ... For example, 'Nothing can be both red all over and green all over' is tantamount to 'There is no such thing as being both red all over and green all over'. And that in turn is equivalent to saying that it is senseless to predicate these two predicates of the same object at the same time, i.e. that this conjunction is a form of words that is excluded from the language. These, and many other forms of sentence, even though they may not appear to be expressions of rules, are in fact employed normatively. Their typical (although not uniform) role is to provide standards of correctness for the use of an expression and licenses for specific inferences.

The rules for the use of words that are of philosophical relevance cannot be unknown to speakers. For one cannot guide oneself by reference to unknown rules, and one cannot use unknown rules as standards of correctness. It would be absurd to suppose that we must wait upon future discoveries by linguists, logicians or philosophers in order to find out what we mean by the words we use and by the sentences we utter. We are not parrots, that emit words without understanding. We speak and know what we thereby say. To learn to speak is to learn to act, and our acts of speech are, for the most part, done knowingly and for a purpose. We can say what we mean and, other things being equal, what we mean and what the words we utter mean in the context of utterance coincide. So the logico-grammatical observations that are to be mustered in order to resolve philosophical problems must be news from nowhere. Indeed, one might say, with only a little exaggeration, that in philosophy, 'If it's news, it's wrong'. It is no news that events occur, happen and take place, but do not *exist*; that they have no coloured surfaces but may emit a smell or make a noise;

that there are colourful events, but no coloured ones; that they have phases, but no spatial parts; and so on.

If a salient method of philosophical clarification consists in no more than reminding people of the way in which they use words, then it may seem mysterious that the problems of philosophy are not solved with the greatest of ease. If every intelligent speaker of the language is perfectly familiar with the sense-determining rules for the use of the words he uses, and if these rules are *a* key to resolving philosophical problems, then it may seem that any intelligent speaker ought to be able to resolve such problems *ad libitum*. But it is not so. Why not?

Every competent speaker of the language has, by definition, mastered the use of the ordinary (non-technical) expressions of his language. Every English speaker knows, for example, how to use the words 'nearly' and 'almost'. But few are able, off the cuff, to identify the differences in their use, namely: that they behave differently under negation. Nevertheless, every speaker will notice that the sentence 'Although there were a hundred students already seated, the lecture room wasn't almost full' is ungrammatical. The criteria for knowing what an expression means consist of correct use (and recognition of incorrect use), intelligent responses to use, and giving correct explanations of the meaning of the expression in utterances in given contexts. But mastery of use does not imply mastery of *comparative use*. To have mastered the uses of 'nearly' and 'almost' one does not have to have reflected on their similarities and differences. Nor does mastery of the technique of use of an expression mean that one can readily describe the complex relationships between it and the uses of related expressions in the web of words that one takes for granted in one's normal linguistic activities. *A fortiori*, it does not imply that one can order the expressions and types of expression whose use one has mastered so that light will be shed upon conceptual problems. But it is precisely these skills that are necessary for resolving philosophical problems.

The differences between 'nearly' and 'almost' are of no philosophical interest. The differences and relationships between the uses of the expressions 'the mind' and 'the body', and 'my mind' and 'my body', are of the greatest philosophical moment. Everyone knows how to use phrases in which the word 'mind' occurs – for example, to make up one's mind, to be in two minds whether to do something, to have a mind of one's own, to call something to mind, to have a thought at the back of one's mind, to have an enquiring mind, and so forth. But when confronted with the question of what the mind is, of what it is to have a mind, we are typically at a loss. For mastery of use does not require mastery of a synopsis of use. We all speak of our own and of other people's bodies. We are proud of our graceful body, complain about our aching body, are pleased with our healthy body, dislike having a sweaty and dirty body – and so forth. But when confronted with the question of what it is to *have* a body, how the body one *has* is related to the body one *is*, what it is that *has* both a body and a mind, we stumble and lose our grip on these familiar expressions. For mastery of their use does not require an overview of use. But that is precisely what is needed for the solution and dissolution of philosophical problems.

Philosophical understanding consists in possessing an *overview* of a conceptual network that one can bring to bear upon philosophical problems in such a manner that they dissolve, or are answered by a description of the relationships between parts of the network. To put the same point slightly differently, as both Wittgenstein and Ryle did, it consists in the mastery of the logical geography of concepts in a given domain. If one can describe the conceptual landscape, then one can (a) select from, and (b) order, the familiar grammatical rules for the uses of expressions, and (c) present a comparative morphology of uses, in a surveyable representation that will shed light upon the philosophical question, puzzlement or confusion at hand. The ordering of what we know is an ordering of the rules for the uses of expressions with which we are perfectly familiar. The comparative morphology consists, for example, in comparing the familiar use of the problematic expression with that of expressions with which it is commonly wrongly conflated, in order to highlight differences. It is noteworthy that in philosophy we already have *all* the information we need to solve our problems. No new information is required – only reminders of the familiar. If we do not solve our problems, it is not due to lack of information, but to lack of insight. The difficulty, the *immense* difficulty, is to bring into view the right aspects of usage – right for the purposes at hand; and to make the right comparisons that will bring out overlooked differences and unexpected similarities; and then to order all these in the right way – the way that will illuminate the problem, and resolve or dissolve it.

It is as if we were confronted by a pointillist painting from close up. We can see all the coloured dots, but cannot stand back to see the pattern. With the greatest effort, we can move our heads a little, and discern (and often only think we discern) a small fragment of the picture. Only the greatest geniuses, such as Plato and Aristotle, or Kant and Wittgenstein, have the ability to stand back and to see – unclearly – a significant part of the pattern, which they then describe. That is one reason why we need to study the history of philosophy.

7. Philosophical understanding: elaboration and qualification

That philosophy is a quest for understanding, rather than for knowledge, needs elaboration and qualification. It is correct to say that philosophy cannot discover new empirical truths about the world around us and can offer no theories about it on the model of the theories of the sciences. It is also correct to say that philosophy cannot discover metaphysical truths about the world – for there are none to discover (as we have seen, what masquerade as metaphysical truths are *at best* no more than norms of representation in deceptive guise). However, is it really true to say that in doing philosophy we never come to know things we did not already know? After all, it is not true that everyone who has mastered the use of event-designators knows how the movement of objects differs from the movement of events. Nor is it true that everyone knows that to have a body or to have a mind is not to *possess* anything – even though one can sell one's body and lose one's mind.

Nevertheless, in so far as philosophy provides knowledge *in this sense*, the form of knowledge, unlike that achieved by the natural sciences, is not that of observation, detection or experimental discovery, but of *realization*. And the object of knowledge is not an empirical truth, but a normative feature of our linguistic practices – of our form of representation (and hence too, an aspect of our concepts, and an internal property or relation of things). But philosophy does not teach us any new logico-grammatical nexus; we learn no new rules of inference; by contrast with the enlargement of mathematical knowledge by means of new proofs, the conceptual structure we operate remains exactly the same as before. That is why the achievement is best characterized as a contribution to understanding rather than to knowledge. For we achieve a deeper understanding of our conceptual scheme, a better grasp of its reticulations and of the comparative morphology of its elements, that enables us to avoid the confusions to which we are prone. We realize that, *of course*, this is the way we use these words, that, *of course*, this is how the uses of these apparently similar words (e.g. 'to have a bodkin' and 'to have a body') differ, and the uses of those apparently different words (e.g. 'to sell one's body' and 'to sell sexual services') are similar. The consequences of such realization can be dramatic – light dawns over the conceptual landscape. One sees the road through the woods. And one sees why one took the wrong turning and ended in a morass. That is why the characteristic reaction to an advance in scientific knowledge is 'Goodness me, who would have thought of that!', whereas the characteristic response to a philosophical insight is '*Of course*, I should have thought of that!'

It is true to say that philosophy does not explain phenomena as the sciences do. By contrast with theories in the empirical sciences, there is nothing hypothetical about the conceptual clarifications and elucidations of philosophy. The empirical sciences may postulate entities in order to explain observed phenomena, and go on to validate such conjectures. Philosophy, by contrast, cannot legitimately postulate entities, such as simple natures, noumena, or universals, in order to explain the a priori natures of things, or the structure of our conceptual scheme, or our uses of language. Nor is there room in philosophy for deducing the existence of such entities, on the model of inferences to the best explanation in the sciences.[18] Nevertheless, there is much that philosophy can and does explain. It explains, *by description*, how the various elements in the web of concepts are woven together. It explains why forms of words that at first blush appear to make sense do not, or why forms of words that appear to fulfil a given role actually fulfil an utterly different one. It explains the sources of conceptual puzzlement and confusion. And it explains how to eradicate such confusions. These explanations are *logico-grammatical* or *conceptual*.

Does philosophy not result in conceptual truths – and is that not a cognitive achievement? That would be misleading. Many of the conceptual truths in question, for example: that we know of the existence of objects in the world around us by the use of our eyes and ears – are news from nowhere. No one would have the effrontery to claim that among the cognitive achievements of philosophy is the discovery that our knowledge of other people's states of mind is warranted by what they do and say. Philosophical achievement does not consist in presenting such logico-grammatical trivialities, but in showing that the apparently powerful reasons for denying that we can know such things on the basis of such grounds are spurious. Other conceptual truths have less of an air of triviality, for example, that memory is

---

[18]   That, I believe, is what Wittgenstein meant by his obscure remark in *Investigations* §599 'In philosophy no inferences are drawn [*werden kein Schlüsse gezogen*]. "But it must be like this!" is not a philosophical proposition.' He did not mean that there are no inferences in philosophical discussion and argument, but that in philosophy one cannot infer the existence of entities on the model of inferences to the best explanation in the empirical sciences. Hence it is illegitimate in philosophy to infer that simple objects, or noumena, or universals, *must exist* on the grounds that if they did not exist then we wouldn't be able to . . .

knowledge retained, and need not be *of* the past; or that the beneficial for artefacts is preventive but for animals also augmentive; or that the imagination is an ability to think up possibilities. Such truths pinpoint adjacent nodes in the web of concepts. We realize that they are true when our attention is drawn to these normative connections between concepts, but they would not otherwise have occurred to most of us. Yet others are even further removed from the obvious – for example, that the limits of thought are the limits of the possible expression of thought, so that the limits of intelligible (true *or* false) ascription of thinking to a non-language using animal is fixed by the animal's behavioural repertoire; or that arithmetic is not a science of the relationships between numbers, but a system of interwoven rules for the transformation of empirical propositions about magnitudes, quantities, etc.; or that the conception of God as an omnipotent, omniscient and benevolent creator is incoherent. Here too we are dealing with realization – but what we have in view is not merely adjacent nodes in the web of our concepts, but a large and ramifying network. To take it in, to grasp the complex conceptual relationships that are thus articulated requires one to discern a pattern that cannot readily be detected, but rather comes into view only when the right logico-grammatical features are deployed in an appropriate manner, when the right analogies are arrayed and the illuminating disanalogies marshalled. Of course, these conceptual truths are not statements of fact. They are descriptions of normative connections within the web of concepts that constitute our form of representation. They are said to be true. Indeed, they are often said to be necessary truths. That, of course, is correct – but misleading. Their truth is akin to that of the proposition that the king in chess moves one square at a time. What we realize when a philosophical insight dawns on us is *a feature of our form of representation*. We attain an understanding of the way in which our familiar modes of description of things hang together.

A final important qualification and elaboration: the picture that I have presented is tailored to theoretical philosophy, i.e. to general analytic philosophy ('descriptive metaphysics' as Strawson misleadingly called it), to epistemology, philosophy of language, philosophy of logic, and philosophical psychology. But although the same kind of intellectual activity is appropriate in practical philosophy (moral, political and legal philosophy), other factors come into play. It is not the business of theoretical philosophy to introduce a better, logically or conceptually more perfect, language – if indeed there is any such thing. Its business is to describe our existing conceptual scheme, not to improve it, to disentangle the knots we tie in it, not to weave a new web. For the problems that plague us are rooted in the language we have, and they can be solved or resolved only by its systematic logico-grammatical description. The only concepts it can fruitfully introduce are new, technical, classificatory concepts within philosophy itself, such as concepts of inductive and deductive reasoning, of *a priori* and *a posteriori* judgements, of species and genus, of determinates and determinables – the purpose of which is to facilitate logical geography. But in practical philosophy there *is* room for the introduction of novel first-order concepts and for the remoulding of existing concepts. Concepts of rights (both moral and legal), of sovereignty, of the nation state, of international law, etc., have been introduced by philosophers and then moulded by fruitful dialogue over centuries between lawyers and legal and political philosophers. Similarly, concepts of liberty, justice, and democracy that were refined and elaborated by philosophical argument, have informed political debate and stimulated political and constitutional reform. Here, in the domain of the rules under which we live, and the rule-governed organization of societies in which we live, the development of the most illuminating, useful, and practical concepts to describe and *prescribe* normative relationships has been an integral part of philosophical reflection.

One might wonder what explains this difference between theoretical and practical philosophy. It is, I think, a corollary of the fact that at the heart of practical philosophy lie our evolving conceptions of the values which we should pursue, the norms to which we should conform, and the virtues to which we should aspire. The concepts of concern to theoretical philosophy are employed primarily in the description and explanation of what is (or is not) actually the case. But the central concepts that engage our attention in practical philosophy articulate our conception of the ideal – of what we ought to be and what we ought to do.

It is, therefore, hardly surprising that practical philosophy has a further task that has no parallel in theoretical philosophy. Since the time of Socrates, philosophers have undertaken the task of rational reflection upon the ways in which human beings should live their lives and organize their societies, of distinguishing the different values in human life and relationships, and of clarifying forms of justification and evaluation. Although conceptual clarification plays a role in such reflections, it is only part of the task. What remains is reasoned debate about the variety of values, their role in human lives, the ways of ordering them, of the incommensurability of values, of what is right and what is obligatory, of the nature of conflicts of duty and of the place of the virtues in human life.

Similarly, it falls to political and legal philosophy not only to clarify (and sometimes refashion) salient concepts in political and legal discourse, but also to reflect on the justifications of various forms of legal and political institutions and to recommend legal and constitutional arrangements suitable for rational beings living under the rule of law.

8. Can there be progress in philosophy?

If, in the sense explained, philosophy is not a cognitive discipline, can there be said to be progress in philosophy? Progress characterizes the sciences. But how can there be progress in a subject that has no subject matter in the manner of the sciences, and that adds nothing to human knowledge save for the realization of the ways in which various elements in our conceptual scheme hang together? Is lack of progress in philosophy not born out by the fact that problems that were discussed by Plato and Aristotle are still being discussed today?

There is no progress *on the model of the sciences*. In the sciences, knowledge is cumulative, and hierarchies of theories are constructed. In the natural sciences, advances in instrumentation make possible new factual discoveries, which lead to new questions, and that in turn leads to new theories that explain the phenomena. Advances in scientific theory and in instrumentation in turn generate advances in technology. Philosophy, however, is not hierarchical. It has no foundations. It erects no theoretical structures on the insights and conceptual clarifications it achieves. There is no instrumentation to aid observation and empirical discovery – but, of course, there is neither observation nor discovery. There is no technological spin-off from theories, since there are no theories that are validated in experience. Nor are there theorems that are proven and then applied to experience. No men are sent to the moon on the back of philosophical elucidations nor is anyone guided through the seas by the charts of logical geographers.

Nevertheless, there are three senses in which there can be progress in philosophy: discriminatory, analytic and therapeutic.

First, clearer distinctions are drawn between forms of reasoning, types of proposition, and kinds of concepts (*discriminatory progress*). We distinguish between deductive, inductive and other forms of reasoning, and thereby are able better to handle conceptual problems that arise out of different kinds of argument. We distinguish between the question of how a truth is learnt and what are its grounds, and so are able to separate questions that were once conflated. We distinguish between determinates and determinables, and between determinate-determinable relations and species-genus relationships. And so on.

P. M. S. Hacker

Progress, in this sense, often appears to be less than it really is. For such distinctions are rapidly taken for granted, and we forget that the articulate differentiation of inference patterns, proposition types and kinds of concepts are hard-won insights obtained from philosophical reflection. So the progress that has been made is sometimes not recognised for what it is.

Secondly, there is progress in the characterization and clarification of problem-generating concepts (*analytic progress*). There has been advance in the *philosophical* understanding of such concepts as truth, existence, probability, mind, person, goodness, rights, obligations, i.e. improvements in the descriptions of the conceptual network surrounding these pivotal, but problematic, concepts. And there has been advance in seeing what was awry with a variety of explanations advanced by past thinkers.

Thirdly, there have been advances in dissolving certain kinds of conceptual confusion (*therapeutic progress*). No longer *need* we puzzle ourselves over the question of whether our knowledge of necessary truths is innate or acquired, or whether the nature of substances is knowable or not, or whether the self is given in experience, presupposed by experience, or is transcendent. No longer *need* we strive to justify inductive reasoning, to prove the existence of the world, of universals, or of events. Here too progress is often not discerned, since *sometimes* the refuted arguments and the futile endeavours vanish from sight, and tempting pathways to illusion and confusion are permanently closed off and forgotten.[19]

Nevertheless, precisely because philosophy is a contribution to understanding and not to knowledge, these forms of progress may be *less* than they appear. For they are distinctly precarious, for two reasons.

First, a conceptual field may be partially illuminated for a generation or two, only to be cast into shadow again. For cultural innovations, technical or theoretical, occur (e.g. the invention of the computer, or of function-theoretic logic) and novel scientific theories are introduced (e.g. quantum mechanics, relativity theory), which cast long shadows over conceptual articulations previously clarified. That may require old ground to be traversed afresh from a new angle, as when the concept of mind needed to be clarified yet again in response to the temptation to conceive of the mind on a computational model, or the concept of natural language reconsidered in the light of the invention of the predicate calculus.

---

[19]   I should like to be able to add a fourth form of progress, namely in moral, political and legal philosophy. But that is a question that requires separate detailed treatment.

Second, if there can be progress of a kind that is not akin to progress in the sciences, so too there can be regress of a kind that does not occur in the sciences. Precisely because philosophy has no foundations, because it is not hierarchical, because it produces neither theories validated in experience nor theorems proven and then applied to experience, because it is not the basis for technology of any kind, distinctions may be lost from sight, methods of clarification may fall into disuse, and the skills they require may vanish. Distinctions that were clearly drawn may become muddied through a novel conundrum that is mishandled − as the insight that all *a priori* knowledge is of necessary truth became muddied by the confused idea that knowledge that the standard metre is a metre long is both *a priori* and contingent.[20] Old confusions may prove irresistible to a new generation (e.g. the attraction of talk concerning the self, mystification about consciousness, the allure of metaphysics, conceived as a science of objective necessities). For conceptual confusions are comparable to diseases − diseases of the intellect. They may be cured for one generation, but the virus may undergo mutation and reappear in even more virulent forms.

Precisely because philosophy is not a quest for knowledge but for understanding, what it achieves can no more be transmitted from generation to generation than virtue. Philosophical education can show the way to philosophical clarity, just as parents can endeavour to inculcate virtue in their children. But the temptations, both old and new, of illusion, mystification, arid scholasticism, scientism, and bogus precision fostered by logical technology may prove too great, and philosophical insight and overview may wane. Each generation has to achieve philosophical understanding for itself, and the insights and clarifications of previous generations have to be gained afresh.[21]

[20]   For the confusion, see S. Kripke, *Naming and Necessity* (Harvard University Press, Cambridge, Mass., 1972). 54−6. For its eradication, see G. P. Baker and P. M. S. Hacker, *Wittgenstein: Understanding and Meaning, Part 1 − the Essays* (Blackwell, Oxford, 2005), 'The standard metre', 189−99.

[21]   I am grateful to Hanoch Ben Yami, Jonathan Dancy, Anthony Kenny, Hans Oberdiek, Herman Philipse and David Wiggins for their comments on earlier drafts of this paper.

Can Philosophy be a Rigorous Science?

HERMAN PHILIPSE

1. Edmund Husserl's Dream of 'Philosophy as a Rigorous Science'

It is difficult to imagine that a Royal Institute of Physics would organize an annual lecture series on the theme 'conceptions of physics'. Similarly, it is quite improbable that a Royal Institute of Astronomy would even contemplate inviting speakers for a lecture series called 'conceptions of astronomy'. What, then, is so special about philosophy that the theme of this lecture series does not appear to be altogether outlandish? Is it, perhaps, that philosophy is the reflective discipline *par excellence*, so that the very nature of philosophy is a topic that belongs to its domain of investigations? Or is there something more serious at issue? Let me first tell you how the question concerning the nature of philosophy arose for me as a young student, and how I tried to answer it, quite naively, by endorsing Edmund Husserl's programme of turning philosophy into a rigorous science. In a second section, I shall offer three diagnoses of the fact that all such attempts seem to have failed. Finally, I'd like to say a few words on my own research agenda in philosophy and on a public function of philosophers.

When I studied philosophy on the European Continent during the years 1969–1976, in Leiden, Paris, and Cologne, the dominant school of thought still was the phenomenological movement, inaugurated by Edmund Husserl. Yet there was no lack of rivalry with other traditions. In The Netherlands, we also read Oxford philosophers, such as Austin, Dummett, Ryle, Strawson, or Hare, and Americans such as Quine or Davidson. We engaged in the fierce debates on the 'open society' between Karl Popper and the Frankfurter Schule, while the Continental – Analytic split was often discussed. In Paris, two triumvirates were adored by the masses of students of La Sorbonne (Paris I, Paris IV). One was the 'holy trinity of suspicion', consisting of Marx, Nietzsche, and Freud. However, many of the more self-consciously serious students preferred the other trinity: 'les trois H's': Hegel, Husserl, Heidegger.

doi:10.1017/S1358246109990099
Royal Institute of Philosophy Supplement **65** 2009

Herman Philipse

You will be able to imagine the abyss of intellectual confusion young students plunged into, when they eagerly read works of all these different philosophers, and attended lectures as diverse as those by Michel Foucault at the Collège de France, Emmanuel Levinas at Paris IV, or Jacques Derrida's interminable ruminations at the École Normale Supérieure. What was it all about? One was supposed to study philosophy, but was there a unified discipline bearing that name? When I moved from Oxford, where I had spent a Hilary Term during the winter of discontent (1973–1974), to Paris, it seemed to me that I had migrated from one intellectual universe to another. Whereas in Oxford one had to write essays and argue with one's tutor about quite precise philosophical problems, what counted in Paris was a vast intellectual erudition. Students were given the impression that one was without intellectual worth as long as one had not read all great philosophers from Plato to the present.

By hindsight I think that this type of methodological pluralism and academic peregrination produced a mental independence that perhaps one could not have acquired otherwise. As was the case in ancient Greece, critical thought often starts with travelling and making the discovery that different ideas about what counts as self-evident dominate the intellectual scene elsewhere. But at the time, the state of intellectual bewilderment and confusion I suffered from merely raised urgent questions to which I did not have an answer. Is philosophy a unified field of investigation? Do philosophers have at their disposal sound methods by means of which they can acquire real knowledge? Should one adopt the descriptive methods of phenomenology and endorse Husserlian *Wesensschau*, or was the austere analysis of language à la Austin the only – and quite modest – thing philosophers could achieve? Edmund Husserl once formulated the question as follows: can philosophy be a rigorous science (in the broad sense of *Wissenschaft*)? Or should we rather conclude that what is called 'philosophy' is a loosely knotted tapestry of opinions and schools, nothing but a contest of world views (*Weltanschauungen*), with no consensus about methods allowing us to decide who is right and who is wrong?

In Paris one could not escape the impression that the second conclusion was apt. I once stood up in one of the great Sorbonne amphitheatres during a plenary lecture by Henri Birault, a follower of Martin Heidegger, who had been talking for a while about Nietzsche's doctrine of the Will to Power. Exasperated by his lengthy and rhetorical exposition, I asked him whether he thought that the Nietzschean teaching that everything is will to power was true, or false, or meaningless. He answered me by addressing the audience at large, saying that 'votre camarade Hollandais' was asking a naive question, since Nietzsche had showed that the notion of truth is deeply suspect. Although I was impressed by French historians of philosophy such as Martial Gueroult or Ferdinand Alquié, whose seminars on Spinoza's *Ethics* I attended with enthusiasm, many philosophical celebrities of the day seemed to be more interested in dazzling rhetoric and in the alleged political implications of their views than in the truth of what they were saying.

In this condition of intellectual turmoil, I felt attracted to the humourless philosophical *Ernst* of Edmund Husserl, the founder of the phenomenological school to which my 'directeur d'études' Emmanuel Levinas claimed to belong. The French translation of Husserl's *Logische Untersuchungen* (1900/01) had been published by the Presses Universitaires the France in 1959–1963, and Levinas devoted a seminar to this seminal work in 1974–75.[1] The more my teacher criticized Husserl's texts, often taking Derrida's early book on Husserl *La voix et le phénomène* as his point of departure, the more I came to admire the rigour of Husserl's arguments, which could be defended quite easily against Derrida's and Levinas's criticisms.[2] I decided to write a doctorate on Husserl's early philosophy of logic, a decision which stimulated me to study also the important logicians of the turn of the century, such as Schröder, Frege, Peano, and Russell. Accordingly, I first went to the University of Cologne, which harboured a centre of Husserl studies, and then worked for a year in the Husserl Archives in Leuven, Belgium. The title of today's lecture is derived from that of an essay Husserl published in 1910/11, *Philosophie als strenge Wissenschaft*, which I have put in the interrogative form.

Initially I tended to believe Husserl's claim that philosophy can be a rigorous science or discipline (*strenge Wissenschaft*) if only one follows what he called the method of transcendental phenomenology. Husserl kept repeating that it is extremely difficult to practice this method, and he devoted all his later books, such as *Ideen zu einer reinen Phänomenologie* (*Ideas Pertaining to a Pure Phenomenology*) of 1913 or *Formale und transzendentale Logik* (*Formal and Transcendental Logic*) of 1929, to pointing out different 'roads' to

---

[1]   Edmund Husserl, *Recherches logiques*. Translated by Hubert Élie, Lothar Kelkel, and René Schérer. (Paris: Presses Universitaires de France, 1959–1963).

[2]   Jacques Derrida, *La voix et le phénomène*. (Paris: Presses Universitaires de France, 1967).

transcendental phenomenology, attempting to convince the readers that they had to perform what he called 'phenomenological' or 'transcendental reductions'. Yet the basic idea of Husserl's method is easy to convey, if one takes Kant's transcendental philosophy as a point of departure.

Kant held that mathematics and physics partly consist of synthetic *a priori* principles, which provide information about reality although they are not based upon experience. In order to explain how this is possible, Kant postulated that such propositions can be known a priori because they are generated by cognitive mechanisms in the knowing subject, and that they can be informative about empirical reality because the empirical world is subjectively constituted out of sense impressions or sensations (*Empfindungen*), which are processed by the very same subjective mechanisms that yield the synthetic a priori propositions. This celebrated 'Copernican revolution' effected by Kant implied that natural science is not about the world as it is in itself (*an sich*), but about a subjectively constituted phenomenal world. The theory also implied an embarrassing contradiction concerning things in themselves, which allegedly cause the sensations in us. Since Kant held that the principle of causality is a synthetic *a priori* proposition, its validity should be restricted to applications within the phenomenal world. How, then, could one claim that our sensations are caused by things in themselves?

Like many critics of Kant in a period when neo-Kantianism was fashionable, Husserl argued that the Kantian notion of a thing in itself is incoherent. As a consequence, he ended up with the Fichtean view that the subjectively constituted phenomenal world is the only material world there is. Since this world is constituted by transcendental subjectivity, it is ontologically dependent on it, so that Husserl became a radical transcendental idealist. His philosophical method can now be characterized as follows. Husserl pretended that by performing a number of 'transcendental reductions', we can become reflectively aware of the intentional mental acts by which our transcendental ego constitutes different types of entities, such as objects of sense perception, other persons, geometrical configurations, or numbers. By describing these mental acts of 'constitution' and their complex interweavings, we can elucidate the 'sense' in which entities of different types exist (their *Seinssinn*). By so doing we allegedly can solve all traditional ontological problems in philosophy.[3]

---

[3] Cf. Herman Philipse, 'Transcendental Idealism', in B. Smith and D. W. Smith, *The Cambridge Companion to Husserl* (Cambridge: Cambridge University Press, 1995), 239–322.

Can Philosophy be a Rigorous Science?

One cannot accuse Husserl of modesty. In his lectures on *First Philosophy* of 1923–24 and later in his essay on the *Crisis of the European Sciences* of 1936, he claimed that his transcendental phenomenology was the *telos* or goal of the entire tradition of Western philosophy, because it finally realized its dream of becoming a rigorous science (*strenge Wissenschaft*). Furthermore, transcendental phenomenology allegedly is foundational with respect to mathematics and all positive sciences, since it elucidates the ontological status of their objects. It is 'first philosophy' in Aristotle's sense and provides a *Letztbegründung* (ultimate foundation) to scientific knowledge. Finally, transcendental phenomenology also provides a philosophical justification of our longing for immortality, because, Husserl argued, the transcendental stream of consciousness goes on indefinitely.[4] Hence, transcendental phenomenology was held to deliver European culture from the crisis of relativism, positivism, and scepticism into which it had plunged during the interwar years.

You will wonder why I am telling you so much about a philosopher who published his most influential works between 1900 and 1936 and who is largely unknown in the United Kingdom. The reason is not only that my infatuation with Husserl produced my first great disappointment concerning a dream of a rigorous method in philosophy. The popularity of Husserl in Paris of the 1970s also tells you something about the influence of politics and fashion on even the most abstruse domains of philosophical thought. Although Husserl was a model assimilated Jew in Germany, having adopted the Christian faith in his student days and having been something of a conservative Bismarckian nationalist during the First World War, he suffered deeply from the ascent of Nazism between 1933 and his death in 1938. This latter fact explains why, after the Second World War, Husserl could be staged as a 'good' German philosopher. Husserl's library and the bulk of his stenograph manuscripts (some 45,000 pages) and letters had been rescued in 1938 from Germany and taken to Leuven, Belgium, by a courageous Belgian priest, father H. L. Van Breda, who founded the Husserl Archives in 1939. After U.N.E.S.C.O. decided to give financial support for the edition of Husserl's collected works, of which the first volume was published in 1950, a small Husserl industry flowered on the European Continent, and Husserl's ideas were widely discussed.

---

[4] Edmund Husserl, *Ideen zu einer reinen Phänomenologie und phänomenologischen Philosophie* (1913), translated as *Ideas Pertaining to a Pure Phenomenology and to a Phenomenological Philosophy. First Book* by F. Kersten (The Hague: Nijhoff, 1982), §§ 81 & 82.

Herman Philipse

My infatuation with Husserl's philosophy did not last long, however. While I was still studying the many thousands pages of Husserl's works, I was beset by doubts about his methodological pretensions. Let me mention four points. First, Husserl assumed, like Kant, the logical positivists, and many others, that the constitution of the perceived empirical world starts with sense impressions, sensations, or sense-data (*Empfindungen*), which we simply find in our stream of consciousness. Husserl argued, contrary to Franz Brentano, that perceptual sensations (colour-sensations, sound-sensations, smells, tactile sensations, etc.) are non-intentional mental occurrences, which we 'interpret' by an 'objectifying' intentional mental act, from which results a perception of something in space and time. But do we really find such perceptual sensations when we reflect on our stream of consciousness? Or is the very notion of perceptual sensations rather a posit of 'scientific' theories of perception first proposed in the seventeenth century?

Inspired by two books, Merleau Ponty's *La phénoménologie de la perception* (1945) and Austin's *Sense and Sensibilia* (published posthumously in 1962), I came to doubt the very meaningfulness of the traditional notion of perceptual sensations as the elementary building blocks of the perceived world. Sensations in the ordinary sense of the word are things that we feel, such as itches or pains, and there does not seem to be any such thing in visual perception, for example. But this doubt destroyed both the basis of Husserlian constitution, since Husserl argued that the objectifying intentional interpretation of sensations is the very basis of (nearly) all mental acts of constitution, and my belief in his reflective and purely descriptive method of phenomenology, for what he claimed to 'find' in the stream of consciousness was in fact a posit of dubious traditional theory construction.

A second point of doubt concerned Husserl's notion of eidetic intuition or *Wesensschau*, which he originally introduced in his *Logical Investigations* with regard to logic and mathematics. Assuming, like so many philosophers of mathematics, that this discipline acquires knowledge about *entities* of some type, he argued like Frege that these entities could be neither physical nor mental. They had to be essences, grasped by a special kind of mental operation which he called the intuition of essences (*Wesensschau*). Husserl then generalized these notions, like Plato had done, and argued that his transcendental phenomenology obtained knowledge of non-mathematical essences, which is synthetic a priori. Inspired by both Popper's and Wittgenstein's criticisms of essentialism, I came to reject this central tenet of Husserl's method. Attempts by Kripke, Putnam, and others in the 1970's, to rehabilitate the notion of essences as structures to be discovered by empirical science never convinced me for a number of reasons, which I shall not spell out here. In other words, I do not think that it is 'anachronistic to dismiss essentialism as anachronistic'.[5]

This second point of doubt automatically led to a third. Husserl had assumed that all problems of theoretical philosophy can be resolved by describing what he called the constitution of entities of different kinds, such as other minds or numbers. But this view seems to presuppose a specific interpretation of our use of numerals or of the word 'mind', which in the wake of Wittgenstein came to be called the 'Augustinian picture' of language or the 'referential fallacy'. Surely, when we say that there are ten people in this room, we refer to the room and to people. But are we also referring to yet a third type of entity, the number ten? Are words always used to refer? Surely not. I came to share the view of the later Wittgenstein that many philosophical problems are generated by misunderstanding our uses of language, and that we should deconstruct, rather than answer, philosophical questions such as 'what kind of entities are numbers?'

A fourth reason for rejecting Husserl's approach to philosophy was inspired by post-Kantian philosophy of science. Like Aristotle, Descartes, and Kant, Husserl had assumed that philosophy has the task of providing a foundation for the special sciences. But this view was completely outdated already in the 1920s, a point I come back to below. By the time I had completed my doctorate in 1982, I had rejected most of the claims Husserl made for his transcendental phenomenology as a result of these and other criticisms. The monumental edition of Husserl's collected works called *Husserliana* now seemed most impressive if interpreted as a memorial to illusions and wishful thinking in philosophy.

2. Philosophy as a Boulevard of Broken Dreams: Three Diagnoses

Edmund Husserl is not the only philosopher who claimed that he was the first to transform philosophy finally into a 'rigorous science'. As you all know, this pretension of being the first to found philosophy as a rigorous discipline is a recurrent theme or trope in the history of modern philosophy. We find it in Descartes' *Meditations*,

---

[5]   Timothy Williamson, 'Past the Linguistic Turn', in Brian Leiter, ed., *The Future for Philosophy* (Oxford: Oxford University Press, 2004), 111.

in Hume's *Treatise*, in Kant's first *Critique*, and in Hegel's *Phenomenology*. The nineteenth century is full of attempts, now largely forgotten, to put philosophy on the secure path of a science, for instance by philosophical naturalists or by positivists in the wake of August Comte. And the rhetoric of founding philosophy as a scientific enterprise for the first time in history did not disappear in the Twentieth century. Compare, for example, Hans Reichenbach's popular treatise on *The Rise of Scientific Philosophy*, published in 1951.

Although on the European Continent the English are still renowned for their understatements, the rhetoric of finally founding philosophy as a rigorous theoretical enterprise has become popular in Oxford quite recently, where it is used by occupants of the Wykeham Chair of Logic. My precursor in this lecture series, Peter Hacker, called it with his usual wit the 'Wykeham chair gambit'. Michael Dummett, Freddie Ayer's successor in the Wykeham Chair, proclaimed some thirty years ago that 'philosophy has only just very recently struggled out of its early stage into maturity'. He argued that philosophers have to construct collectively a systematic theory of meaning, which allegedly 'is the foundation of all the rest of philosophy'. And he claimed that 'the search for such a theory of meaning can take on a genuinely scientific character'.[6]

Dummett's successor but one in the Wykeham Chair, Timothy Williamson, professes in a similar vein that, perhaps, we have just arrived at 'the end of the beginning' of philosophy, pleading for rigorous methodological constraints in philosophical theory construction. He characterizes the 'opponents of systematic philosophical theorizing', who claim that we should not construct theories for answering questions if these questions are conceptually incoherent, as making 'a feeble and unnecessary surrender to despair, philistinism, cowardice or indolence'.[7] But he repudiates Dummett's idea that the primary task of philosophy is to construct a systematic theory of language.

---

[6]   M. A. E. Dummett, 'Can Analytic Philosophy be Systematic and Ought it to Be?', reprinted in *Truth and Other Enigmas* (London: Duckworth, 1978), 457, 442, 454. This text is also quoted by Hacker in his lecture in this series (see next note).

[7]   cf. P. M. S. Hacker, 'Philosophy: A Contribution to Human Understanding, not to Human Knowledge', this volume. T. Williamson, 'Must Do Better', in *The Philosophy of Philosophy* (Oxford: Blackwell, 2005), 278 and passim.

Can Philosophy be a Rigorous Science?

Endorsing criticisms of the linguistic turn in philosophy such as those put forward by Quine and Kripke, Professor Williamson also rejects the view that philosophy should be restricted to resolving philosophical problems by analyzing our linguistic forms of representation. To those who wonder by what methods philosophers might be able to acquire knowledge that goes *beyond* a reflective awareness of the logical grammar of our language, he answers by pointing to the recent revival of essentialism and claims:

> Although empirical knowledge constrains the attribution of essential properties, results are more often reached through a subtle interplay of logic and the imagination. The crucial experiments are thought experiments...

> [W]e should be open to the idea that thinking just as much as perceiving is a way of learning how things are. Although we do not fully understand *how* thinking can provide new knowledge, the cases of logic and mathematics constitute overwhelming evidence that it does so.[8]

Unfortunately, however, none of these attempts to put philosophy on the secure path of a rigorously scientific discipline ever acquired general endorsement in the community of philosophers. Even worse, none of them survived the demise of its author more than a few decades. We may predict the same fate for Professor Williamson's claim that we can acquire 'new knowledge' about 'how things are' by mere thinking or thought experiments. Indeed, the historical track record of mere thinking as a reliable method in philosophy for acquiring knowledge about how things are is not impressive. Williamson's stress on thought experiments strikingly resembles Husserl's method of *Wesensschau* by imaginative variation. Is it surprising that one gets a *déja-vu* experience when one reads such things?

It seems, then, that we may safely perform a pessimistic induction and conclude that philosophy will never be established as a rigorous science. The aspirations of philosophers of the past to transform philosophy into a decent scientific discipline, when collected in a historical survey, now seem to us nothing but a boulevard of broken dreams. Understandably, this pessimistic conclusion has inspired a general scepticism with regard to philosophy as such, even among philosophers. For example, Richard Rorty concluded from his critical analysis of the views of Sellars and Quine that epistemology-centered philosophy should not be conceived of as a distinct

---

[8]   T. Williamson, in Leiter (2004), 111 and 127.

discipline modeled upon the paradigm of empirical sciences or mathematics. Although Rorty saw no 'danger of philosophy's "coming to an end"', he did not tell us either what philosophy would be like in the future.[9]

The German philosopher Odo Marquard drew an even more radical conclusion in a lecture with the telling title 'Inkompetenzkompensationskompetenz?', held in Munich in 1973. He imagined a contest between Chinese executioners. Who could perform the most perfect beheading? The last finalist had to surpass an immaculate decapitation performed by his rival. He swept his sword through the neck of the condemned convict faster than anyone could perceive. Surprisingly, however, the head did not fall and the convict looked up with amazement. Then the executioner smiled affably and said '*Nicken Sie mal*' (just nod). According to Marquard, present-day philosophy is like the thoughts of this convict before he nods.[10]

How can it be, one might wonder, that in a time of unsurpassed scientific progress and rapid specialization, philosophy is in a permanent crisis about its own identity? How should we explain the fact that the numerous attempts to put philosophy upon the secure path of a scientific discipline have failed? Let me briefly mention and evaluate three different diagnoses of this phenomenon.

A first diagnosis is the mother-of-the-sciences conception. The word 'philosophy' originally meant simply each and every search for truth. Whenever this search in a particular domain acquired methodological maturity and results began to accumulate, that domain split off and became an independent scientific discipline. As a consequence, it is not true that philosophy never became a rigorous science. What is true is that whenever a part of philosophy became a scientific discipline, it was not called 'philosophy' any more. This happened to physics in the seventeenth century, to chemistry in the eighteenth, to psychology in the nineteenth, and to cosmology at the beginning of the twentieth. So, the term 'philosophy' as we use it is just a label for immature proto-scientific speculations. All issues that are 'philosophical' today will duly be

---

[9]   Richard Rorty, *Philosophy & the Mirror of Nature* (Princeton: Princeton University Press, 1980), 394. Cf. Herman Philipse, 'Towards a Postmodern Conception of Metaphysics: On the Genealogy and Successor Disciplines of Modern Philosophy', *Metaphilosophy* **25** (1994), 1–44.

[10]   Odo Marquard, 'Inkompetenzkompensationskompetenz', in *Abschied vom Prinzipiellen* (Universal-Bibliothek Nr. 7724, Stuttgart: Philip Reclam jun., 1987), 23–38.

transformed into scientific questions. Marquard would add, however, that by now the womb of philosophy as the mother-of- the-sciences is quite empty.[11]

There is much truth in this first diagnosis. For example, philosophers before Kant used to speculate about the age and size of the universe. Although Kant argued critically that such issues are beyond the reach of human knowledge, they became scientific questions when Einstein, De Sitter, and Lemaître started to apply general relativity theory to the universe as a whole. Nevertheless, there are three reasons why the mother-of-the-sciences diagnosis cannot be the complete story.

First, not all philosophical questions can be transformed into scientific ones. Take, for example, questions of normative ethics, which is a sub-discipline of philosophy. Science can tell us much about what should be our instrumental norms, that is, what means we should use in order to attain specific morally valuable ends. But can questions about ultimate moral ends or values also be transformed into scientific questions? Most philosophers deny this on conceptual grounds, even though the sociobiologist Edward O. Wilson once wrote that 'the time has come for ethics to be removed temporarily from the hands of the philosophers and biologized'.[12]

Second, the sciences that emancipated themselves from philosophy gave rise to new philosophical questions, which are not and cannot be fully absorbed into these scientific disciplines. Physical theories such as general relativity or quantum mechanics sparked off intriguing questions about the status of postulated entities, such as relativistic space-time. And formal logic, once absorbed into mathematics, generated puzzling questions about the relationship between

---

[11]   This was largely Marquard's view, and it is to be found in many authors. Cf., for example, Bertrand Russell, *The Problems of Philosophy* (Oxford: Oxford University Press, 1959), 90: 'Thus, to a great extent, the uncertainty of philosophy is more apparent than real: those questions which are already capable of definite answers are placed in the sciences, while those only to which, at present, no definite answer can be given, remain to form the residue which is called philosophy'. Russell added, however, that philosophy also raises important questions that will always remain without scientific answers, and that it should 'keep alive that speculative interest in the universe which is apt to be killed by confining ourselves to definitely ascertainable knowledge' (90–91).

[12]   At least, Wilson wrote that scientists and humanist should consider this. See his *Sociobiology. The Abridged Edition* (Cambridge, Mass.: Harvard University Press, 1975), 287.

formal-logical calculi on the one hand and natural languages on the other hand. As a consequence, many special sciences are accompanied by philosophical sub-disciplines such as the philosophy of psychology, the philosophy of logic, or the philosophy of law.

The third reason for thinking that the mother-of-the-sciences diagnosis cannot be the whole story is that one of its essential assumptions is false. This assumption is that the distinction between philosophy proper and scientific disciplines such as physics, astronomy, psychology, or theoretical linguistics was made only quite recently, that is, during and after the scientific revolution in the seventeenth century. In fact, however, this distinction was made already by Aristotle in his *Posterior Analytics* and elsewhere.

Aristotle distinguished between particular scientific disciplines, such as physics, astronomy, or psychology, which he called 'second philosophies', and philosophy proper, which he called 'first philosophy', and which his successors baptized 'metaphysics'. This Aristotelian distinction and his concomitant conception of first philosophy, which allegedly is both a universal discipline and the foundation of the special sciences, deeply influenced the philosophical tradition up till Descartes, the early Hume, Kant, the neo-Kantians, Edmund Husserl, Bertrand Russell, the early Heidegger, and even Michael Dummett, who claimed that a general theory of meaning is 'the foundation for all the rest of philosophy'. But if the distinction between (first) philosophy and the special sciences (second philosophies) is as old as Aristotle, it cannot be the case that the mother-of-the-sciences diagnosis is correct for philosophy proper, that is, first philosophy or metaphysics.

This is why a second diagnosis is needed of the fact that philosophy has never managed to become a rigorous science: a diagnosis that explains why first philosophy or metaphysics has never managed to do so. To put it briefly, this second diagnosis is that the very idea of first philosophy or metaphysics is mistaken, among other reasons because it is based upon an inadequate conception of the special sciences. According to Aristotle and many later philosophers, theories in the special sciences ideally should have the logical structure of an axiomatic-deductive system, such as that of geometry in Euclid's *Elements*. It was further assumed that our knowledge of the axioms should be more secure than that of the theorems derived from them, and that apart from domain-specific axioms or postulates, each scientific discipline also presupposes some general axioms about reality as such. First philosophy or metaphysics was conceived of as a theory about reality as such, which would function as a foundation for the special sciences, providing them with their general axioms. Philosophers often thought that they had reliable non-empirical methods at their disposal that would enable them to construe such a general theory of reality without having to engage into empirical research. Methods such as Cartesian clear and distinct intuitions, Kantian transcendental reconstruction, Husserlian *Wesensschau* or Professor Williamson's thought experiments.

However, this conception of first philosophy is flawed, as was brought to light by developments both in mathematics and in physics. Why exactly it was flawed has been shown extensively by logical positivists such as Carnap and Reichenbach, who argued against the German neo-Kantians. In mathematics, the construction of consistent non-Euclidean geometries in the nineteenth century deeply changed our understanding of the epistemological status of axiomatic systems. We do not think any more that, for example, the axiom of parallels in Euclidean geometry is a necessary truth which holds for space as such, as Newton and Kant had assumed. Rather, together with the other axioms it defines a certain conception of space, or a representational system for spatial relations, which can be applied to reality only if it is provided with physical interpretations of its geometrical terms. And in physics, the theoretical revolutions of general relativity and quantum mechanics showed that metaphysical dogmas of philosophers can be disregarded by physics, dogmas such as the truth of Euclidean geometry or a deterministic principle of causality. In other words, the theories of physics do not stand in need of a philosophical foundation, which provides them with meta-physical first principles. And the very idea that philosophers can acquire substantial knowledge about reality by non-experimental methods turned out to be an illusion.

If we conjoin these two explanations of the fact that philosophy has never become a rigorous science, it may seem at first sight that we get a complete picture. To the extent that philosophy had always been distinguished from the special sciences as first philosophy or metaphysics, its very conception was mistaken. And to the extent that philosophy consisted of proto-scientific speculations, the mother-of-the-sciences diagnosis is correct. Nevertheless, the picture is not complete. For, as we saw, new special sciences often beget new philosophical problems, and old metaphysical questions as to the nature of substance, universals, or numbers pop up again and again. With regard to these philosophical problems, which do not seem to be amenable to empirical methods of investigation, I endorse a third diagnosis. It, and the concomitant positive conception of philosophy, have been defended forcefully in this lecture series by Peter Hacker from St. John's College, Oxford, so that I can be brief.

According to this third diagnosis, traditional philosophers misinterpreted the nature of many paradigmatic philosophical problems:

> When bombarded throughout the ages with incompatible claims about the subject and unfulfilled promises of how this is going to be set right, the correct move is to challenge the fundamental assumption that is taken for granted by all participants in the debate, namely the assumption that philosophy is a cognitive discipline.[13]

But if philosophy, as far as many of its core problems are concerned, should not be seen as a cognitive discipline, which aspires to acquiring knowledge about the world, how should it be conceived of?

Inspired by the later Wittgenstein, the logical positivists, and Oxford philosophers such as Ryle or Austin, Hacker defends the view that philosophers should aim at acquiring a specific type of understanding. Their proper activity is to clarify conceptual structures, both of ordinary language and of mathematics and the sciences. Their legitimate aim is to curb the tendency of language users, including scientists, to transgress the bounds of sense. For example, '[e]xplaining that alternative geometries are not alternative theories of space but alternative grammars for the description of spatial relationships contributes to a better understanding of the enterprise of geometry'.[14] We find many conceptual confusions in the works of cognitive scientists, for instance, where they misinterpret the results of their empirical investigations due to confusions between everyday psychological terminology and the terminology of brain sciences, thereby producing scientific mythologies.[15] It is the proper business of philosophy to criticize such mythologies by elucidating the linguistic confusions that produce them.

There are many misunderstandings about this analytical conception of philosophy, according to which philosophy is an a priori conceptual investigation of a specific kind. For example, some critics say that it is an armchair exploration of empirical languages,

---

[13]   P. M. S. Hacker, 'Philosophy: A Contribution to Human Understanding, not to Human Knowledge', this volume, 7.
[14]   Ibid, 7. Cf. for example, Hans Reichenbach, *Philosophie der Raum-Zeit-Lehre* (*The Philosophy of Space and Time*) of 1928.
[15]   Cf. M. R. Bennett and P. M. S. Hacker, *Philosophical Foundations of Neuroscience* (Oxford: Blackwell Publishing, 2003).

which should be transformed into a branch of empirical linguistics.[16] Others claim that it has been refuted by Quine's criticism of the analytic/synthetic distinction, or that it implies a sterile conceptual conservatism. In his lecture and elsewhere, Dr. Hacker effectively dispels these misconceptions, and I shall not repeat what he said.[17] Yet I want to illustrate by one example the inconclusive manner in which a Wittgenstein-style conception of philosophy is criticized by some present-day philosophers.

In a paper called 'Past the Linguistic Turn?', Timothy Williamson intended to refute the view that (all) traditional metaphysical questions should be resolved or dissolved by conceptual analysis.

> Dummett claimed... that the way to answer [the traditional questions of metaphysics] was by the analysis of thought and language. For example, in order to determine whether there are numbers, one must determine whether number words such as '7' function semantically like proper names in the context of sentences uttered in mathematical discourse. But what is it so to function? Devil words such as 'Satan' appear to function semantically like proper names in the context of sentences uttered in devil-worshipping discourse, but one should not jump to the conclusion that there are devils. However enthusiastically devil-worshippers use 'Satan' as thought it referred to something, that does not make it refer to something. Although empty names appear to function semantically like referring names in the context of sentences uttered by those who believe the names to refer, the appearances are deceptive. 'Satan' refers to something if and only if some sentence with 'Satan' in subject position (...) expresses a truth, but the analysis of thought and language may not be the best way to discover whether any such sentence is indeed true.[18]

The implied conclusion seems to be that in order to discover whether, in general, there are numbers, we have to investigate some kind of reality instead of analyzing how numerals are used. But Williamson's argument contains a fallacy of ambiguity, since it

---

[16]   Daniel Dennett, 'Philosophy as Naive Anthropology', in Maxwell Bennett et al. *Neuroscience and Philosophy* (New York: Columbia University Press, 2007) 80–86.

[17]   Cf. also the discussion between Hacker, Searle, and Dennett, in Maxwell Bennett et al. (2007), 73–162, and the appendix on Searle in Bennett & Hacker (2003), 436–443.

[18]   Timothy Williamson in B. Leiter (2004), 111–112.

mixes up two different distinctions. One is the distinction between successful reference and unsuccessful reference. By using the name 'Timothy' I may refer successfully to Timothy Williamson, but if Satan does not exist, I cannot refer successfully to Satan by using the name 'Satan'. The other distinction is the one between referential uses of words and non-referential uses of words. Surely, only if a word is used referentially it makes sense to engage in an investigation as to whether an entity exists that corresponds to the word used in a sentence, with the further aim of discovering whether the assertion made by using the sentence is true or false. Hence, a linguistic analysis concerning the former issue logically precedes an investigation concerning the latter.[19] Only if 'Satan' is used referentially, it makes sense to engage into an investigation in order to find out whether Satan exists.

Edmund Husserl thought that the words 'and' and 'or' are used referentially. As a consequence, he looked for elements or aspects of reality corresponding to these words and he tried to trace phenomenologically the 'constitution' of these elements. However, the logical constants 'and' and 'or' are not used referentially. Husserl was mistaken, not primarily about what exists, but about the logical grammar of the words 'and' and 'or'. Quite a few philosophers of mathematics assume that number words such as '7' are used referentially in the sense that they must refer to entities of some kind. Then they go on to wonder what kind of queer entities numbers are, and by what superior intuition mathematicians are able to know these queer entities. But if number words only *seem* to be used referentially in this sense, whereas conceptual analysis can show that they are not, such questions are misguided products of conceptual confusion.

Many philosophers, such as Karl Popper or John Searle, hold that it is futile to engage in debates about the nature of philosophy. Admittedly, the term 'philosophy' does not stand for some essence, so that one may risk becoming embroiled in verbal disputes when one discusses the nature of philosophy.[20] We should also admit that

---

[19]   Elsewhere, Williamson seems to agree with this point, for in his (2007), 284–5 he writes: 'Philosophers who refuse to bother about semantics, on the grounds that they want to study the non-linguistic world, not our talk about that world, resemble scientists who refuse to bother about the theory of their instruments, on the grounds that they want to study the world, not our observations of it'.

[20]   Cf. Karl Popper, 'The Nature of Philosophical Problems and their Roots in Science', in *Conjectures and Refutations* (4th edition, London: Routledge and Kegan Paul, 1972), 66–96. Cf. Herman Philipse, 'The Nature of Philosophical Problems: Popper versus Wittgenstein', in *Karl*

quite often debates about this theme tend to be fruitless because they merely express preferences for different research agendas.[21] Yet, I would not have accepted the invitation to give this lecture if I had agreed entirely with Popper and Searle. One reason why discussions of the nature of philosophy may be useful is that philosophers often have pursued imaginary research agendas, such as the project of Aristotle, Descartes, and Kant to establish by some non-empirical method a foundational discipline of metaphysics that contains first principles of the empirical sciences. Such imaginary research projects should be criticized. Another reason is that although philosophers may engage in different research projects, they should be clear about the nature of the projects they are engaging in and refrain from pursuing incompatible objectives.

Searle claims, for instance, that what he did in his books was to advance 'general theories' about speech acts, intentionality, the mind, rationality, and the nature of society.[22] But what, exactly, does Searle mean by a 'general theory'? Is he engaging in proto-empirical theory building, as present-day string theorists are, hoping that his theories will become empirically testable in the future? If so, what are the empirical tests he is dimly envisaging for his theories, and what are the predictions he derives from them? Or is he just proposing a somewhat simplified and systematized picture of how we are using segments of ordinary language, such as words expressing intentions or mental characteristics of human beings? Or, finally, is he engaging in a descriptive study of mental phenomena in the tradition of phenomenologists such as Brentano and Husserl, making some new conceptual distinctions when necessary? But such a descriptive enterprise should not involve any theory-construction, as Husserl used to stress.

Maybe there are yet other interpretations of what Searle is doing. But if, inspired by Kripke or Quine, philosophers claim to advance 'theories' about reality without envisaging empirical tests, arguing, for example, that 'mere thinking' is a good method for acquiring knowledge, I think that they are under the spell of an illusion.

Popper. A Centenary Assessment, Volume II. *Metaphysics and Epistemology*. Edited by Ian Jarvie, Karl Milford, and David Miller (Ashgate, 2006), 73–85.

[21]   Cf. John R. Searle, 'Putting Consciousness back in the Brain', in Bennett et al. (2007), p. 122. Cf. also: 'The Future of Philosophy', *Philosophical Transactions of the Royal Society*, **B** 354 (1999), 2069–2080.

[22]   Searle, in Bennett et al. (2007), ibid.

Herman Philipse

What they are doing in such a case sometimes is advancing conceptual truths in the guise of metaphysical statements. However, when Martin Heidegger said that 'thinking' should replace traditional philosophy, he was advancing a religiously inspired world-view, a new myth, with quite disturbing moral implications. Given the deep influence Heidegger had in Germany and on Continental philosophy in general, I devoted some time to developing a properly historical interpretation of his works and to criticizing his views, using the toolbox of analytic philosophy.[23]

3. Socrates as a Role Model

Let me finish by saying something about my own research agenda in philosophy, however modest it is. Traditionally, philosophy was divided roughly into three broad areas: logic, ethics, and metaphysics or theoretical philosophy. In the philosophical tradition from Aristotle to Kant, metaphysics was conceived as a theory about reality in general, which had a foundational role for the special sciences. I argued above that the idea of such a foundational role was misconceived and based upon an untenable conception of scientific knowledge.

Yet I think that the motivation of traditional metaphysics to acquire an intellectual overview of reality and to determine the 'place of man in the cosmos' is of great value. As Wilfrid Sellars once wrote, '[t]he aim of philosophy is to understand how things in the broadest possible sense of the term hang together in the broadest possible sense of the term'.[24] Roughly speaking, there are two different responsible ways in which such a large-scale picture can be obtained. One is in the material mode, to use Carnap's phrase, that is, by constructing scientific theories. For example, if one wants to know what is the place of man in the cosmos, one should take the neo-Darwinist synthesis and modern Big Bang cosmology as a point of departure for one's reflections, because they are the best theories available. In this case, the objective may be described as 'philosophical' but the manner of achieving it is by doing empirical science and empirical research in the humanities.

---

[23] Cf. Herman Philipse, *Heidegger's Philosophy of Being. A Critical Interpretation* (Princeton: Princeton University Press, 1998).

[24] Wilfrid Sellars, 'Philosophy and the Scientific Image of Man', in *Frontiers of Science and Philosophy*, edited by Robert Colodny (Pittsburgh: University of Pittsburgh Press, 1962), 37.

The other way is the formal mode, by engaging in conceptual analysis, focused on how different conceptual systems of representation are logically related. One may wonder, for example, whether a scientific analysis of matter and perception implies that material things do not really have properties such as red and blue or hot and cold, as many physicists and philosophers since the scientific revolution have argued. More generally: how do everyday descriptions of the perceived world on the one hand and the scientific analysis of matter and perception on the other hand hang together conceptually? This was one of the foci of Sellars's own work: the celebrated problem of the alleged incompatibility between what he called the scientific and the manifest image. It is also a topic of my own writings, and I would deny the incompatibility. Sorting out such issues by conceptual and logical analysis is the proper business of the philosopher.

Another question that philosophers might raise is to what extent it is legitimate to use successful scientific theories, such as the theory of evolution, in order to explain phenomena that lie outside their domain of origin. For example, can we use the theory of evolution in order to account for cultural phenomena like religion?[25] Many conceptual points have to be clarified in order to decide this issue. For example, how is the notion of 'fitness' defined in such applications of the theory of evolution? Do these applications generate empirical hypotheses that are testable?

Many philosophers today think that they have to construct 'theories' about how things hang together. For example, in his early work Paul Churchland developed a theory of language, inspired by Quine, according to which all language is entirely theoretical. He concluded that our everyday ways of describing reality and ourselves are part of 'folk theories' such as 'folk psychology', which should be eliminated in the course of scientific progress. I have argued elsewhere that this doctrine of 'eliminative materialism' is a dogmatic metaphysical myth, which should be dispelled by careful logical and conceptual analysis.[26] In general, such a critical analysis of philosophical views and ideologies or world views is more to my taste than constructing ones of my own. Like Hacker I hold that the

[25] Cf., for example, books such as David Sloan Wilson, *Darwin's Cathedral. Evolution, Religion, and the Nature of Society* (Chicago: The University of Chicago Press, 2002) and Daniel C. Dennett, *Breaking the Spell. Religion as a Natural Phenomenon* (London: Penguin Books, 2006).

[26] Cf. Herman Philipse 'The Absolute Network Theory of Language and Traditional Epistemology', *Inquiry* **33**: 127–178.

business of theory construction belongs to science rather than to philosophy proper.

However, I also think that the methodological toolbox of the philosopher should contain more techniques than merely the Wittgenstein-style analysis of conceptual confusions. In order to analyze philosophical theories and ideologies critically, one equally needs the instruments of formal logic, an extensive knowledge of informal fallacies, and one has to be acquainted with many different areas of empirical research. Let me illustrate this thesis of methodological pluralism with regard to critical philosophy by saying something about my present topic of research, the philosophy of religion.

When I was a student, I did not think that I would ever be interested in criticizing religious systems of beliefs. Most of us assumed, naively perhaps, that the world would become ever more secularized. Furthermore, it seemed that the philosophy of religion could not yield any new or interesting insights. But today we live in different times, and a critical analysis of religious systems of beliefs is more urgent than ever. There are three reasons for this urgency. One is purely demographic. Since the alarming population growth on our planet takes place predominantly in religious countries, the secularized societies of Western Europe have a dwindling share of the world population. If we want the tolerant tradition of the Enlightenment to survive, we will have to engage in a battle of ideas and to criticize religious and other ideologies to the extent that they are incompatible with the Enlightenment tradition. For this reason, a philosophical critique of religions has great public utility.

Second, because of globalization, air travel, and internet, ideological conflicts between different cultures tend to become frequent and more passionate. Furthermore, because of migration, these conflicts emerge at home, in our own countries. Let me just remind you of the cartoon crisis in 2006, which was essentially a clash between Islamic religious absolutism and the value of freedom of expression. Or let me remind you of the murder of the Dutch film-maker and journalist Theo van Gogh by the Islamist Mohammed Bouyeri on 2 November 2004, because he had made a film with Mrs Hirsi Ali, criticizing the discrimination against women in Islam.

A third and more philosophical reason for engaging in a critique of religious ideologies is that during the last forty years, there has been a surprising revival of apologetic philosophy of religion in the Anglo-American world. A philosopher such as Alvin Plantinga argues on sophisticated epistemological grounds that a religious believer may be entirely within his epistemic rights and fulfill all his intellectual obligations although he does not put forward any argument for his religious beliefs.[27] And a philosopher such as Richard Swinburne claims that the thesis that God exists can be shown to be probably true on empirical evidence by using exactly the same logical apparatus which scientists use implicitly when they confirm their hypotheses about nature by evidence, to wit, Bayesian confirmation theory.[28] These and other apologetic philosophers of religion intend to bestow on religious beliefs an aura of reasonableness which these beliefs lack, at least so I suggest. It is a challenging and urgent philosophical task to point out the flaws in the arguments of these and other apologetic philosophers.

In order to be well equipped for a critical philosophical analysis of religious ideologies, one should have more intellectual baggage than the mere ability to perform Wittgenstein-style linguistic analysis of religious texts, however indispensable that ability is. For example, one should be widely read in the anthropology of religions, in order not to be narrow-minded about the manifold manifestations of this cultural phenomenon. One should also be informed about the history of the great clashes between science and Christianity in the West, which show in detail why scientific methods for acquiring knowledge are vastly superior to alleged religious methods such as receiving revelations. Furthermore, one should be aware of the failed empirical attempts to validate by double-blind tests religious methods of influencing the course of events, such as prayer.[29] And in order to understand what happened in the early stages of Christianity or Islam, one should be informed about the psychology of collaborative storytelling and the research on cognitive dissonance produced in sects whose messianic expectations were refuted by the facts.

When all these trunks of background knowledge are in place, the real philosophical work can begin. I would claim that this work strikingly resembles what Socrates did in Athens according to Plato's early dialogues. Let us confront the defendant of a religious ideology with two very simple questions. One is: what, exactly, do you mean by what you are saying? The other question is: how, exactly, do you

[27]   Alvin Plantinga, *Warranted Christian Belief*. (Oxford: Oxford University Press, 2000).

[28]   Richard Swinburne, *The Existence of God*. Second Edition. (Oxford Oxford University Press, 2004).

[29]   Cf. Mantra II (*The Lancet*, 16 July 2005) and STEP (*American Heart Journal*, 4 April 2006.).

know what you are claiming to know, or why do you believe that what you believe is true? I predict that after hours of discussion, or after hundreds of pages, in which the answers are analyzed meticulously, the outcome will be one of two. Either the defendant of a religious ideology has to admit that what he was saying does not make sense, after all. Or, if it makes sense, he will have to admit that very probably, what he was saying is false. And of course, we should apply this same type of Socratic and analytical critique of ideologies to other world-views than the religious ones, such as reductionist scientistic ideologies.

Let me end, then, by quoting Socrates, who exemplifies the type of critical philosophical analysis that I want to practice. For it is Socrates whom we have to imitate, rather than those philosophers who pretend to turn philosophy into a rigorous science.

> I went to one who had the reputation of wisdom, and... the result was as follows: When I began to talk with him, I could not help thinking that he was not really wise, although he was thought wise by many, and wiser still by himself; and I went and tried to explain to him that he thought himself wise, but was not really wise; and the consequence was...[30]

I suppose you all know what the consequence was.

---

[30]   Plato, *Apology*, 21c.

The Doctor of Philosophy Will See You Now

CHRISTOPHER COOPE

1. Put not Your Trust in Philosophical Advice

Papers about philosophy, as distinct from papers within it, are like homeopathic medicines – thin in content. We can only hope to provide some substance if we confine ourselves to some particular aspect. The aspect I have chosen to discuss is this. What hope should we have of finding from within this rather curious and academic subject of ours a help in the affairs of life? Could we expect a doctor of philosophy to give practical advice, rather like a medical doctor?

As we all know, many philosophers in recent decades have fostered the expectation that the knowledge and understanding gained by themselves and their colleagues in the course of their studies can be put to work, helping us to resolve many the great controversies of the day. Often these issues have been "ethical", and countless courses in what has come to be known as practical or applied ethics have been devised. A certain pride has been taken in this practical turn. Philosophers have rediscovered their role! And to be sure, these courses have not been a waste of time. They have done wonders for student recruitment and brought in funding from corporations and charities.

Practical philosophy in an academic context naturally tends to offer its findings in general terms and to the world at large. But philosophical services are also available on an individual basis. Recent years have seen the rise of the philosophical counsellor, a professional who 'listens carefully to the person's problems before applying the insights and methods of any number of great philosophers'. (I quote from a report in *The Independent*, Oct 2, 2005.) In the United States such counsellors are established enough to have a professional body 'The American Philosophical Practitioners Association', or APPA, with its headquarters at City College, New York. As we would expect, there is a professional code of conduct: fees must be announced before the consultation begins; and one is not supposed to have sexual relations with one's clients. A similar

doi:10.1017/S1358246109990105 © The Royal Institute of Philosophy and the contributors 2009 association can be found in England, with a similar hands-off code.[1] No doubt there are such things in other countries. There will be conferences, learned journals, accreditation.

What attitude then should we have to all this industry? In a nutshell, my answer is as follows:

Anyone who expects practical guidance from philosophers can't be serious. Philosophy if anything simply makes things more difficult. If it saves us from some errors it puts us in danger of others. 'Making things more difficult' might almost be a definition of our subject. I must however make one exception. For there is one sound item of practical advice philosophers can always give: *Look elsewhere.*

This at any rate is what some of us would spontaneously be inclined to suggest. The answer is, no doubt, a bit abrupt. I want to argue, however, that it is nearer the truth than one might at first suppose. One of the reasons for studying our subject is to come to appreciate that this is so. The very limited help a philosopher can hope to give will usually take the form of undoing the "help" already supplied by practitioners. Not so much practical as remedial ethics.

Not wishing to pretend to novelty, I will start by offering several supportive opinions. First, as to the thought that philosophy simply makes things more difficult, Philippa Foot puts the point succinctly: 'You ask a philosopher a question and after he or she has talked for a bit, you don't understand your question any more.'[2] With respect to the hope of finding in metaphysics a guide to morals, McTaggart was pleased to think that people would have more sense: 'What is the practical utility of Metaphysic? Does it give us guidance? I do not think that a man's views are much affected by his views on metaphysical problems. This is fortunate, since there is so very little agreement about metaphysic that, if it were otherwise, our moral life would...'[3] Russell, our next witness, remarks with admirable brevity: 'Science is what you more or less know and

---

[1] A glossy leaflet put out by my own university, offering ethics to the public, promises 'an exceptional client experience', but sadly gives no further details.

[2] From Steven Pyke, *Philosophers* (Manchester: Corner House Publications, 1993) In this book, the photographer Steven Pyke presented a collection of striking portraits, each philosopher being asked to make a brief remark to epitomise their conception of the subject. This was Philippa Foot's contribution.

[3] 'Introduction to the Study of Philosophy', *Philosophical Studies*, (London: Edward Arnold, 1934) 184.

philosophy is what you do not know'.[4] From this perspective applied philosophy can be little more than applied ignorance. And lastly, and somewhat to the same effect, we have the estimate of Peter van Inwagen: 'If you are not a philosopher, you would be crazy to go to the philosophers to find anything out – other than what it is that the philosophers say.'[5] In this talk I will argue that the drift of these various opinions, gathered from philosophers of rather differing outlooks, is about right. A guide, philosopher and friend, if one is fortunate enough to have one, had better be wearing more than one hat.

2. What is to Count Here as an Application of Philosophical Understanding?

We need first to determine, roughly, what is to count as philosophy and as an application of philosophical findings. As to philosophy itself I propose to define our subject for purposes of this discussion quite casually. It is what goes on in these various universities under this name, a subject that is obviously akin to what we find in the *Theaetetus* and the *Nicomachean Ethics*. It would be tedious to attempt to spell things out further. Should we confine ourselves to *analytic* philosophy for example? Let us by all means agree to confine ourselves in this way, though I am not sure that this honorific description still amounts to much, apart from indicating a vague commitment to be moderately clear, plain, careful and unpretentious. What I shall take to be philosophy for the purposes of this lecture is at any rate what someone who talks about 'applying philosophy' will most likely have in mind.

Although it makes sense to define philosophy with a wave of the hand in this way, it is necessary, if our discussion is to have any interest, not to be too lax in what we are to count as an application of it. Michael Dummett, recalling a controversy he had had on the interpretation of the New Testament, remarked: 'I was struck how greatly many of the participants would have benefited from a short course in philosophy'.[6]

---

4   "The Philosophy of Logical Atomism", *Collected Papers of Bertrand Russell*, Vol. 8, (London: Allen and Unwin, 1986) 243.

5   *God, Knowledge and Mystery* (Ithaca: Cornell University Press, 1995) 189–190. See also 186, fn. 17, as to the peculiar difficulty in philosophy of passing on what one has learned.

6   *The Philosophy of Michael Dummett*, R. E. Auxier and L. E. Hahn, (eds.) (Chicago: Open Court, 2007) 29. The controversy itself is in *New Blackfriars*, 1987–8.

That might well have been so. I am naturally not proposing to argue that in deciding what to do about this and that issue no one should ever take thought, or consider arguments, or make distinctions, or try to be clear and orderly. If merely taking thought, etc. is to be counted as an application of philosophy, then no doubt philosophy can help. Our question is rather different: whether it would be useful in the discussion of practical affairs to draw on hoped-for insights gained from the study of metaphysics, philosophy of mind, personal identity, moral theory, etc.? We can hardly count every academic discussion going on in the name of philosophy to be a philosophical discussion by this standard. The difference would not of course turn on the absence of professional jargon – an entirely superficial matter. What we are here regarding as an application of philosophical understanding need not employ terminology of this kind. But we must surely have in mind something more than what one might read in a well-argued leader column in a newspaper.

Philosophy teachers will sometimes find themselves discussing with medical students the proper limits of medical confidentiality, probing these boundaries with the help of case studies. Though the class might be conducted under the umbrella of a department of philosophy the students might have little or no background in the subject, and the discussion could well be entirely on the level of ordinary good sense without anything more or less distinctive of philosophy getting a look in. It might indeed be all the better for that. (I only say 'might' because nothing that I say in this talk should be taken as an endorsement of the judgment of the common man.) But, good or bad, it would not count as an application of philosophy, at least as I am here regarding it. The fact that discussion can often proceed on the level of ordinary good sense, with perhaps some philosophical decorations, no doubt explains how H. Tristram Engelhardt, who has first-hand knowledge about what is going on in this area, can report that in his experience 'no particular educational background is necessary ... for succeeding as a bioethics consultant'. According to Professor Engelhardt people have often been accepted as consultants 'after a one-week "total immersion" course at the Kennedy Institute of Ethics at Georgetown University'.[7]

[7]   'The Bioethics Consultant', *HEC Forum*, 2003, 378, 367. (The initials 'HEC' stand for 'Healthcare Ethics Committee'.) Professor Engelhardt is surely here reporting without endorsing. Anyone who knows his work will know just how pessimistic he is that much by way of truth or wisdom will emerge from courses in practical ethics.

The Doctor of Philosophy Will See You Now

It might be suggested that there are clear examples from the history of our subject which illustrate how eminent philosophers have been able to help the public deal with practical questions. Think for example of Hume on suicide, Kant on perpetual peace, or Mill on capital punishment. These might be thought to be classic examples of *applied philosophy before its time*, that is to say before anyone began to think of 'applied philosophy' as a category. But if we examine each of these offerings, it is not at all clear whether philosophical insights are being put to work at all. Hume indeed starts with a reference to the benefits of taking a philosophical approach. But by this he evidently means no more than an orderly consideration of argument.[8] Kant's essay has the subtitle 'a philosophical sketch', and there is even a reference to the categorical imperative. But does it play any role? It is mentioned *in an appendix*.[9] And we should remember here that none of these writers were exclusively philosophers by present day standards. Hume was also celebrated as a historian, Mill as an economist. And both were prepared to write essays on a great variety of topics. Aristotle attempted to answer a surprising range of practical questions in his *Problems* – whether cabbage might cure a hangover, etc – but not we would judge *as* a philosopher, at least as we nowadays conceive of this subject. Leibniz would offer advice to newly-weds, as amusingly recorded in Russell's *History of Western Philosophy*. Given a piece of writing which presents a case for action we can always ask whether the substance of what is said could have been put together by an intelligent academic in some other discipline, medicine, social policy or economics. Could it have been written by someone with little or no familiarity with epistemology, metaphysics, philosophy of mind, or moral theory? In our day Michael Dummett has written a book about a pressing practical issue, *On Immigration and Refugees*. He recently said of it: 'I consider that Part 1 of that book is a work of philosophy.' However he immediately went on to say: 'From what I can judge, few professional philosophers have treated it as such'.[10] I am not surprised at this reaction. This material, interesting as it is, seems to me to fail our admittedly rough-and-ready test.

---

[8]   I notice that Mossner, after quoting a passage from 'On Suicide' remarks: 'This is eloquence, no doubt – but is it philosophy?'. E. C. Mossner, *The Life of David Hume*, (Oxford: Clarendon Press, 1954) 333.

[9]   It is of course a very 'Kantian' essay. Thus there is a passing characterisation of conscription as 'mere using,' and of the state as a 'a moral person' which is not to be reduced to the status of a thing.

[10]   *The Philosophy of Michael Dummett*, 844.

Chris Coope

There is indeed a passing reference to Rawls and to Nozick. But that is surely not enough. I recently re-read an old article of my own, strictly in the line of duty; that is to say with just this question in mind. The article was on justice in employment, and published as it happens in the *Journal of Applied Philosophy*. Was this an example, I asked, of what the journal purported to be about? I had to say, quite frankly, no.

Someone might suppose that Mill in particular *must* have been writing philosophy in his speech in defence of capital punishment, since what are called "utilitarian considerations" were invoked. A "utilitarian argument" was on offer. And if this is not an application of philosophy what is? But, if I may put it epigrammatically, there is nothing particularly utilitarian about an appeal to utilitarian considerations. The simple wisdom in fire precautions turns on what are called utilitarian considerations and is intelligible quite apart from any philosopher's doctrine about good states of affairs and our alleged obligations to "maximise them" or to produce a positive balance of good states over bad.[11]

With this rough division in hand between philosophy and methodical but untheoretical writing on practical issues generally, let us return to our main topic. If we think, as I am sure we do, that there is something comical in the very idea of a philosophical practitioner, sitting in a consulting room with a polished brass plate on his door, we still need to ask *why* it is comical, *why* we are right to think it so. Is it because there cannot be such a thing as philosophical authority? Or is it because particular philosophical views or doctrines are incompatible with the enterprise of advice? Or is it simply because the subject happens to be too difficult? Or too difficult in a special way? (for medicine and law are difficult enough, and we expect to find advice *there*). We must in particular distinguish the thought that the project of practical philosophy is *impossible* from the thought that it is so very *unpromising*. I will spend some time arguing against the first suggestion, that is to say the impossibility, before turning to argue in favour of the second.

[11] Compare Elizabeth Anscombe's remark in "Contraception and Chastity", that temperance in regard to eating and drinking, or honesty about property, "has a purely utilitarian justification" (*Faith in a Hard Ground*, Exeter: Imprint Academic, 2008, p. 188). No one could suppose that Anscombe was any kind of utilitarian or was invoking anything which deserved to be called a philosophical discovery.

3. Philosophical Authority

Advice presupposes authority. This is plainly so in regard to medical or legal advice, but is also the case even with the non-technical advice of a friend with 'experience of the world'. A friendly and perhaps useful chat among companions equally at sea is not consultancy. The possibility and the usefulness of advice depends on the evident truth that one is often better off trusting an authority, fallible though he be, than attempting to work things out for oneself. Aquinas's well-known opinion (well-known I suppose because unexpected) that 'an argument from authority founded on human reason is the weakest of arguments' (ST I Q1 Art 8 ad 2) is misleading here, and it is perhaps unfair to quote it outside of its context. Someone who boldly says 'I have thought it out all for myself, and have concluded that p' is often in a weaker epistemic position than the trusting man who says 'I consulted Robinson, and he told me that p'.

Now someone might say that there cannot be such a thing as authority *in philosophy*, that it is in the nature of the subject that everyone has to be his own judge.

This is in part something of a pretence, and in part a caricature of what authority here would look like. I talk about a pretence because I suspect the influence of a high and heroic ideal: that of thinking for oneself as much as possible, the ambition being: to achieve maximal independence of mind. This would be an aspect, these days, of a more comprehensive obsession, often to the fore in medical ethics, which I call autonomania. Autonomaniacs would for example burden patients with decisions they would rather not have to make, 'forcing them to be free'. Philosophy, it might be supposed, is somehow the guardian of this high do-it-yourself ideal. There is indeed something Cartesian about it. One works out everything on one's own, sitting snugly by one's very own stove. Nothing in philosophy is to be accepted without scrutiny and one's own reflective endorsement. Some of you learned in ancient philosophy will remember the immortal words of Socrates:

The unexamined thought is not worth thinking *Third Alcibiades*, 541c

Despite the giddy attractiveness of this remark, however, it must be evident by now that such an ideal is deeply misguided.

The ideal of thinking for oneself is in fact a little difficult to describe. It would perhaps best be achieved by the student or enquirer being let loose in an *ideally anonymous and undiscriminating library*. This would be an unusual library which collects every book, each of which is then edited to eliminate as far as possible the mere effects of prestige. The author's name and qualifications and place of employment would carefully be removed from every volume, together with the usual list of eminent names from the acknowledgments page. There would be no information about the press which published the item in question. Any phrases of puffery from the covers of the volume would carefully be blanked out. In the ideal case, the text would all be translated into a standardised English, and every humanising digression would be deleted. Articles would all appear as if they had been published in a single journal, *The Pure Reason Review*, and each would be accompanied with an official Government Diversity Warning, in bold at the top of the page: 'Caution. What follows might be an article by a well-known Harvard philosopher, but it is equally likely to be a student essay. You must judge the content for yourself'. Now I am not saying that there might not be certain advantages for those who are already philosophically educated having on occasion to read anonymised materials. I once read the first few pages of a print-out which I took to be from a student essay. It turned out to *be* by a well-known Harvard philosopher. This is an instructive experience we all need from time to time. But needless to say, as a way of finding one's way in this subject of ours, confinement to the anonymised library from the outset would, I believe, be quite hopeless.

There is to be sure a virtue of independent mindedness. It is a matter of 'sometimes', and is far too dull to go on about except at a school speech-day. Otherwise 'thinking for oneself' is I suspect a description with uncertain conditions of application, a mere flag to wave in the air. In practice it would mean: not believing one's priest but believing the *New York Review of Books* instead.

Authority has a fairly large place in philosophical enquiry, and it has a larger place the more complex the field becomes and the more people there are at work in it. This is a matter of vulgar necessity common to many human endeavours. If we are rational, we will want to know not just *what* is said but *who* has said it. One has, up to a point, to accept, with proper caution, what one hears from those with a different competence from one's own. Books are relegated to the philosophical stacks on the whole for good reason. The fact that mistakes in relegation are sometimes made makes us forget how much is justly laid aside.

A reluctance to admit the role of authority in part depends on a misconception of what authority would here look like. Teaching authority in philosophy would not, or not characteristically, be a matter of simply saying to the uninstructed – *this is how things are, take my word for it.* 'Theirs not to reason why. Theirs but to say, Aye, Aye.' Jumping-to is a response to authority of a different kind, rational in its place: that is to say, the right to demand obedience. Think of how a parent says to a young child 'Fetch my slippers!' The thing is just to be done. Sometimes indeed even in the case of teaching authority, something just has to be believed, to be taken in, as once again in the case of small children. But this case is special. Acceptance of philosophical authority will rarely if ever be blind acceptance. Still, someone can rationally believe *largely* on the basis of authority that, let us say, non-existence does not count as a defect, having discovered that this is a view rather generally endorsed by those who seem to know what's what. It might even be sensible *wholly* to rely on authority, on the basis of a report that a proof of what one accepts exists somewhere among Saul Kripke's unpublished manuscripts.

Prima facie then we must allow that the project of practical philosophy does not fail simply for the reason that there cannot be philosophical authority. But there is more to be said. Let us consider the implied rejection of practical philosophy we find in Wittgenstein.

4. . . . Only Saying What Everyone Admits

Wittgenstein, we can be sure, never embarked on a course of lectures in applied philosophy. And we could hardly imagine him setting up as a metaphysical agony aunt, despite the talk in his later writings of 'therapy'. This is not because he lacked a practical bent. He had been educated as an engineer, and designed the house built for his sister down to the smallest detail. He was even willing to advise his friend John King to think twice before getting married: 'Haven't you enough troubles already...?' Still, from his perspective, philosophy could not conceivably get itself involved in the advising business. Naturally, the study of philosophy might help one to think more clearly. But this would be a consequence of properly cautious habits; it would not take the form of putting philosophical discoveries to practical use. In 1939 Norman Malcolm deeply offended Wittgenstein by making a remark about the British national character. Later in 1944, Wittgenstein wrote to Malcolm, remembering the incident: 'What is the use of studying philosophy if all that it does for you is to enable you to talk with some plausibility about some abstruse questions of logic, etc., and if it does not improve your thinking about the important questions of everyday life'.

Chris Coope

But there seems no question here of the application of metaphysical insights.[12]

Now Wittgensteinian austerity in this matter is something for which we should have a certain respect. I leave aside here a superficial but not wholly inconsiderable reason: that philosophical advising would involve popularising the subject, with the thought that this could only offer the illusion of understanding. One thinks here of Wittgenstein's reaction to Russell's *Problems of Philosophy* or Eddington's *The Nature of the Physical World*. Wittgenstein would however have offered a more fundamental objection. There had been much discussion in those decades, no doubt stimulated by Wittgenstein's own work, about the character of philosophical enquiry: how there could be any place for an enquiry that wasn't scientific, historical, geographical, bibliographical, etc. This question, which seems always to have been in at least in the background of Wittgenstein thoughts, has a bearing on our present topic. This emerges in a somewhat different way in the *Tractatus* and the *Investigations*.

In the view of the *Tractatus*, as is rather emphasised, there can be no 'ought' or 'must', no necessity, apart from logical necessity. This is simply a consequence of the ingeniously interwoven account of meaning, understanding, truth and the nature of logic presented in that book. That there was therefore no place for 'ethical' pronouncements in particular was seen by Wittgenstein not as an unwelcome or paradoxical consequence to be put up with for the sake of the whole. It was an advantage. As he explained to Ludwig von Fricker, the book's point was 'an ethical one'. 'My work consists of two parts: the one presented here plus all that I have *not* written. And it is precisely this second part that is the important one.' The second part contained, as it were, what *could not be* written: what was 'shown' but could not be 'said'.[13] Later in life Wittgenstein was to express himself more robustly: 'I think it is definitely important to put an end to the claptrap about ethics.'[14] It is hard these days, where ethics is everywhere, not to have a sympathy with that remark. When we turn to the *Investigations* however, it is not so obvious that

---

[12] *Ludwig Wittgenstein, a Memoir* (London: Oxford University Press, 1958) 32–3 and 39.

[13] Letter reproduced in G. H. von Wright, 'The origin of the *Tractatus*', *Wittgenstein*, (Oxford: Blackwell, 1982) 83, italics in text.

[14] Friedrich Waismann, *Ludwig Wittgenstein and the Vienna Circle*, (Oxford: Blackwell, 1979) 68–9.

we can put an end to the claptrap so easily. The idea that the only necessity is logical necessity is no longer emphasised.

We must here distinguish between the second order comments in the *Investigations* about philosophy and what might be called the philosophy itself. The impossibility of philosophical advice, ethical or otherwise, might indeed be settled once and for all by the remarks about philosophical method in the *Investigations*, remarks which catch the eye: such as the provocative aphorism 'Philosophy only states what everyone admits' (Sec. 599). As he explained to his students: 'In philosophy we know already all that we want to know.'[15] In one of the manuscripts Wittgenstein contrasted his work with that of earlier philosophers (here writing in a style uncharacteristically close to the confident positivists of the day):

> A common-sense person, when he reads earlier philosophers thinks – quite rightly – 'Sheer nonsense'. When he listens to me, he thinks – rightly again – 'Nothing but stale truisms'. That is how the image of philosophy has changed.[16]

Clearly, the inability to say anything except what is admitted by everyone precludes advice and authority of any kind.

However, if we exclude the remarks about philosophy, this incapacity does *not* seem to be a consequence of the main philosophical ideas about language and mind in the *Investigations*, the ideas which have served (and still serve) to disentangle misunderstandings in these key areas going right back to Descartes, and which stand on their own. Elisabeth Anscombe began a class on the *Investigations* – which I attended, perhaps in 1963 – by pointing to these eye-catching passages about the limited scope of philosophy. She said, in her characteristically deliberate way, that if anyone thought that the interest of Wittgenstein's book depended upon their truth, it would be hard to see how the rest of the book *could* have much interest at all.

Philosophy cannot *only* say what everyone admits, even if it has to start out from such a base. Some of the things it says will have logical consequences which *not* everyone will admit. It would seem to be a mere stipulation that the drawing of these consequences could not be counted as 'philosophy' as we would now understand it – as the *Investigations* seems indeed to stipulate, where in Sec. 599 it is laid down that 'in philosophy we do not draw conclusions'. We are

---

[15] Desmond Lee (ed.) *Wittgenstein's Lectures, Cambridge 1930–1932*, (Oxford: Blackwell, 1980) 35.
[16] MS 219, 6. Quoted by Anthony Kenny, *The Legacy of Wittgenstein*, (Oxford: Blackwell, 1984) 57.

Chris Coope

right to think of this as a stipulation: it is simply a repetition of what is presented, rather as an axiom, in the very first sentence of what we can take to be Wittgenstein's first effort, the 'Notes on Logic' of 1913.

Apart from this point about consequence, beliefs about the world which *not* everyone will admit can still be reasonable even though they are not established by scientific testing – by conjecture and attempted refutation, let us say – and it would naturally fall to philosophy to point out such beliefs. Our belief in indeterminism – that not every change is determined by causes – would seem to be of this kind. Determinism is evidently not testable. And it is the sort of thesis which should only be believed if it *is* testable. In such circumstances, rational opinion rests with what nowadays would be called the folk belief in this regard – namely, the default taking-for-granted of variability in nature, which is indeed how thing appear.

We find that Wittgenstein himself sometimes relies on what it is 'natural' to think, rather than on what everyone admits. We find this in his interesting remarks on thought and the brain, remarks which stand against a learned or half-learned assumption of our age: 'No supposition seems to me more natural than that there is no process in the brain correlated with associating or thinking...' etc.[17] Wittgenstein's actual practice here opens doors which his *theorising* about his practice had wished to close.

Rather generally it seems, it is as well to pay more attention to Wittgenstein's work and thought than to his comments about it. People like to remember his remark: 'A philosopher is not a citizen of any community of ideas. That's what makes him a philosopher'.[18] This is surely an attractive pronouncement – a declaration of independence. But how did Wittgenstein himself take it? Is it compatible with the Wittgenstein who said that he would be prepared to *combat* someone who believed in oracles:

> I said I would 'combat' the other man, – but wouldn't I give him *reasons*? Certainly; but how far would they go? At the end of reasons comes *persuasion*. (Think of what happens when missionaries convert natives.)[19]

Is it compatible with the Wittgenstein who said that he was writing only for the small number of people who formed his cultural milieu?[20] We

---

[17] *Zettel*, Oxford: Blackwell, 1967, Sec. 608, a step beyond *Investigations* Sec. 158.

[18] *Zettel*, Sec. 455.

[19] *On Certainty*, Oxford: Blackwell, 1969, Sec. 612. Italics in text

[20] *Culture and Value*, Oxford: Blackwell, 1980, 10.

might also remember the Wittgenstein who said to his friend Drury: 'Your religious ideas have always seemed to me more Greek than Biblical. Whereas my thoughts are one hundred percent Hebraic.'[21] Though Wittgenstein was constantly aware of his shortcomings, real or imagined, he was hardly going to conclude that as a citizen of a certain community of ideas he hardly counted as a philosopher.

5. Philosophical Findings Incompatible with Advice-Giving

Let us suppose that we are prepared to admit, abandoning the narrowness of Wittgenstein's remarks on philosophy, that philosophical investigation might came up with particular results. Now certain of these results would, if taken seriously – always assuming this to be possible – quite undermine the project of philosophical advice.

Think for example of the remarkable professions of ignorance so commonly found in the history of our subject. An ancient sceptic seems to have been expected to say 'I know nothing!' – rather in the manner of a certain waiter from Barcelona. What place could there be for a consultant who professed such ignorance? The APPA accredited consultant, made humble by sceptical argument, would have frankly to admit: 'This advice comes to you from one who knows absolutely nothing about anything.' It would presumably be part of his code of conduct to confess such a thing at the outset, along with the information about the fee to be charged. And he might well find himself adding *sotto voce* '... and who maintains that *you* know nothing too'. It is not often realised that one can only advise someone who already knows quite a bit. That is why one cannot advise a new-born baby.

Of course there are particular scepticisms too. It might be argued that although a philosophical consultant can of course know many things, one thing he cannot know, or even reasonably conjecture about, is *in what ways the future will resemble the past*: whether – to use Nelson Goodman's example – the next emerald discovered will strictly follow precedent in being green, or strictly follow precedent

---

21   Rush Rhees (ed.), *Ludwig Wittgenstein, Personal Recollections*, (Oxford: Blackwell, 1981) 175. Wittgenstein was here reacting to the reassuring view, very prevalent as it happens among sophisticated Christians of the present day, that 'at the end of time' everything would turn out well for everyone, even the fallen angels being restored to glory, etc. This had been a teaching in Origen, perhaps influenced by Hellenistic thought, and was looked on with favour by Drury.

in being grue (so that it would appear, and would indeed be, blue). Such an incapacity would thoroughly undermine the consultant's role. Again he might suppose that he has to be forever agnostic as to the existence of other minds since all anyone can actually observe is bodily behaviour. In such a case, it might be argued, he would never know whether he had any clients. Here I must confess there might be minimal opportunities for him. It would be possible to offer advice *in the neighbourhood of a putative client* just in case the client *might* exist. And there is another kind of limited scepticism, which might as it happens correspond to the thought of the real-life sceptics of the ancient world. Michael Frede, in a pioneering article, argued that ancient sceptics were not as radical in their claims as had so often been supposed in the history of thought. The sceptic would not have wanted to suspend belief in regard to everything, but rather *in regard to anything which depended upon learned or philosophical study*.[22] Still, that would be much the same for our purposes here, for the philosophical consultant is hoping to apply these learned opinions.

Knowing nothing is incompatible with competence in advising. But the *second-order knowledge* that nothing first order can be known is quite another matter. That puts the advisor in an absurdly strong position. People are persistently taught that they have duties – to pay their bills let us say – and this thought can be burdensome. A first-order sceptic could helpfully apply his philosophical understanding to their plight, informing them with authority that no one could know that anything was owing. Indeed a more moderate sceptic confining his doubts as to the existence of the past could also offer such liberating advice. And sceptics of either kind might be helpful to those contemplating adultery. Again we all assume that we go in danger of culpable ignorance. A failure adequately to enquire will often put us in a state of bad faith, a fact which renders bad faith exceedingly common. A sceptical advisor could well earn his fee here by putting these gloomy anxieties to rest. Where

---

[22]   Frede admitted that Pyrro himself might have been a total sceptic. For, by report, the helpless Pyrro would have faced all risks, 'carts, precipices, dogs,' were it not for his friends who always accompanied him. But on the whole ancient sceptics tended to lead normal lives without the need for a bodyguard. See 'The Sceptic's Beliefs,' in Myles Burneat and Michael Frede (eds.), *The Original Scepticism, A Controversy*, (Indianapolis: Hackett, 1997). These sceptics believed in the existence of dangerous dogs, but not say, in atoms – in this last respect being like Ernst Mach in more recent times. Modest in comparison to Pyrro, they seem to have argued for an extreme version of the modest reserve defended in the present talk.

nothing can be found out a failure to enquire is no defect. It is very striking that consultants in practical ethics do not appear to be handing out such helpful information – much more worthy to be called the fruits of philosophy than the advice offered by Charles Knowlton in his little volume of that name.

There are other startling theses thrown up by philosophy which would also make the advisor's task impossible. As everyone knows, philosophers in our time have often doubted the existence of God. It has rather been expected of them. What is less well known among the general public is that sober and learned philosophers have recently gone much further, doubting the existence quite generally of persons, people or intelligent agents. This is so to speak a doubt about *minds*, not merely and modestly about *other* minds or the divine mind.

A few brief examples. Russell once thought it arguable that a man, Socrates say, was 'a series of classes' and was hence a logical fiction.[23] In more recent times, Steven Stich has caused a certain amount of philosophical upset by arguing that we might need to 'renounce folk-psychology', where this would 'probably' mean giving up the idea of personhood and agency.[24] Advisors would have to give up believing in the existence of clients – just as they already believe that there are no witches. Peter Unger once undertook to show us *why there are no people* (in his article of that name). And again, if this were so there would obviously be no clients.[25]

Some philosophers deny the existence of consciousness, so that even if they had clients they wouldn't suppose that they had *conscious* ones. It is hopeless to attempt to advise an unconscious client. Galen Strawson has taken a less drastic view, being prepared to accept the existence both of persons and consciousness. But this concession brings little comfort. For according to his view of personal identity it is very likely that any one of us – that is to say 'a subject of experience that is a single mental thing' – will only last for a few seconds, to

[23] "The Philosophy of Logical Atomism", 171.
[24] *From Folk Psychology to Cognitive Science*, (Cambridge, Mass.: MIT Press, 1983) 242. The section in question is entitled: 'Could it turn out that there are no such things as beliefs?' and ends by suggesting that we might, in raising these doubts about belief, personhood, agency, etc. be on the very threshold of a new Copernican revolution. Not an unusual claim in philosophy of course. And far from representing a solitary voice from beyond the philosophical fringe, this sort of thing is by now a recognised 'position' in our subject, going by the name of eliminativism.
[25] P. French et al., (eds.) *Midwest Studies in Philosophy* **IV**, (Minneapolis: University of Minnesota Press, 1979). Peter Unger had earlier defended an even more extreme scepticism, see below.

be succeeded (in most instances) by another such subject.[26] Russell once argued rather more generally that 'the things that are really real last a very short time ... one tenth or half a second, or whatever it might be' – though there *might* be longer lasting things of which we have no knowledge.[27] Minimal longevity will plainly place severe restrictions on the possibility of advice, particularly philosophical advice which we would naturally expect to be given at a somewhat deliberate pace. There would hardly be time for it. Even if there were clients there would be none stable enough to be helped.

But this is not the end of our troubles. The idea that people are really brains or bits of brains is really quite popular among more scientifically-minded philosophers. This would nowadays be the down-to-earth option. Indeed even those who do not make such claims at least purport to take them seriously. Yet if people were brains or bits of brains advice would of course be out of the question. No brain or bit of a brain could be said to offer advice, or to profit from such, any more than could a kidney or corpuscle. Nor would it be necessary to insist that an accredited brain in good standing eschew sexual relations with a client.

It must be admitted then that if any of these views were true, the impossibility of philosophical advising would be established straight away. But this is hardly very interesting as it is quite impossible to believe that any of these views *are* true (or are even clear enough to be considered[28]). Although those who call themselves sceptics may *say* that they or their clients can know nothing, or nothing about the past, or about other minds, or *say* that their clients are unconscious or are bits of brains, their actions will surely proclaim otherwise. They walk the walk all right; they just refuse to talk the talk. Others – pretty well everyone – will regard arguments in this area simply as a challenge perspicuously to say what is wrong with them. They (or we) follow the example of G. E. Moore. This is how people have reacted to Peter Unger's book, *Ignorance*, which

---

[26]   'What is the Relation Between and Experience, the Subject of the Experience, and the Content of the Experience', *Philosophical Issues*, 2004, 289, 291. It can of course be hard to pin a philosopher down. According to Galen Strawson, Dennett not only persists in denying the existence of consciousness, but then persists in denying that he denies it. ('Evolution Explains It All to You', Review of Daniel Dennett's *Freedom Evolves*, *New York Times*, March 2, 2003.)

[27]   'The Philosophy of Logical Atomism', 238.

[28]   Thoughts of 'applying' a fancy philosophical suggestion can be important not because it can be expected to be of practical help, but rather to determine what the suggestion might actually mean.

argued with much admired thoroughness and skill that 'not only can nothing ever be known, but that no one can ever have any reason at all for anything'. If *following the argument where it leads* means trying to accept a conclusion of an apparently valid argument from apparently true premises, no philosopher thinks he ought always to follow the argument where it leads – despite the common rhetoric which advises heroism in this particular.[29] If necessary, 'the most desperate contortions' (in Russell's phrase) will be called for.[30] An argument which purports to show or to suggest that no one knows anything, or nothing apart from *it*, will not be 'followed' even if no suitable remedy or contortion can be invented – though to be sure I am rather leaving aside what it would be to take such an argument seriously. Peter Unger himself, far from continuing to insist that we can know nothing, has since come to the (very reasonable) view that we have 'epistemic responsibilities' to find out certain things.[31]

So we can not say that the project of philosophical advice must founder *here*. Still, something emerges about philosophy from these brief remarks which is very relevant.

6. Waywardness

I have distinguished the thought that the project of practical philosophy is *impossible* – in particular that we can understand from within the discipline itself that this is so – from the thought that it is so very *unpromising*. It is here, I wish to argue, where the trouble lies. Our topic in this section is only in-a-way philosophical, being in part based on what we find by looking around at the academic scene.

---

[29]   Ernest Sosa says, in praise of this book, that 'Unger follows the argument ... wherever it may lead'. I think he must mean simply that consequences are drawn, not that they have had their natural effect on his conduct. After all, Peter Unger is still alive. (Both Professor Sosa's remark and the description of the book's message are taken from Oxford University Press's website.)

[30]   '... and [we] should arrive at solipsism but for the most desperate contortions' *Mysticism and Logic* (London: Longmans, Green, 1918, 210. It is ironical that Russell should in later years have looked down his nose at Aquinas for not setting out 'to follow the argument wherever it may lead,' *History of Western Philosophy* (London: Allen and Unwin, 1946) 484.

[31]   *Living High and Letting Die: Our Illusion of Innocence* (New York: Oxford University Press, 1996) 32.

Chris Coope

The real barrier to the project of philosophical consultancy is the extraordinary waywardness of this subject of ours. We are not here merely thinking in a general way about lack of sense among the bookish. On this broader theme people will remember Hazlitt: 'You will hear more good things on the outside of a stage-coach from London to Oxford, than if you were to pass a twelvemonth with the undergraduates, or heads of colleges, of that famous university'.[32] Our trouble arises from within the ranks of the remote and bookish: it has to do with philosophy in particular. The philosopher only says what no one can possibly admit. He will prove to you that nothing moves. He will swiftly demonstrate that everyone is tall. (Or short, if that is the conclusion you prefer.) 'The point of philosophy is to start with something so simple as not to seem worth stating, and to end with something so paradoxical that no one will believe it', as Russell said.[33] If writing today, he would surely have added: 'on the solid foundation of which helpful advice can then be offered'. A philosopher is a man who will tell you that it is always a waste of time and effort to take precautions (as to one's heath etc.) seeing that what will be will be. That is almost a paradigm of practical philosophy.

Here I must re-emphasise that in all this I confine myself to the kind of philosophy where carefulness in argument is valued, philosophy on a fairly tight rein. I am thinking of something with at least a surface intelligibility. So we shall leave aside the suggestion that justice is the number four, let us say, or that marriage is the number five. That *religious* opinion across the board is so often farcically wayward is not at all to be wondered at. It is in fact a continual cause for wonder that people are always claiming to have a respect for 'faiths' of no matter what complexion. Perhaps it is the concealed expression of a certain contempt. Or perhaps it is thought a social grace to speak in this way. If the Christian Church, despite coming under the heading religious, is able authoritatively to teach, that in itself is as extraordinary as anything else it teaches.

Now we are in no position to say that the truth about the world cannot be strange. On the contrary, it is bound to be very strange. And what it is reasonable to believe for us, here and now, can sometimes be quite extraordinary. When I speak of waywardness I am thinking of a certain impression of folly that so often meets the eye. Not always: certain groundbreaking works in philosophy, often

---

[32] 'On the Ignorance of the Learned', *Table Talk: Essays on Men and Manners*, in *Works*, P. P. Howe (ed.), Vol. 8, (London: Dent, 1931) 75.
[33] 'The Philosophy of Logical Atomism', 172.

regarded as paradigms, seem entirely free of it, Frege's *Foundations of Arithmetic* let us say, or Anscombe's *Intention*. But these examples are rather exceptional. Philosophy is so often simply awry – not so much fallacious as follacious. And in so many directions at once. 'The incredulous stare' is characteristic of philosophical to-and-fro in a way which is hardly matched elsewhere in the learned world. Philosophers rather expect to be laughed at, even – or should I say especially? – by other philosophers. It is a rather playful subject. A current journal displays an announcement of a forthcoming book by 'the maverick philosopher' so-and so. The adjective is about as individuating as *bald* or *bearded* or *bejacketed*. Would you accept advice from members of a profession who, though in good standing, are notoriously *both* so diverse *and* peculiar in opinion?[34] Some feel for the bewildering range of options offered by philosophers on what looks at first to be a rather tractable topic can be gained from reading the opening pages of Eric Olson's recent book *What Are We?* It might seem that when we find ourselves talking about this Tom, that Dick or yonder Harry we already know what *sort* of thing we are talking about. But this appears, on a closer examination, not to be so. What is so very striking here is the range of answers that a clear and painstaking philosopher feels obliged to take seriously. It includes the answer that we are simply talking about nothing at all, to which opinion a chapter is devoted. The book might have been called: *What Are We, If Anything?*[35]

Philosophy is the only subject where something can be tolerated and even praised under the description 'nonsense'. McTaggart wrote a Fellowship Thesis for Trinity College, Cambridge. Sidgwick said of it that it was certainly nonsense, but that it was the right kind of nonsense. A familiar response – so many examiners in philosophy must have thought the same about the material they have felt obliged to judge as satisfactory. Evidently 'the right kind of nonsense' is all that success requires. It may range I suppose from mere absurdity to actual senselessness. (And I am not talking here about a way of talking or hinting, unsatisfactory just as it

---

[34] Of course some *apparent* oddity is easily accommodated. The 'paradoxes of material implication' for example which can look startling are simply a liveable-with consequence of a minimal, truth functional, convention about 'if-then'.

[35] *What Are We?* (New York: Oxford University Press, 2007) The possibility that we are not anything at all is the topic of Chapter 8. Another suggestion considered in this book and not just dismissed out of hand is that 'there is no such thing as thinking' (14).

stands, which we have to adopt in order to get a point across, an utterance which has to be taken, as Frege said when discussing the concept of a function, with a grain of salt.)

I have drawn attention at some length to this waywardness elsewhere, while discussing the range of current philosophical opinion about consciousness.[36] I offer just one further example from this fruitful area. Jerry Fodor recently published in *The London Review of Books* a clear-sighted review of Galen Strawson's *Consciousness and its Place in Nature*. The review was wittily and informatively entitled 'Headaches have themselves'. That, in just three words, well illustrates what I am on about. Incredulity is quite the expected reaction. Strawson himself, after presenting his account of the Self, commented that his account 'strikes nearly everyone as obviously – even hilariously – false'.[37] In turn Strawson finds hilarious falsehood in the views of others. Noting that respectable contemporary philosophers 'are prepared to deny the existence of experience' he comments: 'Next to this denial, every known religious belief is only a little less sensible than the belief that grass is green'.[38]

Philosophical eccentricity undoubtedly makes the subject more enjoyable. Only in philosophy could a serious and possibly important article be published in which the authors state that everything said in their article (perhaps just everything *else* said in it) is untrue.[39] Other philosophers will be overcome with envy. They would just love to have been the first to publish an article incorporating such a claim. The impression one gets as an observer is that philosophers *do not know their way about* – which is of course Wittgenstein's description of the plight of the individual philosopher, pondering his particular topic (*Investigations*, Sec. 123). The very word 'preposterous' seems to have been especially invented for philosophers to use in regard to one another. This marks our subject off from scientific enquiry, where preposterousness (chronicled with such persistence and care by Martin Gardner) remains exceptional and fringy. We remember Cicero's remark, much loved in the trade, and more relevant today

---

[36] Discussed in relation to the question, often rather curiously supposed to be of interest in connection with abortion, whether a foetus at *n* weeks is 'conscious'. *Worth and Welfare in the Controversy over Abortion*, (Houndmills: Palgrave, 2006) ch. 4.2.
[37] 'The Self and the SESMET', *Journal of Consciousness Studies*, 1999, No. 4, 100.
[38] *Consciousness and Its Place in Nature* (Exeter: Imprint Academic, 2006) 5–6.
[39] David Braun and Theodore Sider, 'Vague, so Untrue', *Nous*, 2007, 139, qualified later (everything *else*) 154.

than ever before: that there is nothing too foolish to find its way into the writings of philosophers.[40] This melancholy fact indeed remarkably undermines the usefulness of *reductio*. Berkeley wrote in his notebooks 'If matter is once allowed to exist, clippings of beards and parings of nails may think for ought that Locke can tell ...'[41] That settles that! But such an argument is not going to embarrass a pan-psychist. He will already have taken just such a view of beard clippings, etc. I may remark here, incidentally, that the doctrine of pan-psychism, still taken seriously in the academy, shows us that philosophical waywardness is not always a matter of scepticism about this and that. A pan-psychist claims to have remarkably extensive knowledge.[42]

I have rather suggested that this waywardness can be rather prized. Perhaps it would not matter so much if applications remained inert. How usual it is for articulate philosophers all over the world to find themselves *proving* to their first year students that criminal punishment of all kinds is always unjust, since no once has a real choice to do other than what in fact they do (I mean that their arguments will look rather more like a proof than anything else on offer in philosophy). For all that, no one in the everyday world so much as begins to take the thought seriously. This must be, in part, because these philosophers themselves seem not to take it seriously. A *real* belief that severe and continual wronging is rife in the community has characteristic manifestations, here conspicuously missing. We

---

[40] Cicero, *De Divinatione*, 2, Sec 119. See also Montaigne, 'An Apology for Raymond Sebond', *Essays*, M. A. Screech (ed.) (Penguin, 1991) 613; Descartes. 'Discourse on Method', *Philosophical Works*, Haldane and Ross, Vol. I, (Cambridge: Cambridge University Press, 1911) 90; and Hobbes, *Leviathan*, 'Reason and Science', M. Oakeshott (ed.) (Oxford: Blackwell, 1960) 27. Cicero's particular example is that well-worn illustration of philosophical oddity, the Pythagorean objection to beans – an objection which, ironically, could have been perfectly rational, favism being an inherited condition prevalent in Mediterranean countries.

[41] Berkeley, *Philosophical Works*, M. R. Ayers (ed.) (Everyman, London: Dent, 1975) 321.

[42] There are not only sceptics in philosophy. There are also (what we might call) credulics. A credulic is someone who supposes that every truth can be known. An extreme credulic is someone who supposes that every truth *is* known. Fitch's thesis, that if there is an unknown truth then there is an unknowable truth, when combined with the 'knowability thesis', that no truth is unknowable, yields the conclusion that there is no unknown truth. (Someone who supposes that there must be truths unknown to human beings might find reason here to believe in at least one non-human intelligence.)

should be pleased to find that what might be called metaphysical advice is treated with such reserve. No one familiar with philosophy would be surprised to hear, to take another example, that students in their subject down the corridor are being taught that one cannot actually *harm* others simply by killing them.[43] It would however be quite alarming to think what people might do in the light of such a thought.

As I have said, philosophy is not entirely infected with waywardness. There is a faction among us which is somewhat less willing than the others to tolerate nonsense and absurdity. The very existence of such a faction is significant. The need to adopt 'a commonsense stance' is itself an acknowledgment of the waywardness to which our subject is prone. For the adoption of such a stance represents a determination of the will, not a finding. An innocent, looking over the wall, will surely be intrigued to find there is a division of our subject going under the name of common-sense philosophy – put about by people called common-sense philosophers. No one expects certain doctors, lawyers, and engineering consultants to have to set themselves apart as a common-sense faction. Nor are there common-sense economists, geographers, or historians. To be sure, *common-sense* is not really a satisfactory label to rally around. It hints at a ground for a conviction – not quite sense perception, but like it – although in truth a ground is not invoked and is possibly not needed. But whatever the label, every philosopher takes out a temporary membership in this group when reacting to arguments for scepticism – even when contemporary philosophers claim that the arguments for scepticism are, when presented with care, much stronger than hitherto thought. It is then a question of patiently undoing what has been patiently done. In this way, there is point in Locke's description of the philosopher – or at least a certain kind of philosopher – as an under-labourer, removing the obstacles which lie in our path. We should note however that obsessive carefulness and a devotion to common sense is no guarantee that one will not say the strangest of things, as the example of Moore shows. One only has to think of what he had to say about 'goodness'.[44]

[43]   Perhaps by Galen Strawson, see 'Why I Have No Future', *The Philosophers' Magazine*, 2007. 'You can't harm [people] simply by bringing about their painless and unforeseen death' (23–4). It is worth remarking on this curious qualification. The interesting truth is that we cannot harm people *simply by hurting* them. As we all know, a doctor can often truly say: 'This will hurt you, but don't worry, it won't harm you'. This tells us something significant about the concept of harm.

[44]   This oddity is not however evenly spread. It is very prevalent in the philosophy of mind, and pretty evident in metaphysics and ethical theory, but in my experience modern epistemology is comparatively sane. This no

The Doctor of Philosophy Will See You Now

This particular waywardness in philosophy is a result of three factors. The first factor must be the peculiar combativeness of philosophers, at least when roused. They act as if they would rather be different than correct. Feminists might say *male* philosophers at this point, but I have not myself noticed anything to justify this restriction. Philosophers at the outset of their careers, once they have a safe job, tend to feel obliged to make their mark by saying what will be thought by their immediate predecessors to be off the wall. It can be all right though, if a trifle risky, to return in triumph to the rejected conclusions of *the predecessors* of their predecessors. That nice old saying: 'Two Jews, three opinions' applies pretty well to philosophers too. (No, make that *four* opinions...) I speak in this paragraph about matters of theory only. In social attitude of course we can expect a good deal of the uniformity to be expected in humanities departments.

The second factor is the loss, at least in recent decades, of the insight that philosophers run the risk not only of saying things which are untrue or unwarranted, but also of saying what only appears to make sense. Philosophical enquiry takes place at the edges of our understanding, even when the topics are everyday ones. This is why we continually ask what is time, what is causality, number, action, knowledge, consciousness, etc., when in a sense we already know the answers. But in recent decades we have no longer been so sensitive to the risk of senselessness. So often what is offered as the results of philosophical enquiry should be regarded instead as the raw material for it. It is thought perhaps that as we are no longer logical positivists we can afford to relax in this regard, both in regard to propositions and questions. It is as if we were all now prepared to go along with W. E. Johnson's remark (expressing his exasperation with Wittgenstein) 'If I say that a sentence has meaning for me no one has a right to say that it is senseless'.[45] This subjective reassurance has rather returned to the subject and we are the poorer for it.

---

doubt stems from the nature of the task epistemologists have so often set themselves: of *defeating* the waywardness of scepticism. Political philosophy too often avoids reliance on the uncertainties of theory, setting itself up as 'political not metaphysical'. The metaphysical doctrines in Hobbes – the psychological egoism, the determinism and the materialism – have little bearing on what is of interest in his moral and political philosophy and indeed prove something of a distraction.

[45]   W. E. Johnson to Drury, 1929, *Ludwig Wittgenstein, Personal Recollections*, 118.

The last factor must be the peculiar difficulty of the topic. In Russell's estimation a good philosopher of logic could only think about his subject once in six months for half a minute.[46] I stress the peculiar difficulty, for one does not have to think of philosophy as the hardest subject there is. There is perhaps no one scale of hardness.[47] What gives philosophy its peculiar difficulty, by contrast let us say with chemistry, is that one is working with a thin set of presuppositions. No doubt there are philosophers who would like to be working without presuppositions at all. There is in addition an indeterminacy in the criticism of argument. Arguments even in philosophy are often – and of necessity – the merest of sketches, where the definitive detection of a fallacious step is difficult or impossible. Time and again we have to make do with the impression of validity.[48] Then there is the (related) handicap of not being able to see when one is gradually going wrong. Gains won are thus apt to be lost again like a rare patch of sunlight on a hill. There is an element of truth in the view of philosophy as seen from the perspective of our academic neighbours, the mathematicians. A colleague in mathematics, during yet another bout of anxiety about university funding, was explaining to me, with a wink, just how little by way of resources a mathematician required: no expensive apparatus – simply a pad of paper, a pen and a waste paper basket – the suggestion of course being that philosophy was even more economical, only paper and pen being needed. This rather nice distinction must I think have gone the rounds. It hits home.

7. Problems of Understanding

All this said, we now have to face further troubling factors. Application can stumble over interpretation in a way which seems peculiar to our subject. Philosophers say a variety of strange things about time, causality, personal identity, consciousness; they say these things upfront, with punch and apparent clarity; we think we know where we are with these philosophers; we set out unflinchingly

[46] 'The Philosophy of Logical Atomism', 166.
[47] Wittgenstein told Drury, I do not expect very seriously: If you think philosophy is hard, you should try architecture. Rush Rhees, ed., *Ludwig Wittgenstein, Personal Recollections* (Blackwell, 1981) 121.
[48] It is possible to render an argument trivially valid by adding hypothetical premises, but this of course merely shifts the difficulty. We have now to consider the truth of these new premises.

to 'apply' these teachings. But alas, so often, when philosophers say so forthrightly and clearly that p, it turns out they do not quite mean that p. Or they mean something which could be expressed: 'p strictly speaking' or 'p for philosophical purposes'. This manoeuvre has been familiar since Berkeley made use of it.[49] The phrase 'seriously speaking', as used in the study, tends to become 'frivolously speaking' as soon as we step into the street. It turns out, in the small print as it were, that most of what we ordinarily think gets reinstated by the back door.

Philosophers start with what is bold. There are no clients to be advised, that has to be admitted. Ridicule is not going to intimidate them. They must after all follow the argument where it leads, to return to that heroic formula. However all is not lost. There *are* we shall be told — and no possible doubt about it — surrogate entities: quasi-clients, virtual clients, folk clients, clients unstrictly-speaking, or what might be called clients-for-practical-purposes. And once again we are back in business as if nothing had ever happened.

As an example of what I have in mind we might return to Eric Olson's *What Are We?* As we saw, a chapter of this book takes up the thesis that we are nothing at all, that there are no people ('just as there are no dragons', 183). All the same, the proponent of this startling idea is apparently quite prepared, when put on the spot, to concede that there is *something* right in the thought that there are, let us say, at least six million people in London. 'We can take it for ordinary purposes to be true' he will say (184). Perhaps, after all, there is *almost everything* right in such a thought! Let us contrast the startling view that there are no people with the equally startling view that not only are there people, lots of them — there are also people *with wings*. David Lewis shocked his readers by explaining modality in terms of how things unmodally are. Thus if people with wings are a bare possibility there really *are* people with wings. They simply inhabit worlds which are radically inaccessible from the world we live in. The interesting thing however is that this remarkable discovery, just like the other, appears to have *no* practical implications. We can take it for ordinary purposes to be false.[50] A

---

[49]   *Principles of Human Knowledge*, Sec. 51–3.
[50]   David Lewis in ch. 2.6 of *On the Plurality of Worlds* (Oxford: Blackwell, 1986) says in effect that his doctrine has no practical implications. It has however an ethical upshot, good news for those who devoutly hope that 'the good' be maximised. For the sum total of this quantity in existence 'is non-contingently fixed' (128). It is thus forever maximised, and is indeed maximised whatever we do.

similar reassurance will perhaps be given by those who say curious things about consciousness. In the real world, it's business as usual. Someone who likes to inflict pain need not be disappointed to learn that consciousness does not exist. Nor need the news, purveyed by the next philosopher he meets, that *everything* is conscious, prompt him to flog the pavement.

This saying-and half-unsaying manoeuvre is perhaps not always a cheat, but it certainly lends further uncertainty to the project of applying philosophical discoveries. It is relevant here to note the extraordinary frequency with which philosophers claim to have been misunderstood even *by other philosophers*. Galen Strawson, after expressing his gratitude to all those who had commented on his paper 'The Self,' went on to say that 'the result was a festival of misunderstanding'.[51] Philosophers will not be particularly surprised with this reaction. But where does this leave the project of philosophical consultancy? Applied philosophers take up the work of non-applied philosophers, which quite likely they do not well understand (though perhaps they think they do), and with its aid advise those with little philosophy or none, who are presumably offered arguments which they in turn do not well understand (though perhaps they think they do).

Someone seeking advice from a philosophical counsellor will not simply be told what to do, but, in view of the waywardness I have talked about, will expect to be reassured with arguments. But – will the client be able to evaluate these arguments? Will he be *well* able to evaluate them? It was once part of my job to write a report for my professor on what was called 'the lunatic file' at the Lovell Radio Telescope at Jodrell Bank in Cheshire – then the largest such telescope in the world, much in the news, and the target of much peculiar correspondence lovingly preserved in this file. A few of the items had all the appearance, to untutored me, of rigour and solid content. I was rather in the position of a Diderot confronted by an Euler with a mathematical demonstration of God's existence.

8. The Curious Confinement to Matters Ethical and the Further Problems This Confinement Brings

As we know, the project of practical advice based upon the insights of philosophy is so often supposed exclusively to relate to 'high matters

[51]   'The Self and the SESMET', 99.

of the ethical' – not, for example, to the mere vulgar question of how to get something wanted. A consultant will invariably be found quoting the words of Socrates: 'We are discussing no small matter but how we are to live' (*Republic*, 352d). And this would be taken by readers – by secular modern readers – in a high-minded way, with a heavy emphasis on altruism and ecology.

This exclusive focus seems unnecessary. Might not a philosopher with an interest in metaphysics find gainful employment in a firm seeking to build a time machine? Some philosophers have conjectured that there could be cases of backwards causation – so that action could be taken now to ensure that people who might have been killed in an accident long ago in fact survived it. Surely this might have commercial applications? An embarrassed author who had published a mistake in a work of history might be willing to pay to have reality put right. Millionaires troubled about thoughts of death might want to call on experts in the problems of personal identity over time. McTaggart long since showed what could be done, republishing during the First World War the two chapters from *Some Dogmas of Religion* which defended a belief in human immortality.[52] Some people might hope for a different message, and look for a proof that death is the end – like the dying Maugham grasping his reassurance from the confident Ayer.

No doubt the commercial willingness to pay for philosophical insight has tended to focus on matters ethical rather than metaphysical for sound business reasons. For there is an evident necessity in every corporation to encourage honesty among employees. Analogous hopes might be entertained for all the ethics courses so eagerly introduced into our medical schools. They did not have ethics courses in Dr Shipman's time! However this involvement with ethics brings troubles of its own for philosophical consultancy and in more than one way. I shall begin with a *very* practical matter.

A course in practical ethics is supposed to be 'improving'. We need to ask whether this hope is realistic. There seems to be a confusion here between the philosophical and the inspirational. Should a corporation thinking of putting on an ethics course expect pilfering to increase or decrease? Inspirational courses, run by a reverend, might reduce pilfering somewhat. Distinctively philosophical courses on the other hand should increase it. After all, such a course will encourage the employees to question their beliefs.

---

[52] *Human Immortality and Pre-existence*, Edward Arnold, 1916. McTaggart's reasons were quite ungodly of course, he being a devout atheist.

Chris Coope

That – we are continually told – is what philosophy is all about. Now some of these beliefs will be permissive, and some restrictive. Which kind of belief, are we to suppose, is the more likely to be questioned? Employees will have been taught, restrictively, that stealing is wrong. They may not all succeed in challenging this belief at the very first attempt even though it is plainly a barrier to freedom. I leave aside the fiddling of expenses for this can easily be justified without academic assistance. Otherwise inhibitions will remain strong. It will probably not be enough for their ethicist to proclaim "to each according to his need", beautiful principle though this is. Some of the workforce will only set about stealing once they are introduced to the error theory of obligation, the theory which boldly proclaims the *falsity* of moral teachings. Others will hold out till they reach the next lecture, the one on fictionalism, which suggests that we should all nevertheless *pretend* that stealing is wrong; or the next and somewhat exotic lecture after that, the anthropological bit about guiltless thievery among the uk. Even then a pious and unadventurous remnant will cling to mother's knee morality, at least until the lecturer turns to the embarrassing but inevitable question: why be moral? For the only rational response to this would seem to be: 'Why indeed?', or 'I was just about to ask you'.[53]

The question why anyone need care to be 'moral' (the scare-quotes rather force themselves upon us) is made the more difficult because there is little agreement among the learned about what constitutes a reason for action. There is indeed little agreement about what morality is all about: the more the thought the more the variety. 'Doesn't he understand the difference between right and wrong?' 'No, he's a philosopher.' This lack of agreement, if known about, must undermine the confidence of those who somewhat unaccountably wish to obey the demands of morality and simply hope to obtain guidance as to what these demands might be.

Philosophical advising which calls upon moral philosophy intro-duces its *own* layer of difficulty – that is to say, apart from what might *already* arise from our difficulties with the concepts of knowledge, personal identity, consciousness, etc, which we have touched on above. The accounts of morality and its demands on offer are very confidently expressed and yet are hopelessly diverse. Philosophers, unless their education has been very confined, will be

---

[53] Well, that is a little hasty and cynical. The employees might be asked to read the careful and well-deployed answer to this important question at the end of Peter Singer's *Practical Ethics*. This answer, if accepted, should increase pilfering considerably.

aware of this, but their clients can hardly be expected to appreciate it. In medical consultation one might occasionally ask for a second opinion. In *moral* consultation, what ought the rational client be asking for? A twenty-eighth opinion? And as the number of philosophers at work increases all over the world so does the diversity. Think of what we have already. There are various incompatible virtue theories, incompatible appeals to intuition, colossal claims as to the interests of sentient beings, and so forth. Isn't compassion at least commended by everybody? Not if Nietzsche is to be included. And among those who stress compassion, some say that we must have a compassion not just for actual people (or perhaps 'sentient beings') but for possible ones as well (perhaps even 'possible sentient beings'). Others will regard this not just as false but as ludicrous. Or is the talk all about intrinsic value and rights? Some people think that trees have intrinsic value, others are absolutely sure they have none, and yet others will argue from the side-lines that this talk of intrinsic value makes no sense at all. Some people say that there are natural rights, others that there are no such things, yet others that the very notion of a natural right is nonsensical. Some say – Wittgenstein for example – that good conduct is simply obedience to God's commands. Their critics will say that this idea has been ruled out of court ever since the *Euthyphro*.[54] Some say that morality is about something called the right thing to do (with due allowance for joint winners) but that it is in principle impossible for us to know on any occasion what this is. Others will allow that we can sometimes know what this Right Thing is, but will then leave it entirely mysterious why people should be so concerned to find out. Would they have to be moved by items called moral reasons, or is there nothing interestingly distinctive of the kind? Isn't morality in any case something of a tyrant or a bully? Wouldn't 'liberals' be particularly anxious about this question? Or is it contrary to morality even to raise it? Philosophers worry incessantly about whether this or that account of morality is 'too demanding'. Other philosophers presumably worry about what 'too demanding' could mean. There are even those who suppose that morality makes no *demands* of us at all, that it simply pats certain backs. And we must not forget all those philosophers who continually say, with great assurance, that no one is ever responsible for what they do ('is never really or ultimately responsible' seems to be the preferred

---

[54] 'If there is any proposition which expresses precisely what I think, offered the familiar *Euthyphro* contrast, Wittgenstein is reported as saying: it is the proposition "What God commands, that is good".' F. Waismann, *Wittgenstein and the Vienna Circle*, 115.

language) so that no one has ever deserved a pat on the back in the first place. Faced with all this, and more, one might be tempted to conclude, gratefully adapting what Russell – so often of assistance to us in this enquiry – once said about mathematics: Ethics is the subject where no one knows what they are talking about, nor whether what they are saying is true.[55]

Perhaps people will want to say that the most recent and up to date moral theorists have at long last turned a corner, that they now have a rather better understanding of all these things, just as we now have better dentistry. However these recent theorists are still not in agreement about the most elementary theoretical matters. I have space for just one example. Here is Hugh LaFolette, trying (admirably) to be very plain and straightforward. He is setting out to explain his subject to a beginner in the very first paragraph of a large anthology he has edited.[56] Surely the first step at least will be on firm ground? He distinguishes two kinds of choice. There are choices which affect only ourselves. These, he says, we do not consider to be 'moral choices'. They are not, that is to say, choices which stand to be assessed 'on moral grounds'. Such assessment is confined to choices which affect others. Of course being a thoughtful writer, he immediately issues a caution. It is often not too clear, he says, just when a choice 'affects only the agent'. This cautiousness is of course in order. But it might encourage the reader to suppose that he is in safe hands. This however is not the case. A huge and controversial move has been made. What has gone wrong? I will simply say this, that neither Aristotle nor Kant would have recognised such a divide. For Aristotle what was of central importance was practical wisdom, or more colloquially good sense. For Kant, what was of central importance were the duties we have to ourselves. Hugh LaFollette in effect sides with Mill. Or rather I should say with the Mill of 'On Liberty', Chapter 4, where the distinction is indeed clearly made. Insofar, however, as Mill *was a utilitarian* – as most people are still determined to say – the LaFollette divide would make little sense. After all, if there is a duty to maximise the good (pleasure, or what have you) then the agent's own good must count. Choices which affect only the agent would then be among the choices 'we should assess on moral grounds'. If therefore, *either* Aristotle, *or* Kant *or* the utilitarians are right, something has gone importantly wrong in the first step, the step which looked so innocent. This will not be a rare event in philosophy.

---

[55]   Russell's original remark is in 'Mathematics and the Metaphysicians', *Mysticism and Logic*, 75.
[56]   *Ethics in Practice* (Oxford: Blackwell, 1997) 1.

9. The Pretended Appeal to Something Independent

Moral theorising – that is to say, what we are called upon to apply – is supposed to provide a check, is supposed to be able to put us right. But it is always giving us (what we take to be) the wrong results in actual cases, sometimes indeed quite comical results – as with the suggestion that one must somehow be able to 'justify' going out for dinner or walking down a country lane. By contrast, we are far more sure that murder and rape are outrages than we are of any philosophical understanding of the matter, an understanding which eludes us if we attempt to go much beyond initial simplicities. Theorising is only taken to give us the right results when it more or less tells us what we think we know already, and the more we recognise our need to distrust it the more pronounced this tendency must be. Utilitarian theories have had continually to be 'corrected' in this way. Indeed, as Philippa Foot has said, the modifications seem never to have been able to catch up with the objections.[57]

Kant is commonly regarded as the most profound of moral theorists, he being the philosopher who thought most deeply about human dignity. But what good was that to him, so many philosophers will say, when the time for application came round? I mean application by the man himself, not by others who might well be misunderstanding him. His own applications indeed could well be taken as a guide to what he actually meant. His modern admirers however – and how many of them there are – will almost always consider that his applications, even those most closely related to the idea of human dignity, were profoundly misguided, and even offensive. Think what he would be telling them about lying, equality, animals, homosexuality, suicide and capital punishment. Think too about what he would be saying about 'self defilement', surely very much a Kantian notion. All very unpopular. If Kant were to say these things today he would be prosecuted for 'hate-speech'. In recent decades support for abortion has almost come to define the decent mind. We can readily glean what *he* would have had to say on the topic. It would not be what his admirers would like to hear.[58] People will say that

---

[57] 'Utilitarianism and the Virtues', *Moral Dilemmas*, (Oxford: Clarendon Press, 2002) 60.

[58] For Kant's view that that a human offspring is 'a person' and is not an item of parental property, see the discussion of procreation in *The Metaphysics of Morals* (Mary Gregor, trans., Cambridge: Cambridge University Press, 1991, 98–100). And concerning suicide, Kant maintains that it is not a crime only against oneself but is sometimes a crime against

Kant was simply carried away by the prejudices of his time. What makes them so sure that *they* are not being carried away by the prejudices current in present day academic circles? The one claim does not exclude the other of course. And in either case we are left with the solid result: that the application of ethics on the part of philosophers is strikingly susceptible to prejudice.

In practice all this will mean that people will accept philosophical doctrines when the application seems to fit what they would like to maintain. This is what we expect to happen in regard to claims about 'personhood' for example, gratefully pressed into service in order to excuse what we want to have done: not so much the application of philosophical insight as the philosophical decoration of an opinion. Concepts are here chosen to suit practical ends. In 1859 a black slave girl in the US tried her hand at a little practical philosophy, as we would nowadays call it, no doubt as advised by a skilful lawyer. On being accused of theft before Roger Taney, at that time Chief Justice of the United States Supreme Court, she ingeniously pointed out that she was not classified as 'a person', whereas the relevant statute said quite plainly: 'Any person who...' Naturally this was not going to produce the wanted result. It was ruled that she was a person after all, it being a matter (as the District Attorney said) of what was evident to the eye.[59]

10. Our Pessimism as to the Prospects for Moral Advice Unexpectedly Reinforced

In 1977, when the movement for applied ethics had rather got under way, R. M. Hare, himself something of an inspiration to this movement, wrote an optimistic paper about its prospects: entitled 'Medical ethics: Can the moral philosopher help?'[60] Despite the restriction in the title, this essay was concerned with 'applying ethics' rather generally. 'The problems of medical ethics', Hare said, 'are so typical of the moral problems that moral philosophy is supposed to be able to help with, that a failure here really would be a sign either of the uselessness of the discipline or of the incompetence

---

others too, and mentions the case of suicide in pregnancy. Parents who commit suicide, he says, can violate their duty to their children (218).

[59]   *United States v. Amy*, 1859, 24 Federal Cases, No. 14445.

[60]   Reprinted in Hare's *Essays on Bioethics*, (Oxford: Clarendon Press 1993).

of the particular practitioner' (1). Hare, though he can't have known it, offers some welcome support for the thesis I have been defending.

If the project of practical assistance is on track, Professor Hare suggested, this can only be because philosophy itself has turned a corner. Until quite recently, Hare was happy to admit, philosophy would have been totally incompetent to give advice, since it lacked a vital ingredient: rigour.

> It is only very recently in the history of philosophy that general standards of rigour in argument have improved to such an extent that there is some hope of establishing our discipline on a firm basis. (1)

And it seems undeniable that standards of care and clarity in argument have rather risen since the mid nineteenth century, at least in philosophy of a broadly analytic character. But it matters how this 'rigour' is characterised. This is what Hare had in mind:

> I mean such things as the insistence on knowing, and being able to explain, exactly what one means when one says something, which involves being able to say what logically follows from it and what does not, what it is logically consistent with, and so on. If this is not insisted upon, arguments will get lost in the sands (2).

Now if this is a precondition of the enterprise of advice, I wish to argue, the enterprise cannot possibly get under way. For where in philosophy is it possible to observe this standard of rigour? Philosophy discusses concepts about which we are unclear – cause, time, change, reason for action, knowledge, obligation, wisdom, possibility, intention, person, thought, and so on. In regard to all these we remain in difficulties even after considerable progress has been made. Arguments which essentially involve such concepts are going to be hard to evaluate. People think that it must be pretty easy for someone competent in formal logic to tell whether or not an inference is valid. This might be an artefact of the kind of exercises offered in logic textbooks. When Elizabeth Anscombe towards the end of her life produced a version of (or an improvement of) Anselm's *Proslogion* argument for God's existence, she said – interestingly – 'I could not determine whether it was a valid argument'[61]

---

[61] 'Anselm or Russelm', *Philosophical Quarterly*, 1993, 500, commenting on her earlier article 'Why Anselm's Proof in the *Proslogion* is not an Ontological Argument', *Thoreau Quarterly*, 1985.

Chris Coope

Hare went on to say

> Even now it [i.e. 'rigour' thus described] is insisted on only in
> certain parts of the philosophical world; one is very likely to
> meet philosophers who do not accept this requirement of
> rigour, and my advice is that one should regard them in the
> same light as one would regard a medical man, whether or not
> he had the right letters after his name, who claimed to have a
> wonder drug which would cure the common cold, but was not
> ready to submit it to controlled tests.

The upshot is clear, either we will pretend to a standard of 'rigour'
which has always been impossible and will ever remain so, or we shall
properly regard the purveyors of applied ethics as a bunch of quacks.

11. The assumption of Simple, Honest, Goodness

If philosophers are to become not just our advisors but our spiritual
directors one last difficulty must now be faced. We naturally tend to
make the kindly and civilised (or perhaps just lazy) assumption, that
consultants on matters ethical are nearly always going to be simple,
honest and good − to borrow Nestle's language from the Shredded
Wheat packet. But might they not quite often be shifty, bent or
spoiled? I mean, somewhat more than is usual? And here I am not
so much concerned with the case of a teacher who in the past might
have acted 'unethically' in some spectacular way, such as the
Safeway Poisoner, a onetime lecturer in biochemistry hired to teach
medical ethics at the University of Manchester, having served 7
years of a 12 year sentence for attempted murder.[62] Such a teacher
would, in my view, be somewhat more likely to have a sounder
view of the sanctity of life than prevails among ethics teachers generally. I am thinking of rottenness embraced rather than rottenness
repented of.

True enough, we are very willing to accept that human beings *can*
be corrupt as distinct from incompetent. This is how people view
contemporary holocaust-deniers. Or our minds will return to
certain horrible exemplars from history. It might be thought that
these exemplars could not include academics like ourselves, seriously
concerned with ethics. But take the case of the eminent academic
Joachim Mrugowsky. Professor Dr. Mrugowsky (as he was called,
in Continental style) once edited, with a new Introduction, a work

[62] *The Times*, March 11, 2004.

in medical ethics by the celebrated nineteenth-century doctor, Christoph Hufeland, a man who had corresponded with Kant and had treated Goethe. In demonstrating this concern for ethics Mugrowsky was indeed something of a pioneer, for the practical ethics enthusiasm with which we are now so familiar had yet to take hold: we follow in his footsteps. Yet only a few years after the book was published we find Mrugowsky being sentenced to death for ordering lethal typhus experiments on prisoners at Buchenwald. In his Final Statement to the Court he actually mentioned this work on ethics and claimed always to have lived by its principles.[63]

However a focus on such exotic examples is misleading. No one should suppose that those who are prominently concerned, often to good effect, with what are called 'human rights abuses' could not themselves be advocating human rights abuses.[64] Peter Singer artlessly divides humanity into those who are 'vicious, violent and irrational' and 'the rest of us'.[65] This is surely a divide appropriate only to the world of the Western movie or to the novels of Dickens. This them-and-us distinction is made easier by the inclusion of the word 'violent'. But we should remember that so many outrages, including murder, need not be in the least violent. Poisoning is a gentle thing. If someone is tempted by the thought that corruption is what happens elsewhere, it is something of an antidote to reflect how corrupt we in the West must appear to far-away Muslims. Alternatively, we could usefully imagine how practical ethics would probably have developed, and been taught, if the idea had taken hold in the American South before the Civil War. When Hume said that the errors in philosophy tended to be ridiculous rather than dangerous he cannot have thought how philosophy would one day be 'applied'.

There are two ways in which we will almost inevitably underestimate the extent of corruption. Firstly, we tend to think of corruption as a rottenness which spreads through our whole being, as with apples in the apple barrel. We might think here of the drawing of the boy

---

[63] 'As far as my own concepts of the ethical duties of the doctor are concerned, they are contained in my book regarding medical ethics, and I believe always to have acted according to the principles of that book and lived according to them. My life, my actions, and my aims were clean. That is why now that at the end of this trial I can declare myself free of personal guilt.'

[64] An organisation might usefully be devoted to second-order vigilance – 'Human Rights Watch *Watch*' it might be called.

[65] *How Are We To Live?*, London: Mandarin, 1994, ix.

who smoked in *Scouting for Boys*, his vice seeming to affect his very posture. It is surely important to recognise that a corrupt person can also show perfectly admirable and attractive traits. 'Dissonance' of this kind is perfectly common. Who is more despised than a child molester? But such an individual might be the very person who saves your life, even at the risk of his own. Secondly, we tend to work with a relaxed standard of good faith. More particularly we work with a *subjective* notion of good faith: a man has subjective good faith when he thinks – 'sincerely' thinks, I suppose it would be said – he is acting well. I say that this is a relaxed standard since almost everyone (not excluding Professor Mrugowsky) will be pretty well permanently in subjective good faith. This robs the notion of interest. It lacks interest rather in the way a concept of 'subjective knowledge' would lack interest. (I talk about 'good faith' rather than 'integrity'. The word 'integrity' is indeterminate in sense, its chief use being to lend to one's writing a certain tone. A concept-dropper's notion.)

In considering this topic in the context of this talk let us leave aside the unlovely enthusiasm for 'the unsanctifying of human life' which is such a remarkable feature of the practical ethics movement. For there is a special kind of corruption relevant to teaching or advising. Nowadays the word 'corruption' suggests bribery. This represents a dangerous narrowing and trivialising of the notion. A corrupt teacher by this narrow notion would have to be – let us say – a professor of ethics caught taking kick-backs from a manufacturer of windmills in return for suitably scary lectures about global warming. The kind of corruption peculiarly relevant to teaching involves a willingness to lie or improperly to deceive, where there need be no suggestion of bribery. As we have mentioned, certain philosophers of academic standing have been saying in recent years that moral obligations are as mythical as ghosts and dragons, and that in consequence every moral judgment to the effect that this *ought* to be done, or that there was an *obligation* to do that, are all false. The default position would be that everything is permitted, though the very word 'permitted' would naturally drop out of use. Now there is nothing especially surprising about all this. It must indeed be allowed that the concept of a specifically moral kind of obligation is rather suspect. These philosophers however often want to continue to assert or endorse what they do not believe to be true: they want to continue to say that we are *not* permitted to rape or to be cruel. They want to 'mis-speak' as people nowadays say. This introduces a manipulative dishonesty into the heart of the project of practical ethics.

It might be thought impossible that philosophers who are supposed to love the truth could favour the lie. But then we remember our founding father, Plato.[66] Berkeley though a bishop was prepared to suggest that philosophers should be willing to tell the general public all manner of things, 'how false soever they may be' in order to bring about the desirable result: human wellbeing.[67] Sir Isaiah Berlin was a man so greatly admired in our day for his learning and humanity. Yet he thought it right, both at the time and in retrospect, to betray the trust of his dying father.[68] The best known textbook in medical ethics, constantly in demand year on year in our medical school, writes as if telling lies to patients about their condition can be quite permissible, seeing that the Principle of Autonomy is sometimes overruled by the Principle of Beneficence.[69] The most that can be required of us is to be economical with the untruth. A similar message emerges from John Mackie's *Ethics*, a much reprinted work. 'A prudent man will not squander his limited stock of convincing lies, but use it sparingly to the best effect'.[70] That sounds like irony, but the context suggests not.

People who acknowledge that some prohibitions must be exceptionless have sometimes wondered whether the prohibition of lying should be included. They might mention jokes, or the conventional untruths which are part of etiquette. Or they might be thinking

---

[66]   *Republic*, 389b, 414c.

[67]   *Principles of Human Knowledge*, Sec. 52.

[68]   'Why I do not regret lying to my father about life after death', *The Times*, 19 July, 1996, p. 16. 'We did not talk about death at home. I think my father hoped that there was a future life. In fact, when he thought he was dying, he asked me if I thought there was going to be a life after death. I said that yes, I did. That was a lie. A lie, a lie which I uttered because he obviously wanted it to be so and hoped we would be able to meet again, and I did not want to tell him what I saw as the bleak truth. So I did not tell the truth, and I do not in the least regret it. Since I believed that nothing would follow one's death, why should I cause a dying father pain?'

[69]   T. Beauchamp and J. Childress, *Principles of Biomedical Ethics*, 4th edn., New York: Oxford University Press, 1994, 126: 'on balance the lie may be justified in this context...'. In Case 2, 512–3 it is referred to as 'a bald lie', so we know pretty well what we are talking about. Google-searching suggests that no one finds this passage in Beauchamp and Childress to be worthy of note. (This thought runs through various editions up to the present day.)

[70]   *Ethics, Inventing Right and Wrong*, (Harmondsworth: Penguin, 1977) 183. The chapter is called 'Elements of a Practical Morality'.

of answers to be given to the Gestapo about the Jews in the attic. If so, we should narrow the description. We are dealing here with a special case, *lying in a fiduciary relationship*, that is to say a case of lying which is betrayal of trust, no doubt about serious matters. A teacher of practical ethics is in just such a relationship.

12. In Conclusion

Where does all this leave the vulnerable client? It leaves him with the prospect of having to rely on an advisor who might think he more or less knows what's what, but whose mind has been filled with a cloud of unknowing: more exactly, with a mass of fantasy, uncertainty, and the occasional insight, put across with much unpleasing earnestness. Furthermore the advisor, being well read in ethics, might well have learned to lie or to deceive his clients – no doubt somewhat reluctantly, perhaps even half-consciously, but in the interest of some good cause dear to his heart or faction. All in all, hardly worth the fee.

I do not want to end however on this somewhat negative note. There is scope in philosophy for an instructive exercise or party game. We might call it 'proving the outrageous'. Nothing could be more practical. Participants take a short course in philosophy and then face certain questions, being expected to show versatility and ingenuity. In how many ways can it be shown that black is white? In how many ways can it be shown that nothing exists? In how many ways can it be shown that it is all right to kill a toddler? And so on. The power of moral philosophy provides enormous scope in regard to this last as I have often been able to demonstrate to my students. Certain elementary moves here will occur to anyone who has attended so much as half the short course. But there is also help to be expected from scholarship. There are insights, for example, in *Nicomachean Ethics*, Book VIII. Sec. 12 – material which has, to date, been insufficiently exploited. It is about parents and their children, parts and wholes, shared identity and the ownership of teeth.

Plotinus: Charms and Countercharms

STEPHEN R. L. CLARK

A Very Personal Beginning

For the last few years, thanks to the Leverhulme Trust, I've been largely absent from my department, working on the late antique philosopher Plotinus. To speak personally – it's been a difficult few years, since my youngest daughter has been afflicted with anorexia during this period, and my own bowel cancer was discovered, serendipitously, and removed, at the end of 2005. Since then I've had ample occasion to consider the importance – and the difficulty – of the practice of detachment, and also to worry about the moral some have drawn from Plotinian and similar philosophies, namely that the things of this world really do not matter much, and that we should withdraw ourselves from them. Maybe it is true, as Plotinus says, that 'some troubles are profitable to the sufferers themselves, poverty and sickness for example'.[1] But this is not an altogether helpful message for those afflicted by the bundle of disorders that lead to anorexia. It's difficult not to suspect, for example, that Simone Weil would have lived longer but for her Neo-Platonism. It has also been made obvious to me that we are (or at any rate, I am) much less in control of our own mental and emotional states even than I had thought before. None of this, of course, should have been any surprise: I have frequently pointed out – to myself and others – the importance of distinguishing between one's self and the states one finds oneself in, and the extreme difficulty of controlling the thoughts we say are ours (but which, by that very fact, reveal themselves as very far from *ours*). Any delusion that my knowledge of these facts is of itself enough to render me immune to them has been – at least for the moment – thoroughly debunked – though the facts themselves are such that this disillusionment, so to call it, is probably both temporary and almost entirely insincere!

But to return to Plotinus. My study of Plotinus's Ethics and Psychology began from the recognition that Plotinus is seeking not

---

[1] *Enneads* III.2.5, 15: I use Hilary Armstrong's translation throughout (*Plotinus: The Enneads* Loeb Classical Library, Heinemann: London 1966–88).

doi:10.1017/S1358246109990117   © The Royal Institute of Philosophy and the contributors 2009
Royal Institute of Philosophy Supplement **65** 2009   215

Stephen R.L. Clark

merely to advise but to offer techniques of self-improvement through the use of imagination and – in a sense which I shall try to explicate – invocation. It is also important to be ready to recognize that Plotinian Ethics may seem harsh or irrelevant to moralists who have come to take it for granted that the object of moral action must be to 'improve' things, and that it is the outcome, in terms of human or maybe sentient 'happiness' that is the proper criterion of good judgement. Plotinus, like other ancient moralists, is less concerned about pains and pleasures, and less inclined to judge actions by their outcomes. His is an ethic that could reasonably be described as 'otherworldly', but may still have implications for action and political organization in this world. Though, as I have just hinted, there are elements in his philosophy that might appeal to depressives, his own character, so it seems, was more sanguine than melancholic. It is quite likely that *Porphyry*, his disciple, friend and eventual editor, was depressive: he records that Plotinus spotted his condition, and ordered him away from Rome to Sicily to recover.

Sorting out what the aim of ethical action should be, why all *action* is held to be, in some sense, second-best, and how he suggests we should learn to be properly virtuous, has been my principal task. My conclusion, so far, is that a Plotinian framework, and Plotinian accounts of the good, can serve both individual and global ends – in particular it is worth recalling that Neo-Platonic reasonings lie near the root of Islamic as well as Western tradition, and is also, at least, very similar to elements of Hindu and Buddhist traditions. Neglect of this background has sometimes meant that debates between proponents of the separate traditions have been unnecessarily antagonistic (which is not to say that there are no serious disagreements between them). More than most moral philosophers Plotinus actually provided some workable suggestions for how we might achieve virtue (rather than simply telling us to try harder, or perhaps to lower our expectations), and some clearer conception of what virtue is. By changing the 'metaphors we live by', in a phrase made famous by Lakoff & Johnson,[2] we can begin to change the way we live. Plotinus's goal was both to clarify our thinking and to facilitate our virtuous living.

So what is it that he urges us to do? The point is not simply to believe a set of metaphysical doctrines that, however well reasoned, will inevitably seem obscure, contestable or at least supremely odd. Nor can it be to live exactly as he lived. Plotinus's world, the social

---

[2]   George Lakoff & Mark Johnson *Metaphors We Live By* (University of Chicago Press: Chicago 1980).

and imaginative world of third-century Rome, is certainly not ours.[3] He could reasonably suppose that each of us, upon our first entry to the natural universe, was and is incarnate as a star,[4] and that such trials and tribulations as we suffer here and now are often, though not always, just retribution for the crimes we have committed in past lives. 'There is no accident in a man's becoming a slave, nor is he taken prisoner in war by chance, nor is outrage done on his body without due cause, but he was once the doer of that which he now suffers; and a man who made away with his mother will be made away with by a son when he has become a woman, and one who has raped a woman will be a woman in order to be raped'.[5] His contemporaries had another example of such karmic retribution, to which I shall return shortly:

> God's other name is 'father' because he is capable of making all things. Making is characteristic of a father. Prudent people therefore regard the making of children as a duty in life to be taken most seriously and greatly revered, and should any human being pass away childless they see it as the worst misfortune and irreverence. After death, such a person suffers retribution from demons. This is his punishment: the soul of the childless one is sentenced to a body that has neither a man's nature nor a woman's.[6]

There are still people, even philosophers, prepared to believe in karmic reincarnation (though they had better not say so in public if they wish to be football managers), but I know none who seriously think that their own higher selves are still embodied in the stars of heaven, which we now must conceive as very distant and indifferent suns, not as the innumerable eyes of night. Some theorists imagine that any moral feeling at all widespread in our species must have been selected by neo-Darwinian nature, without regard to any 'objective rightness'. Others believe them merely feelings designed to serve the changing interests of more influential classes. At best such feelings are occasional aids in the business of getting on with things and people, getting on with business. We know, or at least we think we know, that there need never be a single goal, a good that serves all natures and desires. And unlike most Hellenic thinkers we think

---

[3]   This paragraph also features in another paper of mine, 'Plotinus on Becoming Love', in Michael McGhee & Michael Chase *Philosophy as a Way of Life* (forthcoming).

[4]   *Enneads* IV.4 [28].5.

[5]   *Enneads* III.2 [47].13, 11ff.

[6]   *Corpus Hermeticum II:* Brian P. Copenhaver *Hermetica* (Cambridge University Press: Cambridge 1992), 12.

pity is a virtue, and for grown men to love boys a vice (notwithstanding the obvious contradiction between the thought that these are moral truisms, and that there are no moral truisms).

Much of our instinctive or unthinking disagreement can be traced to a reaction against Plato, who puts the following words in Socrates' mouth on his last day:

> The body is a source of countless distractions by reason of the mere requirement of food, and is liable also to diseases which overtake and impede us in the pursuit of truth: it fills us full of loves, and lusts, and fears, and fancies of all kinds, and endless foolery, and in very truth, as men say, takes away from us the power of thinking at all. Whence come wars, and fightings, and factions? Whence but from the body and the lusts of the body? All wars are occasioned by the love of money, and money has to be acquired for the sake of the body and in slavish ministration to it; and by reason of all these impediments we have no time to give to philosophy; and, last and worst of all, even if the body allows us leisure and we betake ourselves to some speculation, it is always breaking in upon us, causing turmoil and confusion in our inquiries, and so amazing us that we are prevented from seeing the truth. It has been proved to us by experience that if we would have pure knowledge of anything we must be quit of the body – the soul by herself must behold things by themselves: and then we shall attain that which we desire, and of which we say that we are lovers – wisdom; not while we live, but, as the argument shows, only after death; for if while in company with the body the soul cannot have pure knowledge, one of two things follows – either knowledge is not to be attained at all, or, if at all, after death. For then, and not till then, the soul will be parted from the body and exist by herself alone. In this present life, we think that we make the nearest approach to knowledge when we have the least possible intercourse or communion with the body, and do not suffer the contagion of the bodily nature, but keep ourselves pure until the hour when God himself is pleased to release us. And thus getting rid of the foolishness of the body we may expect to be pure and hold converse with the pure, and to know of ourselves all that exists in perfection unalloyed, which, I take it, is no other than the truth. For the impure are not permitted to lay hold of the pure.[7]

---

[7]   Plato *Phaedo* 67b (tr. Benjamin Jowett).

We are very easily persuaded that this distrust of bodies is pathological, or at any rate mistaken. What has Plotinus, or the Platonic tradition, to do with us and our necessities?

One answer might simply be that we might, after all, be wrong. When modernists deny even the *possibility* of metempsychosis, or of non-rational intelligence, or of the thought that we are indeed asleep and dreaming, they unduly restrict our options – and incidentally create great difficulties for their own, unreflective theories. If it is truly impossible, for example, that I have been a woman, it is also absurd to ask me to imagine what I would feel if I were,[8] and so absurd to demand of me the sort of moral imagination that is the root of justice. If it were really *impossible* to conceive that I'm asleep, it would also be impossible to conceive that there is a real world independent of my feelings and experience. If the only intelligence were strictly rational (that is, founded only in self-evident truth and purely logical inference), none of us would ever know a thing, or care. And if we really trusted *bodies* or our bodily sensations we would hardly realize that anyone else existed, or much mattered. It is possible to feel a sympathetic twinge when we notice someone else in pain, but it would be quite wrong to suggest that our *knowledge* of their pain rests on any bodily affection. The discovery that other creatures really do exist, and feel, is, in effect, a revelation, an intellectual intuition. Our better selves, at least, aim at reality:

> Certainly the good which one chooses must be something which is not the feeling one has when one attains it; that is why the one who takes this for good remains empty, because he only has the feeling which one might get from the good. This is the reason why one would not find acceptable the feeling produced by something one has not got; for instance, one would not delight in a boy because he was present when he was not present; nor do I think that those who find the good in bodily satisfaction would feel pleasure as if they were eating when they were not eating or as if they were enjoying sex when they were not with the one they wanted to be with, or in general when they were not active.[9]

So Platonists might be right after all – and Platonism is indeed a more popular option among working scientists than modern philosophers have realized. But even if we're right, there is always something to be

---

[8]   This is not to say that I *cannot* imagine the impossible, but that I could not infer any definite practical conclusion from what I know to be impossible.

[9]   *Enneads* VI.7 [38].26, 20ff.

learned from other ways of thinking. To modify a remark of Chesterton's, it is the main purpose of historical philosophy to show that humanity can be great and even glorious under conditions, and with beliefs, quite different from our own.[10] But my concern is rather with phenomenology than physics. What is it like, for example, to be a Platonist in love, and what is recommended for our own lives here-now? What is it to become love, to be possessed, to be 'drunk with nectar', to be – and see – Aphrodite? What is it to bring the god in us back to the god in the all? And how do we do it?

Mysticism, Morality and Magic

It is a common error – at least among philosophers – to contrast Mysticism and Morality, and thence to conclude that either Plotinus can have little to say about everyday moral concerns, or else that what he does say is too robust and uncompassionate to convince us now. It is true that, on the one hand, Plotinus seems to suggest that we should detach ourselves from all earthly concerns, turning to more and more abstract goals, and regarding events here-now as no more than children's games.[11] On the other hand, he is confident that we should care for whatever is kin to the Father (and therefore should care for every living soul[12]), and supposes that Minos' communion with Zeus issued in laws for the proper conduct of society.[13] My argument is that 'the flight of the alone to the Alone', to use the most familiar translation of Plotinus's slogan[14] is misinterpreted. Seeking solitude is the very essence of the fall: 'as if they were tired of being together, they each go to their own',[15] and the inward turn that Plotinus recommends is actually a turn towards community. 'When we look outside that on which we depend we do not know that we are one, like faces which are many on the outside but have one head inside. But if someone is able to turn around, either by himself or having the good luck to have his hair pulled by Athena herself, he will see God and himself and the all

---

[10] G.K. Chesterton *Fancies versus Fads* (Methuen: London 1923), 176.
[11] *Enneads* I.4 [46].8; III.2 [47].8.
[12] *Enneads* II.9 [33].16.
[13] *Enneads* VI.9 [9].7.
[14] *Enneads* VI.9 [9].11. This is McKenna's translation in his great version of *The Enneads*, but *monos*, in this context, actually means 'pure' or 'uninfected', not 'solitary'.
[15] *Enneads* IV.8 [6].4, 11f.

... He will stop marking himself off from all being and will come to all the All without going out anywhere'.[16] Similarly those passages that now seem to us robust and uncompassionate are a recipe for a more genuine love: seeing the beauty of each living soul, but without concupiscence and without projecting our own desires, sets each soul free to help the World Soul make the world. 'The flight of the alone to the alone' is actually a movement of the pure, the naked, to the pure.[17] It is not its *solitude* but its detachment, from everything that gets in our way, that matters. This is not easy. 'When the feeling of pleasure or pain is most intense, every soul of man imagines the objects of this intense feeling to be then plainest and truest, though they are not so'.[18] Remembering otherwise takes effort.

So what is 'the Alone', or the One? And what is it to 'go' there? Strictly, 'it' isn't anything at all, nor is going there 'a journey for the feet'![19] But a way of making Plotinus's meaning a little clearer to us is to accept the gloss he offers: 'the productive power of all things'.[20] Plotinus shows how intellect is carried out of itself, how we depend on myths and theurgic meditations and the passion of love, to fall in love at last with Love Himself. The One is unique, indeed – but very far from solitary. The One is everywhere – but not because it fills a pre-existent space. Rather every place and every entity exists in love. The One *is* Love.[21] Which is why Plotinus would, I think, have had some sympathy with the remarks about 'the childless' that I quoted, though he would also have included within the class of 'children', offspring, any new creation, pupils, works of art or accurate philosophies (notwithstanding his occasional suggestion that external production is a sign, in a way, of weakness).

This is to touch on a suggestion of Hilary Armstrong: 'Many people are looking for an unorganized and unorganizable Good as the only true object of worship, the source of value and the goal of desire, whose light shines everywhere in this ever-changing world as we contemplate it with our ever-changing

---

[16]   *Enneads* VI.5 [23].7, 9f.
[17]   I have examined the metaphor of nakedness at greater length in 'Going Naked into the Shrine: Herbert, Plotinus and the Constructive Metaphor': D. Hedley & S. Hutton, eds., *Platonism at the Origins of Modernity* (Springer: Dordrecht 2008).
[18]   *Phaedo* 83c
[19]   *Ennead* I.6 [1].8, 23.
[20]   *Ennead* III.8 [30]. 10. See Eric D. Perl 'The Power of All Things': *ACPQ* **71** 1997, 301–13.
[21]   *Enneads* VI.8 [39].15.

minds'.[22] That Good promises a future which is always other than our present, an infinite realm of possibility that will be forever filled to overflowing with the forms of beauty, 'boiling with life'.[23]

Plotinian philosophy is not a merely abstract nor a merely individualistic or intellectual affair. When Plotinus planned to found 'Platonopolis' it is easy to suppose that what he had in mind was, in effect, a University: an assembly – with supporting staff – of scholars dedicated to unravelling the truth, by various 'reasonable' means. But perhaps we should take more seriously the thought that he had Plato's *Laws* in mind: a genuine city, all of whose citizens would share in the liturgical year. He would have agreed with Plato:

> Man's life is a business which does not deserve to be taken too seriously; yet we cannot help being in earnest with it, and there's the pity. Still, as we are here in this world, no doubt, for us the becoming thing is to show this earnestness in a suitable way... I mean we should keep our seriousness for serious things, and not waste it on trifles... while God is the real goal of all beneficent serious endeavour, man... has been constructed as a toy for God, and this is, in fact, the finest thing about him. All of us, men and women alike, must fall in with our role and spend life in making our play as perfect as possible... What, then, is our right course? We should pass our lives in the playing of games – certain games, that is, sacrifice, song, and dance... [Mankind should] live out their lives as what they really are – puppets in the main, though with some touch of reality about them, too.[24]

He himself, according to Porphyry, celebrated the birthdays of Plato and Socrates 'with sacrifice and philosophical discussion'. He finds nothing odd in appealing to oracles about honouring the dead – or as themselves the heroic dead.[25] And the mysteries are constantly invoked as meaning what Plotinus himself has come to see, with Plato's help, as true.[26] Even the star-gods, though they do not determine what we shall do, may serve as examples, and we may request their aid.[27] 'In the *Laws*', according to Catherine Pickstock's

[22]   Armstrong 'The Escape of the One' *Studia Patristica* **13** 1975, 77–89 (reprinted in *Plotinian and Christian Studies* (Variorum: London 1979), ch. XXIII), 88.
[23]   see *Ennead* VI.7 [38].15.
[24]   Plato, *The Laws*, 803–4, tr. A.E. Taylor.
[25]   *Ennead* IV.7 [2].15.
[26]   *Ennead* I.6 [1].6; VI.9 [9].11.
[27]   *Ennead* IV.4 [28].30.

reading, 'it is the divine gift of the liturgical cycle with all the concomitant sustenance which the deities bring to these festivals, which
distinguishes human beings from the wild animals which have no
such gifts of order, rhythm or harmony'.[28] I am not so sure that
Plotinus, any more than Porphyry, makes so radical a distinction
between the 'human' and the 'non-human' – one might as well, as
Plato said, divide the world into 'cranes' and 'non-cranes'.[29] But
the main point, that such liturgies embody and reinforce the
themes which souls should rehearse at all times, seems a fair one.
That, after all, is what the Egyptian priests – perhaps – intended:
by using paintings and statues to convey their messages they
allowed the gods an entry into the human soul.[30] The imaginative
exercises that Plotinus himself devises are *theurgic* in intent.[31]
Progress is not made exclusively by intellectual, argumentative
means – indeed such arguments depend upon the real existence of
an intellectual grasp of 'immutable justice and beauty',[32] for which
we can have no *argument* if we cannot already see it. Even when we
do have arguments for a conclusion we may need to reinforce them
if we are to stay convinced: as Pico della Mirandola argued: 'the
magic of Zamolxis is the medicine of the soul, because it brings temperance to the soul as medicine brings health to the body'.[33] We need
something to counteract the effect of natural enchantments, the
charms of my title.

> But how is the good man affected by magic and drugs? He is
> incapable of being affected in his soul by enchantment, and
> his rational part would not be affected, nor would he change
> his mind; but he would be affected in whatever part of the
> irrational in the All there is in him, or rather this part would be
> affected; but he will feel no passionate loves provoked by
> drugs, if falling in love happens when one soul assents to the
> affection of the other [that is, to the life of the living body].
> But just as the irrational part of him is affected by incantations

[28] Catherine Pickstock, After Writing: *on the Liturgical Consummation of Philosophy* (Blackwell: Oxford 1998) 40, commenting on Plato *Laws* 653dff; 42 further cites *Laws* 803d, 644dff on *paideia*.

[29] Plato *Statesman* 263d.

[30] *Ennead* V.8 [31].6; IV.3 [27].11; see *Asclepius* 37: Copenhaver op.cit., 90.

[31] See Gregory Shaw 'Eros and Arithmos: Pythagorean Theurgy in Iamblichus and Plotinus' *Ancient Philosophy* **19** 1999, 121–43.

[32] *Ennead* V.1 [10].11.

[33] *On the Dignity of Man*, after Plato *Charmides* 156dff.

so he himself by counter-chants and counter-incantations will dissolve the powers on the other side.[34]

Those counter-chants and counter-incantations are mostly *arguments*.[35] As Armstrong has written, 'philosophical discussion and reflection are not simply means for solving intellectual problems (though they are and must be that). They are also charms, counter-charms, for the deliverance of the soul'.[36] But not all Plotinus's charms are simply argumentative: some require us instead to use our imagination.

Understanding the uses of the star-gods, for example, depends on changing our point of view. Armstrong may speak for many: 'It would be difficult for us, imaginatively as well as intellectually, to recognize and venerate the goddess Selene in the dreary, dusty receptacle for excessively expensive junk with which we have all become so boringly familiar of late years'.[37] But on the contrary, we have cause to be grateful, in a way, to just that goddess. Looking only at the material, we may suppose that the Moon, Selene, is indeed no more than rubble. But consider instead what it is to look back from the Moon. Consider the images of Earth seen from the Moon which have decorated websites and student bedrooms for the last thirty or more years. That vision of our little segment of the wider world, the blue and silver bubble against a darkened sky, has helped to remind us – at the deepest imaginative level – that we do indeed inhabit a single, beautiful world, and that our political and social divisions must fade before that insight. Looking in turn towards the Moon herself what we should see is the love that binds, the universal sympathy that makes causality possible. What Plotinus called magic we now recognize as universal law – but our words make no clearer than Plotinus's what explains that law, that magic. Those who can think of the Moon – or the Earth itself – as no more than rubble may indeed feel themselves to be in that imagined hell which Armstrong evoked in his – somewhat exaggerated – account of third-century sensibility: 'It was a period in which the sense of individual isolation in a vast and terrifying universe was

---

[34]   *Ennead* IV.4 [28].43: Armstrong op.cit., vol. 4, pp. 269ff.

[35]   *Ennead* IV. 4 [28].43, 19ff: Armstrong op.cit., vol. 4, p. 271.

[36]   Armstrong 'Plotinus': *Cambridge History of Later Greek and Early Medieval Philosophy*, ed. A.H. Armstrong (Cambridge University Press: Cambridge 1967), 195–271: 260, after Plotinus *Ennead* V.3 [49].17.

[37]   Armstrong 'The Apprehension of Divinity in the Self and Cosmos in Plotinus' in R. Baines, ed., *The Significance of Neoplatonism* (Studies in Neoplatonism vol. 1 Old Dominion University: Norfolk VA 1976), 187–98.

perhaps more intensely felt than even immediately after the break-down of the city-state into the Hellenistic world. For in the Roman Empire, under Babylonian influence, the view of the ruling power of the universe as a cruel, inaccessible Fate, embodied in the stars, worship of which was useless, had come to its full development. The individual exposed to the crushing power of this Fate, and the citizen also of an earthly state which seemed almost as vast, cruel and indifferent as the universe, felt to the full the agony of his isolation and limitation'.[38]

One factor in Plotinus's occasional gesture towards an 'astrological' religion which I have not yet managed to disentangle is the difference between planets and fixed stars. The background assumption of his day, expressed by both his immediate predecessors and his successors, was that individual souls, in their descent from the heaven of the fixed stars, picked up planetary aspects of which they must be purged in their ascent. Some commentators are convinced that Plotinus must have been too sensible to believe this, and they may be right. But Plotinus's chief *reason* for not believing it was that he did not wish to insult the planetary angels by suggesting that their influence was entirely bad. They may need to be purged, but rather in the sense of being cleaned than being evacuated.

A passage in the *Corpus Hermeticum* is at least suggestive: to escape the twelve zodiacal torments (ignorance, grief, incontinence, lust and so on), we are to invoke 'the powers of god'. These are, initially, seven in number: knowledge of god, knowledge of joy, continence, perseverance, justice, liberality and truth. Life, light and the good arrive thereafter, to make up the decad.[39] Those seven powers look very much as if they are to be conceived as planetary, though this connection is not made explicit even in the *Hermetica*, let alone Plotinus. What the powers have become in us may not be wholly virtuous, but they are not therefore to be despised.

In the words of a later, Neo-Platonically inspired witness: before Adam fell 'what is now gall in him sparkled like crystal, and bore the taste of good works, and what is now melancholy in man shone in him like the dawn and contained in itself the wisdom and perfection of good works; but when Adam broke the law, the sparkle of innocence was dulled in him, and his eyes, which had formerly

---

[38] Armstrong 'Plotinus and India' *Classical Quarterly* **30** 1936, 22–8: 28.
[39] Treatise XIII, 8–9: Copenhaver op.cit., 51.

beheld heaven, were blinded, and his gall was changed to bitterness, and his melancholy to blackness'.[40]

I'm moved to suggest, very cautiously, that this idea can be joined up with Plotinus's advice to polish our internal statues! Those statues, I suggest, are to be conceived as typical Roman statues of personalized virtues, or of the planetary gods we have internalized 'on the way down'.

The Romans, and their many imitators, chose to depict Virtues on their public monuments as clothed female figures: the four statues ornamenting the Library of Celsus in Ephesus, for example, are of *arete, ennoia, episteme,* and *sophia* (though what the sculptor intended by these titles may remain obscure). Roman coins carry similar figures to represent equity, good faith, modesty and the like. Whether those who admired the statues or glanced at the coins ever sought to invoke these personified virtues, constructing moving images of them in the way advised by sundry modern esotericists, I do not know. It is also not altogether easy to understand what any of these virtues actually amount to: *sophrosune,* for example, is translated, by Armstrong, variously, as 'self-control', 'chastity' and 'integrity'. Possibly, 'self-possession' would be the fittest version. Nor are public, 'civic', virtues all that Plotinus praised: such virtues, indeed, can barely qualify as human, and their exemplars can expect to be born again as ants or bees, in happy service of society.[41] 'Real' virtues are not dependent on a fallen world to give them sense. *Sophrosune,* as seen by those who gaze on the divine beauty, is 'not the kind which men have here below, when they do have it (for this is some sort of imitation of that other)'.[42] The detail of Plotinian ethical theory is another story, but we can get some way towards an understanding of his pedagogic practice, by enlisting the aid of more explicit guides. Consider, for example, John Makransky's summary of Tibetan Buddhist practice:

---

[40] R. Klibansky, E. Panofsky, & F. Saxl *Satum and Melancholy* (Nelson: Edinburgh 1964), 80, citing Hildegard of Bingen: Kaiser ed., *Hildegardis Causae et Curae,* Leipzig 1903, 43. See ps.Denis *Celestial Hierarchy* $14: 'the Celestials' fury of anger represents an intellectual power of resistance of which [our sort of] anger is the last and faintest echo' (taken from http://www.esoteric.msu.edu/VolumeII/CelestialHierarchy2.html, accessed 27th May 2008).

[41] See *Ennead* VI.3 [44].16,28ff; *Ennead* VI.8 [39].5.

[42] *Ennead* V.8 [31].10, 14ff.

Sitting in correct posture on a comfortable seat, one takes refuge (*skyabs 'gro*) in Guru, Buddha, Dharma and Saṅgha, receives their blessing envisioned as light and nectar, and generates the thought of enlightenment for the sake of all beings (*sems bskyed*). That thought is the highest possible motivation for action (*karma*) of any kind. It directs all the ritual activity which follows toward the highest soteriological ends. One then recollects the field of karmic merit (*tshogs zhing gsal gdab pa*). A vast array of lineage gurus, tantric deities, buddhas, bodhisatt-vas, *pratyekabuddhas*, *śravakas*, *ḍākas*, *ḍākinīs*, and protector deities is visualized and their presence invoked by ritual pro-cedures. Each element of the visualization has levels of significa-tion based on Tibetan systematizations of Sūtra and Tantra, the whole array being viewed as a manifestation of enlightened mind, the gnosis of bliss and void, the inseparability of *bla ma* (*guru*) and *yi dam* (*iṣṭadevatā*). Offering one's practices to that 'field' is said to generate enormous karmic merit, to purify, and to bless, the three fundamentals of spiritual progress. In fact, from a Tibetan perspective, no meditator is ever actually alone. A practitioner in 'solitary' retreat not only visualizes the field of deities, but feels their presence, repeatedly entreating them for inspiration and blessing.[43]

The historical question, whether Plotinus and his friends actually did something like this, is probably unanswerable, and is less important, for my purposes, than the psychological, whether such practices have the desired effect, or the philosophical, what they tell us about the way things are – or at least the way we are. The particular terms and images employed by Tibetan Buddhists, of course, are unlikely to be familiar to most inheritors of the European tradition, and there is no need to explore them here – except to note that 'light' and 'nectar' at least are metaphors we hold in common.

---

[43]   Makransky 'Offering (*mChod pa*) in Tibetan Ritual Literature' in José Ignacio Cabezón & Roger R. Jackson, eds., *Tibetan Literature Studies in Genre: Essays in Honor of Geshe Lhundup Sopa* (Snow Lion: Ithaca, New York 1995), 312–330: 318f (housed at http://www.thdl.org/collections/literature/genres/book/show.php). See Stephan Beyer *The Cult of Tara: Magic and Ritual in Tibet* (University of California Press: Berkeley, CA 1973).

Stephen R.L. Clark

Many Selves, One Self

The first thing to note is that the 'vast array' of apparently alien presences is nothing strange.

> 'Know yourself' is said to those who because of their selves' multiplicity have the business of counting themselves up and learning that they do not know all of the number and kind of things they are, or do not know any one of them, not what their ruling principle is or by what they are themselves.[44]

The point about visualising this array is not to summon them from somewhere else, but to identify the work they already do in us, and maybe to give them their appropriate ranks. 'The Unity of Self' is something, in a way, to be achieved, or eventually uncovered, not merely, placidly, assumed. Finding a new way of seeing is also to find a new way of being.

> Not only must the practitioner visualize the deity as vividly as possible, but he must also, in any ritual of evocation (that is, whenever he generates himself as the deity), exchange for his own ordinary ego the ego of the deity, which is the subjective correlate of the exchange of ordinary appearances for the special appearance of the deity and his retinue of mandalas.[45]

Just as Tibetan Buddhists find a vocabulary for their multiplicity in 'lineage gurus, tantric deities, buddhas, bodhisattvas, *pratyekabuddhas, śravakas, ḍākas, ḍākinīs*, and protector deities', so Plotinians found them in Hellenic myth, the myths of Plato, and contemporary culture. Armstrong suggested that Plotinus did not take myths seriously because he used them inconsistently, or strained their sense. But that same fact is actually evidence of the use he made of them. The images, the stories, are changed in action, to embody his particular meanings. And the second thing to note is that for Plotinus as well as for Buddhists all these images and opinions only float past consciousness: they are not of our essence,[46] and must in the end be discarded (which they can't be, if we don't know what they are).

There at least two ways of developing all this. The first, which I have been sketching, is to take the Plotinian or the third-century astrological story as a convenient fiction, which doesn't depend for

---

[44] *Ennead* VI.7 [38].41,22–27.
[45] Beyer op.cit., 76–7.
[46] *Ennead* III.6 [26].15.

its efficacy on any actual astronomical accuracy. The second is to draw corresponding morals from our present, and putatively far more accurate astronomy. We aren't actually down at the bottom of the sidereal universe, but orbiting a minor star some way out in a galactic spiral of an undistinguished galaxy. That story has been used by many moderns to drive home the supposed utter insignificance of human life – though rather few of those who urge that moral seem really to find their own lives insignificant! It is of course easy, and probably even advisable, to make fun of those who pretend to be affected by those thoughts. But maybe we can still learn from them. The universe, assuredly, is very big and very old. But of course its age and size are only large, precisely, in *human* terms. Just insofar as we manage to conceive the world beyond we see that its largeness may as well be smallness, and our very *knowledge* of its being shows that we, or our intellects, are larger still.

John Dillon, commenting on a particular image:

> Here we are being called upon to use our imagination creatively, to attain to a purely intellectual conception. It is worthwhile, perhaps, to try to perform the exercise as Plotinus prescribes. I have attempted it repeatedly, and the sticking point is always the instruction, once one has conjured up the universe (as a luminous, diaphanous globe, with all its parts distinct and functioning), then to think away the spatiality (*"aphelon ton onkon labe"*) – and not just by shrinking it! It is in fact an excellent spiritual exercise. Calling upon God here is no empty formality. If it is done effectively, it has a quasi-theurgic result: "He may come, bringing his own cosmos, with all the gods that dwell in it – He who is the one God, and all the gods, where each is all, blending into a unity, distinct in powers, but all one god, in virtue of that divine power of many facets." In other words, if you perform the exercise correctly, you will achieve a mystical vision of the whole noetic cosmos. And Plotinus knew what he was talking about.[47]

And again:

> If one likens it to a living richly varied sphere, or imagines it as a thing all faces, shining with living faces, or as all the pure souls running together into the same place, with no deficiencies but

[47]   John Dillon 'Plotinus and the Transcendental Imagination' (J.P. Mackey, ed., *Religious Imagination*, Edinburgh University Press 1986) 55–64, reprinted in Dillon *The Golden Chain* (Variorum Press: Aldershot 1990), commenting on Plotinus *Ennead* V.8 [31].9.

having all that is their own, and universal Intellect seated on their summits so that the region is illuminated by intellectual light – if one imagined it like this one would be seeing it somehow as one sees another from outside; but one must become that, and make oneself the contemplation. But we should not remain always in that manifold beauty, but go on still darting upwards, leaving even this behind.[48]

The cosmos as Plotinus conceived it has, of course, some likeness to the unified, fixed cosmos of Stoic and modern scientific myth. What is different is that the whole cosmos is, as I said before, *alive*, and infinite in energy and diversity. One step on the way to its discovery may indeed be the recognition of our merely *personal* insignificance, but this is only to open the way to realizing something more. The *dead* world of modern myth is the outward replica of depression. Plotinus asks us to wake up to the obvious truth that the cosmos *boils* with life, and the less obvious revelation that the order we can see out there reflects a greater, intellectual order by which we can ourselves be moved.

Anorexia, founded as it so often is, in a sense of personal unworthiness, a conviction that we clutter things up by existing, that our perceptions are like dirty fingerprints upon a world that is better without us, is a perversion of a genuine insight, a perversion that prevents that insight's true development. Not *minding* about the body is not at all the same as passionately despising it. Accepting its dissolution is not the same as using violence against it. 'There is disgust or grief or anger: one must not act like this.'[49]

---

[48]   *Ennead* VI.7 [38].15, 25–16, 3. Armstrong, *Enneads* op.cit., vol. VII, 136 suggests that the image of many faces might have been inspired by the sight of 'some small Indian image'. It seems just as likely that the inspiration was Ezekiel's vision of the four living creatures, each with four faces and four wings, and each with a wheel full of eyes, before the throne of God: *Ezekiel* 1.4–28. *Merkabah* symbolism has a long Rabbinic history. Gershom G. Scholem remarks: 'The throne-world is to the Jewish mystic what the pleroma, the "fullness", the bright sphere of divinity with its potencies, aeons, archons and dominions is to the Hellenistic and early Christian mystics of the period who appear in the history of religion under the names of Gnostics and Hermetics', (*Major Trends in Jewish Mysticism* (Shocken Books: New York 1974; 1st published 1941), 44). Plotinus doesn't mention these various inmates of the pleroma, but they may well be there in his imagination.
[49]   *Ennead* I.9 [16].

And to conclude with Socrates: 'A man of sense ought not to assert that the description which I have given of the soul and her mansions is exactly true. But I do say that, inasmuch as the soul is shown to be immortal, he may venture to think, not improperly or unworthily, that something of the kind is true. The venture is a glorious one, and he ought to comfort himself with words of power like these, which is the reason why I lengthen out the tale.'[50] We need both *arguments* and 'words of power', enchantments, to subvert the sorcery of nature, the constant conviction on the one hand that what we individually *feel* is real, and that there is nothing worth considering beyond it, and on the other, that we are really insignificant. On the contrary, we need to remember that it is Soul that gives life to all.[51] Polishing those internal statues, invoking immortal presences, perhaps we come a little closer to the life the ancients praised.

---

[50] *Phaedo* 114d, tr. Benjamin Jowett.
[51] *Ennead* V.1 [10].2.

What is Humane Philosophy and Why is it At Risk?

JOHN COTTINGHAM

1. Introduction

Let me begin with what may seem a very minor point, but one which I think reveals something about how many philosophers today conceive of their subject. During the past few decades, there has been an increasing tendency for references in philosophy books and articles to be formatted in the 'author and date' style ('see Fodor (1996)', 'see Smith (2001)'.) A neat and economical reference system, you may think; and it certainly saves space, albeit inconveniencing readers by forcing them to flip back to the end of the chapter or book to find the title of the work being referred to. But what has made this system so popular among philosophers? A factor which I suspect exerts a strong subconscious attraction for many people is that it makes a philosophy article look very like a piece of scientific research. For if one asks where the 'author-date' system originated, the answer is clear: it comes from the science journals.[1] And in that context, the choice of referencing system has a very definite rationale. In the progress-driven world of science, priority is everything, and it's vitally important for a career that a researcher is able to proclaim his work as breaking new ground. Bloggs (2005) developed a technique for cloning a certain virus; Coggs (2006) showed how certain bits of viral DNA could be spliced; and now Dobbs (2007) draws on both techniques to develop the building blocks of a new vaccine. The idea is that our knowledge-base is enhanced, month by month and year by year, in small incremental steps (perhaps with occasional major breakthroughs); and in the catalogue of advances, the date tagged to each name signals when progress was made, and by whom.

---

[1] Often known as the 'Harvard' system, author-date referencing was apparently first used by a Edward Laurens Mark, a Professor of anatomy at Harvard University, in an article published in 1881 in the *Bulletin of the Museum of Comparative Zoology*.

doi:10.1017/S1358246109990129

There's nothing whatever wrong with this in science. We have all benefited, in countless ways, from the competitive, progress-driven march of scientific research. And science, by its very nature, looks forwards rather than backwards. The dates of references in science journals seldom go back more than a decade or so. But is this method suited for the humanities? Because of the way funding mechanisms are organized, we have all, almost without being aware of it, slipped into a mind-set where we think of ourselves as doing 'research'. In funding applications we have to specify our 'research methods', and any philosopher who answers this honestly ('reading some books and thinking about some ideas') will probably have their application turned down. Above all, research, perhaps not by definition, but by common implication, is thought of as innovative, progress-oriented, competitive, forward-looking.

Are the humanities really suited to being cast in this mould? Aristotle, Leonardo da Vinci, Shakespeare, J. S. Bach ... Do we really think of these names as ones that should be cited, if at all, only occasionally and accidentally – in the way in which Democritus' theory of atoms, or Harvey's work on the circulation of the blood, might appear in an incidental footnote in a science article, the authors remembered simply for antiquarian reasons, rather than as great canonical figures who deserve to be principal subjects of study in their own right? In the case of philosophy (unlike art or literature or music), some practitioners might indeed be eager to bite the bullet, and say that the only really important philosophy is that being done by the latest state-of-the-art researchers; witness the bumper-sticker reportedly seen on some campuses in the USA, 'Just say NO to the History of Philosophy'. But the majority of philosophers would surely have a few qualms about such a radically anti-historical stance; it seems significant, for example, that almost all university departments of philosophy still insist on including at least some classical and early-modern texts as an essential part of the teaching syllabus.

Nevertheless, the science-based model exerts a subtle influence. Even when the great canonical figures are referred to in modern philosophy books and articles, the increasingly popularity of the 'author-date' reference system has led to an extraordinarily cavalier way of citing them. What would we make of a literary scholar who used expressions like 'see Shakespeare (1958)', when citing a passage in *Hamlet*, or who provided no dates other than that of the edition they happened to have on their shelves? And yet countless philosophy books appearing today will casually use references like 'Kant (1962)', very often with nothing, either in the footnotes or the bibliography, to give even the faintest indication that Kant was not an English or American philosopher writing in the latter twentieth century. Quite apart from issues of pedagogy (we surely owe it to our students to be a little more informative), there is something unappealingly parochial about a citation method that reduces the entire sweep of Western thought to a set of modern English editions.

Instead of being proud of our intellectual heritage, and instead of reminding ourselves that our philosophical reasoning is never a neutral, ahistorical process, but has been conditioned in countless ways by the long sweep of Western culture, stretching from the Enlightenment back to the Renaissance and beyond, to the Medieval and Classical worlds, we often seem determined to situate ourselves in a narrow anglophone world that is exclusively or very largely focused on the latest 'cutting-edge' theories advanced by our contemporaries, either supposedly out of the blue, or through debate with other current theorists, or those of the recent past.

My main purpose in this paper, however, is not to mount a defence of the history of philosophy, nor to underline the need for a more nuanced historical awareness of the influences that shaped our modern understanding of the world and our place within it. Highly important though I believe these things to be, there are deeper questions at stake, which I want to address: questions about philosophy's self-conception – about the kind of subject we take ourselves to be doing when we say we are 'philosophers'.

2. Shifting conceptions of philosophy

Uncertainty about the precise nature of its subject-matter may be a sign of malaise in a philosophical culture. And it is striking that the last hundred years or so have seen an uncanny number of shifts among philosophers in their conception of what their subject is supposed to be about. To summarize very crudely and schematically, at the start of the twentieth century a somewhat baroque kind of idealism conceived of philosophy as propounding grand theories of the supposed 'ultimate' nature of reality. G. E. Moore and Bertrand Russell provided an antidote to this by developing a self-consciously dry and down-to-earth style of philosophizing, devoted in large part to questions of logical analysis. Then came Logical Positivism, with its programme for the elimination of metaphysics and the reduction of all philosophical theorizing to claims capable of empirical verification. There followed, around the middle of the century, the therapeutic conception of the later Wittgenstein, according to which the

John Cottingham

job of the philosopher was to dispel the conceptual confusions generated either by other philosophers or by the power of language to
bewitch us into accepting false models of reality. 'What is your aim
in philosophy: to show the fly the way out of the fly bottle'[2] There followed a phase of so-called 'ordinary language philosophy', which in
turn gave way in the final quarter of the century, to a rather different
but still linguistically oriented approach to philosophy, when
Michael Dummett proclaimed that 'only with the rise of the
modern logical and analytic style of philosophizing was the proper
object of philosophy finally established, namely ... the analysis of
the structure of *thought*, [for which] the only proper method [is]
the analysis of *language*.'[3] About the same time, though coming
from a completely different direction, there appeared a cluster of
so-called postmodern thinkers such as Richard Rorty who
proclaimed nothing less than the end of philosophy as traditionally
conceived – the collapse of the image of the philosopher as a kind
of 'cultural overseer' who could pass judgement on the validity and
coherence of various types of discourse.[4] Once such pretensions
were abandoned, it was argued, then philosophy would, in effect,
fade away, leaving us simply with various forms of more specific
inquiry – literary, political, historical or whatever – each necessarily
embedded within the relativities of a given mode of discourse. To
complete this strange catalogue of shifts in philosophy's self-
conception, we have seen, beginning with the work of W. V. O.
Quine,[5] and gathering speed in the last few decades, what one commentator has called a 'naturalistic revolution' in philosophy – the
rise of a science-inspired model according to which philosophy
should 'either ... adopt and emulate the method of successful
sciences, or ... operate in tandem with the sciences, as their abstract
and reflective branch.'[6]

[2] Ludwig Wittgenstein, *Philosophical Investigations* [*Philosophische
Untersuchungen*, 1953] (New York: Macmillan, 1953), Part I, §309.
[3] 'Can Analytic Philosophy Be Systematic?' [1975], in *Truth and Other
Enigmas* (London: Duckworth, 1978), 458.
[4] Richard Rorty, *Philosophy and the Mirror of Nature* (Oxford:
Blackwell, 1980), 300ff.
[5] For Quine's view of philosophy as continuous with science, see his
'Epistemology naturalized', in *Ontological Relativity and Other Essays*
(New York: Columbia University Press, 1968), 69–90, and 'Two Dogmas
of Empiricism' in *From a Logical Point of View* (Cambridge, MA;
Harvard, 1953; rev. 1961).
[6] Brian Leiter (ed.), *The Future for Philosophy* (Oxford: Clarendon
Press, 2004), Editor's Introduction, 2–3.

236

What is Humane Philosophy and Why is it At Risk?

There is perhaps no inherent reason why there should not be many ways of practising philosophy, each with claims to be valuable in different ways. Among the writers from all the various schools so far mentioned there are many who have interesting things to say; and it is certainly no part of the purpose of this paper to run down anyone else's work. Nevertheless, we do, I think, need to be wary of many of these models, in so far as their advocates have typically been imperialistic, proclaiming a supposedly final destiny for philosophy, or some ultimate norm which is supposed to represent the only authentic way of doing the subject. In the case of the science-inspired model of philosophical inquiry that appears increasingly to be gaining ground, there is, I want to argue, serious cause for concern. It is not that much of the work done under this banner does not meet high philosophical standards of rigour and clarity, or that it is not, in many cases, worth doing. The point rather is that if philosophy gets *entirely* confined within this mould, it risks losing its very *raison d'être*.

3. Analysis

The scientifically inspired model of philosophy has strong links with the notion of 'analysis', which has been very influential in determining the shape of so much twentieth and twenty-first century philosophy. Etymologically, to 'analyse' something is of course to break it up or dissolve it into its component parts; and this explains why, in many of its uses, analysis is a scientific notion. Analytical chemistry, for example, aims to separate out substances into their constituent elements. That philosophy should be aiming at this kind of 'analysis' was a view that attracted Pierre Gassendi in the seventeenth century, and he drew on this view in attacking Descartes's definition of the mind as a *res cogitans*, or 'thinking thing':

> When you say that you are a thinking thing, this was not what we were asking you to tell us. Who doubts that you are thinking? What we are unclear about, what we are looking for, is that inner substance of yours whose property is to think ... If we are asking about wine, and looking for the kind of knowledge which is superior to common knowledge, it will hardly be enough for you to say 'wine is a liquid thing, which is ... red, sweet, intoxicating,' and so on. You will have to attempt to investigate and explain its internal substance, showing how it can be seen to be manufactured from such and such ingredients in

such and such quantities and proportions ... Similarly, it is not enough for you to announce that you are a thing that thinks and doubts and understands etc. You should carefully scrutinize yourself and conduct a kind of quasi-chemical investigation of yourself, if you are to succeed in uncovering and explaining to us your internal substance ...[7]

Gassendi is after the kind of analysis that will offer a genuine explanatory advance, and this, he argues, cannot be provided by the Cartesian definition of the mind as a 'thinking thing', which merely re-introduces the *explanandum* (the phenomenon to be explained in the first place). What Gassendi demands instead is an analysis of the mind's workings either in terms of material properties, or (as the 'quasi' in 'quasi-chemical' suggests) in terms of properties that are at least analogous to material properties.[8] Yet in the context of his debate with Descartes, such a demand seems to be a malicious attempt to beg the question against the Cartesian view of the mind by insisting that our explanatory hunger can only be satisfied by an account which makes some reference to the material domain. Descartes (though he was happy to give physical or mechanistic accounts of many other human and animal functions)[9] always held, of course, that the nature of thought and rationality was such as to place it entirely beyond the reach of explanation in anything remotely like material terms.

---

[7]   Pierre Gassendi, Fifth Set of Objections, published with Descartes's *Meditations* [*Meditations de prima philosophiae*, 1641], AT VII 276: CSM II 193. 'AT' refers to the standard Franco-Latin edition of Descartes by C. Adam & P. Tannery, *Œuvres de Descartes* (12 vols, revised edn, Paris: Vrin/CNRS, 1964–76); 'CSM' refers to the English translation by J. Cottingham, R. Stoothoff and D. Murdoch, *The Philosophical Writings of Descartes*, vols I and II (Cambridge: Cambridge University Press, 1985).

[8]   Gassendi himself actually seems to have held that the mind is an incorporeal substance, though he took this to be something known by faith. His empiricist view of knowledge, however, led him to insist that our understanding of the mind must be based on analogy with something perceived by the senses, and hence that the basis of the analogy will always be something corporeal. For an excellent discussion of his views in this area, see Antonia Lolordo, *Pierre Gassendi and the Birth of early Modern Philosophy* (Cambridge: Cambridge University Press, 2008), ch. 10, 230–1.

[9]   See J. Cottingham, 'Cartesian Dualism', in Cottingham (ed.), *The Cambridge Companion to Descartes* (Cambridge: Cambridge University Press, 1995), ch. 8.

Though Gassendi himself was not, in fact, a materialist about the mind, his general approach to scientific analysis (based on an Epicurean or atomistic framework) may have paved the way for the kind radical naturalistic reductionism about the mental that has attracted some later philosophers.[10] This is an extreme form of scientism that need not detain us long; the arguments against it (though I cannot explore them here) seem conclusive. Of course there are, we know, physiological structures and events of various kinds that support consciousness, just as there are gastric structures and events that support digestion. And there is no reason why scientists should not investigate them, or why philosophers, like everyone else, should not be interested in the results. But if we are operating at the conceptual level, at the level of Descartes's 'thinking' (in which he included doubting, understanding, willing, affirming, denying, sensing and imagining),[11] then we are involved in the realm of *meaning*. And here the reductionistic demand seems to be wholly misplaced: even if the existence of a semantic domain may in some way presuppose the existence of an underlying physical domain, it seems hard to see how the relevant truths and concepts could be wholly analysed in terms applicable to the realm of physical structures or events. Spinoza's non-reductive monism (later followed in a certain fashion by Davidson) seems, as far as this particular issue goes, far more plausible: even if it is true that thinking could not occur unless it was realised in some kind of physical process, the kind of explanatory clarification we are looking for, when we ask what thought is, will be at the level of meaningful human activities, not, or certainly not exclusively, at the level of micro-processes.[12]

But supposing, in response to Gassendi's demand for a deeper explanation of the mind, a different kind of 'analysis' were offered – not a reductionistic and materialist one, but a conceptual one? Descartes explains, in another context, that he would be wary of this too:

> You exist, and you know you exist, and you know this because you know you are doubting. But what are you? [Suppose you

---

[10] See for example J. Smart, 'Sensations and Brain Processes', in V. C. Chappell (ed.), *Philosophy of Mind* (Englewood Cliffs: Prentice Hall, 1962).

[11] Descartes, *Meditations*, Second Meditation (AT VII 28: CSM II 19); see further J. Cottingham, *Cartesian Reflections* (Oxford: Oxford University Press, 2008), ch. 4.

[12] Benedictus Spinoza, *Ethics* [*Ethica ordine geometrico demonstrata, c.* 1665], Part II, prop. 7, scholium; Donald Davidson, *Essays on Actions and Events* (Oxford: Clarendon Press, 1980).

say, you are a *man*.] This reply would plunge you into difficult and complicated problems. For example, if I were to ask ... what a man is, and [you answered] that man is a 'rational animal', and if, to explain this, we were to delve into all the levels called 'metaphysical', we should be dragged into a maze from which no escape is possible. For two other questions arise. First, what is an *animal*? Second, what is *rational*? If, to the first question, one answers 'it is a living and sentient being' and that a living being is an 'animate body', and that a body is a 'corporeal substance', you see immediately that the question, like the branches of a family tree, would rapidly increase and multiply. Quite clearly, the result of all these admirable questions would be pure verbiage, which would elucidate nothing and leave us in our original state of ignorance.[13]

The implied target here is the philosophical approach Descartes learned in his youth in the philosophy classes he attended at the college of La Flèche – the standard kind of Scholastic analysis, in terms of genus and differentia. But there is something more general about Descartes's general complaint that will strike a chord for anyone who has worked through a piece of analytical philosophy, hoping to find enlightenment about some fundamental aspect of our human nature, and instead has found themselves drawn deeper and deeper into a maze of definitions and sub-definitions, each raising further philosophical puzzles. Such work can of course boast of being terribly painstaking and precise; but although such precision is often (in Bernard Williams' delightful phrase) 'rather mournfully equated' with analytic philosophy's vaunted 'rigour and clarity', it can often boil down to a specious *mimicry* of scientific procedures, where the practitioners 'persuade themselves that if they fuss around enough with qualifications and counter-examples they are conducting the philosophical equivalent of a biochemical protocol'.[14]

'Fussing around' is perhaps a little unfair. Breaking a concept down into its component elements can certainly on occasion be a useful exercise. But it always needs to be borne in mind that that such a process cannot take us very much further than making explicit what we intuitively grasp anyway. We start with an ordinary

[13]   René Descartes, *The Search for Truth* [*La recherche de la vérité*, ?1649], AT X 516: CSM II 410).
[14]   Bernard Williams, 'Philosophy as a Humanistic Discipline' [2000], in Williams, *Philosophy as a Humanistic Discipline* (Princeton: Princeton University Press, 2006), p. 184.

competence in using a word, supported by basic awareness of correct and incorrect uses, grasp of paradigm cases, and so on. The philosopher then puts forward his favoured analysis, and this is then tested back against our intuitions, and the suggested definition is perhaps refined and modified until a more or less comfortable fit is achieved. But in the first place, the terms of the proposed definition will often themselves raise further problems (this is the labyrinthine worry raised by Descartes); and in the second place (which is the Williams point), it would be sheer self-deception to suppose that such definitional and conceptual work could offer the kind of explanatory enlightenment that scientific research into of a physical phenomenon can provide.

The basic disparity between the scientific case and the conceptual case is this. In the scientific case, the aim is to find some inner constitution, mechanism, or micro-structure whose workings will account for the phenomenon to be explained. Once we know the molecular structure of opium and the structure of the human nervous system, then, as John Locke envisaged, we may be able to see why opium puts someone to sleep with the same kind of transparency as we can see that a certain key will open a given lock.[15] But if we wish to understand meaning-involving activities or states like consciousness, belief, knowledge, intention, desire, goal, purpose – and indeed any number of the other classic problematic concepts in the philosophy of mind – there is not, even in principle, the possibility of this kind of explanation. We may break the concepts down into their conceptual components, but however deep we go, we shall never (as we may hope to do in the scientific case) discover a simple explanatory *key* that makes us say 'ah, *that's* how it operates!' The philosophical analyst may be temped to invent such a key – invoking notions like 'rational substance' or, perhaps in more modern guise, 'central processing module'– but such notions invariably turn out to be relabellings of the phenomenon to be explained, rather than genuine generative mechanisms. What they contribute is likely to be (in Descartes's scathing phrase) 'verbiage', as opposed to genuine enlightenment – ultimately of no more explanatory value that explaining the soporific qualities of opium by invoking its 'dormitive power'.

When I was an undergraduate, there was a great deal of discussion of the nature of moral judgements: what did it mean to say you ought not to steal? A popular view at the time was such judgements merely expressed personal *feelings* or *attitudes*; but then, since these were

---

[15]   John Locke, *An Essay concerning Human Understanding*, [1690], (ed.) P. Nidditch. (Oxford: Clarendon, repr. 1984), Bk IV, ch. 3, §25.

clearly not just any old feelings, it was necessary to add '*moral* feelings' or '*normative* attitudes'. Nowadays, the prevailing fashion has swung right the other way: moral judgements are not at all about subjective psychology but about objective *facts*. But clearly not any old kind of facts. So it is necessary to add '*moral* facts' or '*normative* facts.' But what kind of normativity is involved here? Answer (according to some 'theorists'): a 'metaphysically irreducible' kind of normativity.[16] Such labelling may give a useful indication of where someone locates him or her self in a particular academic dispute, but we should not be lulled by the theoretical-sounding terminology into supposing it does very much more than this.[17]

Of course there may be right or wrong answers to be had when we ask about the nature of consciousness, or of morality, and the point of these examples is not to disparage any particular piece of philosophical analysis. The doubts raised by Descartes and by Williams are of a rather different kind – not that the proposed 'theories' are necessarily flawed in themselves, but rather that there are limits on the kind of explanatory clarification they can provide. The very word 'theory', as used by analytic philosophers, often seems to indicate a very over-ambitious conception of what philosophical analysis can achieve. It is not uncommon, for example, for a philosopher to say he has produced a 'theory' of pleasure, or a 'theory' of action, when all that is being offered is an extended definitional and conceptual discussion. It is very easy to be caught up in the intricacies of analysis, and to mistake the introduction of more and more technical terms for a substantive explanatory advance. There are serious difficulties in the notion that our explanatory hunger can be satisfied by analysis, by breaking a concept down into its conceptual components. There will always be a suspicion that the path travelled will end up being circular, even though the circle may be masked for a time if the terminology introduced along the way is sufficiently technical and impressive-sounding. How might such circularity be avoided?

---

[16]   R. Wedgwood, *The Nature of Normativity* (Oxford: Clarendon Press, 2007), 6.

[17]   What is more, the multiplication of new terminology may give the impression of real new research, or quasi-scientific progress, when what is really happening is yet another swing back of forth of a pendulum, in a continuing piece of philosophical dialogue about the objectivity (or otherwise) of morality that goes back to David Hume versus Richard Price in the eighteenth century and ultimately to Plato versus Protagoras in the fourth century BC. See David Hume, *An Enquiry concerning Human Understanding* [1748]; Richard Price, *A Review of the Principal Questions in Morals* [1758]; Plato, *Theaetetus* [*c.* 370 BC], 160 D.

What is Humane Philosophy and Why is it At Risk?

One model for philosophical theory that has found much favour in the domain of ethics since the work of John Rawls in the 1970s is that of 'reflective equilibrium'. Here the basic idea is that philosophers can indeed make genuine advances by systematizing our pre-philosophical 'intuitions', subsuming them under a simple and elegant generative principle or set of principles. At first this looks very scientific: the aim, as with science is, as Hume put it, to 'reduce the principles productive of natural [or, in this case, moral] phenomena to a greater simplicity'.[18] But there is a radical disparity with the descriptive or scientific case, namely that in science *all* the data have to be subsumed if the theory is to count as successful, whereas in the ethical case, as Rawls famously pointed out, some of our intuitions may need revising or discarding. The object therefore must be to systematize not all, but a sufficient number of our intuitions, either modifying the theory or setting aside some of the 'data', until we end up with principles which 'match our considered judgements duly pruned and adjusted'.[19] A long-standing worry about this kind of 'theory' is that it is merely an elaborate way of trading off one intuition, or set of intuitions, against another. But there is a more serious concern, which connects with our theme of the dangers of a science-inspired model of philosophy.

Thinking of moral intuitions as a set of 'data' disguises the fact that the great moral teachers in history have characteristically called for radical *shifts* in our moral perceptions and sensibilities. This casts serious doubt on the idea that the moral philosopher's job is to construct a 'theory' that will account for prevailing intuition. A telling illustration of this is the current debate over the so-called problem of 'demandingness', where philosophers expend much energy trying to adjust their generative principles until they can reach a result that requires people to give up not too much of their wealth, or quite a lot, or more or less what they now give but perhaps a little bit more, or whatever suitably qualified amount seems 'reasonable' to 'me and my mates' (to use a phrase once coined by David Lewis). There is the obvious problem here that intuitions conflict from individual to individual or group to group. But the deeper problem arises from the fact that serious moralizing, outside the seminar room, is never a static and abstract academic exercise, but is characteristically a call for personal change and individual

---

[18] Hume, *Enquiry concerning Human Understanding*, Sectn IV, part 1, penultimate paragraph.
[19] John Rawls, *A Theory of Justice* (Oxford: Oxford University Press, 1972) ch. 1, §4.

John Cottingham

growth. The teachings of Jesus of Nazareth, to give one famous example, sound extraordinarily demanding (to the rich young man: 'sell *all you have* and give to the poor'; to the disciple who wanted time to bury his father, 'follow me and *leave the dead to bury the dead*').[20] But such injunctions are also coupled with a remarkable claim: 'my yoke is *easy* and my burden *light*'.[21] The implication is of a call not merely for certain actions, but for the kind of total interior change that will completely alter the subject's perspective about who he is and how he proposes to live.

The concern I am raising here about Reflective Equilibrium methodology is not that it necessarily operates in a way that is complacently conservative of the social status quo; clearly, some of its practitioners, including Rawls himself, have advocated quite radical approaches to, for example, social justice.[22] The Rawlsian method, to be sure, allows for some intuitions to be discarded in the course of the reflective process. Nevertheless, the very nature of reflective equilibrium ensures a substantial degree of match between the results of the eventually favoured theory and the content and strength of the central intuitions its proponents start with (albeit partly modified as a function of how they fare under the constraints of coherence and systematicity). By contrast, the kind of demand or 'call' invoked in the Christian morality just mentioned is precisely aimed at exposing a gulf between what we now are and what we are to become. My purpose in referring to such teachings (and they are not confined to Christianity) is not to pass judgment one way or the other on such calls for 'change of heart' or *metanoia*, but to point up a serious psychological 'thinness' in the science-based model of moral 'theorizing'. Abstract, decontextualised, psychologically jejune, detached from the drama of the human journey (the journey from complacency, through suffering, toward moral and psychological growth), the 'equilibrium' it promises seems all too abstract and intellectualised a notion to provide a proper way of addressing the deep ethical challenges of the human condition.

If reflective equilibrium is a flawed methodology,[23] and definitional and conceptual analysis cannot provide genuine explanatory

---

[20] Matthew 19:21. Luke 9:59–60.
[21] Matthew 11:30.
[22] Compare Rawls's 'maximin principle', that requires inequalities to be justified by showing that they benefit the least advantaged (*A Theory of Justice*, §11).
[23] It would take far more space than I can spare here to assess this question thoroughly. Among the extensive recent literature addressing some of

244

advance, where do we go? Here it is worth stepping outside the seminar room for a moment, and remembering that in our ordinary human life and experience, the characteristic way in which we normally achieve understanding within the domain of meaning, as opposed to the domain of physical phenomena and their explanation, is not analytically but holistically: not by taking things apart but by reaching across and outwards.[24] The significance of thoughts and desires and beliefs and intentions is typically revealed when they are located within a wider network, connecting up, both synchronically and diachronically, with the current actions and the continuing lives both of individual human beings and of the groups of which they are necessarily a part. By appreciating the importance of the holistic dimension we can come to see why certain kinds of analytical and science-based model of the philosophical enterprise threaten a radical impoverishment of the subject. What is needed is not philosophical analysis but philosophical *synthesis* – not chopping things into parts, but linking them together.

4. Specialisation

If the direction of explanation appropriate for understanding the domain of human meaning is holistic rather than analytic, requiring us to move outwards rather than inwards, locating our thoughts and actions within a broad network of individual and social activity, then there is one extremely prominent feature of modern academic philosophy that ought immediately to sound alarm bells, namely its increasing *fragmentation* into specialised sub-disciplines. Much of the impetus for specialisation comes, once again, from the needs of science. A biochemist will rarely, if ever, attend a seminar on mathematical astronomy. For one thing, the mechanisms of nature are so

---

the issues involved, see especially G. Sayre-McCord, 'Coherentist Epistemology and Moral Theory', in W. Sinnott-Armstrong & M. Timmons (eds), *Moral Knowledge: New Readings in Epistemology* (New York: Oxford: Oxford University Press, 1996), 137–189, and M. DePaul, *Balance and Refinement: Beyond coherence methods of moral inquiry* (New York: Routledge, 1993).

[24] Compare P. F. Strawson's account of 'connective' as opposed to 'reductive' analysis in his *Analysis and Metaphysics* (Oxford: Oxford University Press, 1992), discussed in H-J. Glock's illuminating study *What is Analytic Philosophy* (Cambridge: Cambridge University Press, 2008), ch. 6.

exceedingly complex and intricate that it is just not humanly possible for any one individual to master the relevant theories in more than one specialised field. And for another thing, he or she would simply not understand the discussion. Anyone who doubts this should talk to a research scientist, or take a look at some recent abstracts of scientific articles. So specialised is the vocabulary used that it is no exaggeration to say that the layperson will be very lucky to understand one word in ten or fifteen. And even a highly qualified scientist may be hard put to it to understand the specific terms of the debate even in a research area which is relatively close to her own, let alone in a more distant field.

That situation has not yet quite arrived in philosophy. But it is, I think, remarkable that many philosophers now working would apparently have no objection whatever if it *did* arrive. It is already noticeable that faculty members and graduate students working on, say, the philosophy of language are often disinclined to attend seminars on, say, ethics, and vice versa. The reason for this is not, as it is in the scientific case, that the papers being delivered are impossibly hard for a non-specialist to understand: there is very little decent analytic philosophy that cannot be deciphered if you are prepared to put in the time and read the sentences enough times. The point rather, is that the debates have become so much the property of specialists who have devoted prodigious energy to devising the most intricate arguments and counter-arguments to support their views, that it is unlikely that anyone who did not have a professional or career motivation for putting in the requisite effort would willingly wade through the resulting conceptual treacle. Consider the following sentence from a recent book on ethics – and I am deliberately choosing an extract not from some philosophically dubious or pretentious piece of writing, but from a serious, high-quality publication which is a recognised contribution to current debates:

> Let us define what it is for a proposition to be [practically] realizable by A at t, [that is] realizable by means of A's *intentional behaviour at t*. To say a proposition p is practically realizable by A at t is to say that there is some way of behaving W such that there are possible worlds in which all the actual truths that are causally independent of whatever A might do or think at t hold, and A intentionally behaves in way W at t, and in all those worlds p is true.[25]

----

[25]   Wedgwood, *The Nature of Normativity*, p. 110.

What is Humane Philosophy and Why is it At Risk?

Extracting a passage from its surrounding context does not, of course, give a fair impression of the accessibility of the whole. But if we move away from this particular example to the general style and content of the great bulk of contemporary analytic philosophy, it is I think fair to say that the way in which most philosophy books and articles are now written has been strongly influenced by the demands of professional academic life. We learn our trade by writing doctoral dissertations, and few dissertations have been failed for being too technical or laborious, whereas a bold and transparently-stated claim to which a counter-example can be found may lead to a thesis being referred back. Or again, if a journal submission manages to work through current technical debates in a manner so impressively complex that the referee cannot easily spot any flaws, it may get the benefit of the doubt. In the fierce jungle of competition, donning heavy armour against possible attack, however exhausting, sweaty, and hampering of movement, may be the safest survival strategy.

Again, this is not a piece of sniping. Much current specialist work is clearly most impressive as far as intellectual acumen is concerned, and there is nothing whatever wrong with intricate argument as such. But we do need to remember that the greatest philosophy, the kind that not merely boosts an academic career but shapes the thinking of a generation, or even inspires new ways of looking at the world, is generally not of this specialist kind. If we look at Plato, or Aquinas, or Descartes, or Spinoza, or Hume, or Kant, what is striking is the *wide reach* of their thought – the extent to which it spans a great many of what we now think of as distinct specialities or subspecialities of philosophy. Plato, for example, has a philosophical worldview which has implications for ethics and politics, for science and mathematics, for metaphysics and aesthetics; and the stamp of his philosophical vision can be clearly seen in his writings in all these areas. Descartes too has a 'synoptic' vision of philosophy; indeed he famously used an organic image, that of a tree, to describe his philosophical system – metaphysics the roots, physics the trunk, with the fruit-bearing branches comprising more specific disciplines such as ethics.[26] In fact all the canonical figures just mentioned had a grand synoptic vision of the nature of the world, of the place of

---

[26]   Preface to the 1647 French translation of the *Principles of Philosophy* [*Principia philosophiae*, 1644], AT IXB 14-15: CSM I 186. For more on Descartes's 'synoptic' conception of philosophy, see Cottingham, *Cartesian Reflections*, ch 1.

humankind within it, of the extent and limits of human knowledge, and of the best way for human beings to live.

We cannot, of course, all be a Plato or a Descartes. But we can all be participants in what Bernard Williams calls the 'wide humanistic enterprise of making sense of ourselves and of our activities'.[27] The kind of 'humane' philosophy which I want to advocate would certainly form part of this general enterprise; and some indication has already been provided of how it may be at risk from hyper-technical and overly specialised conceptions of the subject. To develop a comprehensive worldview, which would make sense of who we are and how we should live is, of course, an exceedingly ambitious aim; but I hope it is by now clear how one might move at least a little way in this direction by cultivating a more synthetic or holistic approach to philosophical inquiry.

One example which may serve to flesh out the kind of thing I have in mind is provided by the work of Charles Taylor, and in particular his critique of Derek Parfit's account of the self. Discussing Parfit's view that there are no 'deep' facts about the identity of the self, and that selfhood itself is reducible to certain relations of psychological continuity across time, which are merely matters of degree,[28] Taylor adopts a much wider perspective which reaches out and across, beyond the specialist confines of the sub-discipline known as 'philosophy of mind'. Approaching the problems of selfhood from an ethical perspective, Taylor argues that to make sense of our lives, and indeed to have an identity all, 'we need an orientation to the good'; we need to have some sense of our lives as reaching towards moral growth and maturity. It follows from this that our lives have a *narrative* shape: as I develop, and learn from my failings and mistakes, there is always a story to be told about how I have become what I now am, and where my current journey towards improvement will take me. Just as my sense of where I am in physical space depends on how I got here and where I am going next, so it is, Taylor argues, with 'my orientation in moral space.'

This involves a radical rejection of the 'neutral' and 'bleached' conception of personhood, which tries to abstract from the framework of moral significance which gives shape to my life as a whole. According to Taylor, '[A]s a being who grows and becomes I can only know myself through the history of my maturations and regressions, over-comings and defeats. My self-understanding necessarily has temporal

---

[27] Williams, *Philosophy as a Humanistic Discipline*, 197.
[28] See Derek Parfit, *Reasons and Persons* (Oxford: Oxford University Press, 1984; repr. 1987), sections 95 and 96.

depth and incorporates narrative.' If Taylor is right, there is something misguided about the approach to the self that attempts to treat it simply as a topic for analysis in the philosophy of mind, as if it could be understood merely in terms of certain purely descriptive psychological or biological properties. Taylor's conception, by contrast, sees the self as inescapably linked with evaluative notions – it is a concept that is defined in terms of values, goals, and moral standards. Human persons exist only, as Taylor puts it, 'in a certain space of questions' – questions about the meaning and purpose of my life as a whole.[29]

It is not my aim here to adjudicate in the debate between Parfit and Taylor, nor indeed to criticize Parfit, who is in fact someone who makes strong connections between psychology and ethics, and who shows in some of his writings that he is interested in the kinds of large-scale inquiry which I am proposing as subject-matter for the best philosophical work.[30] My reason for referring to these particular remarks of Taylor is that he provides a paradigm case of a writer with a synoptic philosophical vision of the kind which seems to be becoming steadily less fashionable, and which would certainly be seriously at risk if the current process of fragmentation into specialised, quasi-scientific sub-disciplines ever became irreversible.

5. The perils of ratiocentrism

So far I have said something about what humane philosophy is, and of current analytic and/or science-based conceptions, which – whether their supporters intend it or not – are inimical to its survival. I want in this final section to turn to one further aspect of the prevailing current conception of our subject that is strikingly at odds with what I conceive to be the aims of humane philosophy, namely its suspicion of allowing into philosophical discourse any emotional, symbolic or figurative elements, or indeed anything other than plain literal language.

Philosophers have had a long-standing wariness about the emotions as potential subverters of reason – a wariness which goes

---

[29]   The various phrases in this and the previous paragraph are taken from Charles Taylor, *Sources of the Self: The Making of Modern Identity* (Cambridge: Cambridge University Press, 1989), 46–52.
[30]   See for example Parfit's 'The Puzzle of Reality', *Times Literary Supplement*, July 3, 1992, 3–5, and 'Why Anything, Why This?', *London Review of Books* **20**: 2 (22 January 1998), 22–5.

right back to Plato. Philosophical reason, in Plato's vision, exercises its proper role when it firmly restrains the emotions and controls the life of the individual and of the state by reference to eternal truths apprehended by abstract logical argument.[31] In the Stoic system, itself strongly influenced by Plato, reason and philosophy are more or less identified, as the controlling power that 'sits at the helm' and steers the ship of life on its course.[32] These are somewhat extreme positions by comparison with a lot of subsequent philosophizing, but there is a strong case for saying that, in varying degrees, much Western philosophy has suffered from a ratiocentric bias – the notion that calm and detached rational analysis provides the unique key to understanding ourselves and our activities.[33]

At its worst, ratiocentrism involves a fantasy of command and control, as if by sufficiently careful use of reason we could gain an exhaustive understanding of the human condition, and even construct a kind of blueprint or map of the requisite ingredients for a worthwhile human life. What is remarkable is the extent to which this fantasy has persisted in current philosophy, despite the Freudian revolution which has left its mark on so many other areas of contemporary academic thought. Freud devoted large parts of his writing to exposing what he called the 'last illusion', that the rational ego is master in its own house';[34] but with a handful of significant exceptions, analytic philosophers have been extraordinary resistant to this, and still continue to write as if the mind was a transparent goldfish bowl within which our desires and inclinations and beliefs were all readily understandable and identifiable.

---

[31] See Plato, *Republic* [*c.* 380 BC], Book III (376ff), Book V (474ff).

[32] '[Philosophia] animam format et fabricat, vitam disponit, actiones regit, agenda et omittenda demonstrat, sedet ad gubernaculum et per ancipitia fluctuantium derigit cursum.' ('Philosophy shapes and constructs the soul, arranges life, governs conduct, shows what is to be done and what omitted, sits at the helm and directs our course as we waver amidst uncertainties.') Seneca, *Epistulae Morales* [*c.* AD 64], 16, 3.

[33] I explore many dimensions of ratiocentrism in *Philosophy and the Good Life* (Cambridge: Cambridge University Press, 1998).

[34] 'Man's craving for grandiosity is now suffering the ... most bitter blow from present-day psychological research which is endeavouring to prove to the "ego" of each one of us that he is not even master in his own house, but that he must remain content with the veriest scraps of information about what is going on unconsciously in his own mind.' Sigmund Freud, *Introductory Lectures on Psychoanalysis* [*Vorlesungen zur Einführung in die Psychoanalyse*, 1916–17], trans. J. Rivière (London: Routledge, 1922), ch. 18.

What is Humane Philosophy and Why is it At Risk?

This is not a plea for a mass conversion to Freudianism among analytic philosophers. There is much in the detail of Freud's theories, and those of his successors, that is for various reasons problematic. But leaving the detail aside, the psychoanalytic perspective on the human condition does offer one central insight which it seems to me philosophy urgently needs to take on board: namely, that the way each of us makes sense of who we are and our relation to the world is a fearsomely complex process of which our intellectualising is only the thinnest of surfaces.[35] At the very least this suggests the need for a certain humility about the philosophical project of 'making sense of ourselves and our activities'. We need to recognise the limitations of intellectual analysis, and the way in which insight is achieved not just by the controlling intellect, fussily classifying and cataloguing the pieces of the jigsaw, but by a process of *attunement*, whereby we allow different levels of understanding and awareness to coalesce, until a picture of the whole begins to emerge.

In facilitating this process, we need, it seems to me, to be open to the kinds of insight offered by a whole range of discourse other than the strictly cognitive and logical. The question of style is importantly relevant here, and it connects up, once more, with the technical, 'science-based' model of philosophizing that is currently so prevalent. Scientists, for perfectly sensible reasons, are aiming at results which are strictly controlled and repeatable, irrespective of the vagaries of local conditions and the individual attitudes and commitments of the researchers; and this no doubt explains the widespread convention of using an utterly neutral, impersonal and detached style ('the substance was placed in the test tube'), which as far as possible prescinds from the particularities and individual characteristics of the researcher.

Many analytic philosophers have increasingly adopted this austere scientistic model of discourse, either subconsciously or deliberately cultivating a mode of writing such that any stamp of individuality is ruthlessly suppressed. Take a few sentences from any current book or article of mainstream analytic philosophy, and, I predict, it will be virtually impossible to guess anything about the personality of the writer, or indeed to distinguish author *A* from author *B*, by any cues or signatures of style. This often makes for very stodgy reading, but that is not my main complaint. The underlying worry is that that the scientific model of philosophical discourse – dry, neutral and impersonal – predisposes philosophers to neglect the

---

[35]   See *Philosophy and the Good Life*, ch. 4, final section.

resources of a whole range of linguistic expression, involving for example emotional resonance, and symbolic and other figurative elements, which is often right in the foreground for their 'continental' colleagues (not to mention those working, for example, in literature departments).

Consider, for example, the role of ambiguity. This is something the scientistic mentality sees reason to shun, since (as Raymond Geuss has recently pointed out) ambiguity in meaning is 'regarded as a grave defect in propositional forms of investigation and argumentation', and many disciplines 'emphasise the need to adopt the most stringent measure to eliminate [it] as completely as possible'. Yet Geuss reminds us, drawing on the famous work of William Empson, that 'some of the best lyric poetry is characterised by ... systematic and deep ambiguity, and this gives it a density of texture that is an aesthetic virtue.'[36] It seems to me that the same may very well be true of the best philosophical discourse; and moreover, that the virtue involved is not merely an 'aesthetic' one (which may suggest something essentially stylistic and extraneous to questions of content), but a virtue that has deep semantic implications.[37] What I have in mind is not the kind of sloppy ambiguity that is mere imprecision or vacillation, nor the kind of equivocation that makes for bad argument, but rather a kind of *polyvalence* or *multiple layering*. The 'density' involved here derives from the fact that the discourse in question tends to resonate with us not just intellectually but at many different levels of awareness. And because of this it may have the power to transform our understanding in ways that the precise and colourless propositions of literal discourse are impotent to do.[38]

Admittedly, the importance of emotional resonance and other kinds of layering at the 'ground floor' level of ethical and psychological awareness need not necessarily entail that such polyvalence is appropriate at the 'meta' level of philosophical scrutiny, where, to some extent at least, we need to stand back from our subject-matter.

---

[36]   R. Geuss, 'Poetry and Knowledge', *Arion* Vol. 11 no 1 (Spring/ Summer 2003), 8. Cf. W. Empson, *Seven Types of Ambiguity* [1930] (Harmondsworth: Penguin, 1995).

[37]   This paragraph draws on material from my *The Spiritual Dimension* (Cambridge: Cambridge University Press, 2005), ch. 5.

[38]   Metaphorical language (when the metaphors are fresh and living) provide a striking case of this polyvalence or multiple layering; precisely for this reason the full meaning of a metaphor cannot be reduced to what might be asserted by a literal paraphrase.

Yet the idea that, at the philosophical level, we can slice off all the distracting resonances of emotion and imagination and polyvalence, and engage in pure, logically valid argumentation that will compel the assent of any rational interlocutor is probably a fantasy.[39] What is more, it seems to me that the scientistic tendency in philosophy, with its commitment to an exclusively abstract and purely cerebral perspective for inquiry, can easily blind its practitioners to the true nature of what they are supposed to be investigating. If there is too great a gulf between the modes of awareness found at the meta-level and those found at the ground floor level, then philosophers can end up simply talking to themselves, instead of cultivating the right kind of sensitivity to the actual subject-matter of their inquiries. A notable example of this can be found in much analytic philosophy of religion, which tends to construe religious allegiance in wholly cognitive terms, as entirely concerned with the adoption of certain hypotheses about the cosmos, rather than as a life-changing moral and spiritual quest.[40] By always remaining at a safe distance, philosophers may run the risk of dismissing a certain terrain as barren desert, when, if they only got closer, they would find it teeming with life.

Does this plea for the philosopher to move beyond the confines of austere and purely literal discourse threaten to launch us into a world of purely rhetorical or poetic discourse which leaves behind the traditional goals of philosophy proper? I do not think so. Philosophy, as Pierre Hadot's work impressively reminds us, is, or should be, a *way of life* – a way of caring about how we live.[41] The care involved is, of course, very largely of an intellectual kind – the kind that involves 'following the argument where it leads';[42] and this in turn requires clarity of mind and logical precision, without which our thinking becomes aimless and unsatisfying. But the struggle to reach the truth is never a purely intellectual matter. The truth, or

---

[39]   Compare Robert Nozick's critique of 'coercive' argument in philosophy, in *Philosophical Explanations* (Oxford: Clarendon Press, 1981), Introduction, 4ff.

[40]   See *The Spiritual Dimension*, ch. 1.

[41]   Pierre Hadot, *Philosophy as a Way of Life* (Cambridge, Mass.: Blackwell, 1995), ch. 3. Originally published as *Exercices spirituels et philosophie antique* (Paris: Etudes Augustiniennes, 1987).

[42]   Plato, *Republic*, 394d. The actual phrase is: 'wherever the argument takes us, like a wind, there we must go' (*hopê an ho logos hôsper pneuma pherê, tautê iteon*). This slogan, incidentally, should not be taken to mean that the only reasonable course in philosophy is to accept the conclusions that follow from our premises; where the conclusions are silly or outrageous, it will often be better to go back and question the premises.

at least the interesting truth, involves, as Heidegger famously remarked, the disclosure of what is hidden; and what is hidden, as Freud so acutely saw, cannot be revealed by logic alone.[43] An illuminating philosophy lecture is seldom a just matter of the deployment of a series of arguments in which conclusions are laboriously extruded from premises. Often an image, or example, or metaphor, sometimes dropped seemingly almost by accident into the discussion, will have more power than long pages of intellectual analysis (essential though these may be); for it is by tapping into the imagination, or whatever we call that partly inaccessible creative core of ourselves, that we are suddenly able to see the vision of the world that has energised the speaker and made him or her care enough about the problem at issue to want us to share their perspective. These are the moments that make it appropriate to think of our subject not merely as another way of earning a living or advancing a career, but as what Plato first called it – the *love* of wisdom: the zeal to pursue our ideas not just because they happen to fit into some currently established academic agenda, but from a wholehearted conviction of their truth, their beauty, or their goodness.

The points I have been making connect up with a claim I have tried to advance elsewhere, namely that philosophy at its best is a way of trying to reach an integrated view of the world: in our philosophical activity, as in our lives generally, integrity has a great claim to be considered the master virtue.[44] The fragmentation of philosophical inquiry into a host of separate specialisms, and the associated development of swathes of technical jargon whose use is largely confined within hermetically sealed sub-areas, represents a disintegrated conception of philosophizing. Again, the piecemeal work may be very useful, and I am not at all saying that it should not be done. But philosophy is also equipped, as no other discipline is, to try to see how far the different parts of our conceptual scheme fit together; and the search for such understanding is one which should involve not just the intellect, but the whole of what we are. Humane philosophy, synthetic in its methods, synoptic in its scope, culturally and historically aware in its outlook, open to multiple resonances of meaning that

---

[43] See Martin Heidegger, *Being and Time* [*Sein und Zeit*, 1927], trans. J. Macquarrie and E. Robinson (New York: Harper and Row, 1962), §44, 262; and Freud, *Introductory Lectures on Psychoanalysis*, ch. 18,

[44] This theme, and that of the preceding paragraph, is developed in J. Cottingham, 'The Self, The Good Life and the Transcendent,' in N. Athanassoulis and S. Vice (eds.), *The Moral Life: Essays in Honour of John Cottingham* (London: Palgrave, 2008), 228–271.

come from the affective as well as the cognitive domains – such a grand enterprise need not occupy all our time as professional philosophers. But unless it occupies at least some of our time, there is a risk that what we do will cease to be of interest to anyone but a narrow circle of fellow-specialists.

The ideal of 'humane philosophy' is no panacea. Like any enterprise it can be done well or badly, and because it is so ambitious in its scope, the risks of failure are correspondingly great. But the potential rewards are also great; for by venturing to philosophize humanely, we may perhaps manage to become more truly human.[45]

[45] I am grateful for the valuable comments received from a number of friends and colleagues, especially from Peter Hacker, Brad Hooker and Javier Kalhat, and also for very helpful discussion points raised by Chris Pulman and other members of the philosophy graduate seminar at the University of Reading.

Why is There Something Called Philosophy Rather than Nothing?

STEPHEN MULHALL

My title is intended to invoke at least two primary reference points or associations. The first, and most obvious, is a question that is very often assumed to be exemplary of the kind of bewildering puzzles that philosophers are distinctively preoccupied with – the question 'why is there something rather than nothing?' The second is perhaps less easy to identify. A set of lectures delivered by Heidegger in the short period between his restoration to the academic life after the Second World War and his final retirement from it was published under the title 'Wass Heisst Denken?' Its English translation was given the title 'What is Called Thinking?'; and if that title does not explicitly carry the same layers of significance evident in the German original, the concept of a 'call' at least keeps open the possibility of recovering many of them. For when Heidegger asks 'what is called thinking?', he means to imply, first, that not everything which gets called thinking really merits that honorific label; second, that it is therefore worth thinking about what form of human activity or passivity would really call for the use of that term; third, that this in turn will involve thinking about what, in our present and conceivable forms of inhabiting the world, really calls out for or provokes such a thoughtful response; and fourth (since he deliberately raises this question immediately upon his temporary re-inhabitation of a university post) that we will thereby find ourselves thinking about whether, and if so how and why, genuine thoughtfulness can find a home in the university, and thereby a place in the broader economy of a culture – whether anything recoverable from the venerable traditions of philosophy in the name of thinking might still be something for which any university, and any human cultural form, can see any call for.

Taking guidance from that second association, therefore, I might say that the aim of this lecture is to delineate what philosophy must be like – how its practitioners must maintain it, and so maintain themselves – if it is to continue to merit its description of itself as the love of wisdom, and thereby to make a legitimate call on reflective individuals, the university and the broader culture for a meet and proper habitation. But in doing so I also want to argue that a

doi:10.1017/S1358246109990130 © The Royal Institute of Philosophy and the contributors 2009
Royal Institute of Philosophy Supplement **65** 2009

human life, a university, and a culture that lacked anything deserving of the name 'philosophy' would lack something fundamental to their own flourishing.

Seen in the light of the first of my two intended associations, however, the vaulting ambition signalled by my second might reasonably be regarded as heading for a fall. For if the question 'why is there something rather than nothing?' really is exemplary of distinctively philosophical preoccupations (and of course, both theologians and scientists might have something to say about that proprietary claim), then it might seem – and has so seemed even to many philosophers – that so-called lovers of wisdom have a disabling predilection for emptiness.

It is easy to see the sense of the question 'Why is there something rather than nothing in that laundry basket?', and so it is possible to conceive of an intelligible and informative answer to it (e.g. 'Because I failed to do the washing this morning'), because this question, along with an indefinite range of analogous ones, asks for an explanation of a particular situation or arrangement within a broader context of other objects, processes and forms of understanding. We know what the difference is between a laundry basket's being full of dirty clothes and its being empty; and we also know how the basket fits into the broader economy of human houses, with clothes typically migrating from wardrobes to bodies to laundry baskets to washing machines to ironing boards to wardrobes. Hence when the question is asked, we know that what is needed is an explanation of matters being one specific way rather than another with respect to the interior of the basket (as opposed, say, to the interior of the wardrobe or the washing machine), and we know what specific kinds of event or process would bring about one such state of affairs rather than another; so we can locate – in the broader context within which the basket sits – candidate causes for its being the specific way it is, and we can test the credentials of these candidates in familiar ways (e.g. by accusing one's spouse of wanton neglect). And this indicates that the possibility of answering such a question presupposes two things at the very least: first, that what we are being asked to account for is (roughly speaking) matters being one specifiable way rather than another with respect to a particular corner of the universe, and second, that as a result we can identify equally specific, but independent, features of the broader context whose being one way rather than another might account for the way things are in this particular corner.

The problem with the question 'why is there something rather than nothing?' is that, although it is patently modelled on such familiar explanatory inquiries, it is formulated in such a way as to remove the conditions which make it possible even in principle to answer questions of that kind, and so seems to deprive us of any reason to regard it as asking an intelligible question of that kind in the first place. For if what now has to be explained is not the presence of dirty shirts (as opposed to their absence) in the laundry basket (as opposed to the washing machine) of the Mulhall residence (as opposed to some other house) in Oxford (as opposed to Kuala Lumpur or Mars), but rather the existence of anything and everything that is, then the question no longer directs us to a specific state of affairs in a specific corner of the cosmos, which might therefore have been otherwise in some specific way, with the result that we lose any grip on what exactly it is that is supposed to be explained; and we are no longer able to point to anything independent of what is to be explained by reference to which it might be explained (since any such thing must, *ex hypothesi*, be, and so must be part of what is to be explained). In short, the question looks like a request to specify the cause of a particular (even if a particularly large-scale) effect; but since what it treats as an effect cannot intelligibly be so treated, nothing could conceivably count as a candidate cause for it; so it cannot in fact be (treated as) a request for an explanatory cause. In the absence of any other possible way of taking it, we must accordingly regard it as essentially malformed, or meaningless – the mere appearance of an intelligible question.

My attempt to characterize what is worth calling 'philosophy' will depend upon contesting this dismissive conclusion about philosophical questions by showing how one can and should take this exemplary philosophical question otherwise – otherwise, that is, than as a large-scale instantiation of a familiar pattern of causal explanation. And in so doing, I will draw upon the second of my titular associations: for, as many of you will no doubt know, Heidegger's lifelong project was to recover a space in philosophy for what he called 'articulating the meaning of the question of being' (a project that might, with equal accuracy, be characterized as 'articulating the question of the meaning of "being"') – the question of what it is for something, anything, to be; and he would certainly have taken the question 'why is there something rather than nothing?' as intended to thematize, or at least as interpretable as thematizing, exactly that issue.

1) A Genealogical Myth of Philosophy

Human beings are creatures whose modes of existence pervasively exemplify a comprehending grasp of the phenomena they encounter

Stephen Mulhall

in the world they inhabit. When a castigated spouse penitently transfers the contents of the family laundry basket to the washing machine, sets it going, then spends an hour or two ironing the clean but crumpled items of clothing that emerge, every aspect of his endeavours presupposes an implicit understanding of the various things he utilizes. Unless he were capable of correctly identifying the presence and location, the nature and the functional possibilities of the basket, the clothes, the washing machine and the iron, he would be in no position to atone for his previous neglect of his domestic duties. Human beings are in this sense immersed in a world of comprehensible entities as fish are immersed in water; but they are also capable of reflecting upon their implicit comprehension of that world – that is, of thematizing it and putting it in question. Our penitent spouse might, for example, be struck by the efficacy of the washing liquid with which he loads the washing machine, and wonder exactly how it achieves its cleansing purpose; or he might, as he unloads the machine, wonder how exactly shirts are constructed, by whom, and in the light of what conception of what is needed to be respectably dressed. Any such moment of reflective questioning might be thought of as the beginning of an intellectual trajectory that culminates in the development of a systematic body of knowledge such as chemistry, textile design, social history or economic theory – what Heidegger would call an ontic science, in which a particular domain or dimension of the world is delineated and made the subject of an appropriately specific kind of intellectual inquiry.

But our penitent spouse's capacity to question his own everyday comprehension of the world, and thereby to deepen that comprehension, can also be turned upon the more systematic bodies of knowledge that he now inhabits. For having established himself in the field of chemistry, he might ask himself what mode of understanding of that aspect of the world is implicit in the rigorous procedures whereby he investigates it with a view to building powerful theories of its nature. In developing a theory about the chemical structure of a particular substance, for example, what is he presupposing about the essential nature of the elements from which any such structure must be composed, and their combinatorial possibilities? In assuming that all material entities are possessed of chemical structure, what is he presupposing about materiality as such? And in testing his theory, why does he presuppose that what he can establish about observed instances of the behaviour of this substance will apply to unobserved instances? What mode of reasoning is he employing, and what if anything grounds his confidence in the reliability of its deliverances?

Why is There Something Called Philosophy

In thus thematizing and questioning the conceptual and methodological resources deployed in any given ontic science, our
spouse-turned-chemist is now transforming himself into a philosopher. The purpose here is not to mark a point at which the individual
chemist must acquire membership of a different disciplinary union; it
is to mark the introduction of a particular kind of question – the kind
which naturally arises from the modes of procedure internal to an
ontic science (any answers to which can therefore be regarded as deepening our understanding of whatever kind of knowledge that science
delivers), but which necessarily cannot be answered by utilizing its
characteristic investigative procedures, since every such use presupposes the validity of exactly what is now in question. To raise and
pursue such questions is to find oneself engaged in the kind of philosophical inquiry that Heidegger calls 'regional ontology' – an inquiry
into what it is for something to have a particular kind of nature, and
into what makes it possible for us to acquire genuine knowledge of
that nature. In this case, another name for that regional ontology
would be: 'the philosophy of science'; but such familiar branches of
philosophical inquiry as 'the philosophy of religion', 'aesthetics',
and 'the philosophy of history' can also be thought of as each denot-
ing a distinctive regional ontology.

Thus far, my mythical genealogy of philosophy (my account of its
unaccountable origins) might not seem particularly Heideggerian –
that is, I don't think of myself as having thus far said anything with
which any self-respecting analytical philosopher might want strenuously to disagree. And it is already enough to suggest that there will
be something called 'philosophy' for as long as there are human
beings naturally inclined to put their everyday knowledge of the
world in question, and thereby generate ontic scientific knowledge;
for they will then equally naturally be inclined to put *that* knowledge
in question, and to do so just is to begin to think philosophically.
But there is a further step to be taken in the terms of my genealogical
myth, and it is this step that is often regarded as being the distinctively
Heideggerian one. I, however, want to suggest that it can be seen to
emerge as naturally from the questions of regional ontology as questions of regional ontology emerge from those of ontic science; and consequently, that what is regarded as a distinctively Heideggerian form of
philosophical inquiry is in fact a development to which philosophy
naturally subjects itself as a result of reflexively reiterating exactly the
same human tendency to question, and so deepen, our comprehension
of the world that engenders philosophy in the first place.

What, then, is this next step? In the terms of my myth, its ineluct-
ability begins to emerge when we imagine our penitent

Stephen Mulhall

spouse-turned-chemist-turned-philosopher-of-science being naturally moved to consider the following question: what, if anything,
is being presupposed when we conduct regional ontological inquiries? If each of these modes of inquiry can be thought of as enhancing
our understanding of whatever the relevant ontic science reveals to us
by subjecting its presuppositions to productive questioning, must we
not – sooner or later – be struck by the possibility that whatever is
presupposed in the acquisition of that enhanced understanding
might itself be put in question, and to equally productive effect? If
and when we are so struck, then the question that strikes us is: what
exactly is it to engage in regional ontology?

Precisely because each species of regional ontological inquiry concerns itself with what we comprehend of a particular region or dimension of the world, what most immediately strikes us about it is its
differences from other species of regional ontology. The issues and
problems that preoccupy philosophers of art or religion often
appear to be very distant from those that predominate amongst philosophers of science or mind or language; and that might itself
seem unsurprising, given the obvious differences between the
various ontic enterprises (art, theology, physics, psychology, linguistics) from which each regional ontology emerges. This, one might
say, helps us to answer the question: what makes a regional ontology
'regional'?

On the other hand, even if each such branch of philosophy focuses
on a very different domain of human knowledge, and so of the world
we thereby know, it is equally true that it focuses on a strikingly
similar dimension of that knowledge, and so of that world. After
all, each regional ontology is, precisely, an inquiry into the *ontology*
of that region – an inquiry into what it is for an entity or property
to exist as, to be, an entity or property of the relevant kind (material,
aesthetic, linguistic or mental), and what it is for us to grasp that kind
of entity or property as it is. And once we appreciate this, a second
question naturally arises: what is it for a regional ontology to be 'ontological'? What, if anything, links inquiries in the philosophy of
science to those in aesthetics or the philosophy of religion or the philosophy of language?

Once asked, it quickly becomes obvious that such links exist at two
main levels. First, there will be specific links between questions that
emerge in one regional ontology and those that emerge in another.
For example, one cannot move far into the domain of philosophy of
religion without realizing that an understanding of religious beliefs
and judgements means establishing an understanding of distinctively
religious language; and that understanding cannot be acquired

independently of addressing broader questions about the nature of language as such – the domain of the philosophy of language. Note that I am deliberately refraining from suggesting that either of these regional ontological inquiries has any priority over the other: if philosophers of religion claim to establish certain conclusions about how language works in religious contexts, how exactly those claims are to be brought into alignment with claims made by philosophers of language who may have very different kinds of language use in focus (whether either party should give ground in the light of the results of the other, and if so which) is and should be an open question – something to be settled by a dialogue between the two parties. My point is simply to register the fact that such dialogues are possible, a fact which in turn demonstrates the dialogical openness of any one regional ontology to its others.

But I said that there were two main levels at which such links existed. The second can be articulated in more general terms – terms which will sound more distinctively Heideggerian. If the philosophy of religion concerns itself with what it is for something to be divine, and the philosophy of mind with what it is for something to be mental, and the philosophy of science with what it is for something to be material, then one way of articulating the unity of these distinct enterprises is to say that all are concerned, in their different ways, with what it is for something to be: with what it is for a phenomenon to manifest itself, both as it is in itself and as being rather than not-being, and with what it is for us to be capable of comprehending it as such – as something in particular rather than something else or nothing. This, one might say, is the meaning of the question of being, the question of the meaning of 'being': it is what Heidegger calls the question of fundamental ontology. And what my genealogical myth is intended to demonstrate is that its emergence as a question is not an arbitary 'Continental' imposition on an otherwise perfectly rational and exhaustive cultural economy of knowledge, in which each legitimate ontic science naturally incubates its own regional ontological discipline, and nothing else. For if the mere existence of a diverse array of ontic sciences naturally engenders a diverse array of regional ontologies, that array of regional ontologies will as naturally engender the question of fundamental ontology, and for exactly the same reason – as a result of the natural tendency of human comprehension to thematise and question itself.

I just said that one might think of the question of fundamental ontology as directing us towards linkages between regional ontologies at two different levels. But I hope it is now obvious that the metaphor of different levels is here potentially misleading. For it may be taken to imply that the two levels I distinguished are essentially distinct and self-sufficient. Whereas, in truth, if there is no such thing as something's being (as opposed to not-being) except as a particular kind of thing – if something can exist only as some specific thing or other – then the fundamental ontological question of what it is for something, or anything, to be is internally related to the question of what it is for something to be a particular kind of thing, and so is internally related to the business of some particular regional ontology. And that business is itself internally related to questions that arise in other regional ontologies – internal relations of the kind acknowledged in my earlier discussion of the first level at which the enterprise of regional ontology is unified. In this sense, to raise the question of fundamental ontology is, necessarily, to raise the question of links between regional ontologies on both levels at once; those two levels are simply different aspects of one and the same articulated unity.

Other clarifications are equally in order at this point. In particular, I need to emphasize that recognizing the reality and significance of the question of fundamental ontology does not require that we commit ourselves to the legitimacy or even the availability of a single, specific answer to that question – to, for example, one and only one mapping of any given regional ontology's relations with any other, and so to a single exhaustive taxonomy of the various ways in which things may be, or to a specification of some feature (or some set of features) that all existent beings must exemplify or instantiate insofar as they exist. Some philosophers have thought it possible to give such a specification of what it is to be, and have disagreed with the specifications of others; others still have denied that any such specification is conceivable. Similarly, some philosophers have argued that work in certain regional ontological inquiries should be constrained by results established in others, whilst disagreeing with one another about which regional ontology should constrain and which should be constrained; others have argued against any, even provisional, assignments of relative priority; and others still have denied the existence of any significant relations between any two given ontological regions. For example, many analytical philosophers feel that theories of meaning constructed in the philosophy of language and logic should constrain the interpretative options available to aestheticians and philosophers of religion; some feel that attention to religious and aesthetic uses of language should rather constrain our choice between general theories of meaning; and others again may feel that, once specific accounts of language use in particular circumstances are established and given due weight, there may be nothing left for a theory of meaning to be a theory of.

The point of emphasizing the reality and significance of the question of fundamental ontology is not to adjudicate between these disagreements, or to deny that they may persist beyond any adjudication, thereby betraying a fundamental mutual incomprehension; the point is rather to thematize the sheer fact of their existence – the fact that it is so much as possible to have such intelligible discussions about whether and how the various regional ontologies relate to one another. For the reality of such debates, whatever their terminus in any particular case, serves to make manifest a horizon of intelligibility within which they are conducted. The various positions taken up in such debates adumbrate a determinable and endlessly-redetermined categorial field of diversity-in-unity or unified diversity to which the articulation – more precisely, the sheer articulability, the simple comprehensibility – of the question of fundamental ontology bears witness.

And those who are struck by the articulability of that question are not committed to one particular way of articulating it or making sense of it; in particular, they need not regard themselves as posing a familiar kind of request for causal explanation, only one that (impossibly) aims to treat all that is as an effect of some cause. For to treat the question of fundamental ontology as articulable need not involve assuming that any particular way of making sense of things within the world might be used to make sense of the world as such, or as a whole; it merely involves acknowledging that there is something inherently questionable about the many and various ways in which we do make sense of any and every particular kind of thing. For if we are capable of making sense of whatever we encounter, then that too (the validity, the diversity and the inter-relatedness of the ways in which things make sense) is something of which we can attempt to make sense (to thematize, to put in question, and so – we hope – to grasp more fully).

2) Philosophy, Knowledge, Reality

From one point of view, to take seriously the question of fundamental ontology just is to take seriously the question of the unity of philosophy. For if the question of fundamental ontology is not raised within the precincts of philosophy, then that means that the question of whether and how the various branches of philosophy relate to one another is not being raised, or at least not being raised in a rigorous and thorough-going manner; and that raises the possibility that philosophical work in any given branch might be conducted in ignorance of what is going on in other such branches. And one way in which such a possibility is realized is the accelerating implementation of the idea that, in order to become appropriately equipped to do work in one ontological region, one must specialize in it; and of course, the more such specialized work is done, the more of it one needs to be acquainted with in order to be equipped to contribute to it, and the less feasible it becomes to keep track of the possible relations between what is being done in this field and what is being done in other such fields.

The result of such feedback mechanisms is the disarticulation or balkanisation of the subject of philosophy. It no longer amounts even to the sum of its parts, but is rather reduced to an assemblage of elements whose nominal status as parts of a putative larger, unified endeavour (one for which the question of its unity is at least poseable) lacks any real grounding. In this respect, systematically to neglect the question of fundamental ontology amounts to depriving regional ontological inquiries of their nature as branches of a single, articulated field of ontological inquiry. And if their full nature and significance depends upon the intelligibility of their inter-relations, then work prosecuted within their boundaries on the unthematized presupposition that those inter-relations have no reality would radically reduce their authenticity, and so their authority, even taken solely as contributions to regional ontology.

To pursue philosophy in this way is to pursue it without even contemplating the question of what makes it philosophy; and that is to fail properly to comprehend what one is doing – to fail to see its full significance or meaning qua philosophy. One might say: if philosophical inquiry fails to find room for the question of fundamental ontology, which means finding room to acknowledge that the matter of its own distinctive nature and how it can and should be realized is inherently questionable – call it the question of the meaning of 'philosophy' – then it no longer deserves to be called 'philosophy'.

This may matter a great deal to those who feel themselves inclined or compelled to participate in philosophical inquiry; but why should the question of whether or not philosophy makes sense to itself as philosophy be of any great moment to anyone other than philosophers? The answer to this question begins to emerge when we recall that the various enterprises of regional ontology from which the question of fundamental ontology naturally emerges *themselves* naturally emerge from the various ontic sciences. To put it another way: the ontological questions each branch of philosophy addresses are themselves addressed to the basic categorial presuppositions within which each ontic science produces its distinctive contribution to human knowledge of reality. Hence, to raise the question of whether and how any given regional ontology hangs together with any other regional ontology is to raise the question of whether and how any given ontic science is intelligibly relateable to any other. If the philosophy of history and the philosophy of science have something to say to one another, then so must history and science; if aesthetics and the philosophy of religion bear intelligibly on one another in various ways, then so must art and religion. Or better: the former constitutes one dimension of the latter.

In this respect, one might say that the question of whether or not philosophy hangs together or makes sense is internally related to the question of whether or not human knowledge hangs together or makes sense. So to regard the question of fundamental ontology as worth posing is one way of showing that the unity of human knowledge is an issue for us. For just as one regional ontology is intelligibly relateable to other regional ontologies – each in principle capable of questioning and of being put in question by the others – the same holds true of the various ontic sciences. Each can be thought of as establishing knowledge and raising questions of a kind that might have a bearing on the knowledge claimed and the questions posed by other disciplines; and in each case, coming to grasp the nature and variety of those inter-relations is part of coming to grasp the full significance and implications of the individual ontic science itself. The meaning of each such body of knowledge is in part determined by its relations with other such bodies of knowledge; what it is as knowledge is partly given in the various ways in which it can and does have a bearing on other putative bodies of knowledge, and so by the fact that it is so relateable. To treat any given ontic science as essentially self-sufficient – as something for which the question of its place in the broader human cultural economy of knowledge is irrelevant – is thus to misunderstand its nature.

Once again, of course, the dialogical unity to which the question of fundamental ontology points us here is not that of envisaging, let alone avowing, the idea that each such ontic science does or must form one part of a single, monolithic and exhaustive science of everything. Where some will see critical implications for religion in the deliverances of contemporary biology, others will deny that those implications exist, and still others will deny that there are any significant relations between them at all. Once again, the point is not to adjudicate these disagreements, but rather to note the simple fact that they can be engaged in, and so to bear witness to the fact that whether or not any given body of knowledge does or could have a bearing on any other is at issue for us – that there is an intelligible question to be asked here, whatever one's preferred answer to it may be.

If, however, there is such a question to be posed about the inter-articulations of ontic sciences, and if those sciences are indeed evolving and self-questioning bodies of knowledge about a given domain or dimension of reality, then there must be room for posing a parallel question about whether and how these various aspects of reality hang together. Coming to see that the question of fundamental ontology is askable is thus also a way of getting us to see that it makes sense to ask whether and if so how reality makes sense – to ask about how, if at all, any given aspect of the real world bears upon any other such aspect. And since ontic sciences are Janus-faced – since they not only claim to embody a grasp of (some portion of) reality, but also constitute articulations of human understanding, ways in which the comprehension implicitly guiding our way of inhabiting reality is thematized and questioned – the question of the sense they make in relation to one another is also the question of what sense, if any, accrues to the particular human form of life they help constitute. Seen this way, the question of whether philosophy makes sense just is the question of whether reality makes sense, whether our knowledge of reality makes sense and whether our modes of living make sense. And that, I hope it is clear, ought to be of interest to anyone with a life to lead for whom the question of how to live that life matters – which means, anyone with a life to lead.

3) Philosophy, University, Culture

In Western European culture, the exemplary institutional expression of this sense of the dialogical unity of reality, our knowledge of it and our way of living is the university. The point of bringing a representative variety of ontic sciences (by which I mean sciences, social sciences, humanities and arts) under one roof is not simply to reduce overheads or to corral socially disruptive clerks within an easily-policeable space; the point is to create a context which embeds and embodies a vision of the denizens of each branch of human knowledge as conversing with one another. To be sure, each department pursues its own ways of acquiring knowledge under its own direction; but each does so in a context which makes it as easy as possible for its members to encounter, learn from and put in question the findings and queries of members of any other department.

Why is There Something Called Philosophy

Certain institutional arrangements may make this kind of unregulated and unpredictable intercourse more natural than others – and here, the collegiate model of a university (as exemplified by Oxford and Cambridge) may have something vital to be said in its favour, since each college's self-governing membership amounts to a microcosm on a humane social scale of the university's aspiration to intellectual diversity-in-unity. But that is only one way of aspiring to facilitate this ideal of mutual conversibility in the face of explosively expanding bodies of knowledge, not to mention financial, political and cultural pressures that work to eviscerate both the substance and validity of that ideal.

If, however, the way in which I have attempted to articulate the question of fundamental ontology in the preceding pages is at all plausible, then there is one university department whose existence is of particular importance to the university's raison d'etre; and that is its department of philosophy. That department's internal articulation into various branches reflects as broadly as possible the internal articulation of the university as a whole; and its inherent tendency to put in question the intelligibility of the relations between those branches – to reflect upon the significance of the fact that they are the internal articulations of a single subject – means that it is uniquely committed to bearing witness to the dialogical diversity-in-unity of human knowledge and of the reality it aspires to grasp. Philosophy itself is not an ontic science: it is rather the subject which aims to comprehend and question the very possibility of an ontic science, the subject for which the intelligibility of that possibility (the possibility of knowing something, anything, as it really is, hence as being rather than not-being) is an issue, an inherently questionable matter. Philosophy is the subject for whom that possibility matters because it is a way of posing the question of its own nature – the question of whether its own continued existence matters, or matters any longer, to anyone other than itself.

And of course, sometimes philosophy finds that its own continued existence does not in fact matter to anyone else. It discovered this most recently, in my neck of the political woods, when the British government of the 1980s decided to reconfigure its funding of universities, and many universities responded to this pressure by closing their philosophy departments. In responding that way, those universities made manifest their inability to see the point of the existence of philosophy in the context of a university, and inadvertently made manifest their inability to see the point of their own existence as universities; and in refusing to contest these responses, the British government and the British people made manifest its own inability to see the point of either philosophy or universities in and for the wider culture. And what are we to say of a culture that no longer sees any point in raising the question of whether its own particular formation, its internal articulations of intelligibility, have any point – whether it continues to makes sense to inhabit the cultural forms through which its inhabitants are currently formed?

But philosophers shouldn't repress the question of their own responsibility for this fate. For, when all is said and done, how many of our existing philosophy departments reflect in their internal structures a sense of the vital significance of the question of fundamental ontology? How far does the inner life of our departments make room for raising the question of how its various activities hang together or make sense in relation to each other, as opposed to amounting to an assemblage of self-sufficient enterprises, or a domain within which the relative importance of various branches of the subject are fixed, effectively put beyond question? If, on reflection, we cannot confidently say that our own ways of living as philosophers are marked by the conviction that the question of whether philosophy makes sense is of such importance, then we should not be too quick to heap all the blame for our present cultural irrelevance on either universities or governments, as if confident that our fate could only have been forced upon us from without.

4) Philosophy, Finitude, Mystery

It will not have escaped you that the tone of my remarks thus far has tended far more towards the arrogant than the self-effacing. So it might be worth emphasising a variety of ways in which the significance of the role I have been assigning my discipline – in the university, in the broader culture, and in (what one might call) the cosmos – will naturally tend to condition, qualify and more generally put itself in question.

To begin with, of course, it follows from my mythical genealogy of philosophy that there is something called philosophy rather than nothing only because there are ontic sciences (upon which philosophers can reflect questioningly); and there are ontic sciences only because there is a world inhabited by beings who are always already cognitively engaged with it. One might then say: there is something called philosophy rather than nothing because there is something (knowable) rather than nothing. This captures the sense in which philosophy is an inherently parasitic discipline: it can exist only because other disciplines exist, and the price of its capacity to sustain itself in relation to any and all of those disciplines is its having no disciplinary subject-matter of its own – no body of knowledge, no domain of reality, to which it is wedded. If its interest fundamentally lies in the fact, the nature and the inter-relations of other disciplines and their subject-matters, then what might at first appear as philosophy's unlimited reach could equally well be seen as its absolute intellectual ungroundedness.

Second, whilst my genealogical myth is designed to capture the sense in which philosophy can be said to be rightly and intelligibly interested in everything, in all that is, it may also thereby create the impression that the philosopher must be occupying a position above or beyond all that is – a kind of God's eye view on Creation from without (for how else, it might be asked, could he take it in as a whole?). But in truth, philosophy does and must occupy a position within the domain that it aspires to take in as if from the outside. Just as philosophy's claim to be the university department which uniquely aspires to acknowledge the articulated unity of the university as a whole must cohere with the fact that it is nevertheless also just one more department within that articulated unity, so philosophy's claim to be the singular point within the culture at which its articulated unity is acknowledged must cohere with the fact that it is simultaneously one node in that cultural economy.

Two important conclusions follow from a proper appreciation of this fact, and so of philosophy's dual-aspect status. First, it means that philosophy's various ways of putting the deliverances of other intellectual disciplines in question can themselves intelligibly be put in question from the perspectives afforded by those very disciplines. Practitioners of any ontic science can question the accuracy of any philosopher's characterization of their founding presuppositions; they might claim for themselves a field of inquiry that philosophers have long regarded as their own (as has happened repeatedly in philosophy's history, to the point at which some philosophers have claimed that philosophy can retain any given field of inquiry only until its distinctive nature and resources have been clarified or thought through to the point at which a genuine science of that domain can be founded); others even argue that philosophy can claim to be grappling with anything of any genuine intellectual substance only insofar as it regards itself as continuous with some ontic science or other.

It should be obvious that I don't find the last of these claims at all convincing; but some of my colleagues do, and I can make sense of their sense of conviction. Be that as it may, one can surely acknowledge the way in which other intellectual disciplines might have a bearing on philosophy and its concerns without conceiving of this as a matter of usurpation or reduction. For example, one might think (as does Stanley Cavell) that aspects of the phenomenon that philosophy grapples with under the name of scepticism are engaged with in literature under the name of tragedy; or one might hope to learn something about the roots and the significance of philosophy's apparent aspiration to find a God's-eye view of reality and culture by drawing upon the lessons of psychoanalysis or theology; or one might be brought by the work of historians and sociologists to appreciate the cultural specificity of the terms in which philosophy understands any given aspect of its concerns (in ethics or politics or aesthetics), and so understands itself.

Such possibilities of inter-disciplinary dialogue cannot be rejected *a priori* by any philosopher who recognizes the pertinence to their enterprise of the question of fundamental ontology; for as I have derived that question, it precisely depends upon acknowledging that a culture hangs together only insofar as any of its thematized modes of understanding can in principle intelligibly and fruitfully be engaged in dialogue by any other. Whether any such encounter will in fact be fruitful, or even mutually intelligible, can only be proven through its concrete working-out from case to case; but its bare possibility is surely something that anything worth calling philosophy is obliged (on pain of self-subversion) to acknowledge.

I said that this was one of the conclusions that followed from an acknowledgement of the dual-aspect nature of philosophy – from the unavoidable fact that it forms one part of the phenomenon it aspires to take in as a whole. The second may be no more than a restatement of the first, but it may also help to bring home the central moral of this moment of humility or self-abnegation in my analysis. For what the first conclusion really registers is the fact that any philosophical work is necessarily situated or conditioned by its place in the broader economy of a culture; and that directs us towards the more general point that philosophy is and must be thorough-goingly conditioned or situated insofar as it is (in effect) one step in the reflexive unfolding of the distinctively human mode of comprehending the world.

To say that that comprehension of the world is distinctively reflexive – that is, that it is always capable of putting itself in question – is simply another way of saying that human comprehension is essentially finite (for if it were not, if it were absolute or unconditioned, it would be beyond any possible question). It is a way of acknowledging that any given body of knowledge has limits, that it is always capable of and subject to further refinement (which will sometimes take the form of revolutionary reconceptualisation), and that it will always be conditioned or informed by a variety of presuppositions which can themselves be the subject of inquiry – perhaps within its own precincts, certainly within the precincts of other branches or modes of human inquiry. In other words, there can be no such thing as an absolute end or terminus to human knowledge of reality – nothing that is beyond further interrogation, hence closed to further enrichment or deepening.

Since my genealogical myth of philosophy is driven from beginning to end by a characterization of human comprehension as inherently produced by, and hence inveterately subject to, questioning, it should be no surprise that the conception of philosophy that emerges from that mythical account should be marked by the same acknowledgement of our finitude. What is now perhaps becoming clearer is that philosophy's way of being marked by, hence of bearing witness to, our finitude has to do with the fact that its defining aspiration (to articulate the question of fundamental ontology) is both undismissable and unfulfillable.

For insofar as philosophy is defined as an inquiry into the human capacity for comprehending inquiry as such, beyond any particular way of acquiring understanding of any particular domain of reality, it amounts to a kind of absolutely purified or intensified exemplar of this aspect of the human way of being (one in which questioning comprehension aspires to be both subject-matter and means, with nothing other than itself involved). But insofar as any such inquiry must itself be questionable, because it is no less subject to condition and limitation than any other exercise of this capacity, it is destined to fail to fulfil its own defining aspiration. In the end, then, what is revealed by the fact that there is something called philosophy rather than nothing is the fact that human beings aspire by their very nature to a completeness of understanding that they cannot realize. Philosophy constitutes the place at which finite human understanding endlessly attempts, and as endlessly fails, to take itself in as a whole; and it thereby reveals that it is internal to the nature of finite beings to be subject to the mysterious, unsatisfiable desire to transcend their own finitude. In this way, philosophy's unending struggle with the question of whether it makes sense even to try making sense of the many and varied ways in which reality does (and does not) make sense to us is the most fundamental way in which human beings manifest the essentially enigmatic finitude of their being.

Philosophy and the Sciences After Kant

MICHELA MASSIMI

1. Preamble: HPS and the troubled marriage between philosophy and the sciences

On 11th October 2007, at the first international conference on Integrated History and Philosophy of Science (&HPS1) hosted by the Center for Philosophy of Science in Pittsburgh, Ernan McMullin (University of Notre Dame) portrayed a rather gloomy scenario concerning the current relationship between history and philosophy of science (HPS), on the one hand, and mainstream philosophy, on the other hand, as testified by a significant drop in the presence of HPS papers at various meetings of the American Philosophical Association (APA).

Since my research activity falls primarily into the category of history and philosophy of science, I am delighted to be able to contribute to this volume on *Conceptions of Philosophy*, by discussing what I see as the very important role that history and philosophy of science plays, or ought to play within philosophy. And the aforementioned gloomy depiction of the current relationship between HPS and philosophy invites some preliminary reflections. There is no doubt, I think, that recent years have witnessed an increasing gap between the sort of topics and themes pursued by HPS scholars, and those pursued by their colleagues in mainstream philosophy. HPS scholars are interested in practicing philosophy by looking at science and history of science in the first place, and by exploring the specific ways in which new scientific ideas and concepts historically originated and evolved. They think that good philosophy has to be historically and scientifically informed. Analytic philosophers pursue philosophy as a perfectly independent discipline, which not only does not need to resort to the sciences or to history of science, but it *ought not* to, if philosophy has to remain a logically rigorous and methodologically autonomous discipline (independent of any historical and scientific contingency). This gap concerns methodologies, systems of values, and intellectual priorities: there could hardly be a more profound gulf. Speciation within a

doi:10.1017/S1358246109990142
Royal Institute of Philosophy Supplement **65** 2009

population is *per se* a positive, healthy sign of adaptation to the environment. But I think that the type of speciation that we are witnessing in history and philosophy of science within philosophy should not be regarded as a happy parting of the ways. I want to begin this paper by briefly reminding what is at stake in this parting of the ways and what both parties risk losing, or, sadly, have already lost sight of.

Without denying the methodological autonomy of philosophy as a discipline, we should not forget at the same time that philosophy began – in the words of Aristotle – with the sense of wonder that men experience in front of nature. Philosophy flourished for centuries as the highest expression of men's strive to understand nature and the world they lived in. For centuries, philosophy has gone hand in hand with the sciences. Nor can the sciences dispense with philosophy. In Newton's time, the name for physics was *natural philosophy*, and scientific discussions on the nature of space, time and gravitation were entangled with metaphysical debates on nature. Still in twentieth-century physics, the reception of relativity theory and quantum mechanics in the works of Einstein, Bohr, Reichenbach, Weyl and others was entangled with epistemological debates about *a priori* knowledge and the nature of physical reality, whereas some of the most beautiful pages in history of science were written in the first half of the last century by people such as Alexander Koyré, who came from Edmund Husserl's phenomenology, or Émile Meyerson, who studied Descartes and Kant as well as being a historian of chemistry.

These are just a few scattered examples of how fruitful the interaction among philosophy, the sciences and, I would add, the history of science (which seems to me an important 'third man' in this binary relation between philosophy and the sciences), has been for long time. Speciation is a recent phenomenon of our time.

In this paper I want to go back to what I take to be an important turning point in the relationship between philosophy and the sciences, namely to Immanuel Kant. Kant's critical philosophy marks probably the highest point in the happy long marriage between philosophy and the sciences. At the same time, it marks also a watershed: after Kant, the marriage became increasingly rocky. The aim of this paper is to offer a historical reconstruction and a possible (tentative and surely not exhaustive) diagnosis of why such a happy long marriage between philosophy and the sciences went eventually wrong after Kant.

In section 2, I focus on Kant's view on philosophy and the sciences, from his early scientific writings to the development of critical

philosophy and the pressing epistemological problems he felt the
need to address in response to the sciences of his time. In section 3,
I take a look at the relationship between philosophy and the sciences
after Kant in the early nineteenth century: despite the fruitful
Kantian legacy in some of the greatest achievements of nineteenth
century physical sciences, post-Kantian German philosophy began
to signal an increasing divide between philosophy and the sciences.
In section 4, I turn to the relationship between philosophy and the
sciences in the twentieth century. In particular, I pay attention to
three main episodes in twentieth-century philosophy. The first
episode is the revival of neo-Kantianism with the Marburg school
of Hermann Cohen and Ernst Cassirer (section 4.1); the second is
the emergence of logical positivism, especially of Rudolf Carnap's
philosophy of science with its debt and, at the same time, departure
from the neo-Kantian tradition (section 4.2). The third significant
episode is Thomas Kuhn's establishment of HPS as a new field or
sub-field of philosophy, and the consequences that it still has for
HPS as is practised today. I conclude the paper (section 5)
by foreshadowing what I hope to be a better future for the philosophy
and the sciences of the twenty-first century (and for HPS itself as a
subject area that investigates the relationship between philosophy and
the sciences) by recovering what I take to be the most important
Kantian insight in this respect. Namely, that epistemology should be
informed by the scientific preoccupations of our time, as much as philosophy of science should rediscover the Kantian epistemological soul
that it has long lost.

2. Kant on philosophy and the sciences

For centuries, philosophy and natural sciences went hand in hand.
Newton called his masterpiece *Philosophiae naturalis principia mathematica* to indicate that his aim was to investigate the mathematical
principles of what at the time was still called natural philosophy. It
is within this Galilean–Newtonian tradition that we can find some
paradigmatic examples of the fruitful two-way relationship between
philosophy and the sciences. Immanuel Kant is one of those paradigmatic examples. Kant was educated within this Galilean–Newtonian
tradition, and in all his writings there is a constant reference to
Newton's natural philosophy as the highest example of the secure
foundations achieved by the physical sciences of his time. Kant's
intense and life-long engagement with the sciences of his time
which I am going to briefly summarise in what follows – from his

Michela Massimi

pre-critical writings to his critical period up to his last and incomplete work published in the *Opus postumum* – testifies to what is probably one of the highest points in the troubled marriage between philosophy and the sciences.

In the pre-critical period,[1] Kant composed twenty-five works, of which several on physics and astronomy. Most of these pre-critical works focussed on the then ongoing lively debates concerning physical sciences. For instance, Kant's very first work back in 1747 entitled *Thoughts on the true estimation of Living Forces* (1747) addressed one of the most debated topics at the time: namely, the physical concept of *vis viva* (the ancestor of the current concept of kinetic energy), which Leibniz defined as the product of mass times squared velocity, by correcting Descartes's definition in terms of mass times velocity. Eight years later, in 1755, Kant wrote another scientific essay entitled *Universal Natural History and Theory of the Heavens*, which was bound to have a long-lasting impact in the history of astronomy because of the introduction of the so-called 'nebular hypothesis'.[2] The key idea, later expanded by Laplace in 1796 and now known as the Kant–Laplace hypothesis, was that the universe and the galaxies in it originated from a nebula (a rotating cloud of gases that expanded and gradually cooled down) according to the fundamental laws of physics, in particular Newton's laws as the expression of God's divine providence, Although kant legged to differ from Newton on the exact role of God in the constitution of the universe.

Even more interesting for the relationship between philosophy and the sciences of his time was the theme of *Physical Monadology* (1756).[3] With this work Kant intervened in the then heated debate – triggered by the Berlin Academy of Sciences Prize Question for 1745–7-between the Leibnizians–Wolffians, on the one hand, and the Newtonian Pierre Maupertuis, on the other hand, on the specific theme as to whether Leibniz's monadology was compatible with the Newtonian idea of infinite divisibility of space and time. Kant's original proposal was to try to reconcile the Newtonian idea of the infinite divisibility of space with a physical monadology that regarded monads as physical point-like centers of attractive and repulsive forces filling a space, rather than as Leibnizian metaphysical

---

[1] By 'pre-critical period', it is usually intended the period preceding Kant's Inaugural Dissertation in 1770, when he was appointed Professor of Logic and Metaphysics at the University of Königsberg.

[2] Kant (1755a).

[3] Kant (1756).

substances occupying a finitely divisible space.[4] If the theme of this early writing is *per se* already symptomatic of Kant's engagement both with mainstream (Leibnizian–Wolffian) metaphysics *and* with the physics of his time, on the other hand, the far-reaching consequences of Kant's original attempt to reconcile the two are even more extraordinary. Indeed, Kant's take on physical monads anticipated the dynamical theory of matter that he developed later in 1786 in the *Metaphysical Foundations of Natural Science*, and that was bound to have a huge impact in the development of the physical sciences of nineteenth century from Oersted to Faraday, as we shall see in the next section.

With the *Inaugural Dissertation* of 1770, entitled *Concerning the Form and Principles of the Sensible and the Intelligible World*, which marks a watershed in Kant's philosophy, Leibnizian metaphysics and Newtonian science are finally disentangled. Against both the Newtonian and the Leibnizian tradition and their respective attempts to reconcile physics with a metaphysics of space, time, and physical substances, Kant's critical philosophy for the very first time introduced a distinction between the faculty of sensible cognition and the faculty of intellectual cognition, and relegated the monadic realm to the second, and space and time as autonomous forms of sensible intuition to the former.

With the beginning of Kant's critical period, the relationship between philosophy and the sciences was completely reconsidered. The task for Kant was no longer to reconcile physical discoveries with metaphysical debates on the nature of space, time, and physical

---

[4]   To this purpose, Kant resorted to a slightly modified proof already present in the *Introduction to Natural Philosophy* by the Newtonian John Keill (1726). The idea of physical monads was at odds with Leibnizian–Wolffian metaphysics, according to which monads are indeed constituted by primitive active and passive forces which are however distinct from derivative active and passive forces at work in the dynamics of moving bodies (Leibniz's *Specimen dynamicum*, and Wolff *Cosmologia generalis* §§183–4. I thank Silvia De Bianchi for helpful research collaboration on this issue). As Watkins (2005), 70 notes, the main problem for Leibniz was to try to harmonize 'the realm of final causality' (monads) with the 'realm of efficient causality' (bodies), i.e. the 'freedom of monads with the determinism of bodies'. Watkins goes on to claim that the idea of monads as physical points, and not just metaphysical substances, was defended on the other hand by Martin Knutzen, who was Kant's teacher although the relationship between the two was not very rosy and polemic references to Knutzen can be found in Kant (1747). On the Kant–Knutzen relationship, see Beiser (1992), Schönfeld (2006), and Kuehn (2001).

Michela Massimi

substances. Instead, the main task for Kant's critical philosophy became that of explaining and justifying how the very successful mathematical-physical sciences of his time were possible, by looking at the conditions of possibility of our scientific knowledge of nature. The answer that Kant gave to this question is well-known: our scientific knowledge of nature is the serendipitous result of applying pure concepts of the faculty of understanding to 'appearances', intended as the conceptually still undetermined spatio-temporal objects as given to the mind in empirical intuition. If the task of critical philosophy was to explain why we have achieved such secure foundations in the mathematics and natural sciences of the time, the answer that critical philosophy gave to this epistemological question relied on the way in which our mind contributes to our scientific knowledge, by projecting onto nature *a priori* forms of sensibility such as space and time as well as *a priori* principles of the understanding, such as for instance causality.

It is not my aim in this paper to enter into the details of Kant's critical philosophy. Instead, since the topic of this paper is to analyse the relationship between philosophy and the sciences after Kant, I simply want to highlight some points which I deem relevant to this topic. First, as the above short remarks about Kant's pre-critical writings show, we can legitimately regard Kant's critical philosophy as the final outcome of Kant's life-long commitment to both the philosophy and the sciences of his time (namely, to Leibniz–Wolff metaphysics on the one hand, and Newtonian physics, on the other hand). Second, the original solution that Kant gave to the problem of how to reconcile the two, consisted in relegating traditional metaphysical debates to the noumenal realm and redefining the role of philosophy as mainly centred around the epistemological questions of 'how is pure mathematics possible?' and 'how is pure natural science possible?'. Kant's transcendental method starts from the fact of science and traces it back to the conditions of possibility of our scientific knowledge. Indeed, the exact sciences continued to play a key role in Kant's critical philosophy as the very source of inspiration and motivation for his entire epistemological project.

No wonder Kant opened the Preface to the second edition of the *Critique of Pure Reason* (1787) by programmatically linking his Copernican turn to the work of scientists such as Galileo, Torricelli and Stahl:

> When Galileo rolled balls of a weight chosen by himself down an inclined plane, (. . .) a light dawned on all those who study nature. They comprehended that reason has insight only into what it itself produces according to its own design; that it must take the lead

with principles for its judgements according to constant laws and compel nature to answer its questions, rather than letting nature guide its movements by keeping reason, as it were, in leading-strings; for otherwise accidental observations (...) can never connect up into a necessary law, which is yet what reason seeks and requires. Reason, in order to be taught by nature, must approach nature with its **principles** in one hand, (...) and, in the other hand, the **experiments** thought out in accordance with these principles – yet in order to be instructed by nature not like a pupil, who has recited to him whatever the teacher wants to say, but like an appointed judge who compels witnesses to answer the questions he puts to them. (...) This is how natural science was first brought to the secure course of a science after groping about for so many centuries.[5]

Galileo is here portrayed as the scientist who paradigmatically accomplished the revolutionary shift that Kant was urging for in epistemology: namely, the shift from the view that our scientific knowledge proceeds from nature itself (i.e. that what we *believe* there is proceeds from what there *is*, which is the very source of the problem of knowledge) to the opposite Kantian view, according to which 'we can cognize of things *a priori* only what we ourselves have put into them'.[6] The certainty and secure foundation achieved by natural science from the time of Galileo onwards is – to Kant's eyes – the paradigmatic expression of this shift. Reason must approach nature with its *principles* on the one hand, and with *experiments* thought out in accordance with these principles, on the other hand.[7] And the task of transcendental philosophy is to clarify what are the principles that make our scientific knowledge of nature possible.

Thus, by asking how pure natural science is possible, Kant was trying to justify why we *do* in fact have a science of nature from the time of Galileo onwards. It is from this particular perspective – I want to suggest – that we can read Kant's entire philosophical enterprise from the *Metaphysical Foundations of Natural Science* (1786) until his last incomplete work 'Transition from the Metaphysical Foundations of Natural Science to Physics' published in the *Opus postumum*.

---

[5]   Kant (1781, 1787); Eng. transl. (1997) *Critique of Pure Reason*, Preface to the second edition, B xiii–xiv. Emphasis added.

[6]   *Ibid*. Bxviii.

[7]   I have explored this point in Massimi (2008b) in relation to what I think is Kant's new conception of phenomena and its relevance to current debates in philosophy of science.

Michela Massimi

In the *Metaphysical Foundations of Natural Science* (1786) Kant expressly tried to latch the transcendental apparatus developed in the *Critique of Pure Reason* onto the physical sciences of his time, namely Galilean–Newtonian physics, so as to provide a justification for its secure foundations.[8] The task of this fundamental work is to show how the empirical concept of matter can be schematised according to the table of categories developed in the Transcendental Analytic of the *Critique of Pure Reason*, i.e. namely according to the four categories of quantity, quality, relation and modality. Hence, four corresponding chapters entitled respectively Metaphysical Foundations of Phoronomy, Dynamics, Mechanics and Phenomenology. And while the chapter on Phoronomy investigates matter as a mathematical point-like movable in space endowed exclusively with a certain 'quantity of motion' (namely, speed and direction), in the following chapter 'Metaphysical Foundations of Dynamics', Kant defined the empirical concept of matter according to the category of quality as the *movable* that fills a space through a *particular moving force*. More precisely, he introduced a priori *attractive and repulsive forces* (which featured already in the 1756 *Physical Monadology*) as two fundamental moving forces, through which matter can fill a space by either causing other bodies to approach it or to be removed from it. Kant derived these two fundamental moving forces a priori from two basic properties of matter, namely its impenetrability and its ability to strive to enlarge the space that it fills so as to counteract the opposite tendency expressed by the repulsive force.

The *a priori* introduction of these two fundamental moving forces paves the way to the chapter on Mechanics, where Kant reformulated Newton's three laws of motion, including Newton's second law, which is regarded as instantiating the category of causality (whereby the impressed force is the *cause* of change in the inertial state of the system). Finally, in the fourth chapter on Phenomenology, the empirical concept of matter as the movable in space is defined according to the category of modality. Kant's aim was to show how to transform *appearance* (*Erscheinung*) into *experience* (*Erfahrung*); more precisely, how to

---

[8]   Michael Friedman has discussed in detail Kant's project in the *Metaphysical Foundations* as strictly related to, and almost an instantiation of Kant's epistemological stance in the *Critique of Pure Reason* (see Friedman 1992a, 1992b). For an alternative reading of Kant's project in the *Metaphysical Foundations* that disentangles the enduring significance of Kant's philosophy from the fortunes of Newtonian mechanics, see Buchdahl (1969a), (1969b), (1974); for a similar line of argument, see also Allison (1994).

transform *apparent motions* into *true motions*. According to Friedman,[9] since Kant rejected Newton's view on absolute space and time, he needed to find a way of explaining true or absolute motions without resorting to absolute space as a privileged reference frame. Kant's strategy consisted in identifying the centre of mass of our solar system as a privileged reference frame. To this purpose, he needed to derive Newton's law of gravitation, responsible for the planetary motions in the solar system, as a necessary and universal feature of matter as the movable in space.

Without going any further into this discussion, the point I want to stress is that following Friedman's reading, in the *Metaphysical Foundations of Natural Science* Kant was trying to give an answer to the epistemological question 'how is pure natural science possible?' by looking at the specific way in which Newton's three laws of motion and the law of gravitation could be justified within the conceptual apparatus of Kant's transcendental philosophy.

In this respect, the *Metaphysical Foundations of Natural Science* occupies a central role in the history of epistemological naturalism, namely in the view according to which answers to the **problem of knowledge** can be found by drawing on **natural sciences** (especially, the physical sciences as historically developed from the time of Galileo and Newton onwards). Kant's **epistemological naturalism**[10] starts with the questions 'what is knowledge?', 'how

---

[9]   Friedman (1992a), ch. 4, on which I draw here.

[10]   A terminological clarification is in order here. I shall henceforth refer to Kant's 'epistemological naturalism' in the specific sense clarified above: namely, that answers to the problem of knowledge should be found by drawing on the natural sciences and on their history. If we want to understand how knowledge is possible, we should investigate how the very successful sciences of the time (Galilean–Newtonian mechanics) were possible, in the first place. Kant's epistemological project was patterned upon the sciences of his time. This is what I mean here – in a somewhat liberal sense – by 'epistemological naturalism'. The term should not be confused with a more common usage of the expression in contemporary (post-Quinean) epistemology to indicate that epistemology should be naturalised, and become a chapter of cognitive psychology (see Quine's seminal work (1969), and Laudan (1990), Kitcher (1992) for more recent discussions of the topic). Kant never endorsed what we now call 'naturalised epistemology': for him, human thought has a fundamentally normative role that cannot be clarified in terms of any naturalistic description. As Hatfield (1990), 17 has pointed out, for Kant 'empirical or natural-scientific description of the mind [is] irrelevant to the discovery and application of standards of epistemic valuation'. On the other hand, this was precisely the path

Michela Massimi

is scientific knowledge of nature possible?'. The pursuit of these epistemological questions led him naturally to the **sciences** and to **philosophy of science** in the attempt to understand the growth of scientific knowledge from the time of Galileo onwards.

If physical sciences, in particular the Galilean–Newtonian tradition, is Kant's main concern in the *Metaphysical Foundations of Natural Science*, on the other hand in the final period of his career and life Kant somehow went back to a series of problems that occupied him already in his early (mid-1750s) works, in particular new discovery in experimental physics and chemistry about combustion, cohesion of solids, and changes of physical state. And if back in 1786, he had dismissed chemistry as a 'systematic art' rather than a proper science, now Kant's awareness of Lavoisier's chemical revolution at the turn of the century, and of the then fashionable theories of caloric and ether as the substances for heat and light, features clearly in his last and never completed work entitled 'Transition from the Metaphysical Foundations of Natural Science to Physics', published as part of the *Opus postumum*.[11]

In this last work, which in Kant's intention was meant to fill a gap he felt was still open in his transcendental philosophy after the *Critique of Judgment*, Kant claimed that in order to complete the transition from the metaphysical foundations of natural science to

---

followed after Kant by Hermann von Helmholtz's empirical research on the physiology of spatial perception.

[11] Friedman (1992a), ch. 5, has illuminatingly pointed out how Lavoiser's chemical revolution, and the recent discoveries of pneumatic chemistry underlie and prompted the 'Transition', whose specific aim was to bridge the gap between the *Metaphysical Foundations* on the one hand, and the vast realm of empirical forces recently discovered, on the other hand. In addition to Friedman's analysis, it must be noted that although the characterization of ether as Wärmestoffe, i.e. as a medium for the transmission of heat, betrays Kant's attempt to reconcile Lavoisier's caloric with ether theories, Kant's use of the ether as a medium for the transmission of attractive and repulsive forces is to be found already in Kant (1755a) and (1755b), with some clear echoes of Newton's analogous use of the ether in the second edition of *Principia* (1713) and most importantly in the 2nd English edition of *Optics* (1717). I have investigated the influence of the Newtonian experimentalism of Opricks, and of the ensuing British and Dutch Natural Philosophy of Stephen Hales and Herman Boerhaave, for Kant (1755a) and (1755b) in an paper currently under preparation. It is as if the last Kant of the *Opus postumum* felt the need to go back to some physical problems that originally prompted his philosophical investigation back in the 1750s.

physics, it was not enough to establish *a priori* attraction and repulsion as two fundamental moving forces in nature. It was not enough because there remains a gap between postulating these two fundamental moving forces in nature from a metaphysical point of view, on the one hand, and accounting for the wide range of specific empirical properties of matter discovered by the chemical revolution by the end of eighteenth century, on the other hand. Hence the necessity to bridge the gap between the all-encompassing metaphysical framework canvassed in the *Metaphysical Foundations* on the one hand, and the multifarious range of more specific empirical properties of matter that natural scientists were discovering, on the other hand.

This is the specific task that Kant aimed to accomplish with the 'Transition to Physics', where by physics Kant meant 'the systematic investigation of nature as to empirically given forces of matter, insofar as they are combined among one another in one system' (22: 298). The main concern of the 'Transition' was then to justify and ground bottom-up a *system of empirically given forces* in nature. The problem is that in nature we may observe objects moving in space and time, changing physical state (from solid to liquid to gaseous) or displaying some properties (e.g. being elastic). But these are only appearances [*Erscheinungen*]. Only when we introduce moving forces as the underlying *causes* that make the objects move in space, or change their physical state or displaying some physical or chemical properties, do we have a conceptually determined appearance or *phenomenon* as the proper object of scientific knowledge. Once again, the category of causality was regarded as crucial in our scientific understanding of a variety of physical phenomena involving moving forces (e.g. forces responsible for the solidification, liquefaction, elasticity, and cohesion of objects).[12] Thus, still in this last and incomplete work, Kant was striving to implement and extend his transcendental apparatus well beyond Newtonian physics to include pneumatic chemistry, theories of heat and light, and even biological theories of his time.[13]

[12] I have investigated the relevance of the 'Transition' in relation to a Kantian conception of phenomena and current debates in philosophy of science, in Massimi (2008b).

[13] For an alternative analysis of Kant's project in the 'Transition', and his proof of the existence of the ether as part of his search for a replacement of his earlier dynamic theory of matter – exposed in the *Metaphysical Foundations* – see Förster (2000).

Michela Massimi

To sum up, with Immanuel Kant epistemology, or better what became later known as *Erkenntnistheorie*[14] acquired a central role in philosophy: analyses of the transcendental conditions for human knowledge replaced time-honoured metaphysical discussions about the nature of time and space triggered by Newtonian science and the Leibniz–Clarke debate. But the normative role of epistemology in tackling the problem of knowledge is – in Kant's view-intrinsically related to the role of the sciences as exemplars of human knowledge. Kant's **epistemological naturalism** is entangled with and ultimately leads into **philosophy of science**: the latter is necessary to accomplish the normative task of the former.

I take this as the greatest Kantian insight that unfortunately both current epistemologists *and* philosophers of science in the Anglo-American world seem to have lost sight of. From the 1930s onwards, in the Anglo-American world, knowledge was identified with justified true belief, and the task of epistemology was no longer to investigate the 'fact of science' so as to find the transcendental conditions for human knowledge, but rather to investigate the logical structure and syntax of language so as to find the sufficient conditions for beliefs to count as knowledge. In the rest of this paper, I attempt a diagnosis of how we got to this stage of detaching epistemology from philosophy of science and hence from science itself. I believe that despite the revival of naturalized epistemology in the second half of twentieth-century, there remains a gap between the philosophy and the sciences that has never been bridged since the time of Kant. And the first signs of this increasing gap became soon evident in the Kant aftermath, at the beginning of the nineteenth century.

3. Philosophy and the sciences after Kant.
The nineteenth century

In this section, I take a brief look at some salient aspects of the relationship between philosophy and the sciences after Kant, with a focus on two main aspects of the Kantian legacy for the nineteenth century. The first concerns the impact that Kant's philosophy of

---

[14] As Caygill (1995), 176 points out 'the German term *Erkenntnistheorie* (theory of knowledge) often translated as epistemology is (...) post-Kantian and was coined by K.L. Reinhold as part of his attempt to transform the critical philosophy into a theory of representation in *Letters on the Kantian Philosophy* (1790–2).'

science had for the developments of the nineteenth-century physical sciences. The second is more directly related to the end of Kant's epistemological naturalism, i.e. his project of tackling the problem of knowledge by taking the sciences as exemplars of human knowledge, in the post-Kantian German tradition. Let us take a look at the first of these two aspects.

Historians and philosophers of science have recently begun to pay more attention to the impact of Kant's philosophy of science for nineteenth-century physical sciences.[15] One of the most significant implications was the role that Kant's dynamic theory of matter played for the movement known as *Naturphilosophie* that developed mainly around Friedrich von Schelling's two main works *Ideas towards a philosophy of nature* (1797) and *First Outline of a System of Philosophy of Nature* (1799). As mentioned in the previous section, following Friedmans analysis, in the *Metaphysical Foundations of Natural Science* Kant identified two fundamental moving forces in nature: a repulsive force responsible for matter's impenetrability and an attractive force counterbalancing the repulsive force. Kant's aim was to start with these two *a priori* established moving forces to provide a top-down justification for his three laws of mechanics. Kant saw the three laws of motion as ultimately grounded on the transcendental principles of substance, causality and reciprocity and on the *constitutive* role these principles play for experience. This top-down procedure finds its natural counterpart in a bottom-up procedure that Kant developed from the *Critique of Judgment* (1790) to the 'Transition from the Metaphysical Foundations of Natural Science to Physics' in the *Opus postumum*. According to this alternative bottom-up procedure, we should start instead from empirically given forces of matter and empirical laws, such as those that the chemical revolution was discovering at the end of eighteenth century, and try to subsume them under higher level yet still empirical laws so as to seek after a *system* of forces in nature. *Systematicity* or *systematic unity* in the investigation of nature was presented as an open-ended, *regulative* (as opposed to *constitutive*) principle of scientific inquiry. It is precisely this distinction between constitutive versus regulative principles, which in Kant runs parallel to the distinction between the faculty of understanding

---

[15]   For the multifarious aspects of the Kantian legacy for nineteenth-century physical sciences, see the excellent anthology by Michael Friedman and Alfred Nordmann (2006), on which I draw here (for a review of this volume, see Massimi 2008a).

and the faculty of reason or reflective judgment[16] that the *Naturphilosophen* dismantled.

The *Naturphilosophen* rejected the dualism between constitutive and regulative principles, and gave a constitutive twist to the regulative principle of systematicity. While Kant stressed systematicity as a regulative principle that the mind projects upon nature, Schelling saw nature itself as systematic and ordered. The speculative physics championed by *Naturphilosophen* regarded nature as productivity, i.e. as *natura naturans* (as opposed to *natura naturata*). This idea of nature as productivity prompted an investigation of forces in nature as the causes of variety of phenomena.

The *Naturphilosophen* extended Kant's dynamic theory of matter well beyond what Kant had envisaged: for them, nature as a whole *dialectically* evolved from the inert/lifeless matter described by Kant into the variety of forms described by contemporary chemistry and biology. Under the influence of the Romantics (from Goethe to Novalis) and influenced by the new electrochemistry, Schelling extended Kant's theory of matter beyond attraction and repulsion and regarded magnetic, electrical and galvanic forces as a *dialectical* development of these two fundamental forces of matter.[17] The search for interconversion processes in the name of the unity and productivity of nature was open, and became a dominant theme of nineteenth-century physical sciences. The interconversion of electrical and magnetic phenomena is one example.

Indeed, Schelling's reinterpretation of Kant in his *System of Transcendental Idealism* (1800) had important implications for the history of electromagnetism in the early nineteenth century. Hans Christian Oersted's pioneering discovery in 1820 that the passage of electric current in a wire could twist sideways a magnetic needle marks the beginning of electromagnetic theory. Oersted was deeply influenced by Schelling, who he came to know via Johann W. Ritter, and even more so by Kant's own dynamic theory of matter that was

---

[16]   In the *Critique of Pure Reason*, in the Appendix to the Transcendental Dialectic, Kant defended systematicity as a regulative principle of the faculty of reason; but in the Introduction of the *Critique of Judgment* the very same regulative principle was re-assigned to the faculty of reflective judgment as the faculty responsible for subsuming the particular under the universal.

[17]   For an excellent analysis of how *Naturphilosophie* expanded some Kantian themes and at the same time influenced some physical discoveries see Gower (1973); and Friedman (2006).

the subject of his doctoral dissertation.[18] Moreover, he attended Fichte's lectures in Berlin and Friederich Schlegel's lecture at Jena.

Some historians of science have even stressed the influence that the German *Naturphilosophie* had in the English-speaking world through Samuel Taylor Coleridge, who was a disciple of Kant in his stay in Germany at the end of eighteenth century, and back in England, allegedly inspired his friend Humphry Davy and via Davy, Michael Faraday, who worked for Davy at the Royal Institution in London.[19] It is no surprise then that Faraday's discovery of electromagnetic induction in 1831 was welcomed by Schelling as vindicating the *Naturphilosophie* manifesto of nature as productivity.

Electromagnetism is not the only example of how Kant's philosophy of science, via Schelling's reformulation, had an impact on the physical sciences of the nineteenth century. The interconversion of heat and mechanical work expressed by the first law of thermodynamics – jointly discovered by Julius Robert Mayer, Hermann von Helmholtz and James Prescott Joule in the 1840s – is another eloquent example. While the link between Mayer and *Naturphilosophie* has become a debated issue in history of science after Thomas Kuhn's seminal article 'Energy conservation as an example of simultaneous discovery' in the late 1950s,[20] a more robust historical link between *Naturphilosophie* and Hermann von Helmholtz, whose father was a close friend of Fichte, has generally been recognised.[21]

But the Kantian legacy for nineteenth-century science is not confined to the interconversion processes at work in electromagnetism and thermodynamics. It extends also to more theoretical aspects of mathematical physics in the works of Jakob F. Fries' *The Mathematical Philosophy of Nature* (1822).[22] In the same

---

[18] On Schelling's influence on Oersted's discovery of electromagnetism see Friedman (2006). Shanahan (1989) argues that Oersted owed more to Kant than to *Naturphilosophie*. He had to study Kant as part of the curriculum in natural philosophy at the University of Copenhagen and indeed wrote his doctoral dissertation on Kant's *Metaphysical Foundations of Natural Science*.

[19] The Kant-Coleridge-Davy-Faraday connection is advocated by the historian Williams (1965), (1973), and questioned by the historian Caneva (1997).

[20] Reprinted in Kuhn (1977), 66–104. Against Kuhn's claim that *Naturphilosophie* was an important factor in Mayer's discovery of energy conservation, see Caneva (1993), ch. 7.

[21] For the influence of *Naturphilosophie* on von Helmholtz see Cahan (1993), ch. 7 and 12.

[22] See Pulte (2006).

Michela Massimi

aforementioned spirit of rejecting the constitutive/regulative distinction and affirming the priority of the regulative over the constitutive, Fries saw Euler and Lagrange's principles of analytical mechanics as the result of a bottom-up approach for systematizing mechanical experience before any constitutive principle could be found and any forces of matter identified. Even more striking is the impact of Kant's Transcendental Aesthetic for the discovery of non-Euclidean geometries. For Kant, the universal and necessary status of Euclidean geometry could be traced back to the fact that objects are given to the mind in empirical intuition according to space and time as *a priori* forms of sensibility. Hermann von Helmholtz challenged Kant on the allegedly necessary status of Euclidean geometry by showing that what makes space seem Euclidean is a series of sense-impressions about the free mobility of rigid bodies and paths of light rays, and the very same empirical evidence can acquaint us with the structure of a non-Euclidean space; hence the non-necessary status of Euclid's fifth postulate. In this way, Helmholtz's empiricism paved the way to Poincaré's conventionalism about geometry, and to non-Euclidean geometries in relativity theory in the twentieth century.[23]

While the *Naturphilosophen* rejection of the regulative versus constitutive distinction and emphasis on the unity of nature opened undreamt-of avenues for the physical sciences, on the other hand, it also engendered a swirl of new philosophical problems. One of the central tenets of post-Kantian German idealism, from Schelling to Fichte to Hegel, was the rejection of Kant's distinction between the faculty of sensibility and the faculty of understanding. For Kant, the distinction between these two faculties was central to understand how nature as given to us in sensible receptivity could become an object of scientific knowledge. And, for Kant, the answer to the problem of knowledge was to be found in the way in which concepts of the faculty of understanding are 'schematised' and applied to spatiotemporal objects of the faculty of sensibility (namely, to 'appearances' as given to the mind in empirical intuition according to *a priori* forms of space and time).

In the hands of post-Kantian German idealists, Kant's interplay of the faculty of sensibility and the faculty of understanding received a new twist, and the contribution of the faculty of sensibility was significantly downplayed. Nature was increasingly regarded as embedded in the conceptual realm, and eventually as the historicized

---

[23]   For the link between Kant, Helmholtz's empiricism and Poincaré's conventionalism, see DiSalle (2006a) 55–72, (2006b).

manifestation of the dialectical development of the spirit, according to Hegel. But it is not just the faculty of sensibility that was downplayed to emphasise the conceptual aspect of human knowledge over and above the contribution of sensibility. The same faculty of understanding was in turn downplayed with respect to the faculty of reason. For Kant, there was an important difference between understanding and reason: the former is the realm of *constitutive* principles that enter in the way we constitute experience by 'schematizing' concepts (i.e. by applying them to spatio-temporal appearances); reason, on the other hand, is the realm of *regulative* principles that provide open-ended and never achievable ideals, towards which we should strive in our scientific knowledge of nature. We have already mentioned that a distinctive feature of *Naturphilosophie* was the pre-eminence assigned to regulative principles over constitutive ones. A consequence of this shift was precisely the aforementioned development of a new dynamic theory of matter that – in the name of the regulative principle of systematicity – took nature as *natura naturans* developing *dialectically* from polar forces. This very same shift, however, had also the effect of opening a gulf between philosophy and the sciences. The historicized, dialectical development of human reason, in conjunction with the downplay of the Kantian faculty of sensibility, meant that knowledge of nature was no longer secured by the Kantian interplay of intuitions and concepts; but rather by the spontaneous activity and dialectical unfolding of human reason itself.

The problem of bridging the gap between what we believe there is and what there is was no longer tackled through Kant's Copernican turn of making appearances conform to *our* way of representing. Instead, *our* way of representing became all there is. The very same dichotomy between us as epistemic agents and the external world as an object of knowledge disappeared in post-Kantian German idealism. And with it, the problem of knowledge that had haunted epistemological naturalism from Hume to Kant also disappeared. Or better, in its place now there was a new problem: that of the unbounded autonomy of human reason in its historicised unfolding. The immediate effect of this idealistic twist was of course that the scientific preoccupations that had triggered Kant's Copernican turn were put to rest for some time. The aim of philosophy – for post-Kantian German idealism – was no longer to explain how we can have scientific knowledge of nature. Nor is the aim of science to provide an exemplar of human knowledge: the post-Kantian idealistic tradition rediscovered the importance of the arts and humanities (from music to art) as exemplars of human knowledge alternative to

Michela Massimi

the sciences. Hence the ensuing debate between *Naturwissenschaften* and *Geisteswissenschaften* that became so typical of German philosophy.

But it is from within this idealistic tradition that at the end of nineteenth century and beginning of the twentieth century a new movement developed, whose primary aim was to rediscover the problem of knowledge and to return to Kant's epistemological project and to the scientific preoccupations behind it. This movement was the Marburg School of neo-Kantianism with Hermann Cohen, Paul Natorp, and Ernst Cassirer.

4. Philosophy and the sciences after Kant. The twentieth century

4.1. Marburg neo-Kantianism

It was the impressive progress of the physical sciences at the end of nineteenth century and beginning of twentieth century (from Maxwell's electromagnetic theory to Boltzmann's statistical mechanics, from quantum theory to relativity theory) that brought philosophers' attention back to the problem of knowledge in the distinctive way in which Kant originally posed it. The return to Kant coincided with and was prompted by the advances of positive sciences. And the primary aim of philosophy became that of providing a theory of knowledge – *Erkenntnistheorie* – that could encompass the fundamental principles of knowledge at work not just in the positive sciences but also in other domains of human knowledge (from morality to aesthetics). *Erkenntnistheorie* became the main focus of the Marburg School of neo-Kantianism. Starting from what – in typically Marburgers' style – they called the 'fact of science' (but also of human culture, more in general), the aim of critical philosophy was to identify the transcendental principles that make it possible.

At the same time, the Marburg return to critical philosophy was inevitably filtered through the post-Kantian idealistic tradition. By contrast with Kant, there is an important residue of idealism in the Marburg *Erkenntnistheorie*. The transcendental principles that make the 'fact of science', of art, of human culture possible are primarily 'ideas' (or, to use Kant's terminology, *regulative ideas*) providing an open-ended normative goal to philosophical inquiry, and analysed in their historical unfolding across the history of science, history of art and of human culture, more in general. By contrast with Kant, who saw in the interplay of the faculty of sensibility and the faculty of understanding (of spatio-temporal intuitions and concepts of the understanding) the key to answer how scientific knowledge is possible, the neo-kannans Marburgers rejected what to their eyes appeared as Kant's semi-psychologistic approach. In their hands the Marburgers, Kant's system came out completely transformed, with the faculty of sensibility gone and the faculty of understanding being played down in favour of the faculty of reason.

Despite these important differences with respect to the Kantian system, we owe to Marburg neo-Kantianism the rediscovery of the Kantian insight about philosophy and the sciences. As Alan Richardson has nicely put it, for them 'science serves both as a resource in the fight against metaphysics and its sceptical antithesis and as a problem for transcendental philosophy. More precisely, (...) the fact of science explodes scepticism and humbles metaphysics, while the philosophical account of scientific objectivity becomes the highest speculative burden of transcendental philosophy'.[24] Transcendental philosophy is considered the best safeguard against the risks of both metaphysics and scepticism, and, at the same time, as laying down the 'idealistic' principles that should account for scientific objectivity. The real novelty compared to Kant has to be found both in the quasi-*Naturphilosophisch* insistence on the *regulative* (as opposed to *constitutive*) *principles*, and on the quasi-Hegelian emphasis on the historical unfolding of these principles. In Hermann Cohen's pioneering work on the history of analytical mechanics from Euler to Lagrange,[25] as in Ernst Cassirer's monumental four-volume *Erkenntnistheorie* from Galileo to Hegel and modern times,[26] critical philosophy – or better, **epistemology intended as Erkennstnistheorie** – was intertwined with both history of philosophy and history of science. And history of science, intended as intellectual history, became an indispensable element to understand the historical unfolding of the transcendental principles of human knowledge. As we shall see below, this rediscovery of intellectual history is a distinctive Marburg feature that many decades later Thomas Kuhn himself acknowledged as having played a role in his own conception of the relationship between philosophy of science and history of science.

The emphasis on regulative over constitutive principles, and on the historicised unfolding of human thought through an open-ended series of logico-mathematical structures as a regulative idea of

---

[24]   Richardson (2006), p. 216.
[25]   Cohen (1883).
[26]   Cassirer (1906–1957).

Michela Massimi

reason, is particularly evident in Ernst Cassirer's so-called 'genetic' conception of knowledge.[27] Cassirer reinterpreted the Kantian '*a priori*' in *regulative* terms. This reinterpretation of the *a priori* as a regulative idea finds its natural expression in what Cassirer called the 'invariants of experience'.[28] The *a priori* no longer denotes that which is *prior* to experience in the sense of being the condition of possibility of experience; but rather that which is the ultimate 'invariant' of experience, unattainable at any stage and yet a regulative goal of scientific inquiry. This seminal investigation – carried out in *Substance and Function* (1910) – was further articulated and explored in Cassirer's later books, namely in the one dedicated to the philosophy of the Enlightenment, and in *Determinism and Indeterminism in Modern Physics*.

In *The philosophy of the Enlightenment* (1932), Cassirer offered a long overdue reappraisal of the Enlightenment conception of scientific progress and rationality. Against the dogmatic tendency to build up philosophical systems, the Enlightenment rediscovered the importance of starting from phenomena. Newton's method of deduction from phenomena (paradigmatically deployed in the *Principia*) became the gold standard of the Enlightenment 'systematic spirit' (esprit systématique). Newton's method does not proceed from concepts and axioms to phenomena, but the other way around: reason becomes the form of the immanent connection of phenomena. This is evidently a neo-Kantian reading of the philosophy of the Enlightenment, a way of linking the philosophical roots of the Kantian regulative demand to the *philosophes*' conception of 'reason' and their admiration for Newton's method. From this perspective, Newton's method of deduction from phenomena comes to fulfil a regulative task: it reveals lawlikeness as immanent in phenomena.

[27] In an interesting study, on which I drew here, dedicated to a comparison of Carnap, Cassirer, and Heidegger, Michael Friedman (2000), ch. 6, has noticed that it is typical of the teleologically oriented 'genetic' conception of knowledge of Cassirer (and of the Marburg School, more in general) to replace Kant's conception of the constitutive *a priori* with a purely regulative idea.

[28] 'From this point of view, the strictly limited meaning of the '*a priori*' is clearly evident. Only those ultimate logical invariants can be called a priori, which lie at the basis of any determination of a connection according to natural law. A cognition is called a priori not in any sense as if it were *prior* to experience, but because and insofar as it is contained as a necessary premise in every valid judgment concerning facts' Cassirer (1910), English transl. (1953), 269.

These ideas were further spelled out in Cassirer's later book *Determinism and Indeterminism in Modern Physics* (1936). According to Cassirer, modern physics has not given up the salient features of Kant's philosophical enterprise. On the contrary, quantum mechanics has only made evident the fact that Kant's philosophical apparatus is to be thought of not as rigid but as dynamic. Hence, 'the *a priori* that can still be sought and that alone can be adhered to must do justice to this flexibility. It must be understood in a purely methodological sense. *It is not based on the content of any particular system of axioms, but refers to the process whereby in progressive theoretical research one system develops from another.*'[29]

I cannot go any further here in an analysis of Cassirer's neo-Kantianism. For the purpose of the present paper, it suffices to note that the relationship between philosophy and the sciences in the twentieth century changed dramatically with the Marburg school. It changed in two main ways. First, philosophy of science was rediscovered once again as a branch of epistemology as *Erkenntnistheorie*, along Kant's original lines. Cassirer's works on Galileo, Newton, and quantum mechanics testifies to the new important role that philosophy of science – intended in the Marburg sense, and surely not in the current sense – played within general epistemology. Second, philosophy of science as a branch of epistemology came to be practiced in strict conjunction with both history of philosophy and history of science. The 'genetic' conception of knowledge prompted the Marburgers to look for the conditions of possibility of human knowledge as historically realised in modern science. However, the serendipitous combination of epistemology, philosophy of science and history of science achieved by the Marburgers was not bound to last. The Vienna Circle of Rudolf Carnap, Moritz Schlick, Hans Hahn, Otto Neurath and Waissman soon gave a new twist to the relationship between philosophy and the sciences, which had far-reaching consequences for the way philosophy of science has been practised in the Anglo-American world since.

4.2. Rudolf Carnap

Among the Vienna Circle, Rudolf Carnap is surely one of the figures that owed most to Marburg neo-Kantianism. As Friedman has

---

[29] Cassirer (1936), Eng. trans. (1956), 74, emphasis added.

Michela Massimi

illuminatingly reconstructed,[30] Carnap studied with the neo-Kantian Bruno Bauch in Jena. He read Kant and neo-Kantians, and many references to Cassirer's *Substance and Function* can be found both in his early works, including his dissertation *Der Raum* (1922), and in *Der logische Aufbau der Welt* (1928). In this latter work, Carnap tried to synthesize the Marburg 'genetic' conception of knowledge with the positivistic faith in a rock bottom level of empirically given sense data (without yet falling back to Kant's faculty of sensibility, or to any phenomenalistic foundationalism *à la* Ernst Mach). But the neo-Kantianism that reached Carnap had been filtered through the logicism of Frege and Russell, and through the idea that what Kant thought was pure mathematics is in fact only a branch of logic (and hence analytic a priori, rather than synthetic a priori).

Following up on Frege's logicism that showed that mathematics is not synthetic a priori, Carnap rejected the Kantian idea that Euclidean geometry is the result of pure intuition. Instead, for Carnap what geometry we choose is an entirely conventional matter (following the path originally opened by Helmholtz and later explored by Poincaré). While for Kant, space, time and causality are *a priori* given and hence constitutive of the object of experience, for Carnap what type of spatio-temporal-causal structure (what in a pre-*Aufbau* terminology he referred to as 'secondary world') we pick out is entirely conventional. What is necessary and not conventional is what Carnap called the positivistic 'primary world' of immediately given sense experience.[31]

This fundamental level of immediately given sense experience provides the foundations for Carnap's project of a 'constitutional system' in the *Aufbau*, namely for what – with Kantian terminology – Carnap calls the 'constitution of reality'. The key idea is to replace Cassirer's 'genetic' conception of knowledge, and hence Cassirer's idea of a sequence of *historically given* mathematical-physical structures as a *regulative* idea, with an alternative sequence of increasingly more abstract logical-mathematical structures, as given to each cognitive subject starting from his/her own sense experience. The idea is to ultimately ground the objectivity of knowledge by embedding subjective sense data into an overarching and intersubjectively valid hierarchy of logical structures. It is in this specific sense that the *Aufbau* was meant to reconcile the positivistic faith in the empirically given with the logical idealism of the Marburg School. The final result, in

[30] Friedman (1999), ch. 6, and (2000), ch. 5, on which I draw here.
[31] Carnap (1924). See on this point Friedman (2000), 69.

Friedman's words, was the transformation of 'neo-Kantian tradition into something essentially new: 'logical-analytic' philosophy.'[32] The most important consequence of this 'logicization' of the Marburg School is, in Friedman's words, that 'epistemology (...) is transformed into a logical-mathematical constructive project.... This formal exercise is to serve as a *replacement* for traditional epistemology.'[33] Carnap's project dissolved traditional epistemological debates, such as the debate between idealism and realism, into the *Aufbau* 'constitutional system'. Thanks to a neutral common basis of formal logic underlying the construction of reality, and thanks to physicalism (i.e. the belief in a physical basis to which ultimately all scientific concepts are logically reducible) all epistemological and metaphysical disputes could be dissolved.

Yet the problem with Carnap's 'constitutional system' is that by pushing Kant's Copernican turn to its extreme limits, and by showing that our scientific knowledge is *objective* thanks to its being reducible to a series of logical-mathematical structures, Carnap was in fact not only dissolving traditional epistemological and metaphysical disputes. He was also dissolving epistemology as *Erkenntnistheorie* and replacing it with philosophy of science intended – in a positivist way – as a logical-mathematical exercise (along the lines of Frege's *Begriffsschrift*, Russell's *Principles of Mathematics*, and Wittgenstein's *Tractatus*).

This is the point where, in the history of twentieth-century philosophy, epistemology – intended as *Erkenntnistheory* – and philosophy of science parted their ways, after the short-lived re-union operated by the Marburg School. And this is where we come from, almost eighty years after the *Aufbau*. As I see it, a rather large portion of current philosophy of science seems in some relevant respect still under the logical positivist spell of practicing their subject as detached from epistemology, intended in the original Kantian and neo-Kantian sense as a theory of knowledge. Be it Bayesian networks or decision theory; be it Everettian philosophy of physics or natural kinds in philosophy of biology, most of the current debates in philosophy of science have, on the one hand, revived the epistemological and metaphysical disputes that Carnap's 'constitutional system' was meant to dissolve; on the other hand, they have also engendered a speciation of subfields in philosophy of science, which seem to have lost sight of their origins. Not only have they lost sight of the problem of knowledge that triggered Kant's epistemological naturalism, but they

---

32 Friedman (1999), 141. See also Richardson (1998).
33 Friedman (2000), 82.

have also lost sight of the historical dimension that Marburg neo-Kantianism brought to this problem. Two main episodes in the history of twentieth-century philosophy are primarily responsible for this speciation, in my opinion.

The first episode is of course the failure of Carnap's project by its own means, as pointed out by Quine's compelling criticism. Quine's criticism of logical positivism, and in particular his critique of Carnap's notion of analyticity[34] constituted ultimately an attack to the Kantian notion of *a priori* as the blueprint of Carnap's 'constitutional' project. In 'Carnap and Logical Truth',[35] Quine attacked Carnap's reformulation of *a priori* knowledge in terms of stipulations or conventions: being 'constitutive' of the meanings of some terms of a linguistic framework (in Carnap's conventionalist sense) does not *per se* imply being immune from revision, according to Quine's holism. At the same time, Quine is responsible for a revival of naturalism in epistemology in the 1960s.[36] Epistemology is no longer regarded as a transcendental enterprise, as it was for Kant and the neo-Kantians, for whom the primary aim of epistemology is to answer how scientific knowledge is possible. Under Quine, naturalised epistemology becomes a branch of psychology.

But even more interesting for the purpose of my paper and of my analysis of the relationship between science and philosophy, is the second episode in the history of twentieth-century philosophy. An attempt to recover the neo-Kantian sensitivity to history of science, without however recovering also the underlying epistemological motivation, took place in the 1960s, when Thomas Kuhn launched his anti-positivistic trend in philosophy of science, to which I now turn.

4.3. Thomas Kuhn

If the early signs of the divorce of philosophy of science from epistemology (intended as *Erkenntnistheorie*) were already evident with the Vienna Circle, the real divorce was complete in the 1960s. With the works of Thomas Kuhn, a new era began for philosophy of science. While philosophy of science rediscovered the importance of history of science, it also expressly rejected normative epistemology as an inquiry into the conditions of possibility of scientific

---

[34]   Quine (1951). For the Carnap–Quine debate see Creath (1990).
[35]   Quine (1963).
[36]   Quine (1969).

knowledge. Whereas Carnap's 'constitutional system' in the *Aufbau* still retained some link with the Kantian and neo-Kantian epistemological tradition, although it ended up replacing epistemological disputes with a logical analysis of language; by contrast, Kuhn's philosophy of science dissolved any normative analysis of how scientists acquire knowledge and replaced it with a historical-sociological analysis of what scientists did and believed. Kuhn broke once and for all the link between philosophy of science and epistemology, by rejecting the idea that epistemology has any normative function in an attempt to understand the growth of scientific knowledge. In so doing, Kuhn broke once and for all with the Kantian and neo-Kantian tradition of epistemological naturalism that we have examined so far. With Kuhn's philosophy of science, naturalism is brought to its extreme consequences: philosophy of science should not investigate the problem of knowledge as it may manifest itself in the sciences. Instead, philosophy of science becomes a chapter of history of science, and (even more so after Kuhn) a chapter of sociology of science. What Kitcher portrays as Kuhn's 'radical naturalism'[37] originates from his firm opposition to logical positivism.

In the 1960s, Thomas Kuhn was one of the very first to voice a concern about the neglect of history of science, which he ascribed primarily to the logical positivist tradition, and one of the first to advocate an integration of philosophy of science with history of science. Interestingly enough, he appealed to the neo-Kantian tradition for this integration and for the rediscovery of the historical dimension in philosophy of science: 'There have been philosophers of science, usually those with a vaguely neo-Kantian cast, from whom historians can still learn a great deal. I do urge my students to read Emile Meyerson and sometimes Leon Brunschvicg. But I recommend these authors for what they saw in historical materials not for their philosophies, which I join most of my contemporaries in rejecting'.[38] Kuhn acknowledges here his debt to the historicised philosophy of science typical of neo-Kantianism, stripped of any underlying epistemological claim. To his eyes, the main contribution of neo-Kantianism has to be found in the important role ascribed to the history of science, not in the underlying epistemological program or in the way in which that program engendered a new wave of philosophy of science. Kuhn rejected Cassirer's philosophy of science as much as he rejected Carnap's philosophy of science,

---

[37] Kitcher (1992).
[38] T. Kuhn 'The relations between the history and the philosophy of science', in Kuhn (1977), 11.

albeit for different reasons. He rejected the former because of its link with *Erkenntnistheorie* and its normative role. He rejected positivist philosophy of science, on the other hand, because of its lack of historical dimension.

And to positivist philosophy of science, Kuhn opposed a new 'philosophy of science' that he himself forged and for which history of science may be all the more relevant: this is the philosophical area that Kuhn himself developed with his view on scientific revolutions, paradigm-shift, and incommensurability in *The Structure of Scientific Revolutions* (1962). The only philosophy of science that can be happily wedded with history of science is a *new* philosophy of science that has little in common with positivist philosophy of science. Kuhn the historian *had to create* a brand new philosophy of science to reconcile it with history of science.

In sum, Kuhn could achieve a reconciliation between history and philosophy of science at the cost of 1) rediscovering the historical sensitivity typical of neo-Kantianism, suitably stripped of any underlying epistemological motivations; 2) creating a brand new, anti-positivist philosophy of science for which history could be of some relevance. Is this a cheap price to pay? I think the answer is no, and indeed within the philosophy of science community, many have never accepted the Kuhnian revolution. The divide remains between those that have embraced Kuhn's lesson and try to do a historically informed philosophy of science, and those that following the positivist tradition are still mainly concerned with logical analyses.

We have identified then two main episodes in the twentieth century that mark respectively the divorce of philosophy of science from epistemology (namely, Carnap's logical positivism), and the subsequent divorce of HPS from philosophy of science (with Thomas Kuhn). What these two episodes have in common is the rejection of the Kantian and neo-Kantian program of tackling the problem of knowledge by taking the sciences as exemplars of human knowledge. Namely, what both positivist philosophy of science and Kuhnian HPS share is the view that the sciences cannot really help us answer the problem of knowledge in the sense of identifying the conditions of possibility of human knowledge. On the other hand, sciences can be all the more important in tackling metaphysical problems about space-time, or reductionism in philosophy of biology, or supervenience in philosophy of mind. The detachment of the sciences from the normative role of epistemology as Kant and the neo-Kantians saw it is the distinctive feature of our era, in my view.

I have now finally reached the end of my historical survey of the troubled marriage between philosophy and the sciences after

Kant. I believe that the current situation in history and philosophy of science is just the last episode of this rather long and troubled marriage between philosophy and the sciences that began after Kant. I would like to conclude this paper by foreshadowing possible future directions of research for the field of history and philosophy of science that somehow take their inspiration precisely from Kant.

5. Conclusion. What future for history and philosophy of science after Kuhn? The Kantian legacy

I want to conclude by urging philosophers of science to go beyond Kuhn. In order to reconcile history and philosophy of science, Kuhn created in fact a new sub-discipline within philosophy of science itself, known as HPS. He set his own philosophical agenda, with his manifesto of scientific revolutions, incommensurability, and theory-choice. He clearly and expressly took his distance from positivistic philosophy of science, and identified new problems and new challenges for philosophers of science to address. By contrast with Kuhn, I think that we do not need to set a separate agenda for a historically informed philosophy of science: we do already have a philosophical agenda with a series of compelling and still open questions (from confirmation to scientific explanation; from underdetermination to laws of nature; from causality to foundational issues in physics and biology, among many others). Those questions have traditionally been regarded as falling in the province of logical analyses dear to positivist philosophy of science. They have been regarded as questions that can be addressed in purely analytical, logical terms without any need to engage with history of science. I think that the future of HPS as an integrated discipline consists in showing that those questions do not belong exclusively to the positivist province and can more profitably be addressed by paying due attention to history of science.

But I urge to go beyond Kuhn also in another sense. I think we are still under the Carnapian and Kuhnian spell in thinking that philosophy of science should not only be detached from epistemology, but should in fact replace it. My vision of HPS is different. I see history and philosophy of science as integral part of the overarching normative function of epistemology. The practice of history and philosophy of science, as I see it, is inherent the meliorative project of epistemology. That is why I believe that the current risk that HPS runs of being increasingly isolated from philosophy is not just to be

Michela Massimi

blamed on post-Fregean epistemology, but is to be blamed also on Kuhn's radical naturalism that has broken the link between philosophy of science and epistemology intended in the Kantian way. My hope is that HPS will eventually rediscover Kantian epistemological naturalism as the family to which it naturally belongs: we do history and philosophy of science because we are ultimately interested in addressing the problem of how we can and indeed *do* have scientific knowledge, and why we do have developed such a surprisingly successful science across centuries. In a truly Kantian spirit, I believe that current history and philosophy of science should rediscover its Kantian epistemological soul (to echo a recent paper by Alan Richardson).

Only in this way, can we hope to bridge the gap between philosophy and the sciences that opened wide after Kant. I am not suggesting that like Kant, we should provide a justification for currently accepted scientific theories. Nor am I, of course, suggesting that we have to dust the Kantian apparatus of *a priori* forms of sensibility and categories of the understanding. I am suggesting instead that any inquiry into the foundations of space-time, or the nature of causation, or living organisms in philosophy of biology, should be addressed and pursued in such a way as to make the question 'how is scientific knowledge possible?' at least meaningful (if not answerable). This particular way of reconciling the practice of history and philosophy of science with the Kantian epistemological tradition has been revived in recent times, thanks to the contributions of Gerd Buchdahl, among the first in the 1960s, and more recently Michael Friedman, Robert DiSalle, Thomas Ryckman, Roberto Torretti, Margaret Morrison, among many others.

Gerd Buchdahl was one of the first in the 1960s to voice the necessity of a return to Kant in the treatment of philosophy of science with his marvellous book *Metaphysics and the Philosophy of Science* (1969a). In more recent years, Michael Friedman has been one of the main advocates of the necessity to rediscover not only Kant's own philosophy of science, but most importantly, Kant's epistemological project and its relevance to twenty-first century history and philosophy of science, despite the widespread prejudice that modern science has proved Kant wrong. In the Kant lectures delivered at Stanford University and published as *The dynamics of reason* (2001), Friedman addresses the very delicate and controversial issue of showing how Kant's epistemology can still be fruitfully applied to twentieth-century science. In particular, he set the ambitious task of reconciling Kuhn's view of scientific revolutions with Kant's idea that there are some *constitutive a priori* elements defining

302

the conditions of possibility of experience as displayed by any scientific theory. By *relativising* those constitutive *a priori* elements to different theoretical frameworks, Friedman argues that it is possible to accept the Kuhnian picture of science as a sequence of scientific revolutions and paradigm shifts, while at the same time maintaining the Kantian insight that what makes our scientific knowledge of nature possible is precisely the presence of some constitutively a priori elements within each theory.

The key idea of Friedman's *dynamic* Kantianism consists then in relativising Kant's notion of *a priori*. Friedman refers back to Hans Reichenbachs *Theory of Relativity and A Priori Knowledge* (1920), suggesting that we should distinguish between two possible meanings of the term 'a priori' in Kant: namely 1) fixed and unrevisable, and 2) constitutive of the object of experience. According to Reichenbach, modern physics has only proved the first meaning wrong, while the second can be maintained and applied to modern scientific theories such as relativity theory. As such, we can keep on using Kant's notion of *a priori* even for twentieth-century physics. The *a priori* becomes relativised: it maintains its constitutive function, while at the same time it is allowed to change with time and to become relative so as to make room for scientific revolutions. This is what Friedman calls the 'relativised *a priori*': it is a significant change compared to Kant, but in a way it allows to reconcile Kant's epistemological project with some modern visions of science.

Accordingly, Friedman claims that we should regard mature theories in science such as Newtonian mechanics or special relativity or general relativity as consisting of two distinct parts: (1) a properly empirical part, containing empirical laws such as Newton's law of gravitation, or Maxwell's equations of electromagnetism in special relativity (SR), or Einstein's equations for the gravitational field in general relativity (GR); and (2) a *constitutively a priori* part containing both the relevant mathematical principles used in formulating the theory (Euclidean geometry; Minkowski space-time in SR; Riemannian theory of manifolds in GR) and certain fundamental physical principles (Newton's laws of motion in Newtonian mechanics, the light principle of SR, the equivalence principle of GR). The claim is that even if the elements of part (2) (i.e. both mathematical and physical principles) can and typically do change in the history of science through scientific revolutions, nonetheless they still retain their Kantian constitutive a priori character in making possible the empirical part (1) of the theory.

Friedman points out that the scientific revolutions of twentieth century have made even more clear the constitutive function of *a*

Michela Massimi

priori principles in Kantian terms, and have even more emphasised the distinction between those constitutively *a priori* elements, on the one hand, and the properly empirical part of the theory, on the other hand. The scientific revolution that Einstein brought about with general relativity, for example, has made even more evident the need of finding constitutive principles as coordinating between an increasingly more abstract mathematical framework, on the one hand, and empirical phenomena, on the other hand. Instead of Euclidean three-dimensional space, we now have a four-dimensional Riemannian manifold of variable curvature. In place of inertial trajectories of Newtonian mechanics, we now have the four-dimensional geodesics of the Riemannian metric. In place of Newton's law of gravitation, we now have Einstein's field equations which relate the four dimensional space-time metric with the stress-energy tensor. Hence, there is an increasing need for principles of coordination mediating between the abstract mathematical structures and concrete physical phenomena. In the case of general relativity for instance, the equivalence principle coordinates the four-dimensional Riemannian geodesic paths with the concrete phenomena of free falling particles in a gravitational field. Friedman claims that the equivalence principle in GR and the light principle in SR have exactly the same coordinating function that Newton's laws of motion have in the context of Newtonian mechanics. And like Newton's laws of motion, they too are fundamental mathematical-physical presuppositions without which the properly empirical laws of the new theory (namely, Maxwell's equations for the electromagnetic field in special relativity; and Einstein's equations for the gravitational field in general relativity) have no empirical meaning or application at all.

Against Quine's holism, Friedman then goes on to claim that it is a big mistake to confuse the mathematical-physical part of a theory with the properly empirical part. While we can subject to experiment the latter, we cannot subject to experiment the former. For instance, despite the fact that Riemannian manifolds can be used to formulate both general relativity and a version of classical mechanics, we cannot say that we can test Riemannian manifolds in either of these two different theories, because Riemannian manifolds provide instead the conditions of possibility of either of the two theories and as such cannot be tested in either of them. Riemmanian manifolds together with some fundamental principles such as the equivalence principle in general relativity cannot be subject to experiment or modified because they play a fundamental constitutive function within relativity theory.

In my book *Pauli's Exclusion Principle* (2005), I have latched onto Friedman's dynamic Kantianism by providing an analysis of a scientific principle, namely Pauli's exclusion principle. Discovered in 1924 by the Austrian Nobel laureate Wolfgang Pauli, the principle excludes the possibility in nature of two electrons, two protons and in general two fermions being in the same dynamic state, and as such it explains a wide array of phenomena such as the stability of matter at the level of galaxies as well as the dynamics of coloured quarks at the subatomic level, among others. I wanted to understand how a scientific principle, such as this one, originates and whether or not it could play a constitutive *a priori* role like the one that Friedman ascribes it to other scientific principles. I then reconstructed in some historical and physical detail the origins of Pauli's principle in the history of early quantum theory and its evolution with the development of quantum statistics in 1926 and later quantum field theory and quantum chromodynamics in the 1960s. The history of Pauli's principle was in my intention functional to addressing the philosophical question of what a scientific principle is, and more in general the epistemological question of how our scientific knowledge of nature – as displayed by QM (and Pauli's principle in it) – is possible.

In my monograph, I drew attention to a different perspective about scientific principles, one that is still *dynamically* Kantian in considering them as relative and revisable, and yet is not distinctively Reichenbachian in identifying them with constitutive *a priori* principles 'coordinating' the mathematical with the proper empirical part of a scientific theory. The history of Pauli's exclusion principle lent itself naturally to this alternative perspective, which latches onto Friedman's by highlighting the complementary, *regulative* Kantian aspect. The upshot of my monograph was to show that an empirical and contingent rule such as Pauli's 1924 exclusion rule attained lawlikeness and necessity because of the *systematizing* role it played in the quantum mechanics framework, whereby systematicity is not just a desirable feature of scientific knowledge. Rather, in a truly Kantian spirit, systematicity as a regulative principle underpins the possibility itself of identifying empirical regularities as lawlike. It is only the systematizing role that an empirical regularity plays within a body of knowledge that transforms it into a fundamental law of nature. This approach has the advantage of doing justice to the revisable and experimentally testable nature of Pauli's principle as much as it grounds its nomological validity on the degree of empirical support it receives within quantum mechanics.

I have lingered on Friedman's dynamic Kantianism and my own more recent work simply because they represent a possible way (albeit not the only one) of developing history and philosophy of science along the epistemological lines that Kant originally traced.

Michela Massimi

Or better, they represent a possible way of practising history and philosophy of science in such a way that the underlying epistemological question 'how is scientific knowledge possible?' remains at least meaningful. But many other ways are possible and need to be explored in future research.

To sum up and conclude, I think we should resist two opposite and similarly dangerous temptations. The first is the temptation to make philosophy of science a branch of science itself, where philosophy risks becoming a footnote at the end of a theorem, be it in decision theory or philosophy of physics. Let us leave the sciences to the scientists and content ourselves as philosophers with the perennial problem of understanding how we could reach scientific knowledge in the first place. The second is the opposite temptation of leaving those epistemological questions to the epistemologists, as if an answer to the problem of knowledge should necessarily pertain to the exclusive domain of epistemology as is practised nowadays in analytic philosophy. If philosophy of science has lost its Kantian epistemological soul, similarly current epistemology seems to have in part lost its scientific soul in trying to pursue those important questions beside and beyond any scientific preoccupation.

Kant opened the path by producing an epistemology that was informed by the scientific preoccupations of his time. The burden now is on us to explore the path further and to venture uncharted territories, even if the path may well be rocky and ultimately open-ended. Or better, it is precisely because the path is probably open-ended that the inquiry into the relationship between philosophy and the sciences can and must go on, after Kant, and despite all the limits of Kant's project.

Acknowledgements

I am very grateful to Anthony O'Hear, Hasok Chang, and the audience of the Royal Institute of Philosophy Annual Series for stimulating comments on a shorter version of this paper. In more recent times, I have much benefited from research collaboration with Silvia De Bianchi on Kant's early writings on natural science.

Bibliography

Allison, H. E. (1994) 'Causality and Causal Laws in Kant: a Critique of Michael Friedman' in Paolo Parrini (ed.) *Kant and Contemporary Epistemology* (Dordrecht: Kluwer Academic Publishers), 291–307.

Beiser, F. C. (1992) 'Kant's Intellectual Development: 1746–1781' in P. Guyer (ed.) *The Cambridge Companion to Kant* (Cambridge: Cambridge University Press), 26–61.

Buchdahl, G. (1969a) *Metaphysics and the Philosophy of Science* (Cambridge, Mass.: MIT Press).

———— (1969b) 'The Kantian "Dynamic of Reason", with special reference to the place of causality in Kant's system' in L. W. Beck (ed.) *Kant Studies Today* (La Salle, Ill.: Open Court), 341–74.

———— (1974) 'The Conception of Lawlikeness in Kant's Philosophy of Science' in L. W. Beck (ed.) *Kant's theory of knowledge* (Dordrecht: Reidel), 128–50.

Cahan D. (ed.) (1993) *Hermann von Helmholtz and the Foundations of Nineteenth-Century Science* (University of California Press).

Caneva, K. L. (1993) *Robert Mayer and the Conservation of Energy* (Princeton University Press).

———— (1997) 'Physics and *Naturphilosophie*: a Reconnaissance' *History of Science* **35**, 35–106.

Carnap, R. (1922) *Der Raum. Ein Beitrag zur Wissenschaftslehre* (Berlin: Reuther and Reichard).

———— (1924) 'Dreidimensionalität des Raumes und Kausalität', *Annalen der Philosophie und philosophischen Kritik* **4**, 105–130.

———— (1928) *Der logische Aufbau der Welt* (Berlin: Weltkreis). English translation (1967) by R. George, *The Logical Structure of the World* (Los Angeles: University of California Press).

Cassirer, E. (1906) *Das Erkenntnisproblem in der Philosophie und Wissenschaft der neueren Zeit.* (Berlin: Bruno Cassirer).

———— (1907) *Das Erkenntnisproblem in der Philosophie und Wissenschaft der neueren Zeit. Zweiter Band* (Berlin: Bruno Cassirer).

———— (1920) *Das Erkenntnisproblem in der Philosophie und Wissenschaft der neueren Zeit. Dritter Band: die nachkantische Systeme* (Berlin: Bruno Cassirer).

———— (1957) *Das Erkenntnisproblem in der Philosophie und Wissenschaft der neueren Zeit. Vierter Band: von Hegels Tod bis zur Gegenwart* (Stuttgart: Kohlhammer).

———— (1910) *Substanzbegriff und Funktionsbegriff. Untersuchungen zu den Grundfragen der Erkenntniskritik* (Berlin: Bruno Cassirer). Engl. transl. (1953) *Substance and Function and Einstein's Theory of Relativity*, by W. C. Swabey (New York: Dover Publications).

———— (1932) *Die Philosophie der Aufklärung* (Tübingen: J. C. B. Mohr). English translation, 5th edn *The Philosophy of the*

Enlightenment, by F. Koelln and J. Pettegrove (Boston: Beacon Press).

————— (1936) *Determinismus und Indeterminismus in der modernen Physik* (Göteborg: Högskolas Arsskrift 42). Engl. translation (1956) *Determinism and Indeterminism in Modern Physics*, by O. T. Benfey (New Haven: Yale University Press).

Caygill, H. (1995) *A Kant Dictionary* (Oxford: Blackwell).

Cohen, H. (1883) *Das Princip der Infinitesimal-Method und seine Geschichte* (Berlin: Dümmler).

Creath R. (1990) (ed.) *Dear Carnap, Dear Van. The Quine–Carnap correspondence and related work* (Berkeley: University of California Press).

DiSalle, R. (2006a) *Understanding Space-Time. The Philosophical Development of Physics from Newton to Einstein* (Cambridge: Cambridge University Press).

————— (2006b) 'Kant, Helmholtz, and the Meaning of Empiricism' in M. Friedman and A. Nordmann (eds.) *The Kantian Legacy in Nineteenth-Century Sciences* (Harvard: MIT Press), 123–140.

Förster, E. (2000) *Kant's Final Synthesis. An Essay on the Opus postumum* (Cambridge, Mass.: Harvard University Press).

Friedman, M. (1992a) *Kant and the Exact Sciences* (Cambridge, Mass.: Harvard University Press).

————— (1992b) 'Causal Laws and the Foundations of Natural Science', in Paul Guyer (ed.) *The Cambridge Companion to Kant* (Cambridge: Cambridge University Press), 161–99.

————— (1999) *Reconsidering Logical Positivism* (Cambridge: Cambridge University Press).

————— (2000) *A Parting of the Ways. Carnap, Cassirer, and Heidegger* (Chicago: Open Court).

————— (2001) *The Dynamics of Reason. Stanford Kant Lectures* (Stanford: CSLI Publications).

————— (2006) 'Kant – *Naturphilosophie* – electromagnetism' in Friedman, M. and Nordmann, A. (eds.) *The Kantian Legacy in Nineteenth-Century Science* (Cambridge, Mass.: MIT Press), 51–80.

Friedman, M. and Nordmann, A. (eds.) (2006) *The Kantian Legacy in Nineteenth-Century Science* (Cambridge, Mass.: MIT Press).

Gower, B. (1973) 'Speculation in Physics: The History and Practice of *Naturphilosophie*' *Studies in History and Philosophy of Science* **3**, 301–356.

Hatfield, G. (1990) *The Natural and the Normative: Theories of Spatial Perception from Kant to Helmholtz*, (Cambridge, Mass.: MIT Press).

Kant, I. (1747) *Gedanken von der wahren Schätzung der lebendigen Kräfte und Beurtheilung der Beweise, deren sich Herr von Leibniz und andere Mechaniker in dieser Streitsache bedient haben, nebst einigen vorhergehenden Betrachtungen, welche die Kraft der Körper überhaupt betreffen* (AK 1:1-181); English translation (in press) *Thoughts on the true estimation of living forces*, in E. Watkins (ed.) *Natural Science, The Cambridge edition of the works of Immanuel Kant* (Cambridge: Cambridge University Press).

———— (1755a) *Allgemeine Naturgeschichte und Theorie des Himmels oder Versuch von der Verfassung und dem mechanischen Ursprunge des ganzen Weltgebäudes, nach Newtonischen Grundsätzen abgehandelt* (AK 1:215-368). Engl. translation (1968) *Universal Natural History and Theory of the Heavens*, in W. Ley (ed.) *Kant's Cosmogony* (New York: Greenwood Publishing).

———— (1755b) *Meditationum quarundam de igne succincta delineatio* (AK 1:369-84). Engl. translation *Succinct exposition of some meditations on fire*, in L. W. Beck et al. (1986) *Kant's Latin Writings* (New York: Peter Lang).

———— (1756) *Metaphysicae cum geometria iunctae usus in philosophia naturali, cuius specimen I. continet monadologiam physicam* (AK 1:473-87). Engl. translation *Physical Monadolody*, in D. Walford and R. Meerbote (eds.) (1992) *Theoretical Philosophy 1755–1770. The Cambridge edition of the works of Immanuel Kant* (Cambridge: Cambridge University Press).

———— (1781, 1787) *Critik der reinen Vernunft* (Riga: Johann Hartknoch). Engl. translation (1997) by P. Guyer and A. W. Wood *Critique of pure reason, The Cambridge edition of the works of Immanuel Kant* (Cambridge: Cambridge University Press).

———— (1786) *Metaphysische Anfangsgründe der Naturwissenschaft* (Riga: Johann Hartknoch). Engl. translation (2004) by M. Friedman, *Metaphysical Foundations of Natural Science* (Cambridge: Cambridge University Press).

———— (1790) *Kritik der Urteilskraft* (Berlin: Lagarde). Engl. translation (2000) by P. Guyer and E. Matthews, *Critique of the Power of Judgement, The Cambridge edition of the works of Immanuel Kant* (Cambridge: Cambridge University Press).

———— (1796–1803) *Opus postumum*, Engl. translation (1995) by Eckart Förster and Michael Rosen, *The Cambridge edition of the works of Immanuel Kant* (Cambridge: Cambridge University Press).

Keill, J. (1726) *An Introduction to Natural Philosophy*, 2nd edn (London: J. Senex et al.).

Kitcher, P. (1992) 'The Naturalist's Return' *Philosophical Review* **101**, 53–114.

Kuehn, M. (2001) 'Kant and his Teachers in the Exact Sciences' in Watkins E. (ed.) *Kant and the Sciences* (New York: Oxford University Press), 11–30.

Kuhn, T. S. (1962) *The Structure of Scientific Revolutions*, International encyclopaedia of unified science: Foundations of the unity of science, vol. 2, no. 2 (Chicago: University of Chicago Press).

Kuhn, T. S. (1977) *The Essential Tension* (Chicago: University of Chicago Press).

Laudan, L. (1990) 'Normative naturalism', *Philosophy of Science* **57**, 44–59.

Massimi, M. (2005) *Pauli's Exclusion Principle. The Origin and Validation of a Scientific Principle* (Cambridge: Cambridge University Press).

————— (2008a) 'The Relevance of Kant's Philosophy for the Physical Sciences of Nineteenth Century', *Metascience* **17**, 79–83. Review of M. Friedman and A. Nordmann (eds.) *The Kantian legacy in Nineteenth Century Science* (MIT Press).

————— (2008b) 'Why There are no Ready-Made Phenomena: What Philosophers of Science Should Learn from Kant' in Massimi, M. (ed.) (in press), *Kant and Philosophy of Science Today*, (Cambridge: Cambridge University Press), Royal Institute of Philosophy Supplement 63.

Pulte, H. (2006) 'Kant, Fries and the Expanding Universe of Science' in M. Friedman and A. Nordmann (eds.) (2006) *The Kantian Legacy in Nineteenth-Century Sciences* (Harvard: MIT Press), 101–122.

Quine, W.V.O. (1951) 'Two Dogmas of Empiricism' *Philosophical Review* **60**, 20–43. Reprinted in (1963) *From a Logical Point of View* (New York: Harper), 20–46.

————— (1963) 'Carnap and Logical Truth' in Schilpp P. A. (ed.) (1963) *The Philosophy of Rudolf Carnap*, (La Salle: Open Court), 385–406.

————— (1969) 'Epistemology Naturalised' in *Ontological Relativity and Other Essays* (New York: Columbia University Press), 69–90.

Reichenbach, H. (1920) *Relativitätstheorie und Erkenntnis Apriori* (Berlin: Springer). Engl. translation (1965) *The Theory of Relativity and A Priori Knowledge* (Los Angeles: University of California Press).

Richardson, A. (1998) *Carnap's Construction of the World: the Aufbau and the Emergence of Logical Empiricism* (Cambridge: Cambridge University Press).

——— (2006) "'The Fact of Science" and Critique of Knowledge: Exact Science as Problem and Resource in Marburg Neo-Kantianism' in M. Friedman and A. Nordmann (eds.) *The Kantian Legacy in Nineteenth-Century Sciences* (Harvard: MIT Press), 211–226.

Schelling, F. (1797) *Ideen zu einer Philosophie der Natur*, 1st ed. Vol. 1 of *Schellings Werke* (Munich: C. H. Beck, 1927).

——— (1799) *Erster Entwurf eines Systems der Naturphilosophie*, in 1st ed. Vol. 2 of *Schellings Werke* (Munich: C. H. Beck, 1927).

——— (1800) *System des transcendentalen Idealismus*, in 1st ed. Vol. 2 of *Schellings Werke* (Munich: C. H. Beck, 1927).

Shanahan, T. (1989) 'Kant, *Naturphilosophie*, and Oersted's Discovery of Electromagnetism: A Reassessment', *Studies in History and Philosophy of Science* **20**, 287–305.

Schönfeld, M. (2006) 'Kant's Early Dynamics' in Graham Bird (ed.) *A Companion to Kant* (Blackwell), 33–46.

Watkins, E. (2005) *Kant and the Metaphysics of Causality* (Cambridge: Cambridge University Press).

Williams, L. P. (1965) *Michael Faraday: a Biography*, Basic Books).

——— (1973) 'Kant, *Naturphilosophie*, and Scientific Method' in R. Giere and R. Westfall (eds.) *Foundations of Scientific Method in the Nineteenth Century* (Indiana University Press), 3–22.

The Inward Turn

CHARLES TRAVIS

> Philosophers constantly see the method of science before their
> eyes, and are irresistibly tempted to ask and answer questions
> in the way science does. This tendency is the real source of meta-
> physics, and leads the philosopher into complete darkness. (*The
> Blue Book*, 1958: 18)

Seeing is, or affords, a certain sort of awareness – visual – of one's surroundings. The obvious strategy for saying *what* one sees, or what
would *count* as seeing something would be to ask what sort of sensitivity to one's *surroundings* – e.g. the *pig* before me – would so qualify.
Alas, for more than three centuries – *at least* from Descartes to VE
day – it was not so. Philosophers were moved by arguments, rarely
stated which concluded that one could not, or never did, see what
was before his eyes. So much for the obvious strategy. It occurred to
almost no one to object that this *could* not be right. Frege did, but
no one noticed. Austin, finally, did away with that conception of
good faith in philosophy which had allowed such a thing to pass,
and then with those arguments themselves. Until then, philosophy
was deformed. Robbed of the obvious approach, a *Drang* set in to
gaze inward, hoping to find what it *really* is to see in what *enabled* sensitivity to pigs, or in its byproducts. Gazing inward *can* be science, but
often merely poses as it. It can be difficult to disentangle actual science
(or at least empirical fact) from mere preconception pretending to its
rigour. Most nowadays *feel* rid of the grip of those barriers to the
obvious approach. But, as we shall see, many so feel wrongly. The
Drang still misshapes their thought. I aim here to identify the *Drang*
at work; thereby, I hope, to rid us of it.

1. Seeing

One sees, one would have thought, such things as mangoes, sloths,
the setting sun, the sun setting, the blackened condition of the

I am thankful to Mark Kalderon, and to Mike Martin, for their patient
and painstaking efforts to make me see things better. The usual disclaimers
apply.

doi:10.1017/S1358246109990154   © The Royal Institute of Philosophy and the contributors 2009
Royal Institute of Philosophy Supplement **65** 2009

toast. An account which said otherwise would, one would have thought, thereby be shown mistaken. As noted, for more than three centuries the nearly universal, and unquestioned, view was: 'Not so.' What one *really* saw, it was supposed without a blush, were, in Frege's terms (pointing to the solecism here) *contents of one's consciousness*: objects of awareness such that, first, there is someone one would need to be to be aware of them, and, second, their career as something *to* be aware of was coeval with that person's awareness of them. One saw things in one's surroundings, if at all, only insofar as seeing these other things might pass for seeing that.

H. A. Prichard – an otherwise admirable philosopher – exemplifies the frame of mind. He begins a pre-war essay, 'Perception', by admitting that in the 'everyday attitude of mind' of philosophers and others, one counts '"chairs and tables, boats going downstream", and so forth' as the sorts of things one sees and touches[1] then commenting,

> It need hardly be said that this view, much as we should all like to be able to vindicate it, will not stand examination.[2]

It will not stand examination because of a principle which Prichard expresses in the following ways:**

> If we really see a body ... as ... from a certain point in space ... it must present the appearance to us which any body of the kind in question seen as from this point must present

> A body, if it be really seen and seen along with other bodies, can only present to us just that appearance which its relations to the other bodies really requires.

> This raises the question ... how if we see a body it can ... look other than what it is, and if we press this question home to ourselves we can only answer, as before, that it cannot.[3]

Given the principle, the idea that we see such things as boats, or walls, is refuted by such ordinary facts as that the moon (roughly spherical) sometimes looks flat, or that if you look at a wall in a mirror left and right reverse.

Many of us have, at one time or another, failed to see a wall (in time). But, one might think, if a principle entails that one can *never* see a wall, then, in point of good faith, it is, *ceteris paribus*,

[1]   Prichand (1950), 52.
[2]   Ibid. 53.
[3]   Ibid. 53-4.

false. Prichard offers a reason for thinking otherwise. He reminds us that we are 'concerned simply with the nature of what we see in the proper 'mental' sense of see' and not 'with what we see in the physical sense of what affects our eyes.'[4] So our idea that we see such things as sloths and walls comes from our thinking of some 'physical sense' of 'see', whereas Prichard, and any philosopher of perception, means to speak of another. It is not clear what either of these senses is; nor even that there *are* different senses of 'see'.

All the same, Prichard's talk of physical and mental seeing is suggestive. No one, I think, thinks there is *any* sense of 'see' in which merely to have something 'affect your eyes' – say, form retinal images – is to see it. Why not? A natural, though not inevitable, idea is: before one saw anything, more stuff would have to happen. (Not inevitable: to have images on one's retinas would not be to see something whether or not more stuff needed to happen.) A further natural idea might then be: at a certain point the relevant stuff, or enough of it, *has* happened. At that point, the perceiver goes into a certain 'internal' state, the upshot of the stuff, where this is one of a specified range of states into which a particular device, 'that which enables vision', might go. In such a state, the idea is, one enjoys visual awareness (or experience). One sees only in enjoying visual awareness. The state decides *what* visually awareness one thus enjoys; thus, at least, what it is in which one might be seeing something.

The nature of the state is to be fixed (causally) by that of which it is an upshot. Any retinal state might unleash any of various sequences of stuff happening. Retinal states thus underdetermine what such internal state one arrives in. So, accordingly, for whatever one has in view; whatever formed images on one's retinas. Viewing *that* might place one in any of various internal states, each differing from the others in what one is thereby visually aware of. Conversely, for any such terminal internal state one, what was actually in view before one might be any of many things – *perhaps* even nothing.

A crucial idea here is that such an internal state furnishes all the visual awareness one enjoys. It thereby furnishes *an* answer to the question just what one is then visually aware *of*. So, for one to be in it is for there to be a determinate way one experiences things being (or seeming) visually. For there to be a *determinate way*, as this is usually understood, is for such-and-such to be the way; thus for one to experience things being, or seeming, visually (arranged) thus

---

[4]   Ibid. 53.

and so. *Perhaps* being visually aware of what it thus decides you are, while, in fact, viewing given things – say, a pig – is what it *is* to see (so be visually aware of) something in one's surroundings – say, the pig. If so, then *that* much as to what one is visually aware of, the internal state would *not* determine. Modulo that possibility, the internal state you are in at the time answers the question what you are then visually aware of.

I will call the whole of the above the *SH model* ('SH' for 'stuff happens'.) The mere idea that we are enabled to see by some identifiable states, the products of happenings unleashed by retinal images, *may* be science, or something it presupposes. The rest is not. It is a *picture* of what awareness must be. I will next begin to trace the current career of the SH model. I hope to show a few reasons why that picture will not do.

2. Perceptual Experience

Gareth Evans is concerned with visual experience, a wider notion than seeing; still more widely, with perceptual experience in general. He writes, 'In general we may regard a perceptual experience as an informational state of the subject . . .'[5] – as he insists repeatedly, an *internal* state. Such is an odd start. An experience, where one can speak of one, is, one would have thought, an *episode*, in which one experiences something or other there *is* to experience – in the case of *perceptual* experience, typically, though perhaps not always, something impinging from without – the warm summer breezes, perhaps, the patterns of sunlight on the wall. To regard all that as an *internal* state is, for one thing, to leave *what* is experienced out of the picture altogether. *If* experience is to be an internal state, the SH model provides ones for this to be. Could Evans' talk of experiences as states of a subject be symptomatic (or more) of allegiance to that model?

The informational states in question are not themselves objects of their owner's perceptual awareness. In experiencing, say, the barnyard, I am (visually) aware of that pig in the sty; not of any *internal* state of mine. But, Evans tells us, I *can* be aware of features of such a state, specifically of the information it contains. For experiencing the barnyard *is* experiencing being in the state: being in it, I experience. One can, Evans tells us, exploit this way of experiencing the

---

[5] Evans (1982), 226.

state 'by re-using precisely those skills of conceptualisation that he uses to make judgements about the world.'[6]

> He goes through exactly the same procedure as he would go through if he were trying to make a judgement about how it is at this place now, but excluding any knowledge he has of an extraneous kind. (That is, he seeks to determine what he would judge if he did not have such extraneous information.) The result will necessarily be closely correlated with the content of the informational state which he is in at that time. Now he may prefix this result with the operator 'It seems to me as though . . .'

So, e.g. it seems to me as though that pig is spotted; *ceteris paribus* the relevant state contains the information that that pig is spotted. I thus *can* be aware of the state containing information it does. *Just* so, for Evans, can perception perform its most central task in a *thinker's* life: allowing how things are to bear, according to their bearing, on how to *think* they are; thereby on how to act.

A state which *thus* contains information is also liable to contain *mis*-information. It may seem to me as though that pig is spotted when it is not. (Just the shadows of the branches of that spreading chestnut.) One *could* appropriate 'information' to include that. It will avoid confusion not to. Information, here, will be of what is *so*.

But there are two uses of 'seems'. On one it seems as though Sid did it if, based on how we see things are, such is most probable. On the other, that pig, standing under those branches, in the filtered sunlight, looks as though it were spotted. It looks (just, or rather) like a spotted pig. It may so look even if we *know* it is just the light and shadow. It would be a further claim that it does not just *seem* that way, but seems to *be* so.

These two readings of 'seem' point to two different ways for something to contain information. The scene before me may, in the first way, contain the information that there is a *bísaro* before me: it makes this recognisable (to one who knows his *bísaros*). It may contain the information that *this* pig has swine flu: a decent veterinarian could tell that at sight. That road sign contains information in the second way. It contains the information that Santiago is 48 km. hence: it says so. The information contained in this second way consists of just those things which what contains it represents, truly, as *so*.

---

[6] Ibid. 227.

Charles Travis

The scene before me, in being as it is, instances literally countless ways there are for a scene, and thus countless ways for *things*, to be. It is *recognisably* countless such ways. So any scene contains indefinitely much information in the first way. Which is not a way of containing *mis*information: information contained in this way is available through the exercise of *recognition* capacities; a capacity being, *per se*, one to get things *right*. Thus it is that scenes – signposts and bill-boards aside – are not liable to contain misinformation. If there is something in perceptual experience that *is* so liable, it will have to be something other than the scene in view, or its inhabitants, again signposts and the like aside. There will have to be something about *it*, not present in a scene, which allows it to do so.

By contrast, the second way of containing information is by *representing* something as so. The signpost contains just that information (misinformation) which it represents truly (falsely) to be so. That something was represented as so never means as such that it *is* so. There is always that much room for representing falsely. So this second way of containing information is a way of containing misinformation.

Frege shows why, if perception is going to make the world bear, for us, on what to think, then it had better do so in affording us awareness of what contains information in the first of these two ways. It had better afford opportunity for exercising, on what we are thus aware of, capacities for *thus* extracting information. For, to begin with,

> The fundamental logical relation is that of an object falling under a concept: all relations between concepts reduce to this.[7]

In Frege's working of the point, concepts are satisfied, or not, by objects – items not themselves eligible for being satisfied, or not, by anything. A given concept 'reaches to' a range of objects which are those things which satisfy it (and identifies a range which are those things which do not). Relations purely between some concepts and others cannot *on their own* tell us to what range of cases a given concept reaches (though, given to which ranges certain concepts reach, relations internal to the domain of concepts might tell us to what some further one reaches). To grasp a concept is to grasp both how it relates to other concepts, and – a different matter – how it relates to what are *not* concepts – in Frege's working of the point, to objects: what satisfy, but are not, themselves, satisfied. One must be able to tell, of *such* things, when they would be such as to satisfy the concept. Such capacities are just the sort one would exercise in

---

[7] Frege (1892–1895), 25.

extracting information contained in something in the first way. Without such capacities, one would have no concepts, so would not be a thinker at all. There would be nothing on which the world *could* bear for you. So the possession and exercise of such capacities *must* be fundamental in any story of how perception makes this bear on what to think.

The point is worth reworking. Frege also says,

> A thought always contains something reaching out beyond the particular case, by which this is presented to consciousness as falling under something general.[8]

The thought is of things being a certain way. The generality of a thought, in the present sense, consists in the fact that there are various ways things being as they are might instance things being that way. If the thought is that that pig is a *bísaro*, things might be that way while the pig is in a sty, or in open range, while it eats acorns or yams, in a good or mediocre vintage year, and so on. The thought reaches to a range of cases in which things being as they were would be their being that way. Doing so is intrinsic to being a thought at all. What it reaches to is the particular case, which is: things being as they are. Such a thing *has* no reach to anything.

The generality of a thought is shared by a way for things to be, a way for *something* to be, and by whatever would make a thought *about* a way for something to be (call that a concept). It is lacked by what such (first-order) things reach to. I will call what has it (*the*) *conceptual*, and what lacks it (*the*) *nonconceptual*. The point is now: one is not engaging in thought at all; one is certainly not in a position in which there is *any* way perception could make the world bear for him on what to think, unless he has, and exercises, capacities to see how the conceptual reaches to the nonconceptual: when things being as they are would be things being thus and so; something's being as it is it being thus and so. Without such capacities for extracting information in the first way, one would not be a thinker at all.

This idea appears in Frege's view of *seeing that*. Here are two expressions of it:

> But do I not see that this flower has five petals? We can say this, but if we do, the word 'see' is not being used in the sense of having a mere visual experience: what we mean by it is bound up with thinking and judging.[9]

---

[8] Frege (1882), *Kernsatz* 4.
[9] Frege (1897), 138.

But don't we see that the sun has set? And don't we thereby see that this is true? That the sun has set is no object which emits rays which arrive in my eyes, is no visible thing like the sun itself. That the sun has set is recognised as true on the basis of sensory input.[10]

Sight affords visual awareness of a scene, and of things, happenings, and conditions obtaining in it: that sloth, the waving of the branches, the blackness of the toast. It thus affords opportunity for exercising certain sorts of capacities: I can recognise, of the scene being visibly as it is, that that is that sloth sleeping, or that toast being burnt. Such is a a fundamentally important way for perceptual experience to make the world bear, for me, on what to think.

I return to Evans. In what way does he think one of his internal states contains (retrievable) information? Is it in the first way, so that it would be the pig's *looking* spotted (to me) which is necessarily closely connected with the state containing the information that it is spotted, or in the second, so that it is my *thinking* (in the right way) that the pig is spotted which is thus connected with the state containing the information that it is? The first idea excludes misinformation. Which would exclude representing as so. Evans is attached to the idea of misinformation (what an internal state would be intrinsically liable to provide); but *also* to the idea that perception is occasion for exercising capacities of *conceptualisation*; thus ones belonging to the first idea. So he is ambivalent. On the one hand, he insists,

> The informational states which a subject acquires through perception are *non-conceptual*, or *non-conceptualized.* Judgements *based upon* such states necessarily involve conceptualization: in moving from a perceptual experience to a judgement about the world (usually expressible in some verbal form), one will be exercising basic conceptual skills.[11]

Which looks, so far, like the first idea. But on the other, he insists that a perceptual state

> has a certain *content* – the world is represented as a certain way – and hence it permits of a non-derivative classification as *true* or *false.*[12]

Perceptual states are truth-evaluable. Only containing information in the second way could make something so evaluable. Only the second

10   Frege (1918), 61.
11   Evans (1982), 227.
12   Ibid. 226.

way makes room for misinformation – something *representation* is *intrinsically* liable to provide. In fact, Evans seems to want the best (for him) of both worlds: representation, but representation with nonconceptual content. Representation necessarily reaches beyond the particular case which it represents as a certain way. So it belongs to the conceptual. If we draw a conceptual-nonconceptual distinction as above, 'nonconceptual representational content' is senseless. *Perhaps* Evans understands these notions in some other way. I do not so. I think he simply fails to choose where one must. I will return to that presently. First, how does Evans' story reflect the *Drang* in general, and the SH model in particular?

3. The Inner

Visual experiences, for Evans, *are* certain inner states. These float free of what lies within the subject's view. For all that in that scene there is a pig beneath the oak, that inner state which is the subject's experience of this may or may not contain the information that this is so. For all that it contains the (*mis*)information that there is a pig beneath the oak, there may or may not be one. If the visual experience is one of *seeing* a scene, then that inner state it is is, presumably, the upshot of interactions with the environment; presumably involving, somehow, retinas. So Evans' account just *is* the SH model. The first thing to note is that it is a *necessary* condition for *visual* experience to represent things as so; to be truth-evaluable. For that, experiencing visually must contain something floating free of the scene in view, as per above. There is nothing in visual experience which could do that except, if it exists, something the *subject* puts there; something *inner*, independent, in principle, of what surrounds him.

Scenes do not represent things as so. Nor do their constituents. There is no way things are according to that pig before the oak (unless it talks). There is no way things are according to its being beneath the oak, or according to the spreading of those branches. None of these things is truth-evaluable. A pig is not. *Nothing's* being thus and so is. Correlatively, neither the scene nor the pig nor the spreading contains *mis*information. Perceptual experience would need some other ingredient for *it* to represent anything as *so*. The spreading of those branches no doubt *means* various things. Perhaps it tells us something about the average hours of sunlight per year in that place. But there is no such thing as it telling us this *falsely*. Which highlights the point that such meaning (the factive sort) is not *representing* anything as so.[13]

There are more notions of representing than are found in representing as so. The state of Sid's liver represents years of hard drinking; the state of those rocks aeons of water erosion. Sid's liver thus contains the information that he indulged in years of hard drinking, the rocks the information that this was once a riverbed. Which makes neither Sid's liver, nor its state, truth-evaluable. These do not represent years of hard drinking if there were none. The spreading branches may represent something – say, careful pruning – in this sense. But something else is needed before anything in an experience of seeing them could represent anything as so: *commitment*. *Something* in the experience must make itself hostage to whether something is some given way. (Hostage, that is, for *correctness*. Which *might* mean harbouring *ambitions* – as judging is a posture one aims to hold only in a particular sort of world.) The spreading of the branches is not thus *hostage* to their being pruned; if they were not, it simply does not mean they were.

Representationism – the view that experience represents as so – thus requires the SH model. Does the model otherwise invite it? Adepts of it *have* tended to see visual experience as representing in *some* sense. But not always as representing things to be *so*. Descartes is a good representative of the alternative. For him, all '*cogitationes*' (ideas) represent. But he also holds,

> Ideas, considered in themselves, and not referred to something else, cannot strictly speaking be false.[14]

> The mind finds within itself ideas of many things; and so long as it merely contemplates these, and neither asserts nor denies the existence of something like them outside itself, it cannot be in error.[15]

A room in the Louvre is filled with sycophantic paintings, by Rubens, of Cathérine de Medicis, e.g. astride a horse, in battle armour, leading grateful troops. That painting represents her so doing. Basing one's judgement on the painting, you *could* take it *that* Cathérine once, on horseback, led troops. That would be a mistake, which the painting, rightly understood, in no way encourages. The painting does not represent it as *so* that Cathérine ever did such a thing. The mistake would be all yours.

---

13 See my 2004.
14 Descartes (1641), 78 (3rd Meditation).
15 Descartes (1644), 184 (*Principles* XIII).

So it is, for Descartes, with perceptual experience in general. My visual experience, as I view the scene, represents a pig in the (or a) sty. I may take it that there is a pig in the sty. But in this I am on my own. No such thing is so according to the experience. It does not represent it as *so* that any pig is in any sty. *Nothing*, on Descartes' view, is so according to an experience as such. (*Thus* far Descartes and Austin are one.[16]

An Evansian inner state, where one *saw* a pig in the sty, would represent a pig in the sty in the way that the state of Sid's liver represents hard drinking. It could not represent in that Rubensesque way above. For that it would need something which functioned as a canvas does: (some of) *its* visual features, themselves objects of the subject's visual awareness, would carry representational import, thanks to something paralleling an *intention* that they should be taken in a certain way. Evans explicitly rejects any such thing. Might these states still represent things as *so*? What function, within the SH model, would such representing serve?

Perception's *essential* task in the life of a thinker is to allow the world – specifically his surroundings – to bear for him on what he is to think (and do) according as it bears on what is *so*. If *cogitationes* were, as it were, a mere play of shape and colour, they would play no such role; would make for no such bearing. For that, they must, for a start, carry information as to how those surroundings are. There are two ways for an object of (perceptual) awareness to carry information. It (our its presence) may *mean*, factively, or indicate something; or it may represent things as some way (on some notion of representing as). Suppose that the play of shape and colour *meant* things (as well it might if there is such a play at all). A particular visual arrangement in the play might mean, say, that there is a pig before me. Then, if I appreciate its meaning, I can *conclude* from what I am visually aware of that there is a pig before me.

Frege's point about the conceptual-nonconceptual distinction is *one* reason why factive meaning, so far as it goes, cannot allow perception to do its job. Some display of shape and colour may *mean* there is a pig before me (my porcine warning system), just as some grunting sound, or Aunt Ida's shrieks, might. If I appreciate its meaning, any of these, if taken in, may be reason for me to think there is a pig before me. But that of the *world* which in fact bears on whether there is a pig before me is, in first instance, things before me being as they are. It is *that* which *is*, or is not, a pig being before me. Perception's job is not done unless it makes available to me (at least sometimes) *that* for me then to evaluate, or recognise, as a pig being before me or not.

---

[16]   See Austin (1962), 11.

Charles Travis

Perception must afford me opportunities to exercise my abilities to link the nonconceptual to the conceptual as it in fact links, by that fundamental relation of falling under, or instance, or just being, as per above. If I am cut off from such possibilities, then, as per above, I cannot so much as get the right bits of the conceptual in mind – a pig being before me, say. Then factive meaning, for all that it may still be there in the world, is no use to me when it comes to what I am to think. To appreciate it, I would need to recognise the bearing of something I *do* experience on ... *what*? Anyway, on something of which, so far, nothing furnishes me awareness.

The only alternative, then, is to take *cogitationes* to provide information by, or in, representing things. Descartes wisely resists supposing *cogitationes* to represent things *to be so*. So they represent, roughly, Rubensesquely. But this clearly makes no progress. I will put this by harping on a point. A *cogitatione* is the content of someone's consciousness, in Frege's sense. The scene before me, and its contents – that pig staring at me from the sty – are things for *one* to experience, to witness, to observe, where, crucially, there is no one one must be to be the one. It is precisely *not* a content of consciousness. As Frege insists,[17] it would be a solecism to speak of *seeing* a *cogitatione*, precisely not solecistic to speak of seeing the pig, or the scene. So my *cogitationes* of the moment being as they are is one thing; the scene before me being as it is another. Accordingly, my being *aware* of my *cogitationes* being as they are is one thing; my being aware of the scene being as it is another. Just maybe, I could be (visually) aware of a scene being as it is *in* being (visually) aware of my *cogitationes* being as they are (though I doubt it). But awareness of my *cogitationes* being as they are is *not* awareness of the scene being as it is. My *cogitationes* being as they are *may* be (though Frege, I think, showed not) their being thus and so – e.g. their representing a scene with a pig front and centre. My awareness of their being as they are may make this recognisable to me (if the notion recognition (*Erkennung*) fits here). But *this* is not what representation needs to deliver here. What is needed is that my visual awareness of the *scene* being as it is can make it recognisable to me that *that* is a pig being before me. No such thing is in the cards. Representation is hopeless for its appointed role here.

Representing makes no progress over factive meaning here. Neither offers awareness of what would be, so could be recognised, as things (before us) being thus and so. Such should have been obvious from the moment *cogitationes* came on the scene. Whatever *they* do,

[17] Frege (1918), 67.

324

awareness of them doing it could not be awareness of a scene doing its thing. But Evans will have no truck with *cogitationes*. For *them* to represent would be for their visual features to have representational significance. To take in their representing what they do would be to take in those visual features and appreciate their representational significance. (Anyway, as Frege stressed, *such* things would need (very roughly) an intention attaching to them for *them* to represent. Where would *that* come from?[18]) Whereas Evans explicitly denies that we are aware how experience represents by being aware of some *vehicle* whose visible features bear representational significance. Those internal states which represent, for him, are not objects of perceptual awareness. Which leaves him with nothing that could represent Rubensesquely. Which is fine with him, since, anyway, in his view, doing the job right — making the world bear as perception must — requires representing things *as so*.

So is the representing Evans posits any more fit for its task than Descartes'? Descartes is driven to posit representing because, given what he thinks perceiving is, it is the only hope for perception to give the *world* bearing on what we are to think. Once *cogitationes* are in the picture, they must *somehow* carry information about the world; nothing *else* could make them do so. Evans' hand is similarly forced. Not that he posits sensory *vehicles* of representing. But he holds a version of the SH model. On it, an *internal* state decides what I am visually aware of in experiencing visually: something I might be aware of no matter what the scene before my eyes (visibly) provided. Awareness of *that* must, somehow, make the *scene's* being as it is bear on what I am to think — allow me so much as to think, and then to judge, of the *scene's* being as it (visibly) is that *that* is a scene being thus and so. What else but representing to connect me with that of which I am thus to judge?

Now the *same* considerations that defeated *cogitationes* for this purpose do in as well what such an inner state makes one visually aware of. For awareness of *that* is not, and could not be, awareness of the *scene before me* being as it is. (It is another matter whether *in* visual awareness of the one sort I might sometimes enjoy some awareness of the other.) I am not so far offered so much as the chance to get in mind that which I must judge to be thus and so. All remains just as for Descartes.

If anything, Evans is in a worse position. For representing as so mismatches the conceptual with the nonconceptual. It provides, at best, only bits of the conceptual to bear on other bits of the

---

[18] Frege (1918), 59.

conceptual; where what is needed is the *nonconceptual* – the scene before me being as it is – to bear for me on what I am to think as to how various bits of the conceptual reach to *it*. Experience, on Evans' view, makes available to me, to bear on how I should think of things, at best the fact that the pig is in the sty, where what I need is acquaintance with things being as they are, so that *this* may bear on whether to think that such is the (or a) pig being in a sty.

Some have thought that experience, to do its job, *must* supply one with things shaped like (truth-evaluable) *thoughts*. Christopher Peacocke, for example, tells us,

> By perceiving the world, we frequently learn whether a judgement with a given conceptual content is true or not. This is possible only because a perceptual experience has a correctness condition whose holding may itself exclude, or require, the truth of a conceptual content.[19]

Only what was shapes as a proposition could bear on the truth of a proposition. Such reflects one conception of rational bearing. But Frege shows how so conceiving bearing gets things exactly backwards, at least when it comes to performing perception's task. Experience must provide that on which I can exercise my capacities to recognise connections between the conceptual and the nonconceptual. Only then can it provide me with that by which I can judge, noninferentially, that, say, a pig is in the sty. Representing things as so is hopeless for that task. Leibniz on being (so thinking about) an individual is *à propos*: for no proper subset of an individual's properties (closed under strict entailment) is having them being it.

Experience representing things as so could not be what places us in contact with the world. Such representing would present *our surroundings* to us as falling under a certain generality. It would thus reach to a range of cases of surroundings being as they were, or a scene as it was – just those instancing the relevant generality. *Thus* would it represent things as being a certain way. To grasp such representing we would need to grasp when what does (or fails to do) such instancing would does so or not; so get in mind its doing so. If our only route to getting in mind the particular things which do such instancing is through having it represented to us that they do, or do not, instance this or that, how could we so much as think such thoughts? In which case, what would make *these* the ways our experience represents things to be? (Frege saw the point.[20]

---

[19]   Peacocke (1992), 66.
[20]   Frege (1918), 67–69.

John McDowell made it well[21]) The SH model cuts us off from the world in our visual experiencing-as we must be cut off for representation by, or in, experience to so much as gain a foothold. Once so cut off from the world, it is a nice question how we are ever to be able again to get in touch with it.

4. Nonconceptual Content

So the SH model ends in an impasse. Such are the wages, for perception, of an inward gaze. It can be understandably tempting to fasten on representation for effecting an escape. But it is hopeless for that task. The idea of representing in or by experience – at least as means for experience to bring the world to bear on its subject's thought – positively requires something with just those features of the SH model which condemn it to failure – reason enough to give up on that idea. But it can be hard to abandon the SH model, especially when it masquerades as mere science.

There is, *inter alia*, this tempting picture. On Evans' account (as on the SH model), in a visual experience there is a way things appear, or seem, visually, to us. Call that, if you like, things appearing, or seeming, a certain way (namely, the way they do). It is just this (through the procedure Evans describes) which makes *how* our experience represents things recognisable to us. So we are in contact with *something* belonging to the nonconceptual (things appearing as they do), which we can thus recognise as falling under various generalities – instancing appearing as though a pig were spotted, say. Why cannot *that* opportunity for exercising conceptual capacities on the nonconceptual be all that is needed for the *world's* being as it is to be made to bear on what we are to think? After all, the right sorts of capacities are in the picture *somehow*. Well, it cannot because what is needed is opportunity for exercise of those capacities on the nonconceptual *our surroundings* supply (or bring into view). But, conflating awareness of A *in* awareness of B with awareness of B just *being* awareness of A, that point goes missing.

The very pull of such manoeuvres shows the tension between the SH model's untenability and seeming inevitability. Such tension is, perhaps, reflected in the strange idea of nonconceptual content. Here *content* is to be the content of what is truth-evaluable; what represents as so (or, again, potential components thereof – what may be true *of* something). The content of a given item fixes, or is fixed by,

---

[21] McDowell (1986), See also my (2007).

Charles Travis

what is so according to it; on *what* its truth turns. To represent as so is to represent things as a certain way. For (such a) representation to have nonconceptual content would be for there to be a way for things to be which was (or was in part) nonconceptual. If we draw the conceptual-nonconceptual distinction as it has been drawn here, this is patent nonsense. A way for things to be, so, too, representation (of things as a certain way) – in Frege's terms, a thought – is *essentially* what reaches to the nonconceptual in a particular way so as for a thought to present the particular case (things being as they are) as falling under some particular generality. Representational content belongs *essentially* to the conceptual, on this deployment of terms.

Evans, and his intellectual heir, Christopher Peacocke, are two among many who think that the representational content of experience is 'nonconceptual' (or, in Evans, nonconceptualised). Peacocke (soon to be centre stage) begins his treatment of perception with the remark (for him mere truism) that 'a perceptual experience represents the world as being a certain way.'[22] That way, he further holds, may be in whole or part 'nonconceptual'. If they are not just talking nonsense, they must mean something else by 'nonconceptual' than the use it has been given here. It can illuminate distortions in the SH model to ask what this can be. (This *may* oversimplify. Perhaps Evans, or Peacocke, simply gives in, simultaneously, to the pull of both poles of that above tension.)

It might seem less pressing to say what 'nonconceptual content' might mean if it seemed absolutely *mandatory* that experience represent as so. If, for one or another reason, the content of such representation could not be straightforwardly conceptual, well, we can leave it to later to work out just what else it might be. *Pro tem* 'nonconceptual' will do as a placeholder. But, we have seen, it is a mistake (or two) to think any such thing mandatory. So what *might* Peacocke mean by nonconceptual? It is none too easy to say. 'Conceptual content', he tells us, 'is content of a kind that can be the content of judgment and belief'.[23] If we suppose that nonconceptual content is content which is *not* conceptual, it follows that nonconceptual content is of a sort which cannot be the content of a judgement. I take this to mean: either of things (catholic reading), or of some thing(s) that they are (it is) thus and so. (So that the concept *being a crisp* is not nonconceptual merely because one cannot 'judge that a crisp'. But, for both Evans and Peacocke, an experience was to represent things as a certain way; where that is to

<hr>

22   Peacocke (1992), 61.
23   Peacocke (2001), 243.

be read as a way *there is* for things to be. Just so does Peacocke hope to finesse the 'problem' of how experience can provide something which *bears* on what to think, from which we may *learn* that such-and-such. Experience represents things as thus and so (on their story); the subject then takes experience's word for it – acquiesces in the representing, so judges – or, if ornery, or suspicious, resists – declines so to judge. On Peacocke's own account of conceptual content, it seems, there could be no nonconceptual content.

In such binds one might try relativising. What, for Peacocke, points towards nonconceptual content suggests he has some such thing in mind. For example, he says,

> Some of the nonconceptual content of our experience can be identical with the representational content of the experience of creatures that either possess no concepts, or possess only a set of concepts far more rudimentary than our own.[24]

We, perhaps, could just things to be as represented – just *that* way. But other creatures, whose experience could still represent things as that way, could not so judge. So goes the thought. If my experience represents Sid just to have grunted, that is a way I, but not these other creatures, might judge things to be. But in this case (the idea seems to be) those other creatures could not so much as have experiences which represented things as that way. For that, they would need the concept *grunt*. (I blush at such thoughts. But such are issues for other occasions. Anyway, I suppose something like this must be what Peacocke thinks.) So, the thought is, *conceptual* content would be content an experience could not have unless its subject had the relevant concepts; nonconceptual content is what could be the content of experiences *both* of those who could judge things that way and of those who could not.

Nonconceptual content in this sense would still be conceptual in the sense of having that generality which, for Frege, is the mark of a thought. It would reach in a particular way to a range of cases, so as to present the particular case – what is experienced – as falling under a certain generality. Only then could it so much as be something *we* could judge. The main question, to follow, is how *any* experience could arrange for anything to do *that*. But, again, necessity is the mother of bracketing such issues. This done, Peacocke's idea, above, is, I think, just another manifestation of the original tension: representation *must*, but cannot, make the SH model work. I will call those other creatures, who cannot judge what we can, 'cats'.

---

[24]   Peacocke (2001), 242.

Why think their experience *has* this content, which they cannot recognise, or so much as take it to have (on pain of being able to judge so)? The idea is: (details of cat eyes, etc. aside), if I am looking at a sparrow in a bush, and a cat is looking at a sparrow in a bush, we *might* see, and experience visually, the same thing. It is not as if the cat must be *blind* to some region of the scene where I can see what is going on. But representational content, if there is to be some, must be a function of the character of the experience – what it was like (visually). Accordingly, that sameness in what I and the cat experience visually must be reflected in à shared representational content of our respective experiences. Unfortunately for the cat, that content could not be the content of feline judgement.

So it would be if the sameness here must emerge in a sameness of representational content. And *this* must be so if the information about my surroundings which my experience makes available to me must be made available through things being represented as so. For what it would take nonconceptual content (in Peacocke's sense) to represent as so *is* what I might recognise to be so of my surroundings, given what I see of them – that the blood from the T-bone has made just *that* pattern in the rug, say. But we are not so shackled. I and the cat both see how things are in and about that bush. We *thus* see, and experience, the same thing. We may both, say, be responsive – each in his own way – to those avian movements in the branches. I can recognise things being *that* way as their being thus and so, for various values of 'thus and so'. The cat cannot do all I thus can. But sameness of experience here need not lie in sameness of how anything is represented in our shared awareness of the scene before us looking as it does. Without the SH model, it can just consist in the awareness afforded both of us of the scene being, visibly, as it is.

Which, on reflection, is no doubt a good thing. The scene before the cat and me is, in being as it is, literally innumerable ways there are for a scene to be – one for each way of reaching to a range of cases which reaches this one. I cannot grasp all the ways (condemned as I am to the *human* condition). It is hard to see how my experience could *represent* things as all these ways. So there are our friends the Martians, graspers of many ways beyond our grasp, failing to grasp others within ours. With them in view, it appears that *all* content of *all* our judgements is nonconceptual in the sense suggested by Peacocke's remark above.

Still, there is an underlying picture here which needs to be addressed. It is clearer in Evans than in Peacocke. Their shared idea was: in visual experience, things appear to me a certain way. In

Evans things so appearing makes it recognisable to me what way, or ways, my experience represents things to be: those ways it is as though things are in things appearing as they thus do. Now a thought might be: Why not cut out the middle men? If things appear to me a certain way, let my experience represent things to me as *that* way. Things appear as though *blah*; my experience represents them as *blah*. Here original tension emerges in a new way. Things appearing to me a certain way can just be things appearing to me as they then do – a denizen of the nonconceptual. So we have here something nonconceptual in the Frege-inspired sense I have given that term. The way my experience represents things is (something like) *as they appear*. If their so appearing is their appearing as they do, so something nonconceptual, then, it seems, so to represent them is to represent them as a certain way, where things being that way also belongs to the nonconceptual.

But the 'certain way' in 'represent as a certain way' cannot be read in the same way as that in 'things appear a certain way', where this is to be read just as things appearing as they do. It must be read as *such-and-such way there is for things to be*. Otherwise we have no representation at all. If anything is *represented* as so here – if there is anything truth-evaluable – then things need not be *just* as they in fact are for things to *be* as thus represented; nor for them to be so represented. The particular case is represented as what it would be in doing something (determinate) less than just being all it is; so in what might be done in a *range* of cases. The idea is things appearing as they do, just in being what *it* is – a certain particular case of things appearing – is to determine *how* this representation is to reach; just what it would be for things being as they are to be all they *need* to be to be as represented. But particular cases, have no reach, determine as such no reach for anything conceptual to have. So the idea makes no sense.

What could give the impression that merely things appearing as they do, in itself, while remaining nonconceptual, could, for all that, determine something it would be for things to be as they were *according* to it – a bit of the conceptual? Evans suggests one thing. An ordinary photograph *registers* (digitally, on film, in a print) the scene before the lens. It thus contains information about that scene in our now familiar first way. There is that photo of Pia on the boardwalk. It shows the way she was back then. Her hair was bobbed then, her chin line firmer. There was that sparkle in her eyes, now lost. There is much the photo does not show: Sid's sideburns and bellbottoms (he *took* the photo, was not in it); his then-addiction to chicken nuggets; the lovers *under* the boardwalk. Nor whether Pia was suffering indigestion, or her obscured arm was then freckled. So things would have been as shown in the photo while the world at large was — things were — any of various ways. In a range of cases things would have been as shown — perhaps the range some bit of the conceptual might reach.

So the photo shows Pia to look a way she could have looked while various things were going on. Someone might take that to mean that it *represents* her to be that way — that there is a way things are *according to* it. If photos can do this, it does not seem to require conceptual capacities so to represent things; which *may* want to make us label representation so achieved as 'nonconceptual' (though the achievement would remain presenting the particular case as falling under some given generality).

One tempted by such thoughts should attend to *what* answers questions as to when things being as they were would be their being as shown. Would Pia's hair have been bobbed then if things were as shown? One might consult the photo to see how it presents her. But is what it shows hair being *bobbed*? A photo cannot answer that. What lies in, or behind, what a photo thus cannot do?

If the photo represents things as so, the most it could do is represent it to be so that Pia then was (*inter alia* looked) *thus* — as shown. If being *thus* counts as having one's hair bobbed, then her being as she was according to the photo is, in fact, her having her hair then bobbed. When it comes to which concepts under which to bring Pia's being as thus represented, just *how* being as shown reaches beyond the particular case, and to what, what the photo shows, its photographic image, so far as that goes, leaves us entirely on our own. Someone *might* think of this as just giving further content to the idea of *nonconceptual* content. The thought would be: perceptual experience is just like that. It, too, represents as scene as *thus* — as it thus appears. But we need to look more closely at whether this is really *representing* at all.

We began with the idea that a photo contains information as the nonconceptual does. This has been worked into the idea that it, so experience, too, can do that while representing as so. It contains information *retrievable* in the first way, but in representing things to be such as for that to be retrievable *information*. What, then, decides *what* information the photo thus contains? The photo contains information as to how Pia looked back then, or at least that day on the boardwalk. Obvious first questions: Back when? What day? What answers these is when the photo was taken; *not*, at first blush, information the *photo* contains. Perhaps the information is written on the back (if a print is in question). Otherwise, there is an historical fact, to be sought as such facts are. E.g. ask Sid. By contrast, suppose I *say*, 'Pia wore her hair bobbed then', saying Pia's hair to have been bobbed at a certain time (or in a certain period). When was her hair bobbed according to me? That depends on how my words are to be understood. For all of my uttering them when I did, I may have said, or not said, her to have had bobbed hair at any of an indefinite variety of periods, or moments.

The crucial point has been made. In a court of law we would speak of the photo *meaning* (factively) that, say, Pia wore her hair bobbed when she was 17 (so, further, that she was not then in the cult). Which is just what it might do, depending on the facts: when it was taken, how constant Pia was in her coiffure in that period, whether she might have been wearing a wig. A *caricature* of Pia with bobbed hair, or a photo of her (or a body-double) with bobbed hair, as one frame in a photo-BD titled, 'Pia at 17' *might* mean something as to her coiffure at 17, or her coiffure at 35 (if, say, her flowing tresses then would have made the caricaturist depict hair as bobbed). But it *represents* her hair as bobbed at a time decided by how it is to be understood. For the BD, produced when she was 35, using a body-double, the title is a clue to that. These are all things a photo as such could not do. There is nothing wrong with the idea that that caricature *means* that Pia's hair was bobbed at 35, but *represents* her as with bobbed hair at 17, or that it represents her as with bobbed hair at 17, but does not represent her *to have had* such hair. All things beyond the reach of a photo. Moreover, that frame of Pia in the BD might represent her as with bobbed hair even if she is wearing a wig. If I said, 'Pia had bobbed hair', the fact that she might have worn a wig in those days takes nothing away from the fact that I *represented* her as having bobbed hair; it merely means that what I said might be wrong. Again, if the photo happens to be of a body double, then all it shows is the body-double having bobbed hair, and all it means (pending further facts is that the body-double's hair was bobbed. Such are some of the differences between representing as so and factive meaning.

The differences are manifest throughout. In the photo, Pia's skin is smooth and pale. Her eyes seem preternaturally wide. Does the photo show her as having such skin, or eyes? It depends on how the photography worked. Perhaps the film (or programme) is not true to skin colour, the lens not true to eye dimensions. The camera produced a certain image; now the question is what, given the apparatus, such an image *means*; what we can conclude from it, what *information* is retrievable. If the film is not true to skin colour, then it is not as though the photo *represents* Pia to have skin of some colour other than she did. Rather, to that extent, it contains no information as to her true skin colour. It cannot represent falsely; by the same token it cannot *represent* at all.

Factive meaning is a relation borne, sometimes by the conceptual, sometimes not, to bits of the conceptual. So there is, as a rule, a range of cases in which things would be as meant. But what factively means cannot, in doing *that*, *reach* in any particular way to any particular range, as is intrinsic to what belongs to the conceptual. Photos mean, but cannot represent (though, like anything, they can be *used* to do so, as in the BD). They are no model for how anything could represent nonconceptually.

5. Filling Out Space

The SH model cannot allow perception to bring the world to bear on what to think as perception would do. Representation cannot allow it to. So the SH model of perception is wrong. Representing in or by perceptual experience – notably things as so – requires the SH model. So there is no room for representation in or by perceptual experience. The next question is: if the SH model fails, what is the *right* way to conceive perception? But temptations to think that perceptual experience represents things run so deep, and touch on things so fundamental, that it will help in addressing that question first to consider, from some other angles, why this is something perceptual experience could not do.

Peacocke's idea of how visual experience represents things is, seemingly, inspired by that photographic (mis)conception of how something belonging to the nonconceptual can be conjured into a bit of the conceptual; perhaps by a conception of how a photo can be digitalised. Accordingly, he postulates a kind of content of such experience which he calls *scenario content*. This is content of a visual experience, identified by a scenario. A scenario is a 3-dimensional space with labelled origin and axes, and with each point in the space assigned some set of properties drawn from a stock out of which scenarios are generated. A positioned scenario is assigned a viewer at a time. For example, if the origin is *right between the eyes*, and the axes *right-left* and *up-down*, then to position the scenario for Sid now is to take the origin to be right between Sid's eyes, where he is now, the right-left axis to run from Sid's right to his left, facing as he is now, etc. Sid's present visual experience has the content thus identified just in case things are as they are according to the experience only if each point in the space around Sid has the properties assigned that point in the scenario. One might, in that case, call the scenario *true*, or true relative to that positioning. 'Only if' because scenario content is only one sort that Peacocke thinks visual experience might have. One might say: on this condition, Sid's experience is true *so far*. A wrinkle: Actually, Peacocke tells us, the content of Sid's experience is iden-tifed by a *family* of positioned scenarios. His experience is true so far just in case *one* of them is true. The family is to reflect Sid's inability, e.g. to distinguish fine shades of colour. I will ignore these complications except where they demand attention.[25]

So *if* a given positioned scenario fits Sid's current experience, then that experience is true so far if that positioned scenario is true: for that scenario to fit is for there to be a certain way things are according to the experience; for it to be true (so positioned) is for things to be that way (though this may not be the *whole* way things are according to the experience). Indeed, this *is* what it is for a scenario to fit. If Sid's experience represents things as they are according to the scen-ario, it fits. There need not be a unique scenario which thus fits. Perhaps there is a unique one generated from some given stock of properties. But there may be others generated from other stocks. If a scenario which fits assigns to a given point being blue, and part of a solid surface, that is *one* way of capturing how things are according to Sid's experience. But there may be others. (This is part of the inspiration for *nonconceptual* content.) The question now is: Which scenarios *would* fit Sid's experience, given that it was as it was? About this Peacocke says,

> Of course, I still owe a philosophical account of what it is for one scenario, with one set of labeled axes and origin rather than another, to be the content of an experience. But once we recog-nise the level of the scenario, there is nothing to make this problem insoluble.[26]

Really? Let us see. First, though, for some ground rules. Little in them should be controversial here.

First, how *much* should a visual experience should represent as so? Suppose can just *see* Sid's inebriated look, the red meat on the carpet, the blood seeping into the white fibres. Then, *perhaps*, that visual experience should represent it as so that Sid looks, or is, inebriated, etc. But suppose she only learns he is inebriated later, by seeing the bottle of Old Codswallop he has been at. She may deduce, or infer, from that, correctly, that he is inebriated. But this is not part of

---

[25] Peacocke (1992), 61–62.
[26] Peacocke (1992), 73.

what she is, or is made, aware of in, or by, seeing Sid staring sheepishly at the red meat on the rug. So it is more than *that* experience should represent as so. A visual experience should not represent as so what one would need to deduce from other things one had taken in. It would thus proffer more information than vision, or mere seeing, then makes available. (With rules to come, this should mean that Pia's present visual experience should not represent *more* as so than she could, or *might*, see to be so if her experience is in fact one of seeing a scene before her.)

Plausibly, for Peacocke or Evans, some form of converse point should hold. If Pia just sees Sid going at the Old Codswallop, and can thereby see that he is going at it, then her experience should represent this as so. For, though seeing that *need* not be based on visual input, here it is. Here there is nothing else from which Pia must, or could, *infer* that Sid is so engaged. *Inference* is not in the cards here. Pia can just recognise of what she sees – the scene being as it is – that *this* is Sid going at the Old Codswallop. Peacocke tells us (and I think Evans agrees) that experience representing things as so is *the* way in which it allows us to learn things from it as to how things are. This, we know, is false. But if it were true, then, since Pia's current visual experience allows her to learn, just from *it*, that Sid is so engaged, *it* would have to represent this as so. Given its *ad hominem* character, I will treat this as plausible, but not mandatory. But if experience representing things as so is *not* the only way for it to make the world bear on what to think, what is the point of its doing so at all? Such would just be making the same information available in two ways at once – as where Pia, *really, really,* not wanting Sid to forget their anniversary, sews the place with both wedding pictures and notes.

Second rule. It should be recognisable to the subject *what* way his *visual* experience represents things to be. Something in what he is, or can be, thus visually aware of should *make* this recognisable to him. I am not here disputing Evans' claim that perceptual experiences cannot themselves be objects of perceptual awareness. Nor am I supposing that perceptual experiences bear their content in anything like the way a sentence does. But I recall something Evans himself relies on: enjoying a perceptual experience *is* a way of experiencing being in whatever state enjoying that experience is – being in one of Evans' internal states, if such there be. What I am insisting on is: experiencing what one *thus* does – something one thus experiences – makes it recognisable to one which way one's experience represents things to be. What one experiences can just be things looking to him as they then do. Recognition need come to no more than this: confronted with the way things relevantly *are* (or prove to be), one is able to say (see) that *this* is not, or, again, is, things being as they were according to that experience: the experience was *wrong*, or *right*. And one can recognise, sufficiently often, of sufficiently detailed concrete examples, what *would* be, or not, things being as represented. For only *recognisable* representing (in the present attenuated sense) could make the world bear, for the subject, on what to think and do. Which was to be the point of representing in experience.

Third, it cannot follow merely from the fact that the scene before me is *not* a certain way that my experience did not represent it as that way; nor, conversely, merely from the fact that my experience did represent things as such-and-such way that they *are* that way. For experience, as elsewhere, truth must not be a requirement on representing at all. For suppose that my experience could not so much as *say* that there was a sloth in that tree unless there was one. Then it could not recognisably so claim where it was doubtful that a sloth was present, or where this was something one still needed to *learn*. So experience could represent *only* what there were other ways of ascertaining, or being certain of. Experience would thus reduce to a fillip on what fares well without it.

Fourth, if experience may represent falsely, it cannot lie blatantly. Suppose I plainly see the snake moving in the grass. Then my experience cannot represent it as so that nothing is moving in the grass. Which means: if my experience represents it as so that the snake is moving, I cannot tell just by looking (at the snake) that it is not. My visual experience cannot represent it as so that the snake is moving if things look to me (so far as I can tell how things look) just like a snake lying still. I omit a general formula, but suppose we can recognise instances.

6. Commitment

The curious idea that perception represents overlooks many obstacles. This section sets out one; the next another. The first obstacle is pervasive. It arises wherever there are two ways for things to look the way they do. Suppose I face an effigy of São Mamede. It looks blue. *Suppose* there are three ways for it to look just the way it does: it may be made of blue plaster; it may be painted blue; it may be neutral-coloured, coloured blue by lasers. (The example, inspired by laser-coloured effigies at Amiens, is *not* far-fetched.) Perhaps things would not look just as they do all three ways: you could tell if the effigy were made of blue plaster, rather than being painted. In that case, representing is *de trop*: its looking as it does *means* that it is painted. But suppose things might look just the same one way or the other. By our rules, what I experience visually must make it recognisable to me how things are represented. But how could things being *visually* as they are for me make it recognisable to me that *visual* experience represented things as one of these ways (blue plaster *there*), rather than any of the others?

The effigy looks just like a blue-plaster effigy — as one would or might. It must *be* a blue plaster effigy to be as it thus looks. It looks just like a blue-painted effigy. It must be blue painted to look as it thus looks. It looks like a blue-laser-illuminated effigy. It must be *that* to look as it thus looks. But none of this so much as speaks to the question how *things* must be to be the way they look ('things' here bearing its catholic reading, on which one cannot ask 'Which ones?'). Yet, it seems, visual experience provides nothing beyond things looking as they do to tip me off as to how it represents things to be. So it seems that such experience could *not* represent things as any of these ways. Of course, I may be in a situation in which there could not be lasers, or, perhaps, blue plaster. In that case, things looking as they do might *mean* that there is blue paint there — but then, no representing needed.

A natural reaction here would be some form of minimalism. Let us retreat to it by steps. First, perhaps my visual experience just represents that region as occupied by something *blue*, no commitment to *how* blue. But if the effigy is neutral coloured, the blue thanks to lasers, there is an understanding of something being blue on which it does count as something blue, and a contrasting one on which it does not; on which something blue only in the laser light is not something blue. Similarly for paint. So on what understanding of being blue does my experience represent that region as occupied by something blue? The above form of argument can be repeated here.

Second, perhaps my experience merely represents it as so that things *look* blue in that region of space. But this cannot help. What makes it recognisable to me how my experience represents things (when to say it was *false*) is things looking as they do to *me*. There are two ways for that to happen: they may so look; or it may just be me. Now the above argument repeats itself again.

Third, perhaps my experience merely represents it as so that things look blue now to me. There are several problems with this idea. But one will do for the moment. I am already authoritative as to how things look to me. (Or if I have lost track of that, it is obscure how representation can help me.) Of what is representation supposed to be informing me here? Or is it, again, just a wheel idling. (Aunt Ida as

I stand before the donkey: 'That's a donkey.') Perhaps it informs me that *that* (things looking as they do) is something looking *blue*. But then how am I to understand it? (It would be nice if my visual experience could represent it as so that *that* colour is *heliotrope, that* one burnt umber, and so on, I being bad at recognising those colours. It would then be a sort of cognitive prosthetic. But, though, taking that '*that*' to refer to a region of my surroundings, it may be *so* that that is burnt umber, it is hard to see how experience could commit itself to any such thing. Recall our first rule: visual experience should not represent any more as so than is retrievable from what is visually experienced. If I do not know burnt umber when I see it, then that *that* is burnt umber is not information so retrievable.

So, it seems, there is just nothing visual experience could legitimately represent as so.

7. Status

Using the strategy of the last section, I now develop a second obstacle. I begin, it will seem to some, off target. I then hone my aim. Here the problem is squaring experience's representing with our first rule (and its converse). If I oversimplify epistemology, the main point will be seen, I hope, to withstand the complications. I draw it from Thompson Clarke (1965). It would not touch a view that visual experience represents, not the scene before one as such-and-such ways, but merely (in suitable cases) itself as revealing – as an experience of *seeing* – how things are. *That* idea was disposed of in the last section.

To begin, then, a fresh baguette is on the kitchen table, on a breadboard, facing Sid (seated). What does Sid see? One answer: 'The baguette.' If so, then perhaps, by 1's converse, his experience should represent it as so that there is a baguette before him. So, too, for any ringer for a baguette-seeing experience – say, one of seeing a play-doh 'baguette' – what *visual* experience would not reveal as *not* one of seeing a baguette. Suppose, though, that the right answer is, 'The front surface of a baguette.' Then, by the first rule, Sid's experience should *not* represent it as so that there is a baguette before him. That would be something for him to *infer* from the information *perception* made available. Such is the shape of seeing's bearing on what visual experience might represent as so.

Here Clarke's point: *no* answer is the right one as such to 'the' question what Sid (actually) saw. Rather, different answers would be the right ones on different occasions for *saying* what Sid saw. What counted, on some such occasions, as what he saw would not do so

339

on others. *And there is no further occasion-independent fact as to what he 'really' saw.* Similarly, an undyed cotton shirt, coloured blue by lasers, counts as then blue on some understandings of what its being blue would be, as not blue on others. There is no further fact as to what its colour 'really' is. Besides those occasional ways of drawing a blue-non-blue distinction, there is no other.

The Clarke point, as I will call it, is that there is no one right answer to the question what Sid saw. So there is no one right answer to the question what he would need to infer. So there can be no one right answer to the question how, by our first rule, his experience is to represent things. Neither the samples above, nor any other answer could be right *as such*. Which means that there can be no right answer at all. If Sid's experience is to represent, for him recognisably, then *how* it represented in a given case cannot vary from occasion to occasion of the asking, according to what Sid would *then* count as needing to infer.

One could argue for Clarke's point by cases. If the little imps have been attaching front surfaces of baguettes to play-doh and leaving them in hopes of their muzzy elders preparing play-doh *tartines*; if such impishness may have struck, then, while Sid may *say* he saw a baguette on the breakfast table, we might count him as really having seen only a front surface. Once the children have all been packed off to military school, we can go back to talking about seeing baguettes. What Sid saw in not decided merely by the presence of the baguette, nor by his alertness being as it was to the occupation of that region; nor by whether the children have in fact been packed off. The circumstances of discussing his situation matter.

But there is a better way to see the point. If perception's job is to make the world bear on one's thought, then to see something is to enjoy a certain epistemic status. That thought, worked out, imposes occasion-sensitivity. I start with *perhaps* slight oversimpliction. An experience of seeing a baguette before one is one which allows the world to bear on his thought as a baguette's presence before him bears on what is so. Which means: it makes available, to its subject, the information that there is a baguette before him: given adequate, and functioning, recognition capacities, he can recognise the scene before him as one in which there is a baguette before him; so he can *judge* that there is one there on grounds that he *sees* it. Seeing *can* be, for him, *proof*. There is no gap between seeing a baguette and there being one through which absence might slip. But if one only sees the front surface of a baguette, then no more is made available to him than that there is a front surface: judgements as to baguettes must be conclusions drawn.

Deciding what someone saw is thus deciding how the world has been brought to bear on his thought; what about it has been made available. Cases like the above bring out the need for such decisions to take account of the uses to which such information is to be put. Telling whether there is a baguette or play-doh on the table may be one such use. For Sid to be *thus* enabled would be for him, then, to be able to tell baguettes from play-doh at sight. Where *clever* imps are an issue, he cannot. Ordinary recognition capacities – say, knowing a pig at sight – are inherently dependent on hospitable environments for being that. If there is a tapir which looks just like a pig, or a pot-bellied pig which looks very unlike one, and if the gentlemen farmers of Oxfordshire are stocking their farms with these, then, though, usually, I *do* know my pigs when I see them, I cannot tell a pig by sight in Oxfordshire. It is not the *actual* one-upmanships of Oxfordshire gentry which cost me the capacity. False rumours in Chelsea may cost me it, on some occasions for the reckoning, if Chelsea somehow relies on me. Whether I have lost my capacity on arrival in Kingston Bagpuize all depends on who is asking, and when and why. *Knowlege* would not be in the picture otherwise. All the rest follows from seeing's role in making one knowledgeable.

Such is a simple thought. Perception allows information to bear on what one is to think – given his ability to extract it from a scene by his capacities to identify *what* counts as being *what*. Sid sees that goldfinch with its distinctive goldfinch head. He cannot tell it is a goldfinch: he does not know them by their heads. Seeing may well (though need not) make the information available (on one good understanding of *available*). Perhaps Sid could describe the head so that an expert knew at once it was a goldfinch. Still, that there is a goldfinch on the branch is not something that may yet bear, for Sid, on what he is to think. In the bread case, the problem is not *knowing* what distinguishes a baguette; nor with what distinguishes one from Play-doh. It is that in impish surroundings the marks of a baguette are not on its facing crust. So it is not that perception makes available to Sid information he cannot use. It is rather that it does *not* make available to him information he perfectly well could use if he had it. It thus does not make available to him the information that a baguette is before him – not even as it did that there was a finch on that branch. So he cannot have seen the baguette. Now the question is: for purposes of saying what he saw, *what* count as the circumstances he was in – impish or not? The answer to that question can only be an occasion-sensitive matter.

Can this be right? If I have checked that it was, in fact, a baguette on the table, I might describe Sid (truly) as having seen a baguette, though all he could tell was that there was a facing surface. On the other hand, in impish surroundings, if Sid claimed to see a baguette, we could confront him with the impish possibilities and force the admission that all he really saw was the facing surface. All of which is just what one would expect if it is an occasion-sensitive matter what circumstances Sid counted as being in. When I establish that it was a baguette, I establish that Sid was not in (relevantly) impish circumstances. I now speak of what he saw accordingly – as it is to be spoken of on an occasion where his circumstances so count. This no more shows that what he 'really' saw was the baguette than finding an occasion on which one would not say a shirt was blue shows that it 'really' is not blue. It does not, for one thing, because it no more shows this than confronting him where he counts as in impish circumstances shows that what he 'really' saw was a facing crust. What one sees, so what one's experience *could*, or should, represent as so, depends on the circumstances one is in. What these are depends on when, and why, you are asking. Which destroys the idea that there could be such a thing as a way things are according to an experience of seeing.

Which may tempt a representationist to minimalism. The rough idea would be: what an experience of seeing represents as so is just the *least* one would ever count as seeing (if one is). If there is a least Sid would ever count as having seen viewing the baguette, this would have to be a facing surface, or region of space. Beyond that, the environment drops out and it is seeing no longer. But the Clarke point applies to surfaces and regions. Suppose Sid, lost in reverie, is but dimly aware of the baguette. On the crust is a dark spot which some say resembles São Mamede. Here cracks, there what *might* be an impish thumbprint. Such details are lost on Sid. Did he see the crust? Or only part, or parts, of it? If the last, then which one(s)? Just which surfaces before Sid's eyes are ones he could judge to be present, or thus and so, which regions thus and so, on grounds of seeing their presence, or being that way – that is, non-inferentially?

Suppose we (mentally) place a grid over the facing crust, one square, e.g., taken up with the São-Mamedeish spot, and ask, for each square, whether Sid saw what is in it. Could Sid really judge, of square R6, that that was occupied by crust – on grounds of seeing it so occupied? Suppose imps may have been cutting bits out of crusts, hoping we will suspect mice. Does what Sid sees allow him to say whether R6 is occupied (or even base a judgement on how he has seen R6 to be)? One would, at least, sometimes, suppose not. But this device, if it can be worked at all, can be worked for each region of the grid (not necessarily simultaneously). (Things get worse if, to oblige Peacocke, we try for answers for each *point* on the crust.) If we add up these results, we would seem to get the result that Sid sees *none* of the facing surface (or at least not much, or much of it not), which would be not to see *it* at all.

But suppose we now ask whether Sid, as he then was, was enabled, by sight, to base a judgement that there is a front surface before him on the presence of that surface – whether he might be able to judge such a thing non-inferentially. For each bit of grid, or most, we can build a story within which it would be wrong to say that Sid could judge non-inferentially that there was crust in that region, simply, by his seeing it, on grounds of there being crust there. But this does not seem to preclude a positive answer to the question. Seeing what he did may make Sid authoritative as to the presence of the crust, while being liable, for any, or even many, regions of the grid, to leave him not authoritative as to whether there was crust there. It may be liable to grant such authority over a region even where, if there were no crust in that region, then there would be no facing crust present (but only, at best, a part of one). Which forces some form of occasion-sensitivity: Sid may count as authoritative as to whether there is a crust; basing judgement on the presence of a crust, even where we recognise that, on certain occasions for asking, he would not count as authoritative as to the presence of a crust in region R, and if there is no crust in region R, then there is no facing crust for him to see. He counts as authoritative as to the crust just where his circumstances do not count as ones in which he is not authoritative as to region R (which need not be for them to count as ones in which he *is* so authoritative). Now we need only remember: that kind of occasion-sensitivity is incompatible with squaring experience's representing with the demands of rule 1.

Minimalism is more familiarly worked in a slightly different area. Sid may wrongly, but understandably, take himself to see a baguette where there is only a facing crust. All he really saw was the crust. But it seemed that there was a baguette: so far as he could tell by looking there was. Similarly (it seems), Sid may wrongly, but understandably, take himself to see a facing crust where it is just a facing image, or just all in his head; but where there is nothing he experiences visually to tip him off. (It is none too easy to say *how* it might be all in his head. But let that pass.) Where there is only the facing crust, it seems that he is seeing something he would, or might, also have been seeing where there a baguette. By parallel, it may seem that where there is no facing crust, he experiences visually (seeing now having dropped out) something which he would also experience visually if there were a crust, or, still better, a baguette. This something-visually-experienced, whatever it is, would be the minimal ingredient in an experience of seeing, present independent of the occasion for the asking. The rest can all then be seen as mere seeing-by-courtesy.

The manœuvre can be made lose its charm. Sid sees the baguette. *What* is it that he would see whether there was a baguette or not? *One* answer is: the facing crust. But does Sid see that *whole* crust, or only part of it? That is an occasion-sensitive matter. What was it like visually to see what Sid did? One answer to that would be by holding up the crust. Things – what he saw – looked like *that*. Here, one needs to fix an understanding of looking like. There are understandings on which the crust, when I hold it up, no matter how carefully, does *not* look as it did when Sid saw it. (Light and shadows, for one thing.) But anyway, if we aim to find a minimal feature in visual experience by looking inward, to, say, the features of some internal state, something belonging to Sid's consciousness, as per the SH model, then holding up the crust does not even address the question we mean to ask. What we what to know is how things were visually *for Sid*. How, then, was it visually for Sid if there was a São-Mamedeish spot on the crust he saw? If pointing to the spot on the crust is not an answer, then there is *no* answer to this until something fixes what it would be for things to be one way or the other in this respect. That would be work of an occasion for the asking. Without that – unless, perhaps, the spot was, for Sid, particularly striking – there is no such thing as 'how that region looked to Sid'. In general, there is no such thing as *the* way things looked to someone in his seeing what he did, unless that way is simply: the way they did. So this way of moving inward moves nowhere. It is crucial, if experience is to represent, that it lead somewhere. For, to repeat a now-familiar theme, only determinate objects of visual awareness *other than* what is seen could possibly make room for experience to represent.

8. Gazing Out

It is not for a philosopher to deny that retinal images unleash chains of happenings. Personally, I am inclined to believe this. Nor is it for a philosopher to deny that such chains terminate in states of some characteristic sort. I am officially neutral. Nor is it for a philosopher to deny that without such happenings and states *we* would see nothing. Some such things no doubt *enable* seeing. This settles little as to what it is that they enable. It does not settle *what* someone sees on an occasion, or when someone would count as seeing such-and-such. Nor does it help much to insist that the things he sees must be ones whose images on the retinas unleash things. Nor can we suppose that those terminal states in the enabling story just envisioned, in having the features they do, might *ipso facto* settle something which was *the* way things (then) looked to their possessor. Nor, correlatively, should we suppose that they settle something which, with the presence of given further factors, not themselves seeing, or even visual awareness of anything – pre-retinal aetiology, say – might add up to seeing whatever their possessor happens to see on the occasion – as if seeing were a hybrid of appearings and a friendly world.

How, then, to conceive visual experience? It has taken too long to get this far for me to say very much about this here. But what has been said so far provokes a few suggestions. First, some visual experience is seeing, some is not. Seeing is what is enabled when all goes well – as all is liable not to. If we do not conceive seeing as a hybrid, with an underlying 'way things look to the perceiver', present whether things are going well or not, we might then treat these cases separately. Which, I suggest, would be helpful.

I begin, then, with seeing. One striking difference between seeing (perceiving in general) and testimony is that seeing is, and remains for its duration, *au courant*. If Sid is told, reliably, that his ribeye has just gone on the grill, he may then know how things were *then*. So long as he has the testifier's word for it, he, perhaps, continues to know how things were then. If, meanwhile, the ribeye has been carbonised into inedibility, it takes a new piece of testimony to make him *au fait* with that. If, by contrast, Sid *sees* his ribeye going on the grill, he is thereby afforded, for so long as the experience lasts, constantly *au courant* awareness of the ribeye's career. He can suffer agonies as, helpless, he watches it carbonise, or, a bit less feckless, flip it himself. Seeing is dynamic. (So, perhaps, are enablings, though, again, my philosophic business is not to claim, or hypothesise, so.)

Seeing things is thus following them. Sid, before the baguette, shifts his attention, his eyes, his head; fidgets, swivels, rolls the chair around (it is one of those). Whatever we say as to his seeing the baguette, we do not normally conceive of seeing such that the right answer to that question changes from moment to moment – unless there is some special reason for it to change, as, when Sid swivels all the way around, the baguette goes, momentarily, out of sight. So seeing the baguette is something one qualifies, or not, as doing over an *interval*. It is relevant intervals – whatever counts, on an occasion, as Sid's experience of seeing, or failing to see, the baguette – which are evaluable as ones in which he saw it, or, aain, did not. More reason not to suppose such a thing as 'the' way things looked to Sid in seeing the baguette, or that the momentary features of some internal state could fix what this was. Here, too, we find reason for conceiving seeing sometimes as *affording* aware-ness, if also sometimes as actually conferring it (Sid may see (still) the baguette at a moment at which his attention is fixed on that dark spot) – but, in either case, as a matter of what Sid holds onto throughout the interval.

A second central feature of seeing (and perceiving generally) is that it is occasion for exercise of our capacities for recognising the reach of various bits of the conceptual to various cases of the nonconceptual. For being carbonised to reach to the nonconceptual as it does may be for it to reach to Sid's ribeye's being as it is: Sid's ribeye's so being is a ribeye being carbonised. The very thought that *that* is a ribeye being carbonised is not one which Sid, or anyone, could so much as enter-tain without acquaintance with *that* – the particular case (any more than I can now think, of a certain man in Ulan Bator, that *he* is now drinking tea). Seeing the ribeye is an exemplary way of making that thought available. Such is a most central role of sight – tied up, too, with the idea, discussed above, that seeing has really not made the world bear on what to think as it ought if it falls short of providing acquaintance with the particular case – the ribeye being as it is.

More generally, seeing makes thoughts, and, more generally, atti-tudes available to a subject which are otherwise liable, sometimes bound, not to be. No doubt these extend beyond those involved in seeing the reach of the conceptual to the nonconceptual. So we now have two measures for what it is that someone saw: what one sees must stay in step with one's epistemic status, as per the last section. It must also stay in step with the attitudes one might count as holding. Seeing the man in Ulan Bator allows me (*ceteris paribus*) to think of *him* that he is drinking tea. Conversely, the right thing to say as to whether I *can* so think may bear on what to say as to whether I saw him. These two constraints may allow one to look at a subject, and what is before him, and, without looking *inside* him, say, on occasion, what it is he saw.

Now for visual experiences which are *not* seeing. I confine atten-tion to cases where enabling processes and states have gone wrong, as where, in special conditions of illumination, convex and concave, e.g., on that house across the road, may reverse. I begin with a problem. We can think of seeing as affording, as well as as conferring, awareness – awareness one might enjoy, where one might also have failed to; awareness of what there is anyway to be aware of. We can do that precisely because seeing is a relation to an environment, whose denizens are for *one* to encounter, broadly speaking, in experience. It is just this – that awareness is of what one *might* be unaware of – which calls for enabling, such as might be provided for *seeing* by chains of happenings unleashed by the retinas, and so on.

The task of those chains of happenings unleashed by retinas was to be to enable visual awareness of one's *surroundings*. The SH model assigns them another role: to issue in states *affording* awareness of something else: how things are visually for – how they look, or seem, to – the subject, where this is independent of how *things* (pleonastically, in the environment) are visually, or look, or seem. This goes inevitably with the idea of such a state as with other features (physiological, perhaps) which impose a unique answer to the question how things are visually for one in it. If such a state thus *affords* awareness, as distinct from conferring it, then this is awareness one might enjoy or not (as, e.g. Evans, insists). So it is something which calls for enabling, just like seeing itself. And, to borrow a term from Frege, the game can begin anew.[27] (Nor could the enabling here be self-enabling, accomplished by those very processes and state which provide such further things to be aware of: such would not be for us to be *afforded* awareness of them.) It is not quite *incoherent* to suppose that an enabling internal state produces something its subject must, but may, be enabled to be aware of. But it *is* incoherent to suppose it an intrinsic feature of enabling stories that they involve states which *do* produce such things. It would at least eliminate promissory notes if the story of what enabled seeing did not posit any such thing.

Suppose that what enables seeing also, on occasion, provides something else of which to be aware visually – say, things looking as they then do to someone. Suppose that this something else belongs to the contents of that person's consciousness, in Frege's sense. Then Frege's lesson applies: such contents of consciousness could not be objects of a *judgement*; there is no sense in the idea that they, just in being as they are, might be thus and so – might thus relate to some given bit of the conceptual.[28] Which does in the idea that one might be *afforded* awareness of such things – as if that is awareness one might enjoy or miss out on.

---

[27] Frege (1918), 60.
[28] See Frege (1918), 67–69, and my 2007.

Charles Travis

The idea of seeing as dynamic suggests a way of reading Frege's lesson. On that idea, a stream of impressions on, so chains unleashed by, retinas, over an interval, goes with a certain responsiveness to the scene before the viewer's eyes, stable over that interval – stable opportunities for attitudes, or affordings of them. What one sees is then some sort of resultant of such responsiveness and what there is for it to be responsiveness to. If, say, what enables seeing sometimes provides further things to experience visually, which are *not* things of which to be afforded awareness in the present sense, then that role of the scene in the above co-operative enterprise drops out. Nothing performs it. What may remain is a subject's responsiveness (through intervals) to things being visually as they are for him; where here awareness may be *conferred*, but not (merely) afforded. Responsiveness to *this* could not take the form of *judging* that (in being as it is) it is thus and so. It could still take the form of seeing things being visually as they are *for* their being thus and so (*auffassen*, perhaps *anerkennen*; not *erkennen*). In any event, responsiveness could now take over the role of making such a circumstance one which, in being as it is, is a subject experiencing things being for him visually thus and so – e.g. as though he were seeing a cantilevered upper floor.

But suppose we think of what enabling-gone-wrong provides, not as contents of consciousness, but rather as determined by, say, features of some neural configuration, or, otherwise, facts as to how the visual system reverses convex and concave when it does. Now we can think of enabling as providing something of which to be afforded awareness. For now I am (so far) aware visually of what I am where, say, concave and convex reverse, in and by being a way there is for *one* to be. By the same token, now enabling is called for for me to be aware of what I thus am. Now, too, there is room for enabling to go awry, and in that way among others room for things thus to look *to me* one way or another in being afforded awareness of what I thus am. Again, the game *can* begin anew. But something must allow the chain of enablings to stop. The previous idea shows how it can.

All this is at best the bare beginnings of understanding perceptual experience. The main aim here was to clear away a picture of such experience which positively blocks understanding. It is a picture widely at work even in those who disclaim it. It is (most often) engendered by a false impression of what it would be to ask after perceptual experience in a scientific manner, or while giving science its due. As Wittgenstein predicted, that impression leads only into darkness.

Bibliography

Clarke, Thompson, (1965) 'Seeing Surfaces and Seeing Physical Objects', *Philosophy in America*, M. Black and W. P. Alston (eds.), (Ithaca: Cornell University Press).

Descartes, R. (1641) *Meditations on First Philosophy*, in *Selections From Descartes' Philosophical Writings*, G. E. M. Anscombe and P. T. Geach (eds.), (London: Nelson, 1954).

————, 1644: *Principles of Philosophy* in Anscombe and Geach, selections.

Evans, Gareth (1982) *The Varieties of Reference*, (Oxford: Oxford University Press).

Frege, Gottlob (1882), "17 Kernsätze zur Logik" in *Schriften zur Logik und Sprachphilosophie aus dem Nachlass*, G. Gabriel (ed.), (Hamburg: F. Meiner Verlag, 2001).

———— (1892–1895), "Ausfuhrungen über Sinn und Bedeutung", in Gabriel.

———— (1897), 'Logik', in Gabriel.

———— (1918), 'Der Gedanke', *Beiträge zur Philosophie des deutschen Idealismus* 2, 58–77.

McDowell, John (1986), 'Singular Thought and the Extent of Inner Space', in *Subject, Thought, and Context*, P. Pettit and J. McDowell (eds.), (Oxford: Oxford University Press), 137–168. Reprinted in *Meaning, Knowledge and Reality* (Cambridge, Massachusetts: Harvard University Press), 228–259.

Peacocke, C. A. B. (1992), *A Study of Concepts* (Cambridge, Massachusetts: The MIT Press, 1992).

———— (2001), 'Does Perception Have a Nonconceptual Content?', *Journal of Philosophy* **98** (5), 239–264.

Prichard, H. A. (1950), 'Perception' in *Knowledge and Perception (essays and lectures)*, (Oxford: Oxford University Press), 52–68.

Travis, C. (2007), 'Frege, Father of Disjunctivism', *Philosophical Topics*, v. 33, n. 1, Spring, 307–334.

Philosophy – Wisdom or Technique?

ANTHONY O'HEAR

'Philosophy begins in wonder. And at the end, when philosophic thought has done its best, the wonder remains. There have been added, however, some grasp of the immensity of things, some purification of emotion by understanding. Yet there is a danger in such reflections. An immediate good is apt to be thought of in a degenerate form of a passive enjoyment. Existence (life) is activity ever merging into the future. The aim of philosophical understanding is the aim of piercing the blindness of activity in respect to its transcendent functions.' (A.N. Whitehead, *Modes of Thought*, Capricorn Books, New York, 1938, 232).

Notice the key concepts: wonder, purification of emotion, piercing the blindness of activity, transcendent functions. There are echoes here of the Platonic doctrine of philosophy as the care of the soul, therapy, the turning of the soul from fantasy to reality.[1] Education, says Plato (and not just philosophy), is the art of orientation, the shedding of the leaden weights which progressively weigh us down as we become more and more sunk in the material world and the world of desire, eating and similar pleasures and indulgences. All this is in the context of the Cave, and a form of vision which is to become able to bear 'the sight of real being and reality at its most bright... which is a form of goodness'.

So philosophy and education should be aimed at a form of conversion, certainly moral conversion, but something more as well covering the whole of life. Plato also warns us against the petty minds of those who are acknowledged to be bad, but who are clever, sharp-eyed and perceptive enough to gain insights into what they are interested in, and 'consequently the keener their vision is, the greater the evil they accomplish'.

Evil? Can philosophy be an adjutant to evil? If philosophy can be a force for good, for taking us through to its or our transcendent function, can it, if misused, by a force for harm too? Plato thought this and maybe when we think about it more, it isn't so far-fetched. After all the sophists were philosophers (of a sort) and were well known to Socrates and Plato. Maybe some of what they did, in fostering and

---

[1]   *Republic*, Bk VII, 518b–519b.

doi:10.1017/S1358246109990166   © The Royal Institute of Philosophy and the contributors 2009

Royal Institute of Philosophy Supplement **65** 2009

Anthony O'Hear

encouraging doubts about morality and truth, wasn't too good. Maybe[2] some of what Socrates and his followers did, qua philosophers, wasn't too good either, at least not if you were an Athenian democrat of the time and an opponent of oligarchs and dictators. In *Crito* when the laws of Athens are speaking to Socrates, they speak of Sparta and Crete as constitutions he admires, hardly bastions of democracy. Maybe, more even than *The Republic, The Laws*, with its nocturnal council and its draconian regimentation of life might give intellectual aid to would-be dictators and their repressive laws and inquisitions. This sort of thing is, of course, the burden of writers like Crossman and Popper who attack Plato as politically evil (though usually wanting to exonerate Socrates).

When you think about it, the great philosophies have rarely been neutral on matters of value. Philosophy is always done against a background of commitments, intellectual and other, which the philosophy is in a sense an attempt to work through, even if the working through may sometimes involve refining and modifying the commitments. Aquinas is often criticised for having very explicit commitments which his philosophy would not be allowed to challenge in a serious way; but all philosophers and all philosophies start from some framework of belief, even if that framework is one of fallibilism or even of scepticism. It is just in these cases the commitment is not as blatant as Aquinas's, or in our day as objectionable. So Plato's notion of philosophy (or education) as a turning of the soul one way or the other may not be so far fetched after all.

> 'Winifred Nicolson tells an anecdote of her great-grand-mother, who was also Betrand Russell's grandmother remarking after a visit from her grandson, "I don't know why it is that all my grandchildren are so *stupid*." I don't know why she thought the great logician stupid at that time; but the stupidity of logical positivism lies, if anywhere, in its premises... If it is true that the crassness of English philosophy has lain always in the quality of its premisses Lady Stanley may in this respect have been right about her grandson's "stupidity"'.[3]

Stupidity is strong, some may think, particularly as applied to Russell, though maybe not too strong if one reflects on some of his educational and political adventures; but what Kathleen Raine is talking about is not the intellectual brilliance and acuity of the logician, of however high an order. She is talking about choice of

---

[2] If I.F. Stone is to be believed.
[3] Kathleen Raine, *Autobiographies*, Skoob Boos, London, 1991, 347.

premises. And here it may be that intellectual dexterity, even of the quality of a Russell, is not enough.

'If meinongianism isn't dead, nothing is,' Gilbert Ryle is reputed to have said in the heyday of Oxford Philosophy. I think Ryle was exactly right.' Thus Graham Priest[4] thinks Ryle is exactly right in exactly the opposite sense to that intended by Ryle. Nothing is *ever* dead in philosophy (and in 2007–8, when Priest is but one of a phalanx of defenders of non-being, least of all the meinongianism Ryle took as his touchstone of philosophical moribundity). Some of us might wish for a healthy dose of Ryleanism (as we would put it) in philosophy of mind as well as in the philosophy of possibility and contradiction (where inconsistent beings are now sometimes countenanced, as well as nonbeings), but, as readers of contemporary philosophical journals will appreciate, that is not how it is. And Priest is surely right to point to the transience and power (both) of philosophical fashion when it comes to premises. In a sense, more power to Priest's elbow in shaking us out of a certain ontological complacency.

That said, how are we to chose premises? And further, how are we to judge conclusions, when philosophers like Priest and Williamson are simply not prepared to accept *reductio ad absurdum* arguments when applied to their conclusions about such topics as noneism and vagueness, and can, in a sense, argue for their conclusions against the most robust-seeming objections? Do we simply toss coins here? Are all defensible premises epistemologically equal, so to speak, simply awaiting their time or their defenders? This would not actually be such a surprise, given that at one time or another, just about every imaginable philosophical position has found its time and its able defenders. Or might there be something a bit more at stake, humanly speaking? Do the philosophies of the great philosophers reflect their own values and commitments in ways which lie deeper than the arguments they deploy in their writings?

'I no longer believe that the apparently impervious rationalists who demand so aggressively that we others should 'explain what you mean by...' (God, love, beauty, the good, the soul, the Logos,) are always victims of what the Church calls 'invincible ignorance'.... To judge others by myself, I would judge that in many more it is the will that has at some time denied and rejected spiritual knowledge. In the choice of premises the will is free: logic cannot dictate the ground from which its conclusions proceed; and I wonder whether the loveless, beautyless state is not the cause rather than the effect

---

[4] In *Towards Non-Being: the Logic and Metaphysics of Intentionality,* Oxford University Press, 2005, 1.

of such systems? If, disregarding those superstructures so dazzling to ignorance, we regard their foundations, they will be seen for what they are. Blake never answered Urizen's arguments, but merely drew his portrait.'[5]

Kathless Raine fought a lifelong battle to extricate herself from the cast of mind of progressivist Cambridge natural science and philosophy of the 1920s and 1930s, which seemed to her to push her into the position of denying the insights into transcendence she had had as a girl in Northumberland, so we may perhaps forgive her a degree of stridency here. She knows that of which she speaks. But is the will operative in premise choice? In recent times philosophers have fought against allotting the will *any* role in belief formation (Descartes' brilliant arguments to the contrary notwithstanding, which they usually show little sign of having pondered either deeply or sympathetically). Maybe the denial of the role of the will in belief formation is itself a feature of a form of intellectualism or rationalism neither Plato nor Aristotle would have recognised, for both understood the way that moral and other evaluative dispositions played a role in choice of ends, and maybe of premises too. We do in a sense have to choose for or against Urizen, but can this be done by means of argument, in the sense that argument one way will show the other way rationally indefensible?

It is often at this point that one begins to hear about judgements of sense and robust senses of reality, as if there might be some touchstone available to the worldly-wise, allowing them to brush off those with other fish to fry. I am not denying that to the person of good sense some things will seem whimsical, far-fetched, superstitious and just plain incredible, astrology, ley-lines and homeopathic medicines being among the usual and obvious suspects. To people brought up in a certain way, or with a certain cast of mind, Blake to whom I have already referred, is going to seem just off the wall. To speak personally, and Kathleen Raine notwithstanding, I am in no sense an uncritical admirer of Blake, or even really an admirer. But I'm reminded here that a philosopher friend of mine has used Blake's famous image of Newton for the cover of a book on the philosophy of science. He had not realised that Blake intended this image to be one of repression, of cruelty, of enmity to life and above all of a blindness to all that was not material, below and measurable, or that the primary sense of Blake's expression 'dark satanic mills' was to refer to the reductionist and mechanistic laws the constrained and constricted geometer Newton was mapping out in Blake's image.

[5] Raine, *op cit*, 347–8.

This is not, of course, an argument against the historic Newton or his philosophy, nor does it show that my friend was entirely wrong to take Newton in a positive sense. As I said to him, attempting to soften the blow I had just landed on him, you could even see the Newton of Blake's image as an angel, albeit fallen; and, as Peter Ackroyd has pointed out, there is indeed a monumentality about Blake's Newton, reflecting his creativity and mental isolation, akin to Blake's own, albeit in Newton's case maddened with unbelief.[6] My point is rather that it simply did not enter my friend's mind that Newton's science should be seen as hateful and life-denying, so he was unable to imagine that Blake's intention might be to show Newton as such.

There is a view of philosophy which sees it as primarily critical and analytical, philosophy itself as the organon of criticism, perhaps. We could think here of J.S. Mill's idea that one thing philosophy should do, perhaps the main thing it should do, is continually to challenge and criticise our assumptions and prejudices, even the most apparently solid. In a Millian spirit it would, of course, be easy to come up with arguments against many of Blake's ideas; Blake would be slain by the sword of critical rationalism. His ideas would not survive testing by experience and observation, if only because most of them are not in that sense testable. Nor are his views immune to logical analysis. No doubt there are plenty of contradictions in his writings too. There is, though, this:

> 'once atoms had no color; now they also have no shape, place or volume... There is a reason why metaphysics sounds so passé, so *vieux jeu* to-day; for intellectual perplexities and paradoxes, it has been far surpassed by theoretical science. Do the concepts of the Trinity, the soul, haecceity, universals, prime matter, and potentiality baffle you? They pale beside the unimaginable otherness of closed space-times, event-horizons, EPR correlations and bootstrap models.'[7]

No doubt we will be told that the theories which deal with space-time and the rest have survived severe testing at in the most precise way; but does that make the theories more believable? Does that in itself dissipate the air of paradox and uncertainty which hangs over them? Does it do much to close the gap

---

[6]   Peter Ackroyd, *Blake*, Vintage, London, (1999), 201.
[7]   Bas van Fraassen, 'Empiricism in the Philosophy of Science', in *Images of Science*, edited by P.M. Churchland and C.A. Hooker, University of Chicago Press, (1985), 245–308, at 258.

between the calculations and observations and the extraordinary conceptions these calculations and observations are held by men of impeccable scientific sense to support?

Maybe it does. Maybe critical rationalism, if it leads us to quibble over the best scientific theories of our time, fuss over their apparent contradictoriness and so on, should just be told to get lost here, given that the theories in question are immensely workable, useful and empirically precise to an unimaginable degree. In any case scientists are not going to dispense with them, whatever philosophers might say, any more than you or I are going to stop treating our friends and lovers as free or our inductive beliefs as probable, whatever Hume and his followers tell us. The point here is that if we are thinking of philosophy as the organon of criticism it is hard to cordon off our essential commonsensical beliefs from its strictures. One lesson Hume teaches is that they will fall too, if examined too critically. Too critically, we say. But is excess of criticism a notion available to the Millian critical rationalist? Mill: 'even if the received opinion be not only true, but the whole truth, unless it is suffered to be, and actually is vigorously and earnestly contested, it will, by most of those who receive it, be held in the manner of a prejudice, with little comprehension or feeling of its rational grounds'.[8] *Rational* grounds *after* vigorous and earnest contestation... amazing really that Mill wrote this decades after Hume.

One feels that a perceptive reader of Hume should not be so certain of any of this, and in true anti-foundationalist/rationalist spirit might instead manage at least one cheer for prejudice, or at least for animal belief. If we are honest, we have to acknowledge that there is a sense in which we do not really believe in philosophy as critical rationalism. We will tend to use philosophy's critical edge highly selectively, against believers in fairies and in the literal truth of the book of Genesis, but not against the things which go to constitute our own 'robust common sense', hardly recognising the variability of what over the years has been taken to shelter under the umbrella of robust common sense.

The whole Millian enterprise of continuous criticism, the enterprise of critical rationalism, in other words, is open to question in further way, as Jacob Burckhardt maintained: 'Keeping everything persistently subject to discussion and change... will end up with a host of irreconcilable contradictions'. The point is that continual

---

[8]   J.S. Mill, *On Liberty*, Ch 2, in *Utilitarianism, On Liberty, Essay on Bentham*, Fontana edition, London, 1962, 180.

scrutiny and review of one's assumptions will deprive one of any firm ground from which to base judgements. In the practical, but not only the practical sphere, there can be many starting points and many goals which are not simultaneously reconcilable. To take a standard example, in the political sphere equality will conflict with liberty and liberty may impede security. But similar tensions will arise in the epistemological domain. Certainty may be bought, relatively speaking anyway, but at the expense of content and creativity. In aesthetics concentrating on formal perfection may well produce dullness; on the other hand exuberance may undermine structure and clarity. Trying to achieve all these goals together will be impossible, as they are not reconcilable in a pure state. In so far as criticism may proceed simultaneously from any and all directions, it too will undermine the coherence of one's projects. We are drawn back once more to the adoption of priorities, to premises, in other words.

I say adoption rather than choice here because I do not think that people chose premises or ends in the way they might chose a tin of biscuits. Normally we do not see ourselves as confronted with equally valuable or valid alternatives, for one of which we simply have to opt. Many factors bear on which premises people adopt, social, psychological, stylistic, developmental and, up to a point, rational. Nor do I want to deny that sometimes people do change their fundamental commitments, intellectual and moral, as much as any others. The claim I am making is that intellectual-cum-argumentative factors are not going to be sufficient in the sense that they are rationally compelling in themselves and on their own. Even if they seem to be to the one who loses a faith, they will not really be. Faiths can always be rationally defended as well as attacked, and if a particular line of defence seems to a majority at a particular time to be unconvincing and if a particular convert chooses not to give much weight to the defences offered by those whose group he is leaving, that may not be for wholly rational reasons.

In *The Russell/Bradley Dispute and Its Significance for Twentieth-Century Philosophy*,[9] Stewart Candlish shows convincingly enough that Russell, though defeating Bradley comprehensively in terms of influence and the course of philosophical history (including the later writing of that history), did not actually provide rationally compelling refutations of Bradley's views. In discussing this episode Candlish refers to a remark of Geoffrey Warnock, that philosophical systems such as Bradley's are more vulnerable to *ennui* than to disproof. Comparing the turgid and convoluted texts of the English

[9]   Candlish, *The Russell/Bradley Dispute* ... , Palgrave, 2007.

idealists with the briskness and crispness and day-light feel of Russell and Ayer, one can certainly appreciate Warnock's observation. Further for many, now as then, there is something reactionary and claustrophobic about the atmosphere of idealism, as compared to the progressive and energetic debunking of worn-out pieties and religion, spilt or otherwise, which we find in Russell, Ayer and their successors, as they force their opponents to say what they mean and profess to find their answers incomprehensible. But that does not mean that they are incomprehensible, or that an iconoclast's sense of *ennui* is much of a criterion philosophically. Maybe what Bradley was striving to articulate is complicated and difficult and maybe Bradley himself was not as gifted a writer or arguer as Russell; but maybe a philosophical faith in science as the touchstone of reality is itself cramping and claustrophobic (as Blake intimates in 'Newton'), inducing in its adherents a form of blindness to genuine aspects of experience.

What then is left for philosophy, if there is no absolute rationality over choice of ends and premises, if what is at issue is in part a mood, an atmosphere, a style, a basic intuition about the way things are, a sense of conviction owing as much to one's disposition as to rational argument? Is the claim of philosophy to take us nearer the truth at a deep level not just empty, but deceptive in that these deep truths, or what we take to be deep truths, are not susceptible of rational proof or argument? I must admit that when I reached this point in my reflections as I was writing this, I began to feel rather depressed, having appeared to reach a point of convergence with Athenian sophists and contemporary post-modernists: that there is no ultimate truth in these areas (or if there is we cannot recognise that we have reached it), and that all that is left to philosophy is persuasion, philosophy being, as it was for the sophists, the art of persuasion. Of course, if we could get to ultimate truths by philosophical means, then philosophy would in another sense be the art of persuasion (as I imagine Russell believed it to be).

I want in the rest of this essay to contest the idea that philosophy aims primarily at persuasion, in either sense. It should not aim at the sophistical type of persuasion through rhetoric, because that would be manipulative of others; nor should it aim at persuading others of ultimate truths by means of rational argument, because rational argument cannot take us that far. Although I do not think that philosophy is a matter of therapy (because I do not think that it deals with philosophical illnesses), the view I am not going to sketch has more in common with the therapeutic view than with thinking of philosophy as attempting to persuade others.

Philosophy – Wisdom or Technique?

Philosophy, properly conceived, has as much to do with self-discovery as with making a noise or having an influence in the world outside, taking self-discovery in a wide sense to include discovering my fundamental orientation to the world outside me. It is, in a certain sense (Descartes's sense), meditative; it does involve a Platonic care of the individual soul.

I have suggested that philosophy cannot justify ultimate premises, and that the hostile criticism of rival premises has limited rational power. But it does not follow from any of this, nor do I intend it to follow, that philosophy may not be about premises. Each of us has a world-view, a fundamental orientation to reality and to our fellows. This world view is, as already remarked, formed by all sorts of influences, including philosophical influences, which have worked their way through the culture of our nation, through our families and friends, and through our own biographies. Most people do little to make their world-views explicit, and are often unconscious of their implications and starting-points. Their world-views may, as a result, have a degree of incoherence and certainly a degree of fuzziness. Lives and world-views often remain unexamined, and if we are concerned, as reflective beings, to know ourselves and our world, this must be a bad thing. The unexamined life may not be worthless, as Socrates contended, but, other things being equal, it may be worth less than an examined one.

As self-conscious and reflective persons, once we start to think about who we are and what we expect, this type of incoherence and fuzziness is bound to be unsatisfactory. The initial impulse to philosophy is not so much wonder (as Aristotle and Whitehead may have thought), though wonder may come into it, as a desire to become clear about the world and one's place within it. This will include becoming clear about what science, history, psychology, the arts and other forms of knowledge and experience tell me about the world and myself, and about their reasons for what they tell me. But this cannot be a purely scientific or historical or sociological or psychological or artistic matter, because part of what is involved here will be what I think about the role of science, history, sociology and psychology in the world, by which I really mean their role in my world view.

In becoming clearer about my world-view, I will also inevitably affect it. In making the inarticulate articulate I will be making clear and definite what is fuzzy and inchoate. Here there will be much to be said for reading and studying what others have said about the things I am seeking clarity on, for seeking reasons, in other words, both for and against. I will begin to understand just what I am committed to, just what its implications are. I will realise things about what I think that I did not previously know, just as in reading Proust on love and jealousy or Baudelaire on *ennui* I will come to understand much about my own emotions which I did not previously realise. In this process of intellectual and conceptual discovery or self-discovery, I may also come to change things I originally thought or thought I thought. Some of these changes might be at a high level of argument or exposition, a level which does not really affect my fundamental commitments, as when a physicalist realises that a type-type identification of mental and brain states won't quite work, but does not take this to impugn his commitment to physicalism, but rather to spur him on to further argumentative epicycles, or as when a theist abandons a literal interpretation of Genesis, but does not take this to undermine Scripture's deeper truth, and begins instead to follow Augustine's plea for more mature and spiritual understandings of Holy Writ.

Work at this level is important, but is on a different level from that which involves changes in fundamental commitments. At a more radical level I may find that some of my basic commitments are inconsistent at a deep level with other things I also believe, and cannot be solved in the manner of our physicalist or our Augustinian exegete. But in a case of deep inconsistency, the change will be against a background of commitment I am not altering. Or it may be because when I realise just how one of my commitments looks when spelled out and clarified, I do not like the look of it. I may come to realise that the image projected by a scientistic or Newtonian world-view is not such an attractive one after all. This seems to me to be a perfectly valid philosophical result, which may come from immersing myself in Wittgenstein as much as in Blake – but, in view of our strictures earlier, I should not expect my change of mind (or heart), or the considerations which led to it in my case to convince a Quine or a Paul Churchland. They may simply be, in William James' terms, tough-minded, disposed to be materialistic, irreligious and sceptical, and determined to hold on to these dispositions and work out their implications, striving to bring them into harmony with all of their experience and commitments.

The picture of philosophy which I am here sketching, in which philosophy is part of a rational, but personal quest for meaning might not be recognised in many philosophy departments (or not by their students, anyway), and would be hard to discern in many of the most acclaimed philosophical writings of to-day. This is partly because of the tendency of academic study in all areas to specialisation and impersonality, specialisation because more and

more people concentrate on less and less in an effort to achieve originality (and so get published), impersonality because of an attempt in
philosophy to appear scientific. Of course, some of the people who
write and practice philosophy in these ways will see their tightly
focused work as contributing to a larger vision, but it seems to me
that the overall direction is false to the true nature of the subject.
And although we can all agree that our endeavours are directed to
the truth, and guided by reasons and arguments that bear on the
truth of what each of us believes, we each have to face the fact that
we will not achieve complete rational convergence on premises,
because it is not there to be achieved. Nor will we come to a set of
truths which will be so evident that they will command the assent
of all who embark on the journey and pursue it in a rational and
reasonable manner, aiming as best they can to seek the truth. It is
just this picture which our earlier considerations on the nature and
history of philosophical disagreement seem to undermine. In the
beginning and at the end, philosophy is a personal journey, crucial
to the examined life Socrates thought so integral to human
flourishing.

Index of Names

Ackroyd, Peter 354–355
Ali, Hirsi 174
Alquié, Ferdinand 157
Anscombe, G.E.M. 3n, 182n, 187, 195, 209
Anselm 19, 209
Aphrodite 220
Aquinas, St Thomas 41–44, 50–54, 100n, 105, 108, 134, 183, 247, 352
Aristotle 34, 50, 51, 57, 58, 99, 101n, 102n, 103n, 105, 110, 121, 122, 134, 137, 146, 151, 159, 161, 166, 171, 172, 181, 206, 234, 276, 354, 359
Armstrong, Hilary 221, 223–224, 226
Audi, Robert 93
Augustine 97, 98, 122, 360
Aurelius, Marcus 13
Austin, J.L. 45, 132, 155, 160, 168, 313, 323
Ayer, A.J. 162, 358
Bacon, Francis 71, 79, 102n, 110n
Baudelaire, Charles 360
Bellarmine, 48
Benardete, Jose 16n,
Bergson, Henri-Louis 5, 45

Berkeley 16n, 54, 89, 97, 109, 111, 197, 201, 213
Berlin, Isaiahn 213
Birault, Henri 156
Blackburn, Simon 101n, 125
Blake, William 353–355, 358, 360
Bohr, Niels 276
Bouyeri, Mohammed 174
Bradley, Francis 45, 357–358
Brentano, Franz 160, 171
Broad, C.D. 89
Buchdahl, Gerd 302
Buddha 13
Burckhardt, Jacob 356
Candlish, Stewart 357–358
Carnap, Rudolf 107, 167, 172, 277, 295–298, 299
Cassirer, Ernst 277, 292–295, 296, 299
Cavell, Stanley 272
Charles Ist 75
Chesterton, G.K. 219
Chisholm, Roderick 32
Chomsky, Noam 143
Churchland, Paul 47, 173, 360
Cicero 105, 196–197
Clarke, Thompson 339–342
Clifford, W.K. 15–35

Cohen, Hermann 277, 292, 293
Coleridge, Samuel Taylor 289
Collingwood, R.G. 96, 103n, 104n, 112n, 128n
Comte, Auguste 107, 162
Davidson, Donald 135n, 155, 239
Dawkins, Richard 32,
Democritus 110n, 234
Dennett, Daniel 169n
Descartes, R. 6, 69, 84, 97, 98, 109, 111, 130, 134, 161, 166, 171, 187, 237–242, 247, 248, 278, 313, 322–325
Derrida, Jacques 72, 119, 124n, 125, 155, 157
Dillon, John 228
Duke of Wellington 82
Dummett, Michael 108, 133, 134, 155, 162, 166, 179, 181, 236
Einstein, Albert 72, 85, 165, 276, 304
Empson, William 252
Engelhardt, Tristram 95, 180
Epicurus 110n
Euclid 166
Evans, Gareth 316–317, 320–321, 325–337, 347

Index

Ezekiel 229
Faraday, Michael 289
Feyerabend, Paul 113
Fichte, J. 4, 9–10, 289, 290
Fodor, Jerry 196
Foot, Philippa 178, 207
Foscarini, Paolo 48,
Foucault, M. 1, 119, 125, 155
Frede, Michael 190
Frege, Gottlob 129, 157, 195, 296, 313, 314, 318–320, 324–326, 347
Freud, Sigmund 155, 250–251, 254
Friedman, Michael 281–284, 295–296, 297, 302–305
Fries, Jakob F. 289, 290
Gadamer, Hans-Georg 103n
Galen 134
Galileo 109, 110, 280–281
Gardner, Martin 196
Gassendi, Pierre 110, 237–240
Gently, Dirk 33
Geuss, Raymond 252
Gibbon, Edward 129
Gilson, Etienne 37, 38–40, 44, 45, 49
Gödel, Kurt 28, 121
Goethe 211
Goodman, Nelson 189
Gosling, Justin 37
Gueroult, Martial 157
Hacker, P.M.S. 162, 168–169, 173

Hadot, Pierre 253
Haldane, John S. 67
Hare, Rom 155, 208–210
Hart, H.L.A. 123n
Hampshire, Stuart 37
Hazlitt, William 194
Heidegger, Martin 2, 5, 103n, 121, 155, 156, 166, 172, 254, 257, 258–265
Helmhotz, Hermann von 289–290, 296
Hegel, G. 7, 100n, 106, 155, 162, 290, 291
Hobbes, Thomas 26, 104n, 105n, 106, 110n
Hufeland, Christoph 211
Hume, David 35, 89, 102n, 109, 111, 112n, 121, 122, 123n, 130, 131, 134, 162, 166, 181, 211, 242n, 243, 247, 291, 356
Husserl, Edmund 5, 70, 155–161, 163, 166, 170, 171
James, William 4, 32, 360
Johnson, W.E. 199
Joyce, James 61
Kant, I. 1, 11, 61, 67, 69, 102n, 106, 107, 109, 111, 112n, 119, 121, 130, 131, 133, 134, 146, 158, 160–162, 165–167, 172, 181, 206, 207, 211, 235, 276–306

Kenny, Anthony 37
Kierkegaard, Søren 8
Knowlton, Charles 191
Knox, Malcolm 37
Kolakowski, Leszek 8, 94
Koyré, Alexander 276
Kripke, Saul 45, 90, 153n, 160, 163, 171
Kuhn, Thomas 106, 113, 117, 277, 289, 293, 298–301, 302
Lakoff, George 216
LaFolett, Hugh 206
Laplace, Pierre-Simon 278
Leibniz, Gottfried 84, 90, 97, 109, 111, 112n, 181, 278, 326
Levinas, Emmanuel 155, 157
Lewis, David 24–32, 45, 201, 243
Lindsay, A.D. 37
Locke, John 89, 100n, 104n, 111, 122, 123n, 134, 196, 198, 241
Lyotard, Jean-Francois 94
MacIntyre, A. 96, 101n, 102n, 108, 109, 120, 125–127
Mackie, John 213
Makransky, John 226
Malcolm, Norman 185
Marquard, Odo 164–165
Mark, Edward Laurens 233
Marx, Karl 2, 98, 155

Maupertius, Pierre 278
McDowell, John 327
McMullin, Ernan 275
McTaggart, J.M.E. 45, 178, 195, 203
Merleau-Ponty, Maurice 70, 160
Meyerson, Émile 276, 299
Mill, John Stuart 74, 119, 181, 182, 206, 355–356
Minos 220
Montaigne, Michel de 6
Moore, G.E. 73, 135n, 192, 198, 235
Mossner, E.C. 181n
Mrugowsky, Joachim 210–211, 212
Mulhall, Stephen 3n
Nagarjuna 6,
Nagel, Thomas 47
Natorp, Paul 292
Newton, Isaac 59, 109, 110, 112, 167, 276, 277–284, 294, 304, 354–355
Nietzsche 1, 5, 102n, 109, 155, 156, 157
Novak, Joseph 52
Nozick, Robert 182, 253n
Oakeshott 122, 124n, 125, 126
Olson, Eric 195, 201
O'Neill, Onora 37
Paracelsus 134
Parfit, Derek 47, 248–249
Pauli, Wolfgang 304–305

Pasnau, Robert 52–54
Peacocke, Christopher 326–337, 343
Peirce, C.S. 106, 123n
Pickstock, Catherine 222
Pico della Mirandola 223
Plantinga, Alvin 45, 174
Plato, 28, 35, 50, 57,58, 97, 99, 110, 121, 146, 151, 155, 160, 175, 213, 222, 228, 247, 248, 250, 254, 351–352, 354
Plotinus 97, 215–232
Poincaré, Henri 290, 296
Popper, Karl 66, 106n, 155, 160, 170, 171, 352
Porphyry 222, 223
Price, H.H. 89
Price, Richard 242n
Priest, Graham 353
Prichard, H.A. 314–315
Protagorus 105
Proust, Marcel 360
Putnam, Hilary 45, 160
Pyrrho 5, 190n
Pythagorus 58, 97
Quine, W.V.O. 4, 45, 46n, 84, 90, 113, 117, 155, 163, 169, 171, 173, 236, 298, 360
Quinton, Anthony 37, 93
Raphael 98n

Raine, Kathleen 352–353, 354
Rawls, John 105n, 118n, 123n, 182, 243, 244
Reichenbach, Hans 162, 167, 276, 303
Richardson, Alan 293
Ritter, Johann 288
Rorty, Richard 2n, 4, 5, 8, 45, 94, 125, 163–164, 236
Rousseau 98n
Rubens, Peter Paul 322
Russell, Bertrand 60, 61, 62–64, 89, 100n, 107, 108, 130, 131, 132, 134, 157, 178, 181, 186, 191–193, 200, 206, 235, 297, 352–353, 358
Ryan, Alan 37
Ryle, Gilbert 45, 59, 141, 146, 155, 168, 353
Sartre, Jean-Paul 10, 71, 79
Schlegel, Friederich 289
Schlick, Moritz 107, 295
Scholem, Gershom 229n
Schopenhauer, A. 60, 65, 67–69
Schroder, Ernst 157
Schule, Frankfurter 155
Scotus, Johann 134
Searle, John 107n, 170, 171

Index

Sellars, Wilfred 163, 172–173

Shakespeare, William 234

Sheffer, Henry 123n

Sidgwick, Henry 195

Singer, Peter 204n, 211

Sisyphus 76

Smart, J. 239n

Snow, C.P. 115

Socrates 52, 57, 58, 105, 121, 150, 175–176, 191, 203, 230, 352, 359, 361

Sosa, Ernest 193n

Spinoza, B. 100n, 106, 109, 111, 239, 247

Stich, Steven 191

Strawson, Galen 191, 196, 198n, 202

Strawson, P.F. 1n, 61, 149, 155, 245n

Sutherland, Stewart 37

Swinburne, Richard 175

Taylor, Charles 101n, 248–249

Thales 58

Unger, Peter 191–193

van Frassen, Bas 355–356

van Gogh, Theo 174

van Inwagen, Peter 179

von Schelling, Friedrich 287–288, 290

Warnock, Geoffrey 37, 357–358

Warnock, Mary 37

Weil, Simone 215

Weyl, Hermann 276

Whitehead, A.N. 97, 351, 359

Williams, Bernard 37, 240–242, 248

Williams, Rowan 33

Williamson, Timothy 133, 134n, 161n, 162, 163, 169–170, 353

Wilson, E.O. 165

Wittgenstein 2, 3, 45, 61, 65, 67–68, 103n, 108, 135n, 136n, 146, 148n, 160, 161, 168, 169, 185–189, 196, 199, 200n, 205, 235, 313, 348

Zeno 16

Zeus 220